To Marietta
from Paris
1945–1960

To Marietta from Paris

1945-1960

BY SUSAN MARY ALSOP

DOUBLEDAY & COMPANY, INC.
GARDEN CITY, NEW YORK
1975

Library of Congress Cataloging in Publication Data

Alsop, Susan Mary.
To Marietta from Paris.

1. Paris. 2. Alsop, Susan Mary. I. Tree, Marietta,
1917– II. Title.
DC707.A45 944'.36'0820924
ISBN 0-385-09774-3
Library of Congress Catalog Card Number 74-33628

Printed in the United States of America
First Edition

FOR MY MOTHER

ACKNOWLEDGMENTS

I am grateful to a number of people who got me through the task of preparing my first manuscript. First my editors and wise counselors, Ken McCormick and Carolyn Blakemore and their assistant, Joan Ward, who have been superb friends to me. Then to the girls who typed with enthusiasm and gusto, Peggy Rohrbough, Margi Levy, Harmon Pinney, Sally Ferguson, and Anne Crile.

FOREWORD

Susan Mary Jay, Bill Blair,[1] and I all met at a picnic on the pink granite rocks of Bar Harbor when we were in our early teens. Over the peanut butter and jelly sandwiches we immediately started a hot, three-cornered discussion about United States foreign policy. Bill was a Chicago *Tribune* isolationist then. I was a League of Nations idealist, but Susan Mary's opinions were a good deal more sophisticated and informed. After all, her father was a diplomat, and she had lived in exotic places such as Romania and the Argentine.

She impressed me at the time as far more mature, worldly, and amusing than any of my contemporaries and also far less of an egoist. She appeared genuinely interested in what Bill and I had to say, and questioned us closely on our opinions. Ever since, she has forced me to examine my views and encouraged me to think, especially in the light of the vast amount of information she always has at her command. For she reads the newspapers and journals with the intensity of an editor and, unlike most at a Washington dinner party, she correctly hears and remembers stories, statistics, or slips made to her by the Cabinet Minister or Ambassador she sits next to. She would have made an excellent Mata Hari.

Instead, she chose to communicate her experiences and give her opinions and insights to her family and friends in a way more typical of the eighteenth century than the twentieth, where now nearly all communication is by telephone. Madame de la Tour du Pin and Princess Lieven are her epistolary cousins.

Many years ago a historian strongly advised me to keep a diary and to write letters to friends, since, he said, without diaries and gossipy letters historians in the twenty-first century would have no

[1] William McCormick Blair, Jr., formerly assistant to Adlai Stevenson, Ambassador to Denmark and the Philippines, director of the Kennedy Center, Washington, D.C.

resources of social history—no personal descriptions of people, or the effects of personalities on their circles, no description of an educated woman's typical day—during a war, just after a war, or in so-called normal times—only business letters. People would want to know how children were brought up, he said, and how the parents regarded them; what were the festivities of the time—parties, large and small, in various countries? What were the outlines of public and private morals, mores, fashions, flirtations, food? What was the anatomy of happiness, comfort, frustration, or grief, which changes so surprisingly from generation to generation? The historian flattered me into becoming a social historian for a brief spell; I kept a diary for three days.

But Susan Mary, without any self-consciousness about future history, has spent a good part of her life recording it in letters to friends—not the generalities of "my-life-has-been-hectic-lately-so-I-hope-you-are-all-well-as-we-are" but projecting herself beside you by describing the *bal masqué* that she went to last week in Paris, and making it more real than the rally for Stevenson in Madison Square Garden that one might have gone to on the same night in New York City.

Susan Mary's friendship has been one of the blessings of my life, and I have been fortunate to see her a great deal over the years, as our lives have run closely parallel since before we both married. Our husbands have been friends, and some of our children are the same age, so it was natural for our families to spend weekends and holidays together as we have so often at Ditchley, England, Cintra, Portugal, Lloyd's Neck, Long Island, Barbados, and in Paris, London, Washington, and New York.

She has seen me through some bad patches, taking infinite trouble and giving precious time to help me, but I chiefly remember all the good times—family picnics on a sailboat off the Lido or in the piny woods of Portugal, climbing the goat trail of Pemetic Mountain on Mount Desert Island, Susan Mary unruffled and breathing normally as if she were strolling down Fifth Avenue. I remember her trim and bright going off at 8 A.M. to her ward job at the Washington municipal hospital, after a marathon discussion in the Alsop living room the night before, where several journalists, C.I.A. officials, senators, generals, White House staff, and Mrs. Longworth took passionate part. (Joe Alsop likes what he calls "zoo parties"—two guests from each category.) In all the scenes with Susan Mary, I see her often in the same pose, pensive, listening intently, and then quick to respond, whether to Frankie FitzGerald, aged three, or Duff Cooper, with laughter, a fascinating and pertinent fact, or a searchlight question. When, for instance, my husband admired her beautiful hat of white violets, she took it off and gave it to him as a present for me.

She is stylish, intelligent, loving and good, and very funny. The reader of these letters who has not yet met Susan Mary Alsop will now have the pleasure of being introduced to her entrancing turn of mind, quality of character, and distinction of person.

MARIETTA TREE
New York
January 1975

To Marietta
from Paris
1945–1960

INTRODUCTION

My life has been interwoven with Marietta's since we were children spending our summers on the same island in Maine. In those days one accompanied one's family year after year in the ritual exercise of leaving the city ("Nobody stays in town") for long months that could be traumatic to a shy teenager like myself. I, the only living child of an invalid father and a gallant but harassed mother, greatly admired Marietta Peabody, who was blonde, beautiful, and the belle of the island. One night we were combing our frizzy hair side by side before the mirror preparatory to stepping out on the ballroom floor of the Bar Harbor Club to the strains of "Night and Day" when she said, "The smell of stale face powder in this ladies' room is the smell of fear." This gave me confidence, for I, too, hated the smell of that room. I thought, "Well, if Marietta Peabody is scared, maybe I'm not too peculiar after all." She has remained modest throughout her distinguished career.

In September 1939, Marietta married Desmond FitzGerald, and Mother gave the bridal dinner at our house in Bar Harbor. A month later I married Desmond's close friend and classmate William Patten, and the next year I was proud to become the godmother of the FitzGeralds' baby, Frances.

The spring of 1939 found me rebelliously refusing the annual pilgrimage to Maine with my mother and settled down at *Vogue* magazine at twenty-six dollars a week. My ambition was to be a writer, and I had obtained the job through my friend Barbara Cushing,[1] who was already a glamorous fashion editor. Edna Woolman Chase, the formidable editor-in-chief, asked me to write an essay on the future of the open-toed shoe. I went to Babe, who said to write an ar-

[1] Now Mrs. William S. Paley.

ticle extolling the virtues of open-toed shoes, as Mrs. Chase was mad about them. Babe in fact wrote most of the piece for me, and it got me the job of receptionist in the Condé Nast offices, with vague promises of finer things to come. Delighted, I waved my mother off on the Bar Harbor express and moved in with Uncle Eliot Cross, a summer bachelor. Aunt Martha was off with the children at some other resort and she and Mama corresponded constantly about how "poor Eliot is getting on, with just a French couple and Susan Mary who knows nothing about housekeeping." We were getting on just fine. At the end of the day we would meet in the beautiful Cross apartment on Fifth Avenue to exchange notes, and it amused him to meet the young men I went out with. One of these was Bill Patten, whom I had met one evening when Marietta was away and the lonely Desmond gave me dinner at the Maisonette Russe, a restaurant in the St. Regis Hotel. He had asked a college classmate to join us after dinner, and thirty-five years later I can still see Bill Patten walking across the room to our table.

I fell immediately and irrevocably in love, and we became engaged a couple of months later but not without some hot pursuit on my part. It was the summer of the New York World's Fair, and I spent many an evening out at Flushing, sometimes professionally as a model for *Vogue*. One particular evening sticks in my mind. There was a parachute thing, from which Babe and I floated again and again in evening dresses until the photographers below were satisfied. Always a victim of vertigo, this was a nightmare to me, but what would I not have done for seventy-five dollars an hour?

On other nights we went to the fair with friends. One evening Charles Francis Adams of Boston, Ethel Woodward, and Bill and I were out together. Charlie, who was devoted to Bill, took me aside semi-seriously and told me to lay off Bill, for Ethel was the girl he must marry. She was charming and she was rich, and Bill's friends feared that his poor health would keep him from making money in a business or indeed any other career. To this I paid no heed, and Bill proposed to me over a holiday weekend at the Lake Champlain summer home of Charlie Adams' father-in-law, Mr. Philip Stockton, the Boston Banker. We went to tell the news to Mr. and Mrs. Stockton, who were like parents to Bill. Mrs. Stockton went off to put the champagne on ice but Mr. Stockton, who was an impressive, awesome figure, asked me to come to speak to him in his study. He was kind but he was crushing. Would I please think over what I was doing, and although he was deeply fond of Bill his words chilled me. He reminded me that I was only twenty, that Bill was twenty-nine and a sick man. Since boyhood his chronic asthma had handicapped him; now, Mr. Stockton said, it was surely not just asthma but emphysema, a mortal disease of the lungs. As an old friend of my mother's and a sufferer from the illness himself (he died a couple of years later), Mr. Stockton felt obliged to tell me that he thought my engagement a foolish one.

Of course I paid not the slightest attention. Cocksure and confident of my own ability to find a cure for Bill, we returned to New York. Uncle Eliot was comforting and my brave mother came down from Bar Harbor to meet Bill. She too was worried, for we knew the dread disease well: Papa had had it and died young after resigning from the Foreign Service in his forties.

We were married in October 1939 and spent an ideal winter in a beautiful house in Cuernavaca, Mexico, Bill so well that we played golf every day. Back in Boston, from whence he came, the doctors were delighted with him but urged him to return to a dry climate. We were lent a ranch near Phoenix, said good-by to family and friends in the East, and took the train to live forever in the desert. Two weeks later Bill blew up the worst asthma attack I had yet seen him have. Once over it, he told me that he was damn well taking tickets on the train to return East, that he simply could not stand Saturday nights at the Phoenix country club with its insularity and total lack of interest in Europe at war, that he realized that by abandoning the healthy climate and going to work he would be shortening his life by a good many years, but that he hoped I would understand. Of course I understood, and think his decision was the right one.

The next two years in Boston were hard ones for Bill. His instincts were interventionist and we followed the agony of the fall of France, the Battle of Britain, and the President's magnificent efforts to help our European friends. All our friends were increasingly involved and we used to join Charlie Adams and his wife for dinner at Charlestown Navy Yard on his destroyer when he came in for leave from "routine Atlantic patrol." How unroutine those patrols were! He was, of course, one of the many reserve officers called out to assist in protecting the convoys carrying the vital aid to Europe. One never spoke of the condition of the ship, rust-covered and sea-battered, or asked if the expended torpedoes had been part of routine practice. When Pearl Harbor came, Bill's last friends left for military service; he tried to put his heart into "civil defense" and prayed somehow to be useful to the war effort. Our prayer was granted one summer afternoon sitting on Mama's porch at Bar Harbor. The lawn ran down to the sea, and Mama spied Mr. Sumner Welles, then Undersecretary of State, taking a gentle walk along the Shore Path. In a flash Mama was in action. "Sumner, come up here, I think you need a cup of tea, and I want you to meet my brilliant son-in-law." Mr. Welles, an austere man who hid his great tenderness and kindness from the world, could hardly avoid coming up the lawn, panama hat in hand, for he had worked for my father in earlier years and had affection and respect for Mama also.

Mr. Welles was impressed by Bill, impressed enough to invite him to come to Washington to work for the State Department. He could have shunted him off to some other division, but instead chose Bill for his own office, a very important one as President Roosevelt used Welles, the Undersecretary, perhaps more than he did Cordell Hull, the Secretary of State, and the action was in Welles's office. Bill could not join the Foreign Service as he would have failed the physical examination, so he became a Foreign Service Reserve officer. In August 1944, after two years in Washington, Bill was appointed to the Paris Embassy, still non-existent after the four years of German occupation, and left in December to join the mission. By this time he had decided to specialize in economic and financial affairs, and he was very useful indeed during his long tenure in Paris. His title as "financial and economic attaché" was extremely nebulous, but his ability was enough to make other more permanent officials momentarily jealous—never for long, as his charm won over the most suspicious bureaucrats and he was loved by all. I was less loved. If you read about Japan you read about the *eta,* the non-people, a caste despised. As non-Foreign Service, we Foreign Service Reserve were outcasts but, never having been one before, I didn't realize that I was *eta,* and as Bill had given me confidence during our five years of marriage I expected and hoped to make friends immediately with the other wives at the Embassy and was sad when Mrs. MacArthur,[2] the wife of our political counselor, summoned me to her house one morning and told me not to leave cards on Mrs. Caffery, the wife of our Ambassador,[3] as F.S.R. wives didn't do that. We might never have met the Ambassador and Mrs. Caffery socially, but for Avis Bohlen,[4] to whom I confided my situation by V-mail, which produced immediate results. The Cafferys met us at a dinner that I describe in a letter. I bore no rancor towards Mrs. MacArthur, who received me in bed at 11 A.M. with a bottle of bourbon and two beautiful glasses and ice on a tray beside her. She was the daughter of Senator Barkley and a most jolly soul. I wish that we could have seen more of her but the occasion did not arise, and Bill and I were so happy together that being *eta* among our own compatriots didn't matter much. There were lonely moments but soon, thanks to the Bohlens, we made lifelong friends on the staff.

Embassies are very specialized. For instance, Norris Chipman, who was to become a close friend, covered the left wing of the French political spectrum. This could hardly have been a more important job in Western Europe in those days, as we entered the period of the Cold War. Norris was a highly trained Sovietologist. Bill, in a much more minor position, dealt with officials of the Treasury, the Banque de France, and the great private bankers.

Bill's charm made it very easy to entertain, but when we first arrived we had no social connections in Paris and not one friend. We were lucky enough to be loaned a family house of great beauty but it was lonely not to have one French chum. I had been to France once or twice, briefly and resentfully with my mother during school vacations, to stay with Aunt Harriet, who owned the house we now lived in. It was due to the luck of the times that we made friends quickly. As I say in one letter, the French, having been thrown in on themselves for four years during the German occupation, were bored, bored, bored, and eager for new faces. We had two letters of

[2] Mrs. Douglas MacArthur II. Her husband was General Douglas MacArthur's nephew.

[3] Jefferson Caffery, U. S. Ambassador to France, 1944–49.

[4] Mrs. Charles E. Bohlen was the wife of a young diplomat who became one of America's great public servants. "Chip" Bohlen had specialized in Russian studies from the time he entered the Foreign Service.

introduction from Washington; one led to the ghastly dinner described in an early letter, the other changed our lives.

They became glamorous lives, as will be seen in the letters, very exciting. But I shall never forget an interim period, early on in Paris. Bill was away for two weeks on a mission and I fell ill with the measles, which can be nasty when one is grown up. After a week or so I was convalescent enough to ask the servants if anyone had telephoned; they replied that no one had. I accepted this as normal, as who would have telephoned? Not Mrs. MacArthur, surely, or anyone else from the American Embassy. I hadn't met anyone but Mrs. MacArthur. Another week went by. By this time I was struggling to my feet and taking little walks, hoping maybe that when I came in someone would have rung, just one of the many American soldiers who had been in and out of the house, or a friend from Washington. When Bill returned he discovered that the telephone had been out of order all the time. I look back on this little episode with humility. Bill was extremely annoyed to find that it hadn't occurred to me to have the telephone checked, and that I was sitting there, ten pounds thinner, having read every book in the house, convinced that I was a failure, full of ostentatious self-pity. I write this paragraph in case it might possibly help any young woman finding that the city of her dreams has become the Vale of Tears.

The year 1945 was, of course, the year of Roosevelt's and Hitler's deaths, of the end of the war against Germany and that against Japan, of the atom bomb, of the overthrow of the great war leader Winston Churchill and of the succession to power of Harry S. Truman, the unknown quantity. The background against which I wrote from Paris was clouded and confused by our government's delay in recognizing de Gaulle and his ministers as the French government. "It would be interesting to collect historical instances of harm that has been done by the reluctance of men to accept readily what they know they will have to accept in the end. It was two months after the liberation of Paris that the United States recognized the government of General de Gaulle, which, during the whole of that period, was carrying out the functions of government and plainly had the support of the people."[5]

[5] Duff Cooper, *Old Men Forget* (London, 1953).

De Gaulle never forgave, and I consider the examples of French kindness to two unimportant young Americans that follow in the letters remarkable. An opportunity had been missed. The national feeling was still there, not as in 1944 but still there, and though statesmen cannot create national feeling they can take advantage of it.

While Bill and I were taking our first tentative steps in Paris Marietta remained at her job at *Life* magazine in New York, sharing her experiences with me by letters, encouraging me. Desmond came home from the war and the letters changed in tone, saddening me by what was not written. I worried, but knew nothing until she wrote me a heartrending letter to inform me that the marriage was over. I could not share her pain or be with her except by letter, and I did not see her again until she married Ronnie Tree in 1947 and to my great joy came to live in England. Marietta being Marietta, I think that our close friendship could not have been destroyed by physical distance. But it added immensely to the fun to have her so close. Perhaps my letters will give some idea of it. When the time comes, Marietta's letters, far better than mine, will add her side of the story that now follows.

In many instances, the letters included were written to my mother in Washington, or to Bill, when we were briefly separated. These may be out of sequence by days or weeks, but they fill in the gaps that letters to Marietta fail to provide.

The letters are printed as I wrote them. When it has been necessary to give additional information or to speak from the vantage of the present, I have written rubrics as bridges. These are set in type different from the rest of the text.

• 1945 •

After Bill had flown Pariswards into the skies from Andrews Air Force Base, I moved to my mother's in Georgetown and spent all my time conniving at how to join him soonest. My daily letters show me asking and receiving help from friends high in government agencies such as the War Shipping Board. The State Department gave me the lowest of priorities, as befit my *eta* status, but at last produced a ticket which I treasure to this day. No government department enjoyed wartime secrecy more than the State Department. The ticket was for a ship named X, sailing date X, time X, destination X. Only spelled out was the price, a hundred and fifty dollars, very cheap for a voyage to paradise. The State Department put one up while waiting for the convoy to sail at a really cunningly chosen hotel in the West Forties in New York; no one would ever have expected respectable State Department wives to stay in so disreputable a hostelry. Mama was at the Plaza, and I spent most of those waiting days with her, checking in by telephone every two hours to my source, Mr. X of the State Department, who at last informed me that departure would take place that night and instructing me to be at a certain blacked-out dock on the North River at 10 P.M. Mama returned bravely to Washington and I dined in the Oak Room of the Plaza with Marietta, who had ably acquired two naval officers to join us. I couldn't possibly eat, my tummy was too tight with excitement, reunion with Bill lay ahead. Lieutenant Richard Kernan of the U. S. Navy got me through the blackout and on board ship.

Aboard U.S.N. Troopship
Easter Sunday, 1945

I cannot believe that I am sitting in a deck chair tucked in the protection of a three-inch gun to escape wind, wearing a smart costume consisting of gray flannel slacks, sweater, and a life jacket, the sun streaming down and the ocean calm and blue. I adore it and so far wouldn't trade this ship for the *Queen Mary* or anything else. It is a specially built troop transport, only nine months old, very long and lean and gray and the cleanest thing I have ever seen. My departure was easy. Dick Kernan was wonderful, got onto the dock with me and was a great help with everything. He hired a longshoreman to carry my bag, typewriter, and John-Fred hatbox down the ladders and companionways to my cabin.

I have only three cabin mates, very nice, and the bunks most comfortable. I have the top one—my own choice, as I feared lack of air, but actually the ventilation is wonderful. We were told we would sail at dawn, so went to bed about twelve. Woke up to hear Mrs. Helm from bunk beneath me saying, "My, what a nice ship, there is so little motion, I feel just as if we were still in New York!" Sure enough, when we went up on deck, we were in New York. Had breakfast, grapefruit, coffee, eggs, bacon, cereal, toast, butter, all of which I actually ate, having had no dinner the night before, and was impressed by how immaculately clean the dining room and galley looked. We sailed about nine-thirty and by one-thirty were out at sea and the convoy got into formation. It was and is the most exciting possible sight; from where I sit now, I can count twenty ships of all sizes and shapes—tankers, cargo ships, troopships, etc., with our escort of D.E.s (Destroyer Escorts) darting about angrily and two Catalina flying boats overhead. Our nearest neighbors are an ancient freighter carrying bombers on the deck and a great black liner so heavily loaded with troops that her top looks as if it had been painted black. We are all quite close together. One is mesmerized and can't stop looking.

Our ship is going over to pick up wounded, and we have no troops aboard, only sixty-five wives, WAACs, Quakers, and so on. The officers and men are U. S. Navy, of course, and the officers young and charming—all might well be Charlie Whitehouse or George Thompson.[1] They are overcome by our being civilians and turn handsprings trying to make us comfortable. The deck chairs were brought out with a great flourish, and they almost go crazy keeping track of the children, as there is no place for them to play,

[1] Charles Whitehouse is a cousin of mine; in 1945 he and our friend George Thompson were young officers.

and around the deck only a steel cable, so they are in constant danger of falling overboard. It has been explained to their mothers that if anyone falls overboard the ship can't stop, but they pay little attention. Most of the passengers are very nice. My best friends are Cherry Cook, wife of Don Cook, of the New York *Herald Tribune*'s London bureau, Madame Peter, wife of the Swiss Minister to Washington, a Dutch archaeologist on his way to Germany, and a young Quaker.

Later

Madame Peter solomnly asked me to a sherry party in her cabin tonight before dinner (dinner is at five). The party consisted of her cabin mates, an ancient French lady in a crepe veil, a nice wife on her way to Bern with a five-year-old boy, two WAACs, and myself. We drank the best sherry out of tooth mugs, solemnly dispensed by Madame Peter, sitting on the bunks. Very comic, especially the hour. Dinner was wonderful—steak, potatoes, vegetables, hot corn bread, butter, salad, and cherry pie with ice cream. It is now 6 P.M., so I shall go up on deck before we black out.

I spend much of my time struggling up the deck, holding onto things, to the captain's cabin, as I have made great friends with him and he lets Cherry Cook and me listen to his short-wave radio. We get two or three broadcasts a day of news which we make into a newspaper with typewriters and the purser's mimeograph. The rest of the time I read in my bunk and talk to my friends.

Friday

Things are just about the same. I am still highly entertained by my fellow passengers, all of whom I now know intimately. The food is still awfully good and abundant and remarkably well cooked, especially as for the last forty-eight hours we have been in a terrific storm and it is still rough. I have been so lucky in not being seasick once and have not been bored.

The convoy had trouble. I didn't know how serious until London, when Tommy Brand,[2] who had been watching it from his ministry, told me that it was under one of the last German attacks. I did know some of it, as I slept poorly, unable to get used to being in my bunk and blacked out soon after our six o'clock repast, and one night the zigzags were so unusually pronounced that I broke rules and went out of our cabin with a flashlight to walk up and down the corridor, where I encountered one of the young officers, who was correctly furious with me. He looked very white and burst out that we had lost our sister ship and that the destroyer escort that had darted in to protect us had been hit and was probably going down right now, so would I please go to bed and not cause further trouble by breaking my leg? The next morning I got a note from him, saying that he was sorry he had been rude, but the exec on the D.E. had been his roommate at the Naval Academy and he trusted me to shut up about the incident. This wasn't necessary; the only person I would have told would have been my friend Cherry, but she was six months pregnant, and I had no intention of worrying her.

My luggage was so funny: one suitcase held food and things for friends in England, the other, my wardrobe—a black dress from Lord & Taylor that had cost eighty-five dollars, very expensive, but you will remember that essential little black dress, a black suit with braid from Mother's tailor in Bar Harbor, a gray flannel skirt, blouses and sweaters, shoes, underclothes, and toilet things; then beside me on my bunk lay Uncle Eliot's superb present to me, a made-to-order John-Fredericks hat made of natural straw with long black grosgrain ribbons. This had cost thirty-five dollars, and I would have clung to that hatbox no matter what.

April 12–13

We landed today, several days late due to bad weather, but as you saw from my letter from the boat, the trip was an amusing experience.

[2] Tommy and Leila Brand (now Dowager Lady Hampden) had been in Washington during most of the war. Tommy held a crucial job attached to the British mission.

We docked about eight this morning, and thank heaven, it was that pretty port Southampton. We were met by the United States Lines and Thomas Cook represented by harassed little men who couldn't have been more efficient or nicer but kept apologizing pathetically for the service not being better and explaining that it was the first time in five years that they had managed this kind of party. Everything went most easily and the train trip was thrilling. It was a warm, sunny day, and the lilacs, apple blossoms, etc., were out everywhere. Every ugly little house had a garden full of quinces and on the ground daffodils and primroses, everywhere that wonderful fresh English green. We passed numerous airdromes, and every now and then a block of houses blown to bits, and at one station a detachment of our troops in battle dress lined up, chewing gum and looking bored and gloomy. We leaned out of the windows and yelled to them, and they looked utterly staggered with surprise to hear American female civilian voices, plus children.

Waterloo Station had lots of efficient old porters. We were met by the husbands of the London Embassy girls, and a man from the Embassy who told me to go to the Hotel Cumberland. I took a taxi there and got a very nice room with a big bathroom—wonderful after thirteen bathless days. One of my cabin mates is sharing the room, but it doesn't matter. Actually it does matter, as it is Miss X, an economist who was neurotically certain that we would all be raped. She exhausted me by tugging at my blankets several times a night during the trip, muttering that a sailor was trying to get into the cabin. So up I would get, open the door, examine the empty corridor, report to Miss X, and try to get back to sleep.

I called up the Brands' house and got Lord Hampden (Tommy's father), who was charming and said that they had been awaiting my arrival hourly for a week, that unfortunately Leila was in the country with the children and the cook, and that several men were picnicking in the house, so they couldn't have me to stay, about which he was frightfully apologetic. I then took a bath, unpacked my black suit and best pink flowered blouse, steamed both, and about eight Tommy appeared and took me to their house, which was a lovely Georgian brick one on a square. Then we found a charming brigadier, just back from Italy. He had returned to find his house a hole in the ground from a V-bomb two weeks ago, so was staying at Tommy's.

We had an excellent martini cocktail, then set out in a taxi which happened to turn up and stopped at White's Club where Tommy procured a bottle of white wine. He and I then proceeded on foot to the Carlton Grill. It was still daylight and the streets were jammed with uniforms, as many U.S. as English ones, girls in summer dresses, parks full of flowers, and a barrel organ. Altogether so gay and yet so moving that I had a constant lump in my throat.

At the Carlton Grill, the old headwaiter came forward and said, "I'm afraid we are a bit short tonight, Mr. Brand." So I prepared for utility bread and water, instead of which appeared bean soup (a bit watery but very hot and full of croutons), broiled pigeon, delicious purèed spinach, fried potatoes, rolls, margarine, and strawberry ice cream, which didn't taste like strawberry ice cream at home but was very good. Then, excellent coffee and, of course, the Rhine wine. The place was full of glamorous-looking English officers on leave, and crowded, but the service was perfect, the old waiter so polite, and the silver and linen gleaming. It had been nine when we arrived, but still light. When we left, it was the blackest black I have ever seen. What with the blackness, the Rhine wine, and my nervous excitement, and the traffic going the wrong way, I was sure we would be killed but, clinging to Tommy, made the tube, which brought us to Marble Arch where the hotel is.

The tube was much cleaner and better aired than our subways, but jammed. I stood between an ancient lady wearing one of those high, vertical ostrich-feather hats and two U.S. corporals.

Fell into bed and slept so soundly that I was awakened at nine by the telephone. It was the brigadier I had met at Tommy's, who asked me to have dinner with him tonight, with a pair called Laycock. I found out later Laycock is a major general and took Mountbatten's place as head of Combined Operations. I accepted with alacrity, although I was not at all sure of the brigadier's name. Then he said, "I am desperately sorry about this news." I said, "What?" And he told me about the President's death. I sprang out of bed and rushed downstairs. Of course the papers were all sold out, but after breakfast I found a nice colonel from Portland, Maine, who told me about it.

Went to the Embassy, which was in an uproar over the news, and found most of my shipmates. Arranged to take a boat for France on Monday.

Took a walk all over the West End, getting lost frequently. It was another delicious day, and the Green Park and St. James's Park were lovely and full of people sitting in the sun. I sat on a bench too and thought about F.D.R.—boarding school, the infirmary and me in bed with the measles, fourteen years old, Pauline du Pont, my lifelong friend, in the next bed. "The banks are closed. It's terribly serious. Papa and Mama sound frantic. The President has said, 'The only thing we have to fear is fear itself.' I think that is very fine, don't you?" "Yes, P.L., but is it true?" . . . The wedding of P.L.'s cousin Ethel du Pont to Franklin D. Roosevelt, Jr. A nightmare. Our pink organdy dresses wilting under the heat of the duPont-Roosevelt feud . . . The war in Washington, Bill and I dining at the White House a few times because Franklin, Jr., and Ethel were there. Infinitely grateful, we would arrive early to be led to the President's study where he made the famous martinis on his desk and dispensed "Uncle Joe's present" (caviar from Stalin) and talked. . . . December 26, 1942—pre-Casablanca, post our allied North Africa landing. "Cable in from Ike. He says that Darlan[3] is a skunk, but we have to deal with him. Can't see our way out otherwise. I agree with Ike." Bill and I, hanging on his words, waited for more but we went down to dinner and old sea stories. Who could blame a wartime President? Thank God he could relax, but each time was a shock of disappointment. I could not be impressed by F.D.R. and I wanted so terribly to have him as I had imagined. In St. James's Park I felt very differently. How could we do without him? Truman—an unknown senator replacing our great wartime leader, our New Deal leader, the man on whom one had depended since one was fourteen years old. A sense of bereavement for a national figure was a new sensation; a cold sad feeling of loneliness made the April day seem diminished and I left my bench to walk through London.

The houses all look shabby and every few blocks there is a

[3] The rather forgotten Admiral Jean François Darlan, who shaped Vichy policy during much of the war, a vicious Anglophobe and Russophobe who went over to the Americans in 1942, saving us from an awkward situation in Algiers.

ghastly hole in the ground or a beautiful town house looking perfect until you see that the whole inside is gone, but somehow not as much damage as I expected. Berkeley Street, Charles Street, the Burlington Arcade, St. James Street, and so on look much the same. The shopwindows are full of things, the women's clothes gay colors but poor materials, the leather bags six and seven pounds and bad quality, but the antique shops have superb things in the windows. Asprey's window was pathetic, but Crichton's, for instance, had beautiful Georgian silver. The street Rosa Lewis lives in was badly hit, but Fortnum and Mason had windows full of brandied cherries, green turtle soup, and other wonderful canned things, but apparently they are so expensive and cost so many ration points, no one can buy them. Found my way with the help of several charming bobbies (everyone is so polite in England, aren't they?) to the Connaught Hotel, where I lunched with Jack and Becky Maclay.[4] Jack is in the Cabinet now. He had just come from the House, which had adjourned at noon because of the President, and said he had never seen such an atmosphere of gloom. They were sweet and, like Tommy Brand, kind and affectionate. I gave them some cigarettes and food and only wished I had more. They want to have a dinner party on Sunday night for me, but I am going down to the Brands' for the weekend and don't know if I can get back in time. This afternoon I walked for miles more, and am now in my creased black rayon and John-Fredericks hat waiting for the brigadier. Wish I knew what his name is, but it is such a heavenly evening I don't care. Anyway, I think he was wearing the Victoria Cross. Tomorrow morning Becky Maclay is going to take me to see the area around St. Paul's, then I set off with the ancient Lord and Lady Hampden and Tommy for the country, carrying the rest of my food and cigarettes. Have been trying to get in touch with Jim Cross,[5] but unsuccessful so far. At last, I sent him a wire to call me here, as his flat has no telephone. Feel I am in a pleasant but mad dream

[4] Old friends from wartime Washington. The Honorable John Maclay was one of the many brilliant British businessmen who worked in Washington during the war. In his case war shipping was his specialty, and it was a life line that would surely have snapped and broken if it had not been for the eighteen-hour days of the Jack Maclays. He was rewarded for his services by being given Cabinet rank.

[5] James E. Cross, my first cousin, who had been serving with the O.S.S.

and as if I would wake up any moment back in Georgetown. Am so glad to be able to start for Paris on Monday—the Embassy was really most efficient about priorities and so on.

Jim just telephoned, sounding cheerful and well, and is lunching me tomorrow at Prunier's in St. James Street which is dear of him and will be great fun.

Sunday A.M., April 15

Friday evening was fun with the brigadier[6] and the Laycocks. We dined at a small restaurant, I think in Soho—all very luxurious, as General Laycock had a car and a very smart driver. The food was awfully good—shrimps, sweetbreads with mushrooms and tomatoes, and a savory—quantity small. Everyone in the restaurant knew each other and talked like Evelyn Waugh characters. "Hello, Biffin old thing, haven't seen you since Tobruk—thought you were in Burma," etc. All the women were extremely pretty—was interested to see Daphne Weymouth,[7] with whom half the U. S. Army was in love. Mrs. Laycock was a Dudley Ward and is a real charmer. He is just what you would imagine the head of Combined Operations to be—hard, lean, Central Casting couldn't have done better. Everyone kept asking me about Truman, which was difficult—Jock Whitney was the only other American there—wonder what he said? Sat up quite late—my roommate, the nice but spinsterish lady economist—announced when I got back to the Cumberland that a man had tried to get into the room and she was quaking with fear. Told her it was probably the bootblack and went to sleep, she sitting up with a flashlight gripped in her hand all night. She left in the morning for the safety of a friend in the London School of Economics' house—great relief. Spent the morning with Becky Maclay touring the East End and around St. Paul's to see the devastation—found it more shocking than I had expected. Went to the Embassy and was pleased to find I had a code number and was MX 356 or some such thing for the trip to Paris. Anticlimax to pick up ticket in most nor-

[6] Brigadier Andrew Montagu-Douglas-Scott.
[7] Later the Marchioness of Bath, glamor girl and writer of some delightful books.

mal way from Continental Booking Clerk at Victoria—warning me in a fatherly manner to beware of French looters. I leave at 8:00 A.M. Monday, and arrive Gare du Nord at 6:00 A.M., Tuesday—very slow.

Lunched with Jim, who gave me a good lunch and was sweet and brotherly. Saw his flat afterwards—very nice. Then he kindly got me French money through a man at O.S.S. and went to Claridge's where I cashed some more American Express checks. Took a three forty-eight train to a place called Horbey in Surrey with Tommy and his sweet old father and mother. House is charming, small, and comfortable. (They have rented it as their big one is impossible.) It is surrounded by a moat and a small Norman church on the grounds with graves dating from 1300 to three German airmen, 1940. Tea with chocolate cake and delicious sandwiches—how? Dinner was very good and cooked by former river keeper of Lord Hampden's—ancient one-legged man. Dishes washed by Leila, river keeper, Lord Hampden, and me. Lord Hampden (ancient, white-haired, charming) excellent on the glasses and silver—says pantry work his specialty, but not so good in the kitchen. Cozy evening around the fire, Leila mending pathetic jodhpurs of youngest girl, gone in a hundred places, and listening to news and description of President's funeral cortege winding up Pennsylvania Avenue. Felt very far away and homesick for a moment. Bed about eleven. Can you send me a hot water bottle in the pouch? Poor old Lady Hampden is absolutely longing for one, and it is the only thing she has mentioned minding about the war. Slept incredibly soundly, came down to breakfast to find everybody else had been awake from three to five as hundreds of bombers passed directly over the house. Didn't hear one sound—Brands say the noise was worse than flying bombs. How could I not have awakened?

Have been in the garden since, looking at more streams of Fortresses[8] going to Germany—also gliders. Now must get dressed for church. Have run out of paper—don't dare to ask for any, as even U.S. ration in London one tiny pad a month. Hope you can read some of this scrawl.

P.S. Cannot close this without describing church—tiny little church—pathetic old white-haired vicar with trembling but beauti-

[8] Flying Fortresses, or B-17s.

ful voice—opens service with minute of silence for "our sincere friend and steadfast upholder." Sermon entirely about President with most genuine and sincere sorrow. After church I asked Leila to introduce me to the vicar to thank him. We go to the vicarage. Mrs. Vicar, sweet old lady, tells me not since the death of Queen Victoria has the village been so distressed. Vicar appears on bicycle. I make my speech and then he shows me the church again and says, "The records only go back to 1200, but there was a church before that here." Back to house, Lord Hampden mowing lawn, and we watch six squadrons of Flying Fortresses pass overhead on their way out. Roast lamb, treacle pudding for lunch. Brands very unconcerned about this but children let on what a treat it is. After lunch, solemn rite of Tommy dividing my Hershey bars into small pieces.

21 Square du Bois de Boulogne
80 Avenue Foch
April 18, 1945

My first letter to you from Paris. Arrived this morning at 6 A.M. Gare du Nord, trip easy and interesting. Troops, both English and U.S. returning from English leave, WAACs, and my faithful friends from the ship.

Dieppe a ghastly sight from German devastation but nice clean train waiting. Got aboard at 9 P.M. and was lucky enough to get a seat in a first-class compartment with two WAACs, a sweet sergeant from Brunswick, Maine, a Swiss diplomat, and a smart English officer with a dachshund on a leash. The dachshund was wearing a khaki sweater and slept peacefully on my lap all night like a hot water bottle. The dining car operated, and at five we had coffee, bread, and jam with the officer, the United States sergeant, and the dog.

Bill was at the station, with porters and a car which he had most efficiently borrowed from the Embassy. He looked wonderfully well and was in high spirits. We drove up here between chestnut blossoms and fresh green trees, the most heavenly sunny morning imaginable. The great avenues were deserted.

At the door was Elisa Vallet, the cook, smiling and cheerful, and the house filled with lilacs from the garden. Breakfast upstairs in the sitting room, the sun streaming in, and in the next room my bed turned down with Aunt Harriet's beautiful linen and blanket cover.

Bill and Elisa Vallet have been wonderful, the house gleams and shines and is far more attractive even than I remembered. Everything seems intact. After Bill left for the office, Elisa took me on a tour, proudly showing me all the things she had saved from the Boches. She seemed very nice and Bill and she have been getting on well for about a week. Bill brings home a few things from the Embassy commissary, and she buys bread and a few vegetables. He seems to have had men to dinner every night. Fortunately, the case I sent January 10 got here last week, so they had my silver, toilet paper, soap of all kinds, shelf paper, coffee, tea, and some canned things, enough for about two weeks. I hope tomorrow to find out how I get our rations regularly.

We have a laundress, and Elisa is trying to get a maid. The car is in France. It came in my convoy and is being assembled—wonderful, as there are, of course, no taxis. We have a little coal, enough for hot water about every other day, and it is so warm, we don't miss a furnace. The garden is sweet and full of blossoming lilacs. I don't think I've ever been so happy!

P.S. I have only been here for two hours.

The house was rented to us by my mother's kind and generous first cousins, Mrs. Winthrop Aldrich, Mrs. Arnold Whitridge, and Mrs. Sheldon Whitehouse, who had inherited it from their mother, Mrs. Charles B. Alexander. For the derisory sum of two hundred dollars a month we found ourselves in this happy family house which I knew well from girlhood vacations at Aunt Harriet's. Even her linen was on our bed, and despite four years of German occupation the two lovely drawing rooms retained their Louis XV walnut paneling, the Guardis hung on the wall, and the dining room gave onto a sun-filled garden. Upstairs we had our cozy sitting room, beds for six, and a canoe, left over by the Whitridges, should we wish to take to the Loire. We owed all this to my mother's family.

My father's family, the Jays, came originally from France as Huguenots escaping religious persecution and settled in New York. On the whole they served the state, generation after generation, and supported themselves by marrying heiresses among the Dutch and later the English settlers. Asked about myself by the Chinese in Peking a few years ago, I said that my ancestors were simple people who had felt deeply about their religion during the Ming Dynasty and fled their native country, France, because of it. The Chinese warmed to this and asked respectfully if on arrival in America they had tilled the soil. I felt rather ashamed, in the People's Republic, to reply that I had never heard of much soil-tilling. Pierre-Auguste Jay, the first to arrive, married the daughter of the Dutch governor of New Amsterdam, Pieter Stuyvesant. A hundred years later John Jay married Sarah Livingston and became our first Foreign Secretary and first Chief Justice. He was sent to Paris by Washington to assist Adams and Franklin with the peace treaty that ended our War of Independence, and his fascinating wife Sarah accompanied him. They saw the last of Versailles before the French Revolution and were friends of Talleyrand, who said that he who had not known France before the Revolution had not known how sweet life could be. I think my father, Peter Augustus Jay, who served as a young secretary at our Paris Legation (we had no Embassy then), was the fourth generation of our family to be involved in French affairs. His father, also a diplomat, was married to a dark-haired beauty, Emily Astor Kane, who fell in love with Paris and Paris with her. She was known as "The Black Pearl" and it was whispered that she rouged her nipples. Even in my time I occasionally ran into some old lady in Paris who still remembered the beautiful Mrs. Jay. But, much as I admired my grandmother, she died when I was very young and little of the French connection had rubbed off on me. I was an Anglophile, speaking very poor French and without a French friend, as I have said above.

80 Avenue Foch
Paris, France
April 18, 1945

Dear Cousins Harriet, Janetta, and Mary:

My pen and ink are still in the depths of my bags, but I must write, however illegibly, to tell you that I arrived this morning and everything is wonderful. I left London at 7 a.m. yesterday, traveling with troops, and arrived at the Gare du Nord at 6 A.M. Bill was there, miraculously, with porters and an Embassy car, and he drove me up straight here where he has been ensconced for three days.

It is the most heavenly day you could imagine, and early this morning, with no traffic on the great avenues and the fresh green and chestnut blossoms, it was like a lovely dream. Madame Vallet was at the door, very smiling, and the house was filled with lilacs from our garden and the cleanest, shiniest thing I ever saw. I took a hot bath (Bill and Madame Vallet nobly hoarding it for me—we can have some hot water every other day), and she brought up a lovely tray of coffee and toasted French bread with marmalade for us to the sitting room, the coffee in a gleaming silver pot, the milk naturally in its can.

After breakfast and Bill had gone to the office—he looks very well, by the way—Madame Vallet and I made a solemn inspection of the house, and I heard all her tales of outwitting the Germans. She certainly did a good job. Except for the outside looking shabby, a bit of plaster off ceilings and walls here and there, and a carpet from Aunt Harriet's room, it looks just as I remembered, only I had forgotten how enchanting it is. I have been thinking of Aunt Harriet so much all day and remembering her sitting in this room. Her drawing by Helleu looks down at me. Madame Vallet says it worried the Boches because it looks so *triste*. They asked her about it, and she says she said, *"Mais c'est la patronne—évidemment elle est triste."* Anyway, I still can't believe that I am here with the square full of chestnut blossoms and lilacs on the desk as I write. The only changes in the square are that most of the houses have been taken over by French government offices, and there is a sort of hole in the middle dug by the Germans to make a reservoir but unfinished.

The linen looks fine, and we have Aunt Harriet's laundress. Silver is also fine, and at a quick glance the china and glass also. Madame Vallet promises a *femme de chambre* shortly; in the meantime, she seems quite happy and well, although she lost one eye. She and Bill are a killing pair. They get on like a house afire, and he has become the perfect French *maître de maison*. I listened gaping while he told her about toasting the K-ration biscuits, and they discussed whether asparagus was too expensive for us to buy. He is paying her twenty-five hundred francs per month, and, at the moment she is sleeping in.

Thank heaven, my first case from Washington arrived yesterday—sent January 10—so we have toilet paper, soap, cigarettes, the cocktail shaker, and other necessities of living! Not much food, but tomorrow I hope to get some from the Army. Bill has forbidden the black market, but Madame Vallet tells me that we must use it and that Monsieur need not *se rendre compte.* Can't believe we will have to when my food from America arrives.

Wednesday

My first night was most comfortable. Have been out in the Métro doing some errands and trying to get the army to deliver our rations. The people on the streets are depressing. They look rather fat and well fed superficially, but their faces are all so sad—one never sees a happy face. The women's extraordinary great hats are of such shoddy materials and, on top of those worn, hard faces, strike me as pathetic and ludicrous. Tonight, our first guests. Bill has asked for cocktails the Courty Barneses, Eddie Gage and Eric Wyndham-White from the British Embassy (old friends from Washington), and a man called Lévis Mirepoix who Bill says is as close as anyone to de Gaulle. Regarding the hors d'oeuvres (saltines), Madame Vallet remarked gloomily, *"Que dirait Général Chuff,*[9] *my foi!"* but it seems very gay to me.

21 Square du Bois de Boulogne
80 Avenue Foch, Paris, France
April 19, 1945

My third day here and each day is more beautiful than the last. The wistaria is all out, as well as the chestnut blossoms and lilacs, and with the fresh green and the sun, it is heavenly. Despite this—my joy at being with Bill and this beautiful house—I have been most strangely depressed. I didn't expect to be and, as you know,

[9] Chuff, my aunt's English butler.

had no sentimental memories of Paris, but the people's faces haunt me, and although it is so much shinier and fresher than London, there I felt gay and exultant because, although people looked tired, they looked confident and there was an atmosphere of hope. Here, I step out of this lovely house full of Aubusson carpets and good American soap into the square, which has been taken over mostly by offices of the Ministry of War for Deportees and Refugees and is full of trucks with the returned prisoners in them. On the street one sees well-dressed people (I must admit that, although I can't stand the great hats and long-coated suits, the smart Frenchwomen do look darned smart) and very few people in rags, but the faces are one and all hard and worn and full of suffering in repose. There really is no food except for people who can afford the black market and not much for them. The pastry shops are empty—in the windows of teashops like Rumplemayer's, one sees one elaborate cardboard cake or an empty box of chocolates, with a sign saying "model" and nothing else. In the windows of shops on the Faubourg St. Honoré are proudly displayed one pair of shoes marked "real leather" or "model" surrounded by hideous things made of straw. Outside the Ritz I threw away a cigarette butt and a well-dressed old gentleman pounced for it. Well, as Bill says, there is no point in being emotional about it and one must just concentrate on trying to help. I must get a job but first must get the house organized. The food system seems to be, we have ordinary ration cards, which supposedly supply us. Bill having forbidden the black market, this means that the cook comes back with some potatoes, carrots, both worn and old, and lettuce, thank heaven. No fats, meat, green vegetables, or fruit. Every six weeks we get our rations; no choice about this; just what the army can spare. They arrived yesterday and were marvelous. All the staples, canned vegetables, fruits, fruit juices, bacon, powdered eggs, evaporated milk, etc., and once a week a fresh meat roast, either a chicken, lamb, or whatever, no choice again. I locked up everything, Elisa the cook helping me. I had to have someone help me, and she seems most honest, she caressed the cans, almost crying. The only trouble is the tins are enormous and difficult to deal with—five gallons of tomato catsup, for instance, and canned fruit in ten-pound tins. Our icebox is tiny, and, of course, the ice-making shop can't deliver, so the cook's children run a sort of pony express, carrying it in a wheelbarrow. The cook does her best, but we both have a lot to learn about cooking with dried eggs and so on, and although we are very well fed nutrition-wise, I have got to work hard to make it attractive. Must have people to meals constantly—ten men for cocktails yesterday, and they stayed till nine, and I couldn't ask them to dine, as the army rations aren't enough for heavy entertaining and until my own things come must be careful. I felt so badly. The only thing I could give them was champagne and K ration biscuits. Tomorrow we are having three or four men for dinner—*la bonne soupe* Campbell (carried all the way in my bag), canned chicken army, canned vegetables, and we hope chocolate mousse made of evaporated milk, powdered eggs, and chocolate.

Tommy Brand is staying with us and is bringing René Pleven (Secretary of Treasury). I think we shall have a paying guest, as financially it would be such a help, and I feel guilty not to. Bill has his eye on a perfect one—a boy called Chatfield who is charming and is a courier, so is away a lot. If we do this, I shall get two more servants instead of just one. The house really needs three. Went to an employment agency this afternoon (very nice and atmosphere just like home with the woman running it wailing about it being impossible to get anyone) to try for a maid. Feel sure it will be easy. The woman said, with that gleam in the eye with which I am already familiar, "*Naturellement Madame aura les provisions de l'armée américaine* [Naturally Madame will have American army rations]."

It was a lovely walk there and back (near the Avenue Kléber), rather slow as the streets are jammed with troops, and I was picked up several times by our soldiers speaking halting French—my reply naturally being "Come off it, Sergeant," or Corporal, or whatever it was, which necessitated explanations and twice sitting on benches listening to descriptions of the home town. They are lonely and touching, but killingly worldly wise about Paris. They carry maps of Paris and about eight of them helped me to find the employment agency, gathering more as we went along, so I arrived surrounded by a whole company, very gay except that they worried about me being out alone. "Say, ma'am, you watch out for these people," etc. They wanted to come home with me, but I couldn't face the numbers, especially as several men are coming in for cocktails.

Do not fear that by all the above I am complaining of my lot. I am thrilled to be here, whatever happens. I miss you badly—do write. Is the cook still drinking? I enclose a line to Eileen Maynard—Mrs. Walter. Would you get her address from the John Auchinclosses? I want to write people's wives after I see them.

21 Square du Bois de Boulogne
Paris, France
April 22, 1945

Please tell Mary Whitehouse how helpful her letters about France are—the greatest help. My French is terrible and I couldn't answer the notes I received without the examples she gave me, particularly the correct form of ending letters, which is so complicated. Let no one say again that the French aren't hospitable. At Rainbow Corner, the Red Cross club where I now work three days a week at the information desk, we have far more invitations from French of all classes than G.I.s to fill them, and this with the food shortage.

As for us, we are in thirty-day mourning for F.D.R., during which we are not supposed to entertain formally. It will be ages before I get sorted out who will go with whom. Our first dinner party *out* was disaster, although the hostess was a friend of a distinguished man in Washington who had written to her about us. She had been beautiful but wore an air of tarnish. There was nothing tarnished about her silver, the fellow guests had on beautiful clothes, and there must have been a kilo of butter in each delicious dish, not to speak of the cream. There was whiskey of several kinds—gin, etc., and Camels and Chesterfields all over the place. The house smelled of the black market, of corruption, of the greatcoats of the generals of the German Wehrmacht, who, we later learned, had been honored guests during the occupation of France. Our hosts apologized for the sparseness of the endless meal and told war hardship stories. There were open fires, and the furnace was full on as it had turned very chilly. We could hardly wait to leave and might well never have accepted another invitation had I not gone to call on Philippe de Noailles's mother the next day in order to take the presents for her he had given me in Washington. Their title is Mouchy; the house was as big as the one we had been in the night before, but the atmosphere was as different as day from night. The duchess was coming in as I arrived, and accepted Philippe's pathetic package with pleasure (needles, thread, safety pins, chocolate, and instant coffee) and urged me to ring up Bill and to stay for dinner, if we didn't mind eating in the porter's lodge, which was the only room with a stove. Oh, the wonderful elegant shabbiness of the Mouchys. The main course was canned peas, preceded by very thin, clear, watery soup. There was no apology about the food, no hardship stories about the war. The china was museum quality, and the oldest girl, nineteen, was very pleased with her dress, which was made from some old curtains. The whole family has great charm, like Philippe, and they have very kindly asked us to come in any Sunday afternoon when they have open house. We have been to other houses, but gaiety is impossible, as the prisoners are beginning to return—thousands flown in by us. At first, I was shocked by the calmness with which the French exchange news of them; it's as if I said to you, "Charlie Whitehouse got in from Buchenwald today, weighing sixty pounds." And you said, "Yes, and Mrs. Eliot Wadsworth is alive after all; of course, she has lost her hair and teeth, etc." Then I thought of our Civil War diaries and realized that these people have been through too much to speak in any more emotional way. I think I wrote that the sorting-out ministry for deportees is at the entrance to our square, so I pass them daily on my bicycle, as well as the families waiting. In the Métro, however crowded, even the oldest lady rises silently to surrender her seat when one of the black and white striped skeletons enters the carriage.

Of the American houses, we like most Admiral Kirk's.[10] He is delightful, and the house is not overdone or too luxurious, although pleasant aides see to every want—Gordon Grayson is one and a boy Bill particularly likes, McGeorge Bundy, another. Of the small, competent Embassy staff, we see most of the Norris Chipmans, Bohlen friends. She is French and beautiful.

[10] Admiral Alan Kirk was commander of U.S. Naval Forces in France.

We were so lucky to have bicycles. They were available at the PX, to which we had limited privileges; we were able to buy extra tires also. Bill used the Chevrolet to get back and forth to work, but we were strictly rationed for gasoline so going out in the evening we often bicycled if it wasn't too long or hilly a ride for him. Part of our duty was representational and, besides inviting to meals all the French officials whom Bill found useful in his work, we also were supposed to go out to as many cocktail parties and so on as possible. Bill's hours were 9 A.M. to at least 7 P.M. so I did the cocktail-party bit by bicycle. The word "cocktail" is used symbolically, reception is more like it. Lots of old ladies sitting on gold chairs around the walls, each of whose withered hands I shook, for French manners are formal and a young woman is supposed to show particular reverence to the old. The rest of the party would be standing about drinking either weak tea or sweet port, there was no conversation, many nervous ejaculations of pleasure at seeing each other, and perfunctory questions about health and family, which were never listened to or answered, for the name of the game was to see who was there and, if someone new came in, he or she was scrutinized and whispers of "Who can that be?" stopped such conversation as there was.

21 Square du Bois de Boulogne
Paris, France
May 1, 1945

I have sat down to write to you several times since last week, but the interruptions are endless. A dusty jeep draws up to the front door, just in from Germany with four weary old friends craving food and drink; Elisa, the cook, to torture me with new bad news about the price of onions (with the franc at fifty to the dollar, this is no joke); Bill calling up to discuss a lunch here for the governor of the Bank of France; always the three guest rooms full; and dramas at Rainbow Corner. Today it is snowing—traditionally one leaves Paris on the first of May to pick lilies of the valley in the forests on this holiday—perhaps next year?

To cheer up this rather gloomy day, we are having the Macy's ice cream mix as dessert for dinner tonight and some attractive neighbors to eat it with us. They live just across the square and are called Jacques and Marie T. Beauvois. He is a Lazard partner, and they are gay and cheerful. He was a prisoner for fifteen months and escaped to join the resistance in Normandy, where their country house was until last July when Flying Fortresses dropped thirty-two bombs on it, aiming for a bridge which had actually already been mined by the resistance, only the message to London telling this had gone astray. Jacques was out with the underground at the time, but she was there with the children and servants—twenty in all—the governess and one manservant were killed. They bear no resentment towards us about this and treat it as an unfortunate mistake, which we will see for ourselves as they have asked Bill to go trout fishing when we have enough gasoline for the drive. Another misconception about the French goes—I had been told that they were ungenerous, as well as inhospitable.

There is no question in anyone's mind about their courage. The political prisoners continue to pour in in ghastly shape. I can see on the other side of the square an empty truck and can make out the big letters painted on it, "Stalag IX libéré le 21 avril par l'armée lère de France—vive la France."

It is the greatest help to have a bicycle, and I am exploring Paris with Aunt Harriet's wonderful guidebooks in my basket. The physical beauty makes one catch one's breath in any weather, and it's fun to learn about the architects and the history. Having no traffic is bliss; one can stop in the middle of the Place Vendôme and read about Hardouin Mansart as if one was in the Sahara. My morning trips to the Red Cross job at Rainbow Corner are great treats. Down the Avenue Foch, quite flat, the chestnut trees and the houses have surely not changed much since Proust knew it as l'Avenue de l'Impératrice and Odette de Crécy's carriage joined the cavalcade borne for the ritual noon drive to the Bois. Round the Arc de Triomphe, which is never the same in any light, and down the Champs Elysées at high speed under the high sky, ahead of me the straight perspective that surely is the finest architectural complex in the world. At the Place de la Concorde we have an American M.P.—God knows why—the war goes on, but we are not an occupying army, and I find him embarrassing. He knows me and holds up the traffic to let me make my left into the Rue Royale. This also embarrasses me, as it's the only corner in Paris where there is any traffic at all, and his action throws off the French policemen directing the entrances to the Rue de Rivoli and the Rue St. Honoré. I have tried remonstrating, but it's no good. "Go on, miss, leave the French to me, and you take care of those pedals."

The military collapse of Germany was consummated in four months by simultaneous drives launched by Russian armies in the east and south and American, French, and British armies in the west. So ended four and a half years of war. It was announced on May 1 that Adolf Hitler had died in the Reichschancellery in Berlin and that Admiral Doenitz had succeeded him. On May 7 a group of German army leaders sent envoys to Rheims, where the surrender terms were signed. The following day President Truman for the United States and Prime Minister Churchill for Great Britain proclaimed the end of the war in Europe (V-E Day). On May 9, Marshal Stalin announced the end of the war to the Russian people.

May 10, 1945

I write from bed, having gotten my cold back due to celebrating the victory with it and must kill it this time, boring as it is. However, the celebration was a sight I couldn't ever forget, and I wouldn't have missed it. Monday night the rumor got around Paris, but the streets were fairly quiet until Tuesday afternoon. In the morning I bicycled up to the Etoile, and the flags were all out and fortunately it was a delicious hot sunny day. Bill came home for lunch with two Englishmen and our second secretary. About three I set out with them back to their offices. By this time the Champs Elysées was a wild sight and driving most hazardous due to every jeep and army vehicle in town being out with every possible inch of it smothered in screaming boys and girls—there must have been fifty all over each jeep. Flying Fortresses were buzzing up and down just not hitting the Arc de Triomphe and the noise was terrific. I fought my way on foot from the Embassy to Rainbow Corner (near the Madeleine) and listened to de Gaulle with my French fellow workers, who were far too emotional to give out any information to G.I.s, and I don't blame them. Got back from there to the Embassy about six and met Bill and Freddie Chatfield.

By now the Concorde was packed even tighter and, although the crowd was extremely friendly and well behaved, getting home presented a problem. Due to Freddie's broken leg, which was still in a cast, we had brought the car, as he couldn't have managed the Métro in that crowd. As we came out of the Embassy gates, a man stepped out on the balcony and made the V sign—the crowd went wild, as he was in uniform and yelled "Eisenhower." It was Bill Bullitt,[11] but I am glad they had the fun of thinking it was Eisenhower. M.P.s got us safely across the Concorde, and we got home a back way, to my relief, easily. Dined quietly, then Bill and I went out on foot with Jacques and Marie Thérèse Beauvois, after drinking a toast of champagne with them.

I will never forget that evening—Arc de Triomphe, Opéra, Place de la Concorde all lit up for the first time and the fountains on everywhere—the Madeleine especially beautiful and flares and fireworks and the Garde Républicaine riding down the Rue Royale with their helmets gleaming and sweating police in their blue capes trying to make way for them, and each member of the Guard having at least one girl riding behind him on the horse, clinging to his Napoleonic uniform and screaming. The jeeps still jammed and the French zoot suiters and the singing, especially the resistance song, which is a really good tune. Got home about 2 A.M. completely exhausted.

I am so glad they had such fun, as the peace is certainly going to be so incredibly difficult. For instance, an immediate question is, what is the General going to do with all the 1939 politicians who have been arriving back for the last few days? To my surprise at dinner last night, the French seemed to think Reynaud[12] would be right back in the government, that the General is devoted to him, and that he heeds his judgment. Eric Wyndham White, who lives around the corner (counselor at British Embassy and an old friend from Washington), had an extraordinary experience yesterday. He came home at 2:30 A.M. or so, following the celebration, and was

[11] William Bullitt, former Ambassador to France.
[12] Paul Reynaud, Premier of France from March to June 1940.

awakened at 5:30 A.M. by loud rapping at the door of his flat. He opened it and was brushed aside by three men, two of them carrying masses of baggage. The third man said most cheerfully, "*Bonjour, monsieur, je suis Daladier*[13] *de retour.*" Eric had rented the flat in America from Daladier's brother-in-law, who lives there; so, feeling somewhat shaken, he put him up in the spare room and went to bed himself. In the morning the maid said that the former Prime Minister was enjoying a hearty breakfast in bed and particularly liked the coffee (Eric's rations) and that he sent a message to Mr. White that after breakfast he would be busy writing his diary but would receive him later. So Eric appeared here at 9:30 A.M., looking despairing, to ask our advice, as he said he didn't mind Daladier having the back bedroom but would he always have to have him at meals; also sharing the bathroom with a complete stranger irked him, and there is only hot water enough for one, and it would be hard to tell the former Premier of France to take a cold bath. I think it is very funny and look forward to hearing the outcome. We are among the few people I know who have hot water, due to the four tons of coal left by the Germans. When that is gone, I guess we won't have any more. This summer I am going to raise heaven and earth to get some firewood and a type of Swedish stove that keeps one room warm. Electricity is still rationed, but we can use the heaters a bit.

Daladier stayed comfortably on in his own flat writing his memoirs, and our poor friend Eric was forced to seek shelter elsewhere. The former Premier was much put out at being deprived of the British Embassy rations. I never met Daladier but knew Reynaud fairly well later. His toadlike face was a clever one and he was excellent company. He had succeeded Daladier as Premier during the terrible summer of 1940 as the German tidal wave was engulfing France and he showed brains and courage for a time, followed by a failure of nerve that I will describe more vividly in my accounts of Churchill's desperate efforts to stabilize the French government as they fled farther and farther from Paris. It was thought that the Comtesse Hélène

[13] Edouard Daladier, Premier of France in 1939. He had been interned by the Vichy government and deported to Germany in 1943.

de Portes, Reynaud's pro-German mistress, was largely instrumental in his demoralization during the fall of France. She was killed in an automobile accident in the Pyrenees as they attempted to flee the country. Marshal Philippe Pétain, the hero of the great World War I Battle of Verdun, succeeded Reynaud as head of the French government on June 16, 1940, and the next day asked for an armistice, which was accepted by the Germans and signed at Compiègne.

June 14, 1945

I hasten to write a line to say that about thirty pouch packages arrived together today from you. I have only opened about half of them yet, but I am thrilled beyond measure, and it is just like Christmas. Your thoughtfulness, efficiency, and generosity are beyond measure. Everything I asked for is there, plus dozens of unexpected delights.

For instance, I was overjoyed, on opening the wooden box containing rubber bands and other useful things, to find a lot of thread, pins, and all sorts of things concealed in it. It is a real labor of love, and I can never thank you enough.

21 Square du Bois de Boulogne
Paris, France
June 15, 1945

There have been blue moments. The euphoria of arrival wore off. It then struck me that Paris was the most beautiful city I had ever been in but that it was like looking at a Canova death mask. I am quoting a fragment from an Isaiah Berlin letter which expresses what I mean: "Paris seemed terrifying to me—so cold and abnormally clean and empty and more beautiful than I have ever seen a city be—more so than Leningrad, and I cannot say how much that means—but empty and hollow and dead, like an exquisite corpse; the metaphor is vile and commonplace, but I can think of nothing else." I am sure I am wrong and that the vitality of this magnificent, exasperating, heroic people will return, but this is the period of let-down following the excitement of the liberation last year. Thank God I am beginning to make a few French girl friends. Louise de Rougemont and Odette Pol Roger and her sister, Jacqueline Vernes,[14] are our age, and I feel that I have known them forever. Somewhat older but wonderfully attractive, too, are the Mouchys, cousins of Louise's. The Mouchys and the friends mentioned above had very difficult times during the war, but one rule here is that those who suffered prefer not to talk about it, and it is next to impossible to worm resistance stories out of them. I went to a ceremony at the British Embassy to see the Ambassador thank and decorate members of the underground who had helped the British during the war and was struck as I heard the citations—not only by the courage but by how the resistance cut across class distinctions. The butcher and the baker were as brave as the Ganays, an aristocratic family consisting of four or five heroic boys and a mother whom I met at the Mouchys' the other day, whose task it was to guide Allied soldiers and fliers through the subway to safe houses. This doesn't sound like much but, of course, one word of English and Madame de Ganay would have been off to Ravensbrück.[15] I asked her about it, and she said that the only thing that worried her was that during the rush hour someone might easily have stepped on a soldier's toe and that, disciplined as they were, it is hard to say *ouch* except in one's own language. She didn't look as if she had ever been in a subway in her life.

The Duc de Mouchy had a stroke early in the war, although he is only in his forties, and he still has a withered arm. But he gets about and he and his wife are wonderfully kind showing me Paris and explaining about the French. He tells me not to believe for a second that the French are hospitable; they are simply bored with four years of their own society, so that Bill and I could not be here

[14] Comtesse Jean Louis de Rougemont, Madame Jacques Pol Roger, Madame Georges Vernes.

[15] Ravensbrück was a German concentration camp for female political prisoners. A taint of Jewish blood, resistance of any kind to the German occupation, and above all helping the Allies were crimes for which many brave women gave their lives in this terrible place. Torture was a commonplace; sadistic wardresses added every sort of horror to the prisoners' lives, and the mortality rate was appalling. Those who survived the malnutrition alone were very strong, but the ones I met later told me that they would never, never be quite the same. Belsen and Buchenwald and Dachau were equally terrible camps.

at a more fortunate time if we wish to know the French, which, according to Henri de Mouchy, is not necessarily a pleasurable pursuit. The *gratin,* for instance, that upper crust so familiar to us novel readers, is something I am unlikely to encounter if I live here for a hundred years, according to the Mouchys. I had rather thought that they represented it, but no, they and their friends have generally got an American grandmother or some other sort of besmirching foreign blood, and the true *gratin* are strictly "old France." They crouch in their apartments discussing marriage settlements and degrees of consanguinity, they do not travel, their silver is dirty and their bronzes unshined, and their servants hate them for their meanness.

We are staggered by the number of parades and holidays this summer. As someone said last night, every time anyone sneezes, they close off the Champs Elysées, and it seems just about true. De Gaulle is going in heavily for the "*mission historique de la France, prestige,*" etc., but I don't know how well it is going over. Bertrand de Maud'huy, husband of my delightful friend Maria, and himself a distinguished Lorrainian, said bitterly, "A country is worth what its men are worth," and continued in a vein very critical of the General. The press is curbed and uncritical, but an old Foreign Office hand was here yesterday, practically tearing his hair out and saying the man is mad, completely mad, meaning de Gaulle, and says that Bidault[16] hasn't been on speaking terms with him for months.

One impressive thing is the lack of bitterness towards the Germans. Already very farsighted men like Jean Monnet and Robert Schuman and Maud'huy are talking of future plans of co-operating industrially, and this will produce a head-on clash with de Gaulle and his passion for nationalism and grandeur. Even the unpolitical Mouchys appear to view the Germans with detachment—more than we could do. Their château, Mouchy, near Chantilly, is the most ghastly mess. We took Henri and the children out there last Sunday. Marie couldn't face it. Having bicycled out many times during the war in search of food (forty miles each way), she had a very clear idea of the senselessness of the destruction. Why half ax down a long line of ancient beech trees before leaving? The trees will die. Why laboriously cut the eyes out of all the portraits? But you have

[16] Georges Bidault, Foreign Minister of France.

read and heard so much of this sort of thing that I will not belabor the point, but only say that Bill and I took off our hats to Henri and to his son, Philippe, who had been in Colorado Springs with tuberculosis during the war. We walked around the place with the manager, and they didn't make one sentimental remark—talked briskly about the future—the only possible future is to complete the Germans' work and blow the whole thing up or raze it to the ground somehow. We ended in the guesthouse, which had become a Bavarian-type beer hall, stucco and all. Incongruously, a huge Noailles portrait by Nattier hung over the mantelpiece. Henri remarked on what boring women Nattier's subjects always seem to be and then made his one anti-German remark of the day. "God, how badly hung. One hates them for hanging pictures that way."

June 19, 1945

Am astounded by reports in the French papers that Caffery is to be replaced by Winant.[17] The Embassy is buzzing with gossip, but no facts. We saw the Cafferys on Saturday night at the Chipmans'—a most curious evening. The dinner consisted of a big French publisher and his wife, the André Siegfrieds (he is the best-known conservative newspaper correspondent of the moment), and ourselves. The Ambassador told the French ladies he was sitting by, in ringing tones, that in his opinion France was going into anarchy by their own choice, that he was disgusted by the government having expensive military parades every moment and constant holidays instead of doing something about the dreadful internal disorganization, that the French evidently prefer to go hungry, as nobody takes a stand against the black market or lack of transportation, and a lot more. These ideas are very familiar to me, as expressed by irate Americans in the bosom of the family, but I had never heard anyone tell the French them. I have been wondering ever since whether it is the right line for the Ambassador to take. What do you think? Anyway, the effect on the French ladies was devastating. After dinner I sat in one corner of the drawing room with the publisher's wife, who burst into tears quietly, fortunately,

[17] John Winant, Ambassador to Great Britain at this time.

and she said to me that she never had been so wounded and how could the Ambassador talk like that. Meanwhile, Bill, Mrs. Caffery, and Siegfried were having a terrible row in the other end of the room, due to Siegfried having made remarks about the luxury of the food at the San Francisco Conference and elsewhere he had been in the U.S. Mrs. Caffery got furious (she understands French but does not speak it), so Bill translated her hate admirably. He was pretty mad himself, and that ended with Siegfried backing down and making a handsome speech about how wonderful it was that we could fight a war on two fronts and still have any food at all. Then the Ambassador, who had been in another room with the French publisher and Chipman, came out, the Frenchman white and shaking, as evidently he had got the same line. Shortly after this, the Cafferys left.

The next day, Sunday, we went to Grosbois with the Duc de Mouchy and a genial cousin of his called the Princesse de Murat. It was a beautiful afternoon, and the place looked lovely. Goering had set it aside for his own use after the war, so it is one of the few châteaux untouched by the war. I remembered the inside remarkably well from our expedition there with Aunt Harriet, but it was fun to go with Mouchy, as he is an expert on furniture and explained it all very well. A young Princesse de La Tour d'Auvergne was living there. She was outside dressed in an old cotton dress and sneakers, watching with glee fifty gardeners who were cutting the grass and cleaning up the grounds. This remarkable apparition on a Sunday was due to the fact that the French government had ordered her to have lunch for the Sultan of Morocco this week and had sent the gardeners. They are also sending the food and the servants. "Grandeur."

21 Square du Bois de Boulogne
Paris, France
July 30, 1945

Lunched with David Rockefeller today—our old friend. It was interesting as Harold Callender of the New York *Times* was there and the talk was good. I was most grateful for David's ever kind hospitality, as the Pétain trial is making me physically sick. You will have read it all in the papers, but it is remarkably unpleasant to be in that little courtroom day after day; yet one wouldn't miss it—it's morbidly fascinating. Of course, I shouldn't be there; each embassy has one bitterly fought-for ticket, but an official gave me his own because he didn't want to see it. His reasons were interesting: France is in a bad way. The resistance, in which he played a distinguished role, is *un miroir brisé* (broken looking glass), with many of the men who joined it *after* the liberation in powerful places. There isn't a party in which anyone believes except the communists, and he for one does not wish to relive the decay of French democracy in a hot courtroom. So I have his seat and listen to former members of the government getting up day after day to exonerate themselves from any guilt and bringing tears to the eyes of everyone, including the defense attorneys, with moving descriptions of how the country was plunged into a bath of poison by the nefarious treason of Marshal Pétain. Sometimes they get so far off the point that the Marshal doesn't come into it at all. The witness is never stopped in his monologue, and there is almost no cross-examination. The Marshal sits there looking extremely spry and somehow dominates the proceedings by remaining silent.

It is not for me to judge Philippe Pétain, Marshal of France. Bitter things have been said about him by Frenchmen. I quote Vincent Auriol, later President of France, who says, "Daladier had taken all vitality out of Parliament, and through governing by decree, deprived it of all sense of responsibility. And when the tragic hour struck, the nation looked in vain for an embodiment of its sovereignty. The broken crown had been swallowed up by the abyss. And when the legal government finally disintegrated at Bordeaux, under the pressure of Pétain and his group, the Parliament failed to avert the traitors' plot. Only the team of defeatism and dictatorship, sheltering under the Marshal's oak leaves, was there to triumph."[18]
But Pétain was balm to the wounds of defeat. "France has spared neither her blood nor her labor. She is conscious of having earned the

[18] Vincent Auriol; *Hier . . . Demain* (Paris, 1945).

respect of the world. And she looks to herself for her own survival. Let Mr. Churchill remember this. . . ."

Aching, wounded, proud France accepted Pétain in the main, while the wounds healed and the nation recovered. There was confusion enough in Vichy, the Pétain capital, and in London, the temporary capital of de Gaulle's government in exile, to fill many books, some of which I have read. I do think that amid all the contradictions and bitterness one should remember that Pétain, famous for his vanity, was nearly ninety and it must have been easy to put into the mind of a nonagenarian the thought that he was the man of destiny, loved by the peasants, leading the country into the simple army officer philosophy on "Work, Family, Country." On coins, stamps, and public buildings the great Revolutionary motto, "Liberty, equality, fraternity," was rigorously suppressed. But my views about Pétain are of no importance; what was important was the travesty of justice that was his trial. He was not executed but deported to a remote island off France where he lived to the end of his long life.

Paris, France
August, 1945

I continue after a hurried trip to the Avenue Victor Hugo for ice on my bicycle. Why Aunt Harriet never had a Frigidaire, I can't imagine, as the one icebox simply isn't big enough, and nowdays the iceman only comes three times a week, and often not at all if he doesn't feel like it. The dessert for lunch was melting fast, but fortunately I got some after queuing up for half an hour.

To continue with your questions, the mothers don't seem to do any chaperoning any more as the modern jeune fille is as grown up if not more so as an American girl and just as independent. They are having the first good time of their lives, going out every night with French, English, or American officers alone or in parties to their friends' houses or to Le Forty-Five, which is a night club, and to talk to, they are remarkably mature and independent, but retain their old-fashioned good manners, which makes an attractive combination. A charming young cousin of Louise de Rougemont's was there at tea yesterday. She had been at a Sacred Heart Convent in England when the war broke out, became an anesthetist, and joined Le Clerc's Free French 2nd Division in Africa and followed all the way with her ambulance unit, Tunisia, Italy, Strasbourg. Of course, most of the girls had no such chance and had to sit out the war here, but it was hardly a sheltered life.

On the whole, I would say that the strength of France is all in the women, although I have met a few healthy and attractive young officers, but they are very few and far between, and the little G.I.s of the last class called up for Indochina are pathetic-looking specimens. As you have seen from how nice they have been to us, the poor French felt so claustrophobic from five years of being cut off that they welcome any American who doesn't eat with his knife, so to speak.

Here are more answers to your questions. No, I have not had any materials made up as any dressmaking house charges a minimum of ten thousand francs for a dress, even with the material provided (their excuse is the higher salaries), and as this is two hundred dollars and we are hoping from week to week that the rate will change, I decided to wait. Hats are a hundred dollars. Also, I am completely happy in my American clothes, which are much admired. I soon found that the only people who had the new suits of last spring with long jackets and elaborate hats were the war profiteers' wives and black market queens and a few rather vulgar ladies, collaborators' wives, and so on, and people like my friend Louise de Rougemont or Marie Beauvois wear five-year-old dresses, and if they ever wear hats, they are very simple small ones. The very big hats were already going out when I got here in April, although one still sees them around. I imagine that by this autumn the smart women will have pulled themselves together and will be buying again, although they say the materials are horrible; but so far, the shabbiness of all hands is extreme and the only really smart woman I have seen is Alix de Rothschild,[19] who of course came over from New York after I did. However, I would think that we have seen only the more conservative French so far and don't know what the café society ladies wear. I imagine there still must be a Duke of Windsorish group, don't you?

[19] Baroness Guy de Rothschild.

No, I think it was a little early for café society to start up. There had of course been one during the war, when the fashionable restaurants and night clubs echoed to the tune of "Lili Marlene" but those beautiful French ladies who had hung on the gray greatcoats of the Wehrmacht were somewhat sobered, even the ones I met at our first terrible dinner party in that big, luxurious house smothered in black market butter. This was an interim period.

Paris, France
August 15, 1945

I am still so appalled by the atomic bomb and the atomic future that I can only feel a tremendous sense of relief in thinking of Desmond, Charlie Whitehouse, etc., coming home alive but no real joy. Every time I look at a picture of President Truman, I think what an honest, decent face he has but how incongruous it was to hear from that flat, unimpressive voice those bloodcurdling words about the power of the atomic bomb. One felt that such news should come with a clash of cymbals and the vocabulary of the three witches from *Macbeth.* Truman looks like my dentist in Washington, and the tone was the same as Dr. Osborne's "Open just a little wider, please." Quite right, too, I suppose, rending garments will get us nowhere. I had the perfect companion that strange day, John Walker, the director of the National Gallery, who has been in Europe with the Roberts Commission searching for lost art treasures. He had dined here a few days before with Chip Bohlen, who was on his way home after Potsdam. I don't think I ever say enough about how lovely it is to have old friends arrive. Chip has been here twice, Paul Nitze, too. Freddie Reinhardt drops in from time to time. Their news is always absorbing and one can relax. In any case, Johnny and I had made a date to go sightseeing, but when we heard about the atomic bomb, everything seemed different, and we drove past the Louvre without going in and took a walk on the Ile de la Cité near Notre Dame, talking very little. Then we had a lemonade at a café on the quai and talked and even laughed about things in our pasts, and that was that. He is a most charming man.

I continue to be amused by Philippe in his role as Prince de Poix and mayor of his village, Mouchy, which votes mainly Communist, but he is popular and when they asked him to go out last Sunday to open the annual ball in the main square, an old farmer asked him to buy in Paris a diamond ring for his daughter. Mission accomplished, Philippe brought out the ring, which the old Communist said wasn't nearly big enough. So Philippe returned to Chaumet, carrying three hundred and fifty thousand francs in a paper bag, and bought a whopping great ring. The farmer was delighted and said to Philippe not to worry about it having cost so much because he had seven million francs in a cupboard. There is your classic rural Communist.

In this letter I mention three remarkable American public servants, two of whom, Charles E. Bohlen and Frederick Reinhardt, are, alas, no longer with us. A memory that sticks in my mind is of a dinner that Joe Alsop and I gave in October 1962 to say good-by to the Bohlens as they left for Paris. It was a small party, and the President and Mrs. Kennedy, the French Ambassador and Madame Hervé Alphand, Philip and Katharine Graham, and Isaiah Berlin were the other guests. I always found it nerve-racking to contemplate having the Kennedys come to dinner, which they did occasionally because of their real affection for Joe and their certainty that he would have guests who would not bore them, but once they arrived, running up the steps of our Georgetown house laughing, warm, life-enhancing, my worry left me and I relaxed completely and loved every minute. This night was different. It was warm, although October, and we had cocktails on the terrace. The President casually took Chip Bohlen off to the end of the garden to talk and walk up and down under the magnolias. Up and down they walked, for far too long, while I sat chatting and worrying about two things on my mind. One was Avis Bohlen's back, which was in bad shape, and she had doped herself up with codeine to make the dinner; I didn't want her to be kept waiting. Less important, but gnawing at me, was a leg of lamb which I knew was in the oven. Could I count on my impatient little French cook, Jeanne, to keep it juicy? Probably not. And what was the matter with the President? It was most unlike him to conduct business before dinner. At last the two men joined us. I can see them walking up the brick path by the box hedges, laughing, making a joke, and can hear the President apologizing to me for the delay. What Joe and I could not know was that early that morning he had been shown the first C.I.A. reconnaissance photographs of the Russian-placed missile sites in Cuba, and that he had been informing Chip and asking his advice. I think that it must have greatly comforted the President to talk to Chip before facing confrontation. Entirely apart from substance, Chip's voice was the most attractive I have ever listened to. Deep, rather slow, it held a quality unlike anyone else's. If he told me to jump off the Washington Monument I would have been the first on the elevator to get to the top; if he wanted to make me laugh, as he usually did, three words in that voice did it.

Two more things stick in my mind about that evening. Twice at dinner the President asked the same question—the conversation was general. Twice he asked the Russian experts present, Chip and Isaiah, what had happened in history when the Russians found themselves boxed into awkward situations from which it would be difficult to extricate themselves without loss of face. This startled me, for Kennedy was the best extractor of information I have ever met, and I was most surprised that he wanted to go back for more on a subject that didn't even seem interesting. The other impression was physical. The poor President had to sit by me when he came to dinner. That night he was revved up—I wish I could think of a better simile. It seemed to me that the very powerful engine, say Bentley or Ferrari, beside which I had had the honor of sitting many times, running at fifty miles an hour, had been thrown into the intensity of full power, controlled, the throttle was out and, what was more, he was enjoying it. It was thrilling, like sitting by lightning, but it made no sense. My mind struggled to comprehend, but the news had been very commonplace that week and I couldn't imagine what made me say to Joe as we went to bed that something was up, for sure. As the Kennedys left, I heard the President thank Chip for something, I couldn't hear what—I imagine that he was just thanking him for being there, as we all did, all our lives, until he died.

Paris
August 20, 1945

To our great surprise, Joe Alsop turned up last Friday in a huge C-47 from China carrying General Chennault and lots of emeralds for Tish[20] and rare old Chinese bronzes for the Alsop collection. General Chennault is a very simple, shy man with a face carved out of granite. I kept thinking of Churchill's remark after meeting him: "Thank God that man is on our side." We had a French dinner party and they were much impressed by him. The next day Joe led him off to see Paris. He had never been here before and was as eager a sightseer as the greenest G.I. Joe looked really handsome in his captain's uniform. It was a shame that they stayed such a short time.

The next night Cousin Winthrop[21] arrived and we had thirty-five to forty people for cocktails, after which we dined at the Ritz with Cousin Winthrop and the three men of his party. Most pleasant, although the Ritz is having a hard time, as they have had to go off army rations, and so it is a civilian restaurant, not a mess. They are not black market and do wonders. The waiters and atmosphere are prewar, and they still have good wines. Dinner was barley soup, a small piece of meat, mashed potatoes, turnips, and pears and grapes. But the barley soup was steaming hot and just the right consistency; the mashed potatoes were beautifully puréed; the turnips were presented as a separate course in a chic copper casserole covered with a delicious if thin sauce Béchamel. The grapes, though few in quantity, were peeled and arranged around the skinny pears in a bowl on ice decorated with fresh leaves. The *café national,* as we are obligated to call the strange brownish drink we have everywhere after meals, was served by at least three waiters, their tail coats all but sweeping the ground.

Chris Herter[22] spent the next night, on his way to Yugoslavia and then Poland. He is connected with UNRRA, and it was interesting to hear him talk to Nabokov,[23] who is staying with us again. Nicky gave vivid descriptions of the ten million Germans wandering around in what is now Poland and of the long line of Russian army wagons (horse-drawn, of course) on any road in Poland, proceeding eastward, swaying under the burden of their loot. There isn't a chamber pot left east of Berlin.

[20] Mrs. Stewart Alsop.
[21] Winthrop W. Aldrich, head of Chase Bank, later Ambassador to London.
[22] Christian Herter, later Secretary of State.
[23] Nicolas Nabokov, author, philosopher.

· 1945 ·

Paris, France
September, 20, 1945

Out of the blue came a telegram from Leone Fumasoni Biondi, the *Osservatore Romano* correspondent in Washington in the thirties who was so crazy about both of us, do you remember him? The message said that Bill's sister Jean[24] was very ill and required antibiotics, pronto. She is in the hospital in the village in Italy where their country house is, Fabriano. Bill couldn't get away, so I obtained compassionate leave from the Red Cross and went. Jean, a heroic girl who knocked herself out during the war carrying messages for the partisans and sheltering Allied fliers and taking care of her large family under hideous circumstances, for their house lies near the Gothic Line and they were constantly bombed, is recovering, as a result of the penicillin I carried, and besides the pleasure of seeing her, it was most interesting for me, as I had a chance to see Allied Military Government at its worst and at its best. The worst is lower-level bureaucratic types in Naples, where my bomber landed me. I spent two miserable nights at the Red Cross billet, struggling with potbellied majors in offices who refused me permission to get north but invited me to dine and dance in luxurious officers' clubs above the Bay of Naples. Just getting to the jeeps was purgatory. Picture the poverty of prewar Naples cubed and skeleton children from Hieronymus Bosch pictures clutching at the skirt of one's uniform and the fat army rations and the rum and Coca-Cola served by obsequious waiters with murder in their eyes, and dancing under an obscene moon with an obscene man. The second night I didn't go to sleep but stole out at dawn on the road to Rome and thumbed a ride north. From then on, I have nothing but praise and gratitude to AMGOT.[25] Truck drivers passed me on to jeep drivers who transferred me to command cars. I shared their rations among the scarred olive trees and we never stopped, for they understood my fear that the antibiotics might go bad in the intense heat. By the evening of the next night, my last friend left me at a marker saying Fabriano 2 kilometers. He would have driven me into town, but it was off his route, and he had done more than

[24] Marchesa di Pellegrini-Quarantotti.
[25] Allied Government Occupied Territories.

enough. I walked into the hospital and asked a nun for Jean, who had never seen me before and was quite unprepared for my arrival. She is much like Bill, and I felt at home with her at once. Although very weak, she said she was thrilled to see me, only Bill had described me as very dark and I was blonde. This sent me to the mirror in a hurry. Of course, it was only the dust of the drive and the bad light—I looked like George Washington.

The Italian trip caused the only argument I had with my dear mother during these years. She was living alone in Washington, gallantly supporting me with praise and affectionate letters and dozens of weary trips to the State Department mail room with packages of everything from ice cream mix to safety pins. But my mother is a woman of high principle, herself the widow of an Ambassador of the United States, and she felt strongly that government transport should not be used for personal reasons.

I was furious at my mother's reaction to the trip to Italy, as I thought I had been rather heroic, and wrote back asking if she would have liked me to use the only other possible method of getting from Paris to Fabriano, which would have been to ring up Alexander Kirk, our Ambassador at Rome, and an old family friend, asking him to put me up at the Palazzo Barberini, his residence, and send me up to Jean's in his car. He would have felt he had to do this for my father's daughter (Papa had, after all, been in charge of the Embassy when I was born in Rome), but I know the pressure on ambassadors from their citizens and preferred to do it my way. Bill wrote a placating letter, in which he said that he hoped Mama didn't blame him too much for the Italian trip, but that I had fixed him with "those stern brown eyes" (a family phrase, first employed by my Aunt Harriet when I was three), and there was no way to dissuade me. He went on to describe the Laval[26] trial, which he said was an even more disgusting exhibition than that of Marshal Pétain. It was. The purge trials preoccupied us all that year, and the incoherence with which justice was meted out did much to cause the *crise morale*, or crisis of conscience among the French. One heard wildly exaggerated figures of the executions of French men and women who had collaborated

[26] Pierre Laval, Foreign Minister under Pétain, collaborated with the Germans and was tried and executed as a war criminal.

with the Germans, known as *collabos*. Later figures have shown, I am told, that the repressions in other occupied countries, Belgium, Holland, Norway, were much more severe. Bidault, the resistance leader and Foreign Minister, gave us the figure of ten thousand collaborators summarily executed without trial, half of these before the liberation of France. The regular post-liberation courts sentenced nearly three thousand persons to death but only seven hundred or so sentences were carried out. There were about forty thousand sentences to imprisonment, but by the end of 1952 only fifteen hundred or so were still in prison. What splintered French morale was the unfairness of some of the punishments. A young woman who had slept with a German soldier perhaps deserved to be dragged through the streets with her head shaven, thought my friends, but why should the economic profiteers get off unpunished? The black market flourished for a long time and was run by rings who bought the steaks and the butter from the peasants and sold it to black market restaurants in Paris at a huge profit—the farmers did well out of it too, as my letters show in two instances.

21 Square du Bois de Boulogne
Paris, September 25, 1945

Do you know that I met an optimist in Italy? A democrat who is convinced that his broken country is going to achieve perfect, Jeffersonian democracy. I suppose that six months in Europe have so accustomed me to despondency that that is why this brave little Italian made such an impression on me.

I do think that most American visitors to Paris have a dreary time. It is no place for Mr. Jones, president of some not too important business in the U.S., who has decided to come over for a look-see. First of all, most visitors get off to a bad start by being told in London or somewhere that on their continental trip they are VIPs. This means very important person and thrills them, but it is really like having a Priority 4 on the Air Transport Command and doesn't mean a thing, as all congressmen, actors, people writing magazine articles, minor civil servants, most businessmen, etc., are automatically VIP and only Winthrop Aldrich and the very highest generals are VIPI (very important people indeed), and they have private planes and suites at the Ritz and lead an easy life. Anyway, the ordinary visitor arrives, the VIP label on his bags, bursting with enthusiasm at being on the Grand Tour and in Gay Paree, and disillusion immediately sets in. First, he can't get a taxi, and Lily Pons or some other VIPI has all the cars out of the motor pool. So he has to walk miles from the third-class hotel he has been billeted in and when he gets to the George V or the Meurice or whatever used to be his favorite hotel, he can't get into the dining room because the army has it and he is a civilian. He then goes on a shopping tour and sees bags at Lanvin for the little woman. These are made out of chewed straw, and a disdainful vendeuse indicates that at ten thousand francs she is practically giving one to him. He tries to buy perfume, but there is a queue of several hundred American soldiers at each store, as well as at the booking office where he tries to buy a ticket for the Folies. Sightseeing is out because his feet hurt quite a lot now, and he really hasn't got time anyway because so much of the day is spent walking from his remote hotel to the remote mess where he has to eat. He goes to the American Embassy, and the Ambassador is too busy to see him, but if his business is financial, he probably meets that charming character, Mr. William S. Patten, and is asked to a cocktail party at the Embassy and to lunch at Mr. Patten's residence. He looks forward to the cocktail party, having been given the impression that it is in his honor and that he will meet a great many interesting French people. So he soaks his poor tired feet in cold water (there is no hot water at his hotel) and hoofs it to the Avenue d'Iéna at six o'clock, and the cocktail party consists of several hundred other VIPs who are congressmen, Masons, Rotarians, visiting consuls, CIO officials, and vice-presidents of the Kansas City branch of the Save the Sewer Rats of Paris Society. He sees his friend Mr. Patten and goes over to him, hoping that he will introduce him to some of the resistance leaders who he still feels must be lurking about somewhere. Instead of this, Mr. Patten introduces him to Mrs. Patten and to that gallant figure of the resistance, Monsieur Georges, le sous-chef du Division des Affaires Protoculaires du Ministère des Affaires Etrangères. And so it goes. By the time the cocktail party is over, his mess is closed, and there is nothing for it but a black market restaurant where he is poisoned on bad lobster for twenty-five dollars.

October 1, 1945
Beaumont-le-Roger, Normandy

This weekend at the Beauvois' country home has hurt me and cheered me. The hurt was because although I knew yet once more that it wasn't our fault this must have been an enchanting little town. The remains of the Romanesque church and some houses still standing in the main square give one an idea, and bombers cannot be accurate if there is a small airfield nearby. Bill and Jacques found some trout in the river and Marie and I picked mushrooms in the woods and went calling on the farmers' wives, which was fun; not only could we take real butter and cream back to Paris but the conversation was marvelous. They are making fortunes, and as one can't buy anything like shoes, which they really need, it's all kept in cash. One clean little kitchen had a picture of F.D.R. next to de Gaulle and General Leclerc.[27]

Paris, October 11, 1945
V-mail urgent

Would you please send me some candles immediately preferably white but really any kind. Now the electricity breaks down every night instead of every other and it's a bore as we are suddenly off summer time so it gets dark early.

Paris, October 14, 1945

Thank God the sun has come out and it's Indian summer. It's impossible to be gloomy with the trees yellow and gold and the Arc de Triomphe very white and American soldiers with girls on their arms strolling by nannies sitting on the iron chairs in the warm mornings, while the children roll hoops. My girl friends, Louise de Rougemont and Odette Pol Roger and Jacqueline Vernes and Maria de Maud'huy, on the first good autumn day rush off and buy new hats, just as one would in New York. Here one goes to Reboux, still,

[27] Commander of Free French forces during the war.

and I wonder what will happen when women stop wearing hats as I dare say they will one day, they are not exactly necessary, but what a difference a bit of veiling and a pretty color of velvet make—more than dresses, I think, but I haven't been able to buy a Paris dress yet.

I still bicycle everywhere, and would love a couple of bicycle lights if it isn't too much trouble. I have flashlights, but it's a bore holding one. The lack of complaining of the French is remarkable, no one talks about the dreaded winter, or much about the past.

Paris, October 28, 1945

Dinner at the Vernes', a very gay party, has sent Bill and me to bed with food poisoning. Jacqueline usually has marvelous food, this sort of accident happens only because of transportation difficulties with fish. So we are in bed on our sixth wedding anniversary but feeling more cheerful every moment. I sat by the Duke of Windsor, who talked to me about the war. He said that of course he was quite out of touch now but that it had occurred to him at one time that if Dakar had been taken and the Bahamas invaded he would have sent the Duchess to Miami and fought it out to the last in Nassau, which you will remember he was governing. He meant this—the ring of sincerity was there. Bill says that he had a great time talking food to the Duchess, who gave him her recipe for canned salmon soufflé, which will not be useful right now as the ration is six eggs for two weeks in our household, which is eight people, but I rejoice in the thought of it later.

21 Square du Bois de Boulogne
Paris, France
October 7, 1945

This has been a busy and amusing week. Staying here for a night or two, we have had Fulton Cutting, Chris Herter, Jr., Henrik Kaufmann[28] on his way through from Denmark, Nicky Nabokov from Berlin and a Captain Krinsky, both back from three months in the Russian Zone, and the people who came to the house for meals or dropped in sound like a mad hatter's tea party. Perhaps the two I was most grateful to see were two of my friends from Rainbow Corner, Privates Elliott and Tlusky of the Signal Corps, as our telephone is nearly always out of order. It's true all over Paris and said to be because the hungry rats eat the cables, and it's tiring to come home for dinner from work and not know how many we will be. Mama goes on being superbly generous with pouch packages and we have army rations, but Elisa and I are never quite sure whether there will be enough next week. Don't please repeat this whine; I would feel very badly if people did not realize how pleased Bill and I are to do something for the many people who arrive with letters to us, or the old friends who send friends unannounced, to say nothing of the old friends themselves.

Everyone here has been depressed by the failure of the London conference.[29] While the Russian stubbornness worries us, my friend Nabokov, who has been living in the Russian Zone, tells me that the Russian officers are terrified of an imperialist war by England and America against them and feel that they are on the defensive. The situation in Germany appears more and more improbable. As we have all heard for ages, our zone is a mess. Chris Herter, Jr., is in despair about the quality of our military governors, and feels that the Germans are relishing the spectacle of inefficient and in some cases dishonest Americans running them. In Chris's town, on the Chiemsee near Salzburg, the town major deliberately released one flagrant Nazi, on the condition that the German's daughter become his mistress. The sooner we get in trained civil administrators, the better; but when will that be? The French are having a field day regarding our mistakes. Today, *Figaro* has a leader by François Mauriac, pointing out that America and Russia will soon destroy each other, England will be drawn in, and only France will be left to carry on the great tradition of democracy. Well, I wish them luck.

[28] Henrik Kaufman, Danish Ambassador to United States.
[29] Conference of Foreign Ministers, to discuss the future of Germany.

To Marietta from Paris

Paris, November 11, 1945

I went to an extraordinary sale this week at the Hotel Drouot. It was the jewelry and furs of the collaborating war profiteers. Hideous, huge, bad-quality jewels, furs equally ugly. The prices were very high. A worn gray squirrel went for four hundred and thirty-five thousand and a big brute of a yellow diamond ring for four million—figure this at the eternal fifty francs to the dollar. A strange, avid audience, some poorly dressed, others the black market queens in their new Lelongs.

Going to the theater is a chilly business, one never takes off one's coat and imagine that the hit of Paris is *Arsenique et Vieilles Dentelles,*[30] we have seen it twice.

Thank God for the candles, you were wonderful to get them here so quickly.

Paris, November 26, 1945

Our Thanksgiving went cheerfully, we had a turkey and sixteen guests to eat it and various people dropped in through the day. Eddie Warburg is back from his awful struggles in Germany for the Jews, and I was once more impressed by what a fine person he is and how hard his job is. Nicky Nabokov returned from Berlin, and brought us an interesting friend of his, Clarissa Churchill,[31] who is possessed of a curious and special charm. We took Eddie to dine with General Redmin, and the next day we all lunched with the John Marriotts.[32]

General Marriott is in command of the Guards Division in the British Zone and had some wonderful stories. He lives in great comfort in Godesberg in a schloss belonging to the eau de cologne king, Mr. 4711, and had just been having Montgomery[33] to stay. He said that a few nights ago he had given them the most fascinating

[30] *Arsenic and Old Lace.*
[31] Clarissa Churchill became Mrs. Anthony Eden and later Lady Avon.
[32] General Sir John Marriott. Lady Marriott and her sister, Mrs. John Barry Ryan, were close friends of mine from New York.
[33] Field Marshal Bernard Montgomery, the hero of El Alamein and commander of the British Eighth Army, has charisma, a flair for publicity, and brilliance.

lecture after dinner on the three men he considered the greatest military leaders of history: Moses, Cromwell, and Napoleon. I was struck by this choice, as one thinks of Moses as a leader of displaced persons rather than a military leader—anyway, apparently the talk was wonderful. Marriott says that his Guards were very bored by Monty, as they consider his style of dress unseemly, and when he wanders around they pay little attention to him, which is very embarrassing, as he likes to have the men swoon and is accustomed to the Eighth Army veneration.

Dined last night at the British Embassy, about twelve people and very pleasant. Sat by the Swedish Minister, who is a charming man. The other guests were nice French, plus the Marriotts, Mrs. George, Clarissa Churchill, etc. We dined in the upstairs dining room, which is walled in tapestries, and I loved the beautiful yellow silk on the walls in the room where we had coffee. At dinner I could hardly talk to either of the gentlemen as I was fascinated by what General Gentilhomme, the governor of Paris, was telling the English lady next to him about the present conduct of our troops; a conversation full of phrases like "*des barbares, pire que les Russes, vous ne pouvez pas vous rendre compte, chère madame, de cette situation épouvantable—ils sont des gangsters.* [Barbarians, worse than the Russians, you cannot imagine, dear lady, the horror of the situation—they are gangsters]. (Did you know that gangster is a French word now? Pronounced as you would think it would be in French.) I was longing to rush in across the table in defense of the G.I.s but it was just as well I didn't as in fact they are behaving as you would expect any bored troops to behave, and I am not proud of them.

After dinner to my horror I was forced to play bridge with the Ambassador against the Swedes. I happened to be the only woman there who played at all, and as my bridge is terrible I was miserable. This took place in a great cold drawing room untouched since the days of Wellington, lit by candles. I had hopeless cards and played very badly when I did have them, and although Duff Cooper[34] was very kind to me I longed to be back in Washington

[34] Duff Cooper and his wife, Lady Diana, made the British Embassy in Paris the first postwar center of intellectual, political, theatrical, and artistic life to emerge in shabby, tired Western Europe. Duff Cooper's post as British Ambas-

cozily singing the Eton Boating Song with Lord Halifax.[35] The Swedes won three swift rubbers with merciless Swedish efficiency and left. Shortly after this debacle we left too, I as always cheered by Lady Diana.

Paris, December 2, 1945

Can you bear one more of my endless conversations with the Duke of Windsor? He is pitiful, looks young and undissipated, and the famous charm is still there but I never saw a man so bored.

He said to me, "How do you manage to remain so cheerful in this ghastly depressing place? What did you do today?" So I said, "Well, sir, I work at one of our enlisted men's clubs and I was there all day." He said, "Oh, what fun that must be, do you think I could come down someday and see it?" I said, "Of course, sir, they would be overjoyed." "You know what my day was today," said the Duke. "I got up late and then I went with the Duchess and watched her buy a hat, and then on the way home I had the car drop me in the Bois to watch some of your soldiers playing football and then I had planned to take a walk, but it was so cold that I could hardly bear it. In fact I was afraid that I would be struck with cold in the way people are struck with heat so I came straight home. On the way

---

sador to France followed his year in Algiers representing his government with the French Committee for Liberation (de Gaulle's government). Earlier he had been a member of Parliament, Secretary of State for War, First Lord of the Admiralty, and Minister of Information. His resignation from office in 1938 over the Munich issue caused a world-wide sensation and was thought to be the end of his career. Diana backed him in this, and in everything. Duff Cooper wrote of her physical courage that while he was, in one rather bad moment, repeating to himself the great lines from *Measure for Measure,*

> Be absolute for death; either death or life
> Shall thereby be the sweeter,

which he kept for emergencies, Diana was completely unalarmed. "She was only slightly annoyed at being disturbed when she was comfortably asleep." (*Old Men Forget.*)

[35] The Earl of Halifax, wartime British Ambassador to Washington.

everyone I saw looked green with cold and their coats were so shabby that I became overcome with depression, in fact I saw one fellow who had no socks on and his ankles were blue, and I thought, 'What would happen to me if I didn't have my fur-lined slippers?' When I got home the Duchess was having her French lesson so I had no one to talk to, so I got a lot of tin boxes down which my mother had sent me last week and looked through them. They were essays and so on that I had written when I was in France studying French before the Great War (1914–18) and letters to my family. You know, I'm not much of a reading man." I thought this description of a day was pretty sad from a man who used to be Edward VIII by the Grace of God, of Great Britain, Ireland and the British Dominions beyond the Seas, King, Defender of the Faith and Emperor of India. (I have that wrong but you know what I mean.) They are dining here on Saturday and I couldn't dread it more but as we had been there three times I thought we had to ask them. I didn't know how to go about asking them but, remembering that Mama had said if we asked the Ambassador we should offer several dates, I hazarded a wild guess that the same might apply to royalty so wrote a note doing so and they leaped at the first one. The Duke told me he is dying to go to a night club but as Bill and I never go to them because they are all too sordid for words we are much relieved that they have today closed all night clubs and cabarets because of the famous electricity shortage that I complain about so much. The situation is becoming acute; after the drought this summer there is not enough water power to keep the plants going and instead of the two million tons of coal expected from the Ruhr they only have three hundred thousand tons so cannot supply the plants with adequate coal.

This week has been most exciting from Bill's financial point of view, as Pleven is fighting tooth and nail against the Communists' plan for nationalization of the banks and credit. The government's plan is already very Communistic and makes the hair curl of the bankers and businessmen, but the Communists want even more. Bill was at the Chambre all morning and they must be having a very heated morning as he went back this afternoon and I am now waiting for him to come home for dinner at nine o'clock.

To Marietta from Paris

Paris, December 3, 1945

A wonderful Mouchy afternoon this week. It is great luck to be able to go around with someone who knows so much about pictures, furniture, everything, and all the people in the shops love him and they discuss the fine points, way above my head but it's educational. Marie tells me that it doesn't bore him and in fact is good for him as he has so little to do. His paralyzed arm is getting worse and they don't seem to be able to help him. She is a wonderful woman and neither of them ever complains and they are always so cheerful. They teach me lots of things besides fine arts. Henri says that I will never understand French people or French society, but that there are a few simple rules. One is that if a foreigner puts down a well-cooked chop in the middle of the Place de la Concorde every Frenchman in sight will come running, and that the best parties before the war were given by foreigners who went to a great deal of trouble and expense to entertain the French, who were generally too mean to ask them back for so much as a cup of tea. Marie reminded him of the Beaumont balls and one her father gave (she was born a Rochefoucauld) but they agreed that these were rare occasions. With Henri's advice I have bought Bill some Watteau engravings for Christmas; for some reason engravings are cheap.

Paris, December 6, 1945

Sometimes I get utterly fed up with the sentimentality of the American army towards the "good, peace-loving" German people in marked contrast to the "grasping" French. It would do them good to see some of the cases I deal with.

This one isn't in the least unusual, but the boy's family own one of the finest houses in Paris and when I went to see the father I was struck by the contrast between his surroundings and his powerlessness:

Stein, Jean. Aged 21, No. 77703
Definitely known to have been in Block 4, Sangerhassen, Commando Elrich, until April 1945. Believed to have left Nordhausen, in train filled with ill French deportees, destination Belsen

gas chamber. Train believed to have been stopped, April 14, at Gardelegen, and Germans threw flame throwers into vans. Some prisoners known to have escaped. Family have recently heard rumor that Americans stationed in Gardelegen, as occupying troops, have unearthed some corpses bearing metal identification numbers near scene of train burning. If so, was No. 77703 one of those on list? Who has the list, and are there any further facts? French Ministère des Prisonniers et Déportés has no information.

Months later Bill Patten proved definitely that Jean Stein had died at Dachau.

Martin, Marie. Aged 27, No. 44623.
Known to London under code name "Delphine." Request for help to American Red Cross made by husband, Major Philippe Martin, and British Embassy; the latter wishes to present Madame Martin with citation and decoration for her heroic work aiding British through the underground or if she is deceased would like to present the awards posthumously. Major Martin left France to join de Gaulle in 1940, and eventually fought his way from Equatorial Africa to Paris with Free French forces. Entering Paris at the liberation, he found his apartment empty. Neighbors reported that his wife had been taken off by the Gestapo a few months earlier, and further inquiries produced witnesses who had seen her in dying condition at the concentration camp Ravensbrück, having submitted to torture and suffering from malnutrition. French Ministry for Deportees and Prisoners had no further information, so case seemed closed. Two weeks ago [my memo is dated April 1945] Colonel Martin (he has recently been promoted) received a letter in English from an American soldier stating that he had seen Marie Martin in a hospital in Germany, that she was very weak but gave her husband's name and address accurately and sent the message that she was still alive, but not for very long, she thought. Rest of message very personal and beautiful. The soldier wrote on paper from one of own Red Cross clubs, postmarked Paris, but added that he was on his way home to U.S. He gives neither name of hospital, nor address, nor his

own rank, serial number, name of outfit, nothing, writing very good except for signature, which none of us can decipher. Bryzinski is the best we can do. We are trying every possible way, no leads yet.

We never found the soldier. Nowadays with computers we probably could have.

Sometimes the cases were close to home.

Colloredo-Mansfeld, Franz, Squadron Leader, R.A.F. Title Count Colloredo-Mansfeld. Father Austrian, mother American, graduate of Harvard, 1932. Joined Royal Air Force 1939, missing on mission over Pas de Calais area, flying Spitfire. The losses on the mission were high, but survivors recall Colloredo-Mansfeld leading squadron until German anti-aircraft hit his plane somewhere near Berck-sur-Plage on French coast and he was lost sight of. Request comes from American family, from his father via Red Cross, Vienna, from R.A.F. via British Embassy.

Colly (or Fritz) would have been the best man at our wedding but in the summer of 1939 a laughing voice over the telephone apologized to Bill, explaining his business elsewhere, and asked to speak to me. I never saw him, but I am sensitive to voices and instantly loved his voice. We joked along about how clever I had been to catch Bill Patten, the charmer of that exceptional class, Harvard, 1932, and made a date to meet as soon as the war was over. He must have been a most romantic character, Fritz, everyone loved him and Bill missed him always. To me he sounded like one of the young Englishmen of 1914, Rupert Brooke or Julian Grenfell. No one today reads their poetry.

We found the grave, Bill and I. Berck was a desolate spot, before the war famous for its sanatoriums for tubercular cases. The November winds coming off the Channel caught at our throats, but the mayor and the priest were very kind. We interviewed the fisherman who had gone out to the plane and brought Colly's body in. There were photographs taken by the doctor—Bill identified his friend at once. The little cemetery is protected from the Channel gale and someone had put chrysanthemums on the grave.

Paris, December 18, 1945

In bed with a cold, all my own fault. Snobbishness and passionate love of seeing this beautiful country will bring me to an early grave. My downfall came at Oriane de la Panouse's château on the Loire. Marie and Hope Carter[36] both begged me not to go, as even before the war the house was too cold, but I couldn't resist the chance of being shown châteaux of the Loire by Georges Salles, director of the Louvre, a fellow house guest. I remember nothing of Blois, Chenonceau, Azay-le-Rideau, but I'll never forget a child saying to me in Oriane's drawing room, "Is it true that in America people can sit in salons without a coat on?" I collapsed on the second day—and behaved very badly. Naturally, no hot water so I treated a prisoner of war, German, like a serf and had him boil up relays of kettles for hot water bottles.

21 Square du Bois de Boulogne
Paris
December 26, 1945

Thanks to the Communist Party, we have had a lovely Christmas and pre-Christmas. We haven't had a breakdown in telephone or electricity for ten days and everyone from the cook to the Prince de Broglie firmly believe that it must be because Maurice Thorez[37] has

[36] The Duchesse de Mouchy and Mrs. Bernard S. Carter. The Carters were the most distinguished members of the American colony in Paris. He was the head of Morgan's, later Morgan Guaranty Trust Company. They were wonderfully kind to us, and we owed them the loan of their beautiful manor house at Senlis, Clos St. Nicolas, for several happy summers.
[37] Maurice Thorez, General Secretary, French Communist Party.

moved in two blocks away—the Prince de Broglie says that this sanctum sanctorum is furnished with the rarest treasures of the state reserves of furniture. Elisa the cook says it's rotten bad furniture—I know neither of them well enough to ask how they are so well informed. . . .

The Christmas party here was smashing, I thought. All my favorite sergeants from Rainbow Corner, and friends from the Embassy, and the house full of holly and mistletoe from Corbeil Cerf, which François de Lubersac had brought us the night before. Lunch went on until five, then we dashed off to embrace the Rougemonts, who are back from London on leave, returned to dress and went on to the British Embassy, which was candelit and romantic, Lady Diana beautiful in a pale ivory satin dress trimmed with black lace, giving away presents to every single person there, and there were a hundred and fifty or so, from a big tree, each package marked with one's name in her writing. The mixture was wonderfully odd, all the most attractive people in the French government plus various diplomats and all the artists and musicians. Bérard and Cocteau and Février and Drian and lots I didn't know, all the British Embassy staff and children, and about midnight the Ambassador went around benevolently announcing that the franc had gone to four hundred and eighty to the pound. We were the only Americans there and I was in agony until I could find Bill to tell me what this meant to us—it's a hundred and twenty to the dollar, we had prayed for a hundred and fifty but praise the Lord I may be able to buy a French dress before we are ousted from this paradise.

It's been an extraordinary year for Bill and me, we feel infinitely lucky and blessed, but I miss America because of missing all of you, also I find that I become more and more American each day. Sentimentally, because of all the young Americans who have been in our house, the Herters and Emmets and Dennys and dozens of others in uniform doing their jobs modestly and decently, one is proud of them as one is of the Elim O'Shaughnessys and Norris Chipmans and Bills working long hours in the chancery on the Avenue Gabriel. Intellectually, because I suspect that we are in for trouble, and I suppose that defense mechanisms take over. Ever so long ago, say last year, we used to sit around the house in Georgetown talking about postwar Europe and I never heard anyone say he looked forward to Pax Americana, in fact we groaned and moaned a bit about Roosevelt's wanting to have the English leave India and feared that we might find ourselves biting off more than we could chew. There must have been and there still may be American imperialists but I never met one in my time. Now my instinct is that we are going to be forced into an exertion of global power that we neither desire nor are ready to fulfill. But this is no way to end a letter meant only to say, "Happy New Year."

· 1946 ·

21 Square du Bois de Boulogne
Paris, France
January 3, 1946

Well, I have made an ass of myself. Perhaps, if I write it, it will serve as a catharsis. At the British Embassy Christmas night party, already described, I met and made friends with X, who, after General de Gaulle, is supposed to be the most powerful man in France today. He called me up a few times, proposing that we meet, which I did not mention to Bill, as I thought it would irritate him. Finally, he proposed a perfectly safe invitation—tea at his house with some mutual friends. He lives in a famous house built by Gabriel, which I longed to see, so I accepted for yesterday, telling Bill, who said it was a damn good thing to do, as it was maddening to see him at the British Embassy, as he rarely went to ours, and that making a friend of him could do some good. He told me several things to talk to X about. You will recall that things have been a bit tricky here since the formation of de Gaulle's new government in November. Although the vital ministries of War, Interior, and Foreign Affairs were put in safe hands, the major economic ministries went to the Communists. A Cabinet in which you have five Communist ministers is obviously of extreme interest to the United States, and Bill's field is, of course, financial and economic.

I never got to ask Bill's questions. The house was beautiful, but I was received by a shifty-eyed little manservant who took my coat. There were no other coats in the hall, no mutual friends. Soft music was playing on a record player, a fire lighted, curtains drawn, and after a perfunctory cup of tea X invited me, as an eager student of French eighteenth-century architecture, to visit the rest of the rooms. The only one we reached was the classical bedroom from a farce by Feydeau, with double bed *open*, more soft music, fur rug on the floor, fur rug on the end of the bed, spring flowers from the South of France, and a sickly smell from some sort of perfumed candle. Instead of escaping with dignity, a tussle then took place—back to our Bar Harbor teen-age years. X is a strong man, but I made it out at a gallop, slammed the front door, leaving my hat, coat, and gloves, and ran to the Embassy, which isn't far. Miss Dilkes, the motherly receptionist, said, "Dear me, Mrs. Patten, you seem terribly out of breath; is everything all right?" "Thanks, Miss Dilkes, I'm just fine; I've just been getting some exercise on the Champs Elysées."

Bill gave me a lift home, roaring with laughter. Today arrived my missing clothing. I feel an ass!

X later became a close friend. Frenchmen may be wonderful lovers. I wouldn't know. Certainly they are very good thwarted lovers, bearing no rancor.

Mégève
January 1946

Thank God, the Red Cross has lowered its flag. My uniform is in mothballs, and so is my conscience. I should be at the Sorbonne educating myself; instead, I am near Chamonix, skiing with Daisy de Gourcuff, her husband, Louis,[1] and four or five of their friends. The trip down was no cinch. The train was oversold, and at Dijon there were loads of people waving thousand-franc notes at the conductor to get aboard. This made Louis, ordinarily a charming man, bad-tempered. He muttered all night about there being no hope for France, so I got no sleep. The trouble is that the salaries are so low that every little railroad official, policeman, or minor government servant has to depend on his bribes. This is part of *la crise morale* and the poor old General's government is much blamed.

The French girls never do anything badly in war or peace. It was to drive me mad with jealousy to see our party, all of whom had skis on for the first time in five years and claimed that they couldn't ski, step effortlessly onto their skis and go off like greyhounds running through the woods. Just like my first golfing day with Lally de

[1] Comte et Comtesse de Gourcuff.

St. Saveur,[2] who had been too modest to admit that she was the champion of France. Well, the Gourcuffs and their friends are angels to me, and the sun and air are delicious. Sitting on top of an Alp, lunching in a chalet, we heard the stupendous news of de Gaulle's abrupt resignation, but I could think of nothing but myself, as I was about to do my first *grande ballade* (ski run), and the view of Mont Blanc above me and the vertiginous prospect below me numbed my political reactions. The run takes Daisy, fragile in her Schiaparelli *pantalons fuseaux* (tight, narrow trousers), eight minutes—I took one hour and forty-five minutes. After a few days I got a bit better. We spent two days at Val d'Isère on the Italian frontier, the end of the Route des Grandes Alpes (romantic name). It was nearly the end of me, as it is very high, and we ran into a blizzard getting there and had to leave the cars and walk nine kilometers up the mountain carrying our skis, starting at six in the evening. Abandoned by the two guides, who said they could go no farther, Daisy said calmly, "*Les éléments sont déchaînés, tu ne trouves pas?* [The weather is out of hand, don't you think?]" And without a word, took my skis from me and put them over her own shoulders. We reached the hotel in two hours. It hadn't been open since 1939. So much was made of us. No change of clothes, as the guides had the sleds below; no hot water, but the patron was an old friend and, complaining loudly of the difficulties of living, gave us pâté, truite au beurre noir, veal cutlets in a wine sauce, fried potatoes, cheese, chocolate soufflé, Pommery '26, and U. S. Army coffee. Such fun. And they filled the champagne bottles with boiling water and put them in our beds, into which we sank, taking off our ski boots and nothing else. I shall return immensely refreshed. It's so long since I have had any fresh air.

21 Square du Bois de Boulogne
Paris, France
January 27, 1946

Bill met me on my return from skiing. The Gare de Lyon at 6 A.M. is no fun, and I was deeply touched, especially as he had had two hours' sleep following a merry party with Suzy Solidor and Maurice

[2] Vicomtesse de St. Saveur.

Chevalier. He looks very well and is fascinating about the recent political events. By a happy chance, he obtained yesterday the economic and financial proposals that the new Prime Minister Gouin[3] was to submit later to the Chambre, and delighted the Ambassador, who spent four hours with Bill drafting the cable to Washington. It's not all as gloomy as it seemed to us in the Alps. The program makes sense, apparently, and while Paris is very blue over the weakness of the present government, no one is sobbing over de Gaulle's departure. He must have decided to leave fairly abruptly. Gaston Palewski[4] had asked us for dinner at his official and beautiful quarters just a few days ago. It rather shocks me that people are not more shocked by the end of de Gaulle. But perhaps it is not the end.

It delights me to see Bill so well. He loves working hard and has been dining out a lot. He describes the shock of the De Ligne wedding in Brussels on Saturday, as told to him by the Mouchys, who are aunt and uncle to the groom. There was a dinner dance the night before for three hundred and seventy guests, all the women wearing tiaras and the men in white ties, and a luncheon the next day for twenty-seven hundred guests, eating only the white meat of chickens. There were seventy cars for the guests coming from Paris, all with chauffeurs and footmen on the box, with the footmen wearing the family livery. To the bedraggled French emerging from their third-class carriages, family tiara in paper bag, it seemed most wonderful to see flowers everywhere in January, and the houses all heated.

Bill and I are planning to go to Belgium—it must be another world.

21 Square du Bois de Boulogne
Paris, France
February 1946

We are getting fonder and fonder of Palewski, who gave us lunch this week and read aloud several bitterly satirical pieces from *Le Canard Enchaîné* (a very clever, influential political paper) which

[3] Félix Gouin, Premier of France, January–June 1946.
[4] Gaston Palewski, Chef de Cabinet to de Gaulle.

were about him, speculating on his future. He thought them very funny and is completely cheerful and philosophical about having been thrown with brutal abruptness from a position of great power to complete obscurity.

I am very pleased, as Elim O'Shaughnessy tells me that the Ambassador is crazy about Bill and thinks his work is first class. As both Mr. Caffery and Elim are reserved men, this is really nice; Elim would not have made it up. Both Cafferys are shy, but one likes them more and more. Awful evening at the Windsors' this week, the Duchess determined to play word games, despite her complete lack of education and the competition of Lady Diana Cooper, who learned history with her mother's milk and also is in training, as she plays parlor games all the time. Poor Mrs. Caffery could be heard plaintively whispering that she never had been good at history; the Duke couldn't remember Metternich and Castlereagh and the Duchess to help him screamed, "Your turn, David, now take someone we all know," the last had been the fatal Castlereagh.

Today, pure pleasure and frivolity—Palewski and Etienne Burin de Rosiers[5] for lunch with Maud'huys—later Mrs. Snow[6] came to the house with photographers. I shall be all over the fashion magazines this spring, and you will be ashamed of me, but it does help. Balenciaga is making me two dresses for $108, isn't that exciting? I hope you will like them. Mrs. Snow wants me to write for her. Last year, she asked me for a monthly letter from Paris, but Bill correctly refused to let me. She is still at it, but it wouldn't do. Marvelous letters from Paris, written for *The New Yorker* by our friend Janet Flanner ("Genêt"), cover the scene, and Janet's wide and profound knowledge of France and the French makes me feel like a fool, as I contemplate how little I know.

21 Square du Bois de Boulogne, Paris
February 26, 1946

Sat by General Juin[7] last night at the Belgians, and found him a

[5] Dedicated Gaulliste, distinguished diplomat.
[6] Carmel Snow, editor of *Harper's Bazaar* and a great influence on the French and American fashion scene.
[7] General, later Marshal, Alphonse Juin. Career soldier, always somewhat xenophobic, suspected later of political ambitions.

most attractive, simple, straightforward old French soldier, but it was hard to get out of my mind a description one of the participants had given me of that ugly night in Murphy's[8] villa in Algiers after the North African landings in '42, when we practically captured him and he snarled, "*Rudement bien joué, vous autre Américains.* [Well played, you Americans]." Does he still hate us for that humiliation? I should think so, but he gave me a very good time. I asked him what had been the most unexpected thing that he remembered from his long distinguished career and he answered instantly, "The night I learned to believe in ghosts." This had occurred in Gibraltar during this war, when he was obliged to spend the night with the British governor between two planes. It was a strange story to hear from such a hard, unemotional man. The governor and his wife accompanied him to his bedroom early as he had had a long day, and told him that they hoped he would sleep well and not be disturbed by the young woman who occasionally haunted that room, the daughter of an eighteenth-century governor who, thwarted by her father's refusal to permit her to marry the suitor she loved, had thrown herself to her death from the window of her bedroom, which gave onto the battlements far below. General Juin said that after some merry jokes about what fun it would be to have the ghost of a ravishing young English girl appear he said good night to his hosts and undressed and went to bed. But he couldn't get to sleep, and within an hour or so he began to feel that there was someone in the room with him. The lights on, room empty. Lights off, and instead of sleep came the sound of rustling silk and the voice of a girl murmuring English phrases which he couldn't understand, but he felt the sadness and the poignancy in her voice. This was too much, he was terrified, frightened as he had never been in battle. He put on the lights again, dressed, and spent the rest of the night sitting in a stiff chair in uniform, two *pistolets* on the table beside him. In the morning he came down to breakfast and said good-by, vowing to himself that never, never would he set foot in Government House, Gibraltar, again. Telling the story, he became quite moved; at the end he mopped his brow. I like General Juin.

[8] Robert Murphy, American government official who carried out preparations for Allied landings in North Africa.

21 Square du Bois de Boulogne
Paris, France
March 26, 1946

We spent an evening last night at the British Embassy. Noël Coward played a lot of his old things and then his new waltz, which he thinks is the best he has ever written. It is called "Cadenza" and will be out in the autumn. Watch for it, it is lovely. Then Hervé Alphand[9] did his imitation of the Foreign Ministers' Conference, which is always funny, although he cannot imitate Byrnes's Southern voice. The best is the Bevin-Vishinsky passage which begins with Mr. Bevin saying that he will not be put in the dock to answer questions. He does Chip, interpreting, very well.

Then I had a glass of champagne between Noël Coward and the Duke of Windsor, who both wanted to talk about the Royal Navy. Noël Coward gets a feverish glint in his eye when anyone so much as mentions the navy and would have burst into a stream of naval shop, but the Duke had been to Dartmouth[10] so wasn't to be outdone. Noël's movie, *In Which We Serve,* was what started all of this, and it really was funny. Sample:

Noël: Were you ever in old *Charybdis,* sir? By God, she was a happy ship. I well remember a run in her in '42 from Algiers to Malta . . .

H.R.H.: Most interesting. Reminds me of a curious experience I had in Nassau about the same time. One of our cruisers put in . . .

Noël: Ah, what is there like a cruiser? Curiously enough, the old *Charybdis* was a cruiser. I was just back from doing a bit of singsong for the troops in North Africa and went down to spend Sunday at Chequers.[11] At breakfast, I found the Old Man ready to split a brass rag . . .

H.R.H. and me, simultaneously: What?

Noël: Sorry, sir, I thought you'd know. It's an old Dartmouth term like China plate or Flute-suit.

[9] Distinguished French diplomat and wit.
[10] British academy for naval cadets.
[11] Country residence of the Prime Minister, who at that time was Winston Churchill.

H.R.H.: Oh, quite. Well, go on.

Noël: Winston had a signal from the Admiralty in his hand and looked as black as thunder standing there. He read it to me: "*Charybdis* went down last night off Malta!" For a moment, I couldn't say a word. Then I said, "Winston" . . .

H.R.H.: Most interesting. That was a first-class show that we put up in the Mediterranean. An entirely different problem from ours off Nassau, of course. . . .

And so on went the battle. Men shouldn't talk about the war unless they were in the same theater of operations, don't you agree?

Our food is getting worse. We are so lucky to have the pork chops and the tuna fish and the chicken, but oh, the chicken is so tough, and I am sick of tuna fish hot with sauce creamed with Klim[12] or cold with canned mayonnaise. My fault as I'm sure I will be just as bad a housekeeper when we have fresh things again.

Today for the first time the newspapers are out in four pages. This will only happen once a week for a while, but it is a good sign and thrilling to see the kiosks carrying such thick newspapers—*Combat, Figaro,* etc.

21 Square du Bois de Boulogne,
Paris
March 30, 1946

This has been a week of delicious warm weather. I have just come in from an afternoon of wandering with Ethel de Croisset and Jacqueline Vernes around the Odéon and in the Luxembourg gardens, ending up for tea in that funny little teashop opposite Notre Dame kept by a retired English nanny. She never stopped making plum cake all through the war! It's a treat to go to the Louvre now—there are still only a few galleries open but they contain some of the very best pictures, and I have had two guides, Georges Salles, director of the Louvre, and Henri de Mouchy. The day with Monsieur Salles was thrilling as he explained their new plans and

[12] Powdered milk used as one of the army rations.

hopes, come the day they have the money, but I enjoyed more going with Henri, who is used to my questions, "When was Fragonard, why do you admire him?" Both of them have given me books, but Henri does say that books about pictures are generally no good and one learns by looking, looking. So much for Berenson and Roger Fry and Ruskin? Henri exaggerates, but looking is the thing, he is right, and my self-education is from now on planned to include two Louvre afternoons a week. Mama wants my portrait done, but it's not easy. I can't just pick up John Singer Sargent the way Grandma Jay did, and although I have been to a lot of exhibitions by the younger painters it isn't an age of portrait painting.

We lunched at Maxim's yesterday with Davidson of the London *Times* and Darsie Gillie of the Manchester *Guardian* and when we came out found the Rue Royale thronged with people in masks and costume for the Mi-Carême (Mid-Lent) parade. All the children were dressed up and jumping up and down with excitement, it was the first really warm sunny day with the buds just discernible and the sky so blue, the Seine so sparkling that everyone became infected with the spring fever. Bill grimly returned to the Embassy—the State Department knoweth not the seasons—but it wasn't hard to persuade the two Englishmen that instead of spending the afternoon in the House listening to the debate on the nationalization of gas and electricity they must walk into the Tuileries gardens to spend a happy afternoon watching the children with me. They had both lived in Paris off and on for twenty years and they agreed that the crowd that day had for the first time the gaiety and spontaneity of a prewar crowd. Only we all missed the candy sticks and ice cream that should have gone with the merry-go-rounds and the Guignol (puppet show). Someday the frills will come back. The exuberance was what made it such fun.

You say that it sounds odd for me to talk about having a dinner for the young and our staying at home while they go off to dance. Well, let me tell you that at Le Forty-Five (a sort of night club-club) on Wednesday night I sat against the wall and all the young girls I know stopped dancing to come over and shake my hand, with many a curtsy. IN A FEW YEARS WE WILL BE THIRTY! The Forty-Five has good music and the girls look so pretty, many of them in crinolines and any number of strapless dresses. The really elegant wear hobbleskirts, very narrow, and draped across the side. I wear the crinolines from my Bendel trousseau of 1939 on the rare occasions we go to this place—there was no chance to wear them during the war so they are fresh as daisies. Mrs. Snow of *Harper's Bazaar* has me in a Balmain strapless for the last picture. She took a lot of trouble with it and posed me herself, sitting on a sofa below a fine mirror. The effect she was attempting was described by one of the French assistants as "*très David mais très* ladylike."[13] It will come out with the usual frozen idiotic expression I always have in photographs, alas, but if it's any good I'll send you a print. Could you in return possibly send me three cans of Bon Ami or any other bathtub-cleaning powder?

21 Square du Bois de Boulogne
Paris, France
April 1946

Have been much at the Chambre this week, as pre-election excitement is rising, and I especially wanted to hear old Herriot—he of the golden voice, the great parliamentarian of the twenties and thirties, the defender of the people of Lyon, whose idolized mayor he was, he who did *not* stand up to Pétain in the terrible days of June 1940. "*Adieu la liberté!*" he began this afternoon, thundering out against the Communist Party. Chills ran down my spine. But there are some French who say that he has no more moral force than he ever had and would vote with the Communists in a minute if it seemed politically expedient. Generally, the present debates are very Third Republic and third rate.

Louise de Rougemont is back from London for a month. She is the most beloved of my contemporaries here—serene, clever, restful, and unselfish. All ages adore her. She is having another baby, and I am to be godmother—a great honor, as Louise is a fervent Catholic. She gave a lunch for six women—an unprecedented event, as, of course, women here never lunch with each other, but either with their families or a mixed party. At the lunch, all the women except

[13] David was the great early nineteenth-century painter who posed Madame Récamier on a sofa in the famous portrait in the Louvre.

me had had husbands directly and dangerously involved with the Maquis[14] and had been involved themselves. For once they talked about it, and you can imagine how absorbing it was to me. It's years too soon to judge the resistance. The historians will be arguing for ages about its real value to the war effort, but I do know that women, such as my friends, gained a moral strength which is unchallengeable and which they will never lose.

The British Embassy gets stranger and stranger, and Bill and I adore the mixtures one finds. Imagine Evelyn Waugh, Lord Carlisle, the Bishop of Fulham, Harold Laski, and Peter Quennell all under one roof and none of them loath to speak up at the table, and all outdone by Louise de Vilmorin,[15] who got fed up at not being allowed to tell a story, so she threw her butter ball up to the ceiling with her butter knife. It held there, stronger than the planet Venus, and so mesmerizing was this feat that all conversation stopped, permitting Louise to launch into one of her truly spellbinding tales. Bill and I cannot decide what we feel about Evelyn Waugh, who is a strange man. He is friendly to us and comes to the house and has asked us to stay. Perhaps someday we will know him.

21 Square du Bois de Boulogne
Paris, France
April 5, 1946

We spent a lovely spring weekend near Villers-Cotteret, at the Raoul de Lubersacs.'[16] The men shot boar, while my hostess and I, as usual, went from farmer to farmer trying to buy food. I am beginning to get to know a little more about the new bourgeoisie. These farmers were even more prosperous than the ones I have described in Normandy and the Oise. Immense fortunes were made trafficking during the war, and the *crise morale* will take a long time to sort out. Mimi de Lubersac and Raoul, respectively, were in

14 The wartime French underground resistance movement.
15 Louise de Vilmorin, poet, writer, beauty, and wit. Her charm was so great that Billy and Anne, my children, still remember the magic of an afternoon at Vérrières, the Vilmorin country house, twenty years later.
16 Comte et Comtesse de Lubersac.

Fresnes prison[17] and Buchenwald. Mimi was taken for sheltering American fliers, and when the Gestapo arrived at her apartment at the usual 7 A.M., she cleverly grabbed a box of Kleenex and took it with her, knowing that once a month she would be allowed to send out laundry. On the Kleenex, she wrote letters to her mother, the old Comtesse de Luart, and sewed them into the shoulder pads of her dresses. She had two cotton dresses as her wardrobe, and thanks to the ghastly shoulder pad fashion, Madame de Luart got news of her. I could never have been so clever. Like our other friends, Mimi and Raoul are wonderfully unbitter about the collaborators, and even managed a laugh when we got to one farm to find no one except for some German prisoners who told us that Monsieur and Madame (the farmer and his wife) had gone to Nice with the children and the governess in their new car. Mimi and I have both been to the collections of the big dressmakers, and the only people really buying are the black market ladies, so we instantly imagined the farmer's wife sailing down the Promenade des Anglais at Nice dressed by Molyneux.

Sadness on return. Philippe de Poix has had a relapse of T.B., and the Mouchys are very worried. As usual, no matter what tragedy affects them, they are so kind to us.

Last night, we dined there to meet Professor Montdor, the world expert on Mallarmé, who is the wittiest and most charming man I have met in ages. He told a story about the Bibliothèque Nationale. Every year there is a solemn inspection of their most precious books. The director, the under director, and five assistant directors gather. Seven doors and fourteen safes are unlocked, and at last everyone holds his breath as they arrive at the most closely guarded boxes, from which the pre-original manuscript of the Gutenberg Bible or whatever emerges and is handed from hand to hand and caressed, all this under the sharp eyes of twenty or so policemen. This sensual and intellectual ceremony accomplished, everyone disperses happily for another year. Yesterday was the day for the ceremony, and on top of the priceless books and manuscripts was a Communist tract! Nothing stolen, nothing touched, but how did it get there? This was not told as a funny story. The professor said, "I

[17] In Paris.

can assure you that not one member of the Académie Française closed an eye last night."

Ethel de Croisset has just telephoned, asking me not to repeat this to a soul, but she is disappointed in the chestnut blossoms. Do I not think that the dogwoods in Long Island at this season are prettier? Good for Ethel, she is honest and no snob. Of course, the dogwoods beat anything.

Our weekend at Villers-Cotteret was instructive in several ways. The Lubersac forest of five thousand acres or so was less valuable than it should have been, as some of the timber was as full of World War I shrapnel as a plum pudding is of raisins, for the drive that started the great battle of Villers-Cotteret came out of those woods. What struck one was not that there should have been so few people of the quality of the Lubersacs but that there should have been so many. After all, France lost a million and a half men and the same number disabled in the first war, out of a population of thirty-nine million, and it was only twenty-one years later that World War II began. I don't know the figures for our Civil War—another terrible bloodletting—but the United States recovered remarkably quickly. The French, another vital people, had very little time to recover, but in fact, by 1924, the worst problems of the postwar period seemed to be solved. However, the surface was more impressive than the reality, as was shown by the series of left-wing governments struggling hopelessly with inflation and the instability of the franc. Although the world economic crisis of 1929 affected France less than it did countries which depended on their foreign trade, the cracks in the structure showed up dangerously by 1931, and my generation could remember the Stavisky scandal, the riots of 1934, and the open conflict during the last years of the Third Republic between Parliament on one side and the forces of Fascism and Communism on the other. How could my generation in their early twenties believe in democracy, believe in anything, when faced with the dreadful dilemma of 1940? Those who have seen the film *The Sorrow and the Pity* will understand some of the complexities that split France into those who thought the cause of freedom hopeless and those who joined the resistance.

Historians are still arguing about the value of the resistance. Eisenhower put it very high, and I have read his estimate that, on D-Day, the Allies could count on about three million Frenchmen to resist actively. I would agree with *Combat*,[18] in which Roger Stephane wrote these fine words:

"When all is said and done, the resistance was not so much an action as a refusal. Thanks to this refusal, we were able to look the Russian, American, and British soldiers straight in the eyes without blushing. It may seem ludicrous, but it is this ludicrous little thing—this refusal to submit—which saved our human dignity."

21 Square du Bois de Boulogne
Paris, France
May 1946

Dined last night with Alix and Guy de Rothschild, a pair to whom we are increasingly devoted, taking Chip Bohlen and Ben Cohen.[19] The rest of the party included Momo Marriott, Nin Ryan, and Gaston Palewski. Chip was enthralling, discussing Koestler's *Darkness at Noon*, which has just come out here and has caused a sensation. He feels that it is still the best explanation of the trials and of the Soviet mentality in general. That led him to describing how the Politburo works. He is convinced that they sit around talking like a *Pravda* editorial, using phrases like "capitalist encirclement" completely deadpan, and that they never say to each other, "Frankly, now let's grab Persia," but instead, carry on the game of talking about defending themselves from the imperialists. He said that Vishinsky, who is the only member of the Politburo who has ever talked to a foreigner and who is Chip's closest approach to a Russian friend, has once or twice seemed on the point of saying to him something like this: "Now, man to man, old fellow, this question of democracy in Iran is a lot of trash; let's get down to business." But he never has, because of the mentality described by

[18] *Combat* was perhaps the most influential paper, except for *Le Monde*, during our early days in Paris.

[19] Benjamin Cohen, adviser to F.D.R. and, in 1946, counselor of State Department.

Koestler, i.e., a Soviet must not once get off the narrow path of principles laid down by the Party and start thinking for himself or he is lost. So Vishinsky goes on with his stream of platitudes, and there is no meeting ground, although he did relax enough to say, "Nuremberg trials, pshaw, give me a free hand, and I'd have them all shot in twenty-four hours."

We are much on duty at the Embassy. Mrs. Vandenberg called me Mrs. Chipman today, apologized sweetly (no need, as Fannie is our star beauty), and added, "When I am tired, I forget names, but I know all you dear girls by your hats." Yes, ma'am, Mrs. Vandenberg, Mrs. Byrnes, and Mrs. Connally, we are beginning to know your hats, too.[20]

My favorite friend is Miss Cassie Connor, the Secretary's secretary. I took her shopping to buy souvenirs, and she came back to tea and talked about having been one of the only four women who knew about the atomic bomb and the agonies they went through wondering whether it would work, not to mention the moral side. She is funny about life in the Hotel Meurice. "I said to Mr. Byrnes, when he accused me of looking for Communists under every bed, 'Mr. Secretary, I tried at Potsdam, I tried in London, and I am trying here, but when I find one of Molotov's guards trying to stop Mrs. Byrnes from entering her own sitting room, I tell you frankly that I have the willies.' "

21 Square du Bois de Boulogne
Paris, France
May 4, 1946

As the papers report so much about the conference,[21] I will just add that it is as leaden an atmosphere as it sounds. Even brave Senator Vandenberg said after three hours on Trieste yesterday, "Oh, how easy it was when we were all isolationists." It's lovely to see a lot of Chip, and last night the British put on a splendid

[20] Mrs. James Byrnes, Mrs. Arthur Vandenberg, and Mrs. Tom Connally accompanied their husbands to the Council of Foreign Ministers at Paris, 1946. Senators Vandenberg and Connally were giants of the Senate at that period, Byrnes was the Secretary of State.
[21] Council of Foreign Ministers, 1946.

show, Horse Guards band playing in the ballroom, and the doors open into that wonderful garden. Odette Pol Roger, easily the prettiest girl in Paris, was divine in a dark green satin Schiaparelli ball dress, sitting out with a handsome man in the conservatory, which looked as if Wellington had it designed just for them. Under the chestnut trees wandered the highest in our lands. Vishinsky I met, and Molotov, who looks like the original Russian intellectual revolutionary—a clever face—is followed everywhere by a little man in a shabby brown suit who is Pavlov, the famous interpreter. Bevin has a most impressive face, ugly and strong and totally honest.

The next day we went to beloved Senlis. Can you imagine, because of the Carters' kindess, we have one of the most heavenly houses in the Ile de France all our own?

Clos St. Nicolas
Senlis, France
May 14, 1946

Our second weekend in Senlis is as successful as the first one—the house covered with roses and syringa and other sweet smells coming from the garden.

This afternoon we went to Chantilly to find horses for Bill to ride, and walked in the forest, which I do think is the most beautiful in France, with every day new wildflowers. I'm learning the names and revel in coming in in the evening to study them, and then read old Maurice Barings, after a delicious dinner with Bill by the fire. The food is all fresh from the garden, and I only worry how we can ever thank the Carters for this.

Today, we had people for lunch. Chip Bohlen brought a carload of friends here for the conference,[22] and we had some French, most of whom seemed to be bound for Lourdes. They are very casual about this—I should hate it. They all promised, during bad times in prison camps, to make the pilgrimage if they survived. Last year they were too weak to do so, especially as many had vowed to walk those hundreds of kilometers. My neighbor at lunch had vowed to

[22] Following the Foreign Ministers' Conference already mentioned, this conference was of twenty-one nations to discuss peace treaties and frontier problems.

bicycle, following a nasty moment having nearly been taken by the Germans after parachuting into the Vosges. I asked him why he had vowed to bicycle, as I should have said, "If I get out of this, I'll walk to Lourdes," or perhaps, "I'll go to Lourdes," but I would not have thought of bicycling. He said, "Well, you know, the situation wasn't quite desperate; so I said to myself, I will make a vow to bicycle, but if it gets any worse, I'll change it to walking." I thought this so disarming.

The State Department threw a bombshell yesterday by cutting everyone's living allowance in half, effective immediately. We wouldn't have undertaken Senlis if we had known this, but the angelic Carters make it very cheap, and it is not a house to be missed. I do wish you could see it. It is paradise!

Senlis
September 5, 1946

We shall soon be returning this lovely house to its kind owners. It was hard to leave it last month for three whole weeks, spent at Mont-Dore, a cure place for respiratory diseases in the middle of France, the Massif Central. In this gray, rainy rockbound spot are springs famous since Roman times; the doctor thought they might help Bill. To save money, we stayed at a dreary second-class hotel, and while Bill spent his mornings at the baths, I walked miles, hating the volcanic rock and the rain. In the afternoons he rested; then we would take a drive and return to drink martinis and play gin rummy. We soon became accustomed to the routine, and I have yet to be bored by Bill's company; so it wasn't dreary, and perhaps he will breathe better this winter.

"Cure" finished, we set off in the Chevrolet for the South of France, stopping at Avignon and other dreamy places to sightsee, landing eventually at the Windsors' at Antibes for a long weekend. The villa is huge and comfortable, and one walks down to the best swimming-off rocks I have ever seen. Unluckily, the first night, I was poisoned at the grand villa of your nice friend David-Weill, and for forty-eight hours was very miserable. The Duchess was extremely kind, but I wish someone could tell her not to be such a perfect housekeeper. If one is well and out of bed, the maids just press your sheets daily with an iron they bring in on a long cord, but if one is ill, they come and change the linen twice a day, which involves getting up when one longs to be let alone to writhe. On the third day, the steel-hand-in-the-velvet-glove side of the Duchess emerged for the first time. Bill came back to our room after breakfast looking cross and said that the Duchess expected me downstairs for luncheon today, no matter what, in order to sit by Monsieur Paul Reynaud, as his English is no good; that he, Bill, had said to the equerry, Major Phillips, that this was out of the question—I needed another day in bed. He had just finished telling me when there was a knock on the door, announcing the arrival of a footman with a note for me from the Duchess. This was a crisp little message, saying how happy she was to hear that I would be joining the party at lunch, that I was expected on the terrace at 1:30 P.M., and that I would be sitting next to the former *Prime Minister,* Monsieur Reynaud. Getting out of it would now be about as easy as telling the tumbril driver during the French Revolution to avoid the Place Royale, where the executions took place. Luckily, I was nearly myself again and got through the meal somehow.

I cannot bear to leave Senlis, which will always mean the smell of linden trees. There is a long avenue of them just over the garden wall, and in June the perfume wafted over and filled the house with magic. Paris seems quiet. Lunched at the British Embassy yesterday—just six of us, at a round table in a corner of the gold and white drawing room—the Duff Coopers, Harold Nicolson, Emerald Cunard, Bill, and me. Lady Cunard is said to be the best hostess in London. She looks like a very clever sparrow, and I had heard that she was so hard, one could sharpen diamonds on her; but she was surprisingly friendly to us. Harold Nicolson and Duff have much in common—their love of and knowledge of France and history, literature, and politics of both England and France. Diana, who hates flying, told a wonderful flying story from their Algiers days in the war. Determined to return to her son, little John Julius, in England in order to spend his spring vacation with him, she hitched a ride from Air Vice-Marshal Dawson, whose R.A.F. motto was, "Dawson always flies." This intrepid airman put her into the fuselage of an empty bomber, where she hoped to lie quietly on a mattress throughout the night. But as they took off Dawson told her that she must go to the toilet, which was at the other end of the aircraft. Diana said that she had no need, but he replied, "I insist." And he left her. Diana obediently crawled to her unwanted destination, but on her return slipped, and her leg went right through the fuselage, and there she was, trapped, hanging thousands of feet above the Mediterranean. Hours later Dawson returned; Diana said, "Too sorry, you nearly lost me." Dawson—"Don't worry, the aircraft can be repaired quite easily."

Senlis, France
September 10, 1946

We are ending our heavenly summer. Evenings on the lawn looking up at the cathedral towers, mornings picking *fraises des bois* in the kitchen garden or walking in the forest, old servants to spoil us and encourage us to fill the house on weekends, and, above all, the excitement of living in a small French town. I was in love with Paris; now I am in love with France, as one could never be without living in a small town.

At least three nights a week are spent in Paris, and I have been waiting to write you thrilling letters about the peace conference; but it has been the dreariest tussle you ever saw. Although twenty-one countries are represented, the dominant note is the increasing strain between Russia and us. Harold Nicolson said, "Instead of open covenants openly arrived at, we have open insults openly hurled." Today, at last, a bit of Congress of Vienna-like glamor was introduced by the reception at Versailles given by Georges Bidault, Foreign Minister of France. Versailles suffered terribly from the war, and is still shabby; but one didn't notice it in the courtyard with Goums and Spahis and Gardes Républicaines mounted and wearing their wonderful cloaks, nor on the staircase lined with eighteen-century wigged and liveried footmen, nor in the Galérie des Glaces, to which had been brought the finest Savonnerie carpet I ever saw. The weight of this, plus the delegates and guests, caused the curators to tremble—they were worrying about dry rot. A complete disappearance of the party would have been little loss aesthetically—Communists are really too ugly for Versailles, and their shining gold teeth and padded shoulders and heavy unpolished shoes depressed me into spending much of my time at the windows, looking out at the fountains playing in the sunset, and later at the floodlit trees, each a mile high, and the canal, an endless silver stream.

At the beginning of the summer, the first ball was given in Paris since the war; and guess who gave it—your old friend. Never, never shall I organize another; the very thought of it makes me shudder. My American do-good streak was aroused by the condition of the orphans of devastated Lorraine, as described by our Lorrainian dear friends, Maria and Bertrand de Maud'huy. What could be simpler, I thought, than to have a charity ball like New York? Teddy Phillips, one of Duff Cooper's private secretaries, was enlisted to help, less because he cared about the orphans than because he is a charming bachelor who knows about parties; and we hired Pré Catalan, that romantic restaurant in the Bois de Boulogne, and sent out tickets for a masked ball. Nothing whatever happened except a sinister visit from Philippe de Croisset, who meant to be friendly. "Susan Mary, you must leave Paris—have pneumonia—anything, but cancel the ball. I mean it. No one is going to come to anything in this city for a good cause unless it's fashionable, and you aren't fashionable. Your name doesn't mean a thing nor does Commander Phillips'; you won't sell a ticket." I burst into tears—we were up to our ears in debt to Pré Catalan and the orchestra already. Bill came in from the office and, as usual, lifted the clouds. "Philippe, you read too much Proust; have a drink and stop fussing."

Early the next morning I was at Diana Cooper's bedside, in the famous red damask Pauline Borghese room, begging for help. Diana is as good as she is beautiful and as practical as she is wise. "Leave it to me; I'll talk of nothing else, and meanwhile, we'll visit the dressmakers." We did. Reboux, Schiaparelli, Lanvin, Balenciaga were our first stops. "Could I please see the models for the masks for the ball at Pré Catalan? I'm terribly sorry to be so late; you must be running out of materials already." Not one dressmaker or milliner dared admit to Lady Diana Cooper that they hadn't heard of the ball. "*Mais oui, milady, pour vous tout est possible. Il nous reste quand même quelques petites plumes d'autruche, du velours on s'arrangera* [Certainly, milady, everything is possible if you wish it. We still have some little ostrich plumes, and we'll manage to get the velvet]." Diana said that this was just as well, as some of the English guests who would be flying over for the party might need last-minute help. The bluff paid off. Two weeks later we were oversold and a nice little black market in tickets started. The party was a huge success, helped by the arrival of some of our Peace Conference friends. Chip Bohlen and Joe Alsop were loyal till five in the morning, and I even saw Ben Cohen, our distinguished, serious counsel to the State Department, flirting with the Duchesse de Brissac, who was dressed in skin-tight silver from head to foot, like some lovely bird, her skin-tight silver mask made to go with the costume wings. The orphans of Lorraine will do all right, but never again for Susan Mary Patten.

To my joy, Avis Bohlen arrived to join Chip, and we dined together at the British Embassy, Avis looking lovely and both of us in a dither as we had not met Mr. Winston Churchill before. Balenciaga had made me a dress for fifty dollars, and we swept up the stairs of that most beautiful house beside our handsome husbands to find a dinner that only Diana could have arranged. Not the state dining room, but the small, intimate dining room, with two tables and not more than ten people at each. The seating was utterly incorrect but the greatest fun. I sat by the Ambassador, with Jean Cocteau on my other side, who holds any table in spellbinding conversation, and just as well too, as I innocently mentioned the Secretary of State's Stuttgart speech to the Ambassador and got an icy blast in return. Duff Cooper can be frightening, and it was a relief to have the conversation become more general. In a pause, I heard Mr. Churchill at the other table say to Chip, "Young man, I remember you." "Yes, sir, we met when I was translating for President Roosevelt." Churchill growling, "One cannot be reassured when one remembers the Oder-Neisse line." Chip, very calmly, "I feel sure you remember that it was not the United States that was responsible for the Oder-Neisse." Good for Chip. The Prime Minister was charmed by him, and said to Avis, blowing cigar smoke right into her beautiful face, "You are married to a brilliant young man, my dear." I also overheard him complimenting Avis on her appearance, which was very unusual for Churchill, and while proud of my friend, I couldn't help feeling a pang of jealousy.

Usually, only Odette Pol Roger got the compliments. This was a beautiful December-May relationship, quite harmless and smiled on by Mrs. Churchill, who much admired Odette.
Later, when Churchill named his favorite race horse Pol Roger and took Odette to Brighton to see her run, there was a certain amount of gossip about the outing. But it was only one of the many times that Odette gave the old man innocent pleasure by her presence. For him, she personified France, and he was a romantic about France. Early on, he laid down a rule which was always followed until his death—namely, if Winston Churchill came to Paris, Odette Pol Roger was to be invited to dinner at the British Embassy. When he died, the family paid Odette the great compliment of asking her to attend the funeral service at St. Paul's. She was one of the few non-official foreigners there.

21 Square du Bois de Boulogne
Paris, France
December 12, 1946

Personally, we are going to have a lovely Christmas, which I'll describe later; but I have never felt so blue. The early euphoria about which I wrote just after the war has completely disappeared, and the bitter winter last year looks as though it is being succeeded by another just as cold. If so, many people will die of cold and starvation and some of broken hearts and frustration. The Russians believe in their government, one supposes; so do the British. I can think of no one else in Europe. I feel like a spoiled Roman matron about the year 400 A.D., sitting in her colonial villa in Gaul or Britain, waiting for the barbarians, and almost wishing they would come—the frustration and disappointments are great.

The French government has so far kept the two crucial posts of Interior and Foreign Affairs out of Communist hands, and probably will continue to hang on to them; but it would not be very difficult for the Russians to march to Brest, and we certainly couldn't stop them, as we are down to a couple of divisions; our Allies the same—a far cry from the three and a half million Americans in khaki who were in Europe a moment ago. Serious people take the possibility of a Russian offensive seriously, but I don't feel it like that in my tummy, rather I see a dreary, slow return to the Dark Ages, hungry peasants tearing Poussins out of the Louvre in order to use the frames for firewood, wolves chewing away at rich bindings in the Bibliothèque Nationale.

Forgive a blowing off of steam. We are in luxury—did I confess that I got the central heating going? I am deeply ashamed of this and pretend I did it for Bill's health; he, himself, didn't speak to me for weeks. The first year it was all right—a great joke to have the two wood stoves the Germans left behind them and to dress for dinner huddling around the one in our upstairs sitting room, by candle-light, and drive gratefully to dinner at our lovely warm Embassy; but it got boring not to be able to write to you without stiff fingers—I never caught on to the trick the girls at the Quai d'Orsay had of typing in gloves, which Bill described with admiration. So, I cracked, just as I would under N.K.V.D. questioning, and just before the last of the fashionable non-fighting American generals left, I sat beside one at the Windsors' (oh, the warmth of that house), and he noticed a chilblain on one of my fingers. Presto! The house is full of German prisoners for days repairing the furnace and trucks of coal follow them. I couldn't look the Germans in the eye; they seemed so young, so decent, and no doubt were thinking of their freezing families at home. Elisa Vallet, our concierge and cook, not only adored looking them in the eye but was beastly to them. It is only fair to admit that she had the house full of Germans for four years, but I get tired of her resistance stories; she looked very fat and well when we arrived, and I have probably observed to you before that no French who was a hero of the resistance, as many of our friends were, talk about it.

We go to London next month for Bill to try a new treatment for emphysema under a man called Dr. Croxon Deller. It is unpleasant and radical, but we hear wonderful things of him. The patient is given a general anesthetic, and they go down with a new kind of bronchoscope and clean up the bronchi and the lungs, filling the diseased pockets with antibiotics. The anesthetic technique is, of course, the tricky part, but we are full of hope and the hospital is called the London Clinic and said to be excellent.

December 30, 1946

1946 was a year full of delights for us, as you will have gathered from my letters. But apart from our personal happiness it was a stagnant year compared to last year, which was so full of drama, pain, and hope. The French Fourth Republic still has no President, although the great Socialist Léon Blum will probably become the head of the next government, and there will be a treaty with England, which is very important. But I feel as if all cars were in neutral gear—all sorts of clever people have their feet on the accelerators, but nothing is moving. Sound and noise, movement, no action. I hope I am wrong and would love to get the feel at home but see little hope of coming back as we are pinning our hopes on Bill's London treatments for the emphysema next month.

• 1947 •

21 Square du Bois de Boulogne
Paris, January 6, 1947

I am sending you by ordinary mail some pictures of the Vogüés[1] château near Rheims. This was our first visit to the champagne country, which is lovely and rolling. The château was surrounded by water and there was a pretty park. Unfortunately our troops had painted the best drawing room bright red and blue and torn up the ancient shining floor to build a bar, but there were plenty of other rooms and besides drinking a lot of Moët et Chandon, which is the Vogüés' champagne, we did some thrilling sightseeing. Rheims cathedral, of course, and another fascinating church, St. Rémy, then lots of calling on the neighbors to see their châteaux. The routine is always the same wherever we go, may I describe it?—it's quite unlike England or home. The hospitable owners are waiting at the door, the hostess is dressed in tweeds and a stout felt hat, the host is often red-faced and invariably jolly and very polite. The sons are weedy and look as if they needed cod-liver oil, the daughters are fat, strong, and cheerful. Elaborate minuet of introductions, much handshaking all around, everyone admires our fine car (the old Chevrolet from Washington), and if the children are small they leap into it. Apologies about the château and the park not being properly kept up, protestations from us. Then everyone puts on an extra coat to go inside and begin the visit of the house. I play a guessing game with myself as to dates and periods. There are some lovely things but some monstrosities if there is a rich great-grandfather. There is some horror committed during the war by the Germans or the Americans; if it's us everyone sighs and we all say in unison that troops are alike everywhere, and they could not be more generous or friendly to us about it. We emerge frozen into the garden, which is inevitably laid out by Lenôtre, there is no other land-

[1] Comte and Comtesse Robert de Vogüé. Very unlike local neighbors I describe visiting.

scape gardener. If it is afternoon we go in for a cup of tea and ten minutes' general conversation. Subjects: the high cost of living; the imbecility of the government; the difficulty of getting things done nowadays. Ten minutes of handshaking and off we go. I hope this doesn't sound critical, it just took us a little time to get used to the formality which these nice people wear so easily.

21 Square du Bois de Boulogne
January 16, 1947

The sun is out for the first time in weeks and any other people would be thrilled to have such a beautiful day for the election of the first President of the Fourth Republic,[2] but the French are bored. As someone said the other day, they adore royalty, any royalty, and after the English visit in 1938 they gladly paid ten francs to see the apartments at the Quai d'Orsay in which the King and Queen had stayed, but at no time would they pay fifty centimes to see the presidential apartments complete with the President in them. I love processions, and shall watch this one alone on my street corner; the election takes place at Versailles, so they will come right by us.

We leave for England tonight for Bill to undergo Dr. Croxon Deller's radical treatment for his lungs. It makes such sense to go down with a bronchoscope and clean up the infection, but this is much more profound a bronchoscopy than the one he had in New York and I am sick with worry over their problem with the anesthesia. Bill is gay and gallant, imploring me to accept every invitation I get and to have fun in London, and although I have no desire to go out a lot we are both very touched by the letters and telegrams from our English friends welcoming us. They say that it is the coldest winter in years and the fuel crisis critical. One invitation we have accepted with alacrity is from Ronnie Tree, who asks us to come to Ditchley the moment Bill leaves the hospital for a long convalescent weekend. We are dying to see the house, which is said to be the loveliest of its period in England and Ronnie is an angel to want us. I'll let you know from London how we get on.

[2] Vincent Auriol.

· *1947* ·

London, England
February 3, 1947

Bill has been in the London Clinic for two weeks and will be discharged in a few days for a recuperative, long weekend at Ronnie Tree's. We are full of hope about the treatment, although it was very, very unpleasant. Bill is as usual the bravest man in the world, but it was a blow that they had to go down into the lungs three times. The nursing care is wonderful—pretty little Scotch and Irish nurses pile the blankets and hot water bottles on and are with him at the touch of a bell with boiling hot tea. The best they can do is to keep the room at about fifty-six to sixty degrees.

It seems the worst of luck that the British should be taking the most blows this awful winter. The blizzards have pretty well stopped production of fuel and electric power. One has only a few hours for domestic use a day. Industry has practically ground to a stop, monetary reserves are frighteningly low, and God knows what unemployment is, and people are tired, tired. And yet, there is a reserve of moral strength that is hard to describe. For instance, as you know better than I, the Greeks are going straight into the Russian sphere, politically, unless they get help fast, and the English look like being too poor to help them. This means a demeaning request to us to take over, and I have no idea whether this would be accepted by Congress. My feeling is that Truman and Marshall and Acheson will fill the gap and sell it to Congress somehow—another Vandenberg, or perhaps he, himself, will put it through. How bitterly dislikable, how truly humiliating any Latin nation would find this request. But the British have the humility of *grandeur*—sorry, I used the French word, which is graven on my heart—there must be a better word. To the French grandeur and humility are incompatible, for the moment; I feel sure that the next generation will see things differently.

Bill was an observer last summer at the Fontainebleau conference attended by Ho Chi Minh; to his and my uneducated eyes, this was a turning point in French colonial affairs, and I am grateful to have met Ho Chi Minh. He is a very big man, giving one the creepy, crawly spine-tingling feeling when one shakes his hand that President Roosevelt never gave me, longing for it as I was, and perhaps the French government could have handled him better. We are too ignorant to know. And I'm absurd to be taking you away to a remote Far Eastern worry, for, thank God, I cannot see the United States involved in Indochina. We have enough on our hands, and I pray that the President will pull off the Greek-Turkey commitment, which really means, the English friends say calmly, that the Mediterranean is our baby.

I am staying with the Maclays, old friends from wartime Washington, in Mount Row, just near the Connaught. They are angels of mercy—it's no fun having a guest. All pipes in London are on the outside of people's houses, so all pipes are frozen. Becky and I get up and have a go to see if we can force a little water through in order to heat it—no go; then I walk to the London Clinic, which gets my circulation going, to spend the day with Bill, whose nurses are as nice to me as they are to him, so we joke and drink tea, and the English friends come in hordes to see him, bless them; then I leave and walk back to Mount Row. Jack is a busy Minister, and Becky has her hands full; so quite often I go out to dinner. Dear Louise de Rougemont is here, and I have one American friend, an interesting girl, Kick Hartington; do you know her? She is the daughter of Joseph Kennedy, the former Ambassador, and lives in a little house in Westminster looking out over the beautiful ruins of the church in Smith Square. She used to come to the house in Paris when we were first there, and it is fun to have one American friend to whom one can say frankly, "Why in hell do the English have all their pipes on the outside?" She is full of charm and love of life and uncertainty. I don't know her well enough to understand the uncertainty, but can guess that part of it must have to do with religion. Today, the brothers Sykes were there, Evelyn Waugh, and a brilliant priest whose name I missed. This is high-powered, intellectual Catholicism and must be confusing to someone of Kick's upbringing. She has said enough to make me feel that she is fascinated, disturbed, and intrigued. I want to see much more of her in the future.

Kathleen, Marchioness of Hartington, was killed tragically in an airplane accident over France the following spring, 1948. I heard the news from an English newspaperman whose name meant nothing to me. He rang me up in Paris saying, "Lady Hartington is dead.

We understand that you were a friend of hers, and we know that her father, Joseph P. Kennedy, is in Paris. Have you talked to him? Is it true that they were on very bad terms?"

Of course I hadn't spoken to Mr. Kennedy, I didn't even know him. What I did know, for I had kept up with Kick, was that she had the devoted support of her English in-laws, who were behind her whatever she did. This could not have been easy for them at the beginning, for although I have seen mention of the horror of the Catholic Kennedy family that one of the daughters should fall in love with and marry a Protestant, Billy Hartington, not much has been written in America about the reaction of the Cavendish family, whose head, the Duke of Devonshire, was Kick's father-in-law. An anecdote may illustrate this. My aunt took me to stay with the Duke and Duchess of Devonshire in Derbyshire a year or two later. We were having tea when the Duke, a most engaging and delightful man, looked out of the window. He sprang up. "Moucher"—the nickname of his wonderful wife—"papists in the drive! I see them coming." We all rushed to the window and indeed two nuns in their black habits were coming up the drive, no doubt on some routine charity appeal. This was of course a joke, and treated as such by the Duchess, but I sensed that it wasn't entirely a joke and remembered Kick's description of her engagement. Her husband was killed very early in the war, and she was enormously grateful for the support of his family. The warmth and charm that I mention in my letter made her the most popular young widow in London; one of the reasons is that she remained so American.

I remember a telephone call from her during these ghastly freezing weeks in London, 1947. "Susan Mary, I'm going to cheer us up. I'm giving a ladies' lunch for you, like at home." "But, Kick, do they do that here? What fun, as they don't in Paris." "No, they don't, but I'm going to, it will be you and me and my four best English girl friends, I want you to meet them. And it's so cold in my house that I'm going to have cocktails first, none of this sherry they go in for, then I'm going to have crab meat out of cans from America, which mother sent me, with tomato ketchup, and corn bread, and fried chicken, okay?" "Okay, Kick, you're terrific, I can't wait, Bill will understand if I leave him for once instead of having lunch at the cafeteria on Marylebone Road."

The lunch was a great success, the English girls were as attractive as

Kick had said they would be, and one of them drove me back to Bill's hospital. On the way she said that they couldn't do without Kick, who made life gay when things were desperate, as now. I asked her if she felt at all the subcurrents of uncertainty, which I mention in my letter. She said that of course she did, adding, as we drew up to the hospital, "Kick is the sensitive Kennedy—I've known them all."

21 Square de Bois de Boulogne
Paris, February 15, 1947

I haven't had the heart to write since our return as I rather think that Bill is less well than before that wretched torturing treatment in London. He coughs too much, is emaciated. The Ambassador is so kind—so is Mrs. Caffery, both wrote me notes urging me to persuade him to go south. This would be wonderful, but he wants to go right back to work—you know his courage. Well, someday they will find a cure and meanwhile we must be grateful that he got through this last treatment safely and both of us are deeply moved by the kindness of our English friends. With their country barely surviving, and possibly slipping into total economic collapse and everyone so worried, how could they worry about us too? The weekend at Ronnie's was marvelous, we slithered down through a blizzard to find a huge fire blazing in the hall of the finest house I have ever seen, with Ronnie and Anthony Eden having tea off a round table in front of the chimney. That night Eden talked brilliantly, mainly about the Balkans and England's particular worries about Greece.

Paris seemed the promised land when we got back, peaceful warm, stable. Of course it is none of those things except in comparison to stricken England, and there was an ominous general strike yesterday. The French enjoyed having the police on strike and had a lot of fun driving up all one-way streets the wrong way. The cook says good riddance, the police were just a band of assassins anyway.

I haven't felt like going to look at the dress collections. The girl friends say I must have a look at a man called Christian Dior, no one ever heard of him before but there is something called "The New Look" which he has invented. Apparently Mrs. Snow of

Harper's Bazaar, who is here, says that this man Dior has saved the French fashion industry. I'll go soon and report.

I had no idea that Marietta was destined to marry Ronald Tree in July and become the mistress of his great house, Ditchley. My happiness was great when I learned the news that summer, for *her* because I knew and deeply admired Ronnie, for *me* as this meant that she would be just across the English Channel with my little goddaughter Frankie FitzGerald.

21 Square du Bois de Boulogne
Paris, February 23, 1947

I did go to Dior's first collection, fighting my way through hundreds of richly dressed ladies clamoring to get in. It is impossible to exaggerate the prettiness of "The New Look." We are saved, becoming clothes are back, gone the stern padded shoulders, *in* are soft rounded shoulders without padding, nipped-in waists, wide, wide skirts about four inches below the knee. And such well-made armor inside the dress that one doesn't need underclothes; a tight bodice keeps bust and waist small as small, then a crinoline-like underskirt of tulle, stiffened, keeps the skirt to the ballet skirt tutu effect that Monsieur Dior wants to set off the tiny waist.

As one of the salesladies is a friend of mine I was permitted to go into the fitting rooms afterwards to try on some models. This was more dangerous than entering a den of female lions before feeding time, as the richest ladies in Europe were screaming for the models, shrill cries of "WHERE is Miss New York? I had it and someone has stolen it right from under my eyes!" (The dresses are called Miss Paris, Miss Nice, etc., this season).

The prices are very high, as you can imagine, but I have had a piece of luck—only you mustn't tell a soul. Monsieur Dior has asked me to wear his clothes this season, all I have to do is to ring up in the morning and ask them to send over the model I want to wear. Naturally he would prefer people to think that they are my own made-to-order-for-me dresses, hence the need for discretion.

Other cheering news is that Bill has been persuaded to go to Mallorca in Spain, said to be warm and sunny and everything someone with emphysema should be helped by, and we are to drive down to Barcelona, where one embarks for the Balearic Islands. Teddy Phillips is coming with us; he is a delightful companion and drives beautifully in case we get tired. It will be a wonderful drive, Tours, Carcassone, Perpignan, to the Spanish frontier, which is closed for political reasons but our diplomatic license plates solve that problem. We have turned in the aging Chevrolet for a Buick freshly arrived from home, brand-new tires and everything. My spirits soar. Can you not possibly get away to come to us for a visit? You would look smashing in the Dior dresses. We always have room. Did I write that my mother is coming over this summer and has given us the lovely Senlis house as a present? Too good of her and I cannot wait to see her after two years. This means that we can offer you the choice of two houses!

There was nothing unusual about Dior's offer; the great houses often offered this sort of deal to young women who could not afford the prices they charged. Theoretically, one was supposed to be good publicity and a bait for other customers. Schiaparelli also never charged the top prices to me, and later I found my true love, Balmain.

Dior became a friend, and once when he was dining at the house I told him with pride that a New York friend had cabled me to order three dresses for his wife which he had chosen from sketches sent over by their saleslady. He asked which ones, so I named them, Isis, Venus, Arethusa (he was naming the dresses for goddesses that year), upon which he became pale with horror and cried, "Stop the order!" The point was that all three dresses were embroidered from head to foot, and Dior the artist was revolted by what seemed to him the vulgarity of one woman having such rich finery. He said that he couldn't imagine anyone in the world leading a life that required three embroidered dresses and could I not persuade her to choose instead at least two very plain, understated numbers, of which the collection was full. He explained to me that he didn't expect to sell his embroidered dresses very often, but he put them in because embroidery by hand is an art in France, a minor art but an art, and he wished to keep the embroiderers going, which he could afford to do as he was doing so well with the other dresses, perfumes, etc. By this gesture Monsieur Dior lost about twelve thousand dollars, or rather he would have if my New York friend had agreed to change the order. He did not, and the dresses were made and dispatched. I feel sure that some costume museum is enjoying them now and am delighted that they went to America.

A footnote to the brilliant success of Dior's first collection: although he needed no publicity by then, he learned somehow that my birthday was June 19, and on that day arrived "Miss New York," my favorite dress, to be all my own. He was a kind and charming man. I hung on to "Miss New York" sentimentally until a few years ago when I gave it to Cecil Beaton for the Victoria and Albert Museum's collection of modern costumes which he was arranging. My poor mother in America was horrified by my arrangement with the house of Christian Dior. I still have a letter in which I tried to comfort her by saying, "The mannequins are such nice, clean girls, if you could see them you wouldn't mind my wearing their clothes." If the mannequins had seen this sentence they would have torn me apart with their shining white teeth. They were beautiful and elegant, one often saw them at Maxim's with admirers like Prince Aly Khan.

Another important figure in the world of high fashion was the formidable Madame Lucienne of Reboux, the great milliner. As I never left my house even to mail a letter without wearing a hat and gloves, hats were terribly important. I ordered two each season from Reboux; the decision what to order was made by Madame Lucienne herself after one had sat at a mirror in the sunny showroom on the Avenue Matignon trying on every hat in the collection with the help of minor acolytes. I trembled before this awesome woman. Once she thought that I looked terrible in every hat in that season's models, so after some thought, during which the acolytes and I hardly dared breathe, she snapped her fingers, saying, "I've got it, bring me one of the hats from the period of the great beauty of Madame Martinez de Hos." Little girls went scurrying to the back, where Lucienne must have had her own costume museum of models from the days of Napoleon III, and raced to us carrying a cloche from the twenties with which Lucienne was delighted. The lady for whom it had originally been made would not have been delighted; she was still very much around and I thought her beautiful.

At Reboux's, once the choice had been made, the hat was first made in white muslin and one went to have it fitted. Then it was made in the material of one's choice, and one went back again for a fitting, sometimes twice. At the final fitting Madame Lucienne was sent for to give the okay, and she sometimes did not like it; if so, it was torn off your head and cut into ribbons and one started all over again, despite one's pitiful pleas that one needed the hat that night. By hats for the night I mean the little feathered headdresses of ostrich or paradise feathers that we wore to cocktail parties and to restaurants. I find a letter comparing Maxim's to boarding school—"it might as well be a school uniform, the little black dresses and the feathered headdresses, we can't be told apart except for the colors in our feathers."

21 Square du Bois de Boulogne
Paris, March 17, 1947

Our trip to Spain was wonderful, I don't think any of us will forget the laughs we had, and more importantly, it has done Bill so much good. He looks like a different man, coughs less, is sunburned, put on some weight, and is sure that the London treatment is beginning to work. Cautious as ever, I am keeping my fingers crossed, but at least he is in better shape than he has been in ages and I am beginning to realize that he will never climb stairs easily again, and that I must stop expecting miracles from the doctors. He is happy and pleased that we went, and although we were gone two weeks and two days and did over three thousand kilometers he isn't in the least tired. Thank God we took Teddy Phillips, who is a mechanic as well as a charming companion. Our brand-new horrible sea-green Buick from home is equipped with the new postwar synthetic tires and we had seven blowouts between here and the Spanish border. It was still snowing when we left Bordeaux and very cold in the Pyrenees. On the other side of the Spanish border we created a sensation and children ran out in the streets screaming that the Germans were back (the only foreigners they knew, due to the border with France being closed). I will send you a comic article from the Barcelona paper; it begins, "A sensation was caused at the Hotel Ritz on Monday night by the arrival of an immense green Buick from France, the first car seen from that country since the closing of the frontier. In the car there were three distinguished personages from the Parisian diplomatic world, [then our names], who were dressed in fur coats and fur-lined boots of the utmost richness. Señora Patten even wore heavy green wool stockings and fur gloves, on her head a green Tyrolean hat. This extraordinary manifestation was easily explained by the visitors, who said that it was very cold in France, with snow south of Bordeaux. On hearing of the arrival this newspaper [*El Correo Catalan*] rushed two ace reporters the following morning to the Ritz, where they found Señor Patten still reposing himself after the voyage, but Señora Patten and El Commandante Phillips were in the lobby drinking orange juice. When questioned as to the probable result of the Moscow conference they answered that they hoped for the best and ordered more orange juice. When asked how long he considered that the frontier would remain closed El Commandante remarked that he was not at liberty at this time to disclose the views of His Majesty's Government but that he was free to say for quotation that he found Spain a lovely country, and that this was his first fresh orange juice for many years. On the French political situation the pair were guarded, but ordered a third orange juice. At this moment the American diplomat joined them and all three went out together, their destination unknown, but it was observed that they had discarded their fur boots. El Commandante wore a Leica camera around his neck, the Señora carried a guidebook of our fair city." I swear not one word is made up, I'll prove it by sending the Spanish copy, once unpacked, which also has a fine photo of us guzzling orange juice in the Ritz lobby. Mallorca was almond trees in bloom, Robert Graves to greet us at Deja, and a little boat which Bill and Teddy loved sailing. It was never quite warm enough to swim, but so restful and good for Bill, our greatest excitement an evening game of écarté.

To Marietta from Paris

21 Square du Bois de Boulogne
Paris, April 20, 1947

Your letter of April 16 has come, and I am deeply touched by what you say about your great regret that we haven't been able to talk in two years. Your letters have been the best possible substitute, but I do so wish I could be with you now in your deep unhappiness. If your marriage is going as badly as you say it certainly isn't because you and Desy haven't tried . . . you are both unselfish, gallant people and I hope neither of you will have a sense of failure if you break up. Four years apart is a frightful strain, and guilt is what you mustn't feel. You say that you feel sawed in two, which must be a horrid feeling. I could not be sadder or sorrier, dear Marietta. Come to us the moment you can get away, bringing my darling little goddaughter. As I wrote before, we have this house and Senlis going full blast this summer, waiting for you, and France is the most comforting country I know. I have been blue myself lately, in a minor way, and if one walks the long avenues of Versailles or the little cobbled streets of Senlis or the tortuous, narrow passages that pass for streets in the old part of Paris one returns smoothed out. I put this down to the fact that so many, many men and women have lived and suffered here before us and that their spirit emanates from the surroundings in which they lived, telling us to take courage. And there are so many friends who would love to meet you—above all you would give Bill and me a huge boost in morale.

While we were away in Spain and probably before, a man has been intriguing to get Bill's job, and it is uncertain whether or not we shall be booted out in a few months. (This would not affect our summer plans nor our invitation to you and Frankie.) Bill's health makes his position vulnerable of course; who wants a sick man when a well one would do? Happily he works as hard and well as the strongest, and I hear that Elim O'Shaughnessy, who is closer than anyone to the Ambassador, has written the latter a strong letter saying that Bill's dispatches are first class and that in Elim's opinion we are doing more as a team for the country than anyone in the Embassy. I didn't like the team suggestion when I heard this, as I want Bill to get all the credit, but this is a profession in which a wife can help or hurt and it was nice of him. We know the man well who wants Bill's place, it is rather unpleasant. I often feel so futile compared to you, with your real place in New York City, and what do I do except meet trains and airplanes and order fish for dinner, but it's rather hard to think of a life for Bill without a fulfilling and useful job. But something will come up—his spirit makes my whines seem shaming. Do keep in close touch, and I think of you all the time.

It was a blow and yet a relief to get Marietta's April 16 letter in which she for the first time admitted that her reunion with Desmond had been followed by a failure of readjustment. The blow was because I loved Marietta and Desmond and I could imagine what a devastating effect this period must have had on both of them. Desmond was proud and brilliant, Marietta was brilliant but humble, never really believing in her extraordinary success. I could hardly bear to think of Bishop and Mrs. Peabody, her parents, who I admired. For, admirable and praiseworthy as they were, I could not feel that they would understand. I don't know still what they said, Marietta would never have told me, but I can guess. Eleven generations of her distinguished family—Peabodys, Parkmans, Lawrences, and others—had survived the harsh winds that blow over Massachusetts from the Atlantic and I imagine that few of these hardy people had known the pain and sadness of divorce. My heart ached for her, but I was relieved to know what was wrong, for her delightful letters over the two years that we had been apart held an undercurrent of sadness that none of the amusing stories about life in New York could explain. I was writing and writing, pouring out my happinesses and my disappointments, and Marietta would reply regularly and wittily, sharing in my excitements but never telling me about herself.

As for Bill's problems, the situation was happily resolved by the Ambassador, Mr. Caffery, telling the man who wanted Bill's job to go jump in the lake. For eight years more we felt always like Eliza on the ice floes in *Uncle Tom's Cabin*, one jump ahead of the authorities, but ambassador after ambassador stood up for Bill and insisted on his indispensability, so he was able to continue to serve in Paris, doing one competent job after another.

To Marietta from Paris

21 Square du Bois de Boulogne
Paris, April 28, 1947

With the wolves at the door and Europe possibly about to collapse into barbary, perhaps I should describe our last weekend at the only place I have yet seen that is untouched. This is Bel Oeil, near Brussels, which belongs to the Prince de Ligne. His wife, Philippine, is the sister of our great friend Henri de Mouchy, and it was Henri's son Philippe who took us there. It is so feudal that the Prince de Ligne had written ahead to me saying that he was sorry that a pressing engagement would prevent him from meeting us at the border, however he would send someone to guide us to Bel Oeil. Can you imagine such lovely old-fashioned manners in 1947? For Bel Oeil is as well known to the Belgians as Versailles is to the French, we really could have found it on our own. But Philippe de Noailles, who was with us, shrugged his shoulders and said, "That's Uncle Antoine for you, perhaps there will be a traveling carriage with outriders at the frontier."

Instead there was a shiny new Packard Clipper with a very smart chauffeur. He said to the customs officials, "Guests of the Prince de Ligne," and everyone fell to the floor and there was no question of customs, passports, or papers for the Buick, we whisked into Belgium behind the Packard going all out at a hundred and twenty kilometers with the klaxon screaming and people in villages diving onto sidewalks.

Bel Oeil was all I had expected and more. Besides the comfort of the conversation (they are talking of adding or doing over wings instead of chopping them off, as in most places), the history of the Low Countries was in our rooms, and this is the history of Europe in the late sixteenth and all of the seventeenth centuries. Bill's enormous room was filled with pictures of the Lignes of the period arriving at the court of Charles II of England as ambassadors, resplendent as their Dutch galleons sailed up the Thames to anchor below the Tower of London. I was next door, within easy bicycling distance, in the "Marshal's Tower," and had besides my bedroom a bathroom, two sitting rooms, and a dressing room entirely devoted to souvenirs of the life of this great eighteenth-century figure. Over my bed hung the gayest picture you ever saw, of the death scene in

Vienna, with the Marshal in a pink and white lace bed jacket and Emperor Alexander of Russia and the King of Prussia gossiping away on each side of the bed. One souvenir I shall never forget, my bidet made of solid silver, beautifully shined, carrying the arms of the Talleyrands, as this Prince de Ligne's grandmother was a Talleyrand. The motto of the coat of arms is "Only God is above us." This touch delighted Bill and Alan Kirk, our Ambassador and old friend.

You will be as amazed to hear as I was that in spite of their style of living our hosts could not be more modern in their outlook and no one admires them more than Spaak[8] and the Socialists. In one of the wings are two hundred orphans, the Versailles-like gardens are open to the public, and the government considers the château a sort of national home.

The only sadness on return was to find Henri de Mouchy very ill. He cannot live much longer, for the last months have been a steady slide down. We go to see him all the time, as Marie, who is heroic, thinks that he enjoys hearing us babble away although he can no longer speak. If he is up to it, they want us to go tomorrow to describe our impressions of his sister's house, Bel Oeil.

21 Square du Bois de Boulogne
Paris, 1947

When you come over I think that I must take you to a charity sale, as nothing is more French. Except for charity balls, the sale seems to be the only way to raise money and my friends work like dogs over them. I have just come from one. They are all alike but the place chosen varies in size. However, it is invariably cold, damp, dark, and smells of pork pâté at one end and musty old damask napkins with ducal coronets embroidered on them at the other

[8] Paul-Henri Spaak of Belgium was one of the great postwar leaders of Western Europe, ranking with Robert Schuman of France, Alcide de Gasperi of Italy, and Konrad Adenauer of Germany. A dedicated believer in a united Europe, he never lost hope. I met him in Paris often and loved his optimism and his courage. Soon after the failure on the European Defense Community in 1954 I encountered him at lunch and tried to say something comforting and sympathetic. He waved away my sympathy, saying, "What difference does one tactical defeat make? Our hopes are deferred for a year or two, that's all."

end. As I approach "la stand" of my particular friends happy cries go up, "Good, here comes Susan Mary," and I am offered all sorts of goodies from people's places in the country, really fresh eggs, etc., which are well worth buying, although the prices are necessarily twice the black market prices. If I arrive too late I am in for the doilies "crocheted by the English nurse of my sister-in-law," or worse. All hands have been working since dawn yet I fear that the long day cannot be really remunerative financially. Yet they tell me that it would be out of the question to do as we do at home, send out letters explaining the cause and asking for a check, with a good mailing list and some publicity.

Another very French thing to which, alas, we could not take you is the ceremonial shoot for the Ambassadors at the President of France's country residence, Rambouillet. Duff Cooper told us that this year he was placed between General Juin (chief of staff) and Admiral Le Monnier (head of the navy) and that Le Monnier may be a good admiral but as a sportsman he is comic. A poor old pheasant tottered out about ten feet in front of him walking sedately along the ground, so the Admiral immediately drew a bead on it. General Juin, horrified at his colleague's unsportsmanlike behavior, shouted at him not to shoot a bird moving on the ground, and the Admiral replied coldly, "But naturally, General, I'm not shooting while he is walking, I am waiting for him to stop." Which the bird did and Le Monnier fired both barrels at a range of twelve feet and missed him. I hope you think this as funny a story as Bill and I do.

This letter is hardly worth the stamp, it's just to tell you that I am thinking of you and miss you.

May 12, 1947

We are going to Ditchley this weekend, taking Odette. Never have I known anything like the kindness of Ronnie Tree. He has taken such trouble, and we are to visit Blenheim and many another beautiful house in Oxfordshire. And Odette and I will stay on in London for a few days; we are thrilled about the trip and are packing our best dresses and plan to carry dozens of eggs and other things to eat.

Our most recent visitor has been our cousin Jane Whitridge—such a wonderfully enthusiastic girl. She literally burst into tears the night she arrived over the beauty of Notre Dame when seen from the quays on the Left Bank. Bill and I enjoy having her and look forward to Sylvia's arrival later. It's part of the fun of living here to have the guest rooms full, as it's no effort particularly if the guests are young and keen. I do wish I could have got Jane into our day yesterday, which is worth describing in detail.

Winston Churchill has been here to receive the Military Medal and the French have given him a really spontaneous welcome wherever he went during the three days. I have never felt Paris so alive and enthusiastic. Yesterday morning was perhaps the most triumphant moment, as he and Duff Cooper made a tour of St. Denis, the Faubourg St. Antoine, and other of the poorest quarters of Paris—the "Red Belt"—and he received an ovation in his open car, shouts of *Vive Churchill, Vive l'Angleterre.*" The day before he had worn the uniform you will have seen in the pictures—I think it is the tropical dress of one of the Hussar regiments, with the Military Medal, and looked smashing. Mrs. Churchill said that she had had the greatest difficulty in keeping him from wearing the uniform of an air marshal, I think it was because he liked the color, but that she had said, "Winston, if you must wear a showy uniform please wear something that you really have a right to," and he had given in with bad grace. Yesterday he was in civilian clothes, but I am getting ahead of my story. We had been asked for lunch at St. Firmin, the charming little château at Chantilly which the Duff Coopers take as a weekend home, and arrived to find the house party assembled. Ethel Harriman Russell,[4] who is a great friend of Diana's, Mrs. Montagu,[5] Alastair Forbes,[6] Randolph, Mrs. Sandys, and Mrs. Oliver,[7] and their mother, Teddy Phillips, and poor Diana, who

[4] Ethel Russell, Diana's old friend from America, was the daughter of Mrs. J. Borden Harriman, who became our Ambassador to Norway.

[5] Venetia Montagu, born Venetia Stanley, was another of Diana's oldest friends. As a girl in the London of the First World War she was much admired by the Prime Minister, Asquith, who used to take her for afternoon drives in the park, during which he would confide state secrets to her. It is hard to picture this scene in modern times.

[6] A clever and charming young newspaperman on the *Daily Mail* whose gifts had already attracted Churchill's attention.

[7] Randolph Churchill was the only son of the Prime Minister, Mrs. Sandys and Mrs. Oliver two of his daughters. Bill and I were devoted to Randolph,

had been there since 9 A.M. arranging the flowers and so on. The only outsider besides us and Odette Pol Roger was Mr. Bullitt,[8] more of him later. I thought Mrs. Churchill charming, so gay and friendly and kind, and liked the look of the girls. The château is in the grounds of the big château, off by itself above the lake, with a lawn running down to the water and enchanting planting of chestnut trees and elms. I must have described it often before, but it was at its best yesterday. We sat about for a few minutes, Odette and I felt grossly overdressed just as we had feared we would, as the English ladies wore dank tweeds except for the Ambassadress, who wore gray flannel slacks and a large straw hat. Then Mr. Churchill and the Ambassador arrived, and it was all too evident that the Prime Minister's mood had changed from the early morning when he had been moved almost to tears by the crowd's acclaim, and he had become a tired, grumpy, terrifying old man who wanted his lunch. The Ambassador said that in the car he had found fault with everything: the chauffeur drove too fast, the detective had a German back of the neck, the country was ugly, the French security police was no good, the people didn't really want to see him, and why was he being dragged down to Chantilly for lunch? (It was of course he who had proposed the outing originally.) Diana gave one look at him and ordered champagne, which he likes, and put him on a large sofa with Odette on one side and me on the other. We then waited for three quarters of an hour for Mr. Bullitt, and I do not want to go through such an experience again. The reason they waited was not because he was a former U. S. Ambassador but because he had to be kept happy as the house at Chantilly is his on a long lease from the French government and the Coopers want to keep it this summer, and Bullitt is being filthy about it, won't say whether he wants it or not and for six months has refused to answer any of Diana's letters. She adores the house, and as he was leaving for the U.S. today this was the last chance to placate him. Mr. Churchill's head sank onto his chest, Odette and I tried every possi-

---

frequently exasperated by him. Like all his friends, we feared that his exceptional powers would be dissipated by his violent temper, his impatience, his seeming lack of discipline. But before he died he achieved a work that will live in history, the biography of his father.

[8] William Bullitt had been United States Ambassador to France when World War II started.

ble topic to please him, said that we were so looking forward to hearing him speak at Albert Hall on Wednesday, that the reception in Paris had been so genuine and wonderful, how much the French adored him, and so on, on and on. His only reply was a sound that I can only describe as "Gwumph" and an occasional cold look darted at us out of the corner of his eye. At last Bullitt came prancing in with the most lighthearted and casual of apologies (I heard today that he was drinking at the MacArthurs' before lunch and boasting that he was lunching with Churchill) and came right up to the Prime Minister to ask him how he had liked his book. "Gwumph." Lunch is announced, and very good it is, especially considering the time, and the sun begins to come out. When the ladies leave Mr. Churchill tells the men about his ideas for a United States of Europe, in what Bill said was a most thrilling and inspiring manner. Unless unification comes "this fertile continent will become a cess-pool, a sore spot, a charnel house." Bill said the language and the impassioned tone were worthy of a great foreign affairs debate. After lunch it is decided to walk down to the lake. There is a brook between and we all try to steer Mr. Churchill to the bridge, but he is determined to jump it. We hold our breath, he makes it easily waving the cigar, I take off my shoes to follow him and he turns around and says across the brook, *"N'ayez pas peur, suivez-moi."* [Have no fear, follow me] For he has decided that I am a French relation of Odette's, and nothing will deter him from speaking French to me. You know his French—Later in the afternoon he comes up to me with a childlike smile and says, *"Vous venez en Angleterre, je serais très content si vous et votre mari voulez dejeuner chez moi à la campagne lundi en huit"* [When you come to England, I would be very pleased if you and your husband would dine at my country house at eight o'clock on Monday]." I reply, "Thank you so very much, Mr. Churchill, Bill and I would love to come to lunch a week from tomorrow." *"Très bien, c'est entendu."* The Duff Coopers, rocking with laughter, say, "Winston, Susan Mary speaks very good English and Bill and she are on the staff of the American Embassy." He doesn't listen for a second and, having decided to speak French, turns to Mr. Bullitt and tells him in French that while he approved of part of his book the first chapter is utter nonsense and claptrap. This rolls off Bullitt's back like water off a duck, never have I seen such a conceited man. The Churchill family leaves for Le Bourget with the Ambassador, we all wave good-by from the steps shouting, "*Vive Churchill, Vive l'Angleterre.*" Smiles, cigar waving, V-sign. Duff on return says that on the way to the airport Mr. Churchill never stopped talking for a second about what a wonderful visit it had been, that he had adored every minute of it, and what a beautiful country France is. He caught sight of some large and hideous electric power lines and, turning to Mrs. Churchill, said, "Look, Clemmie, those magnificent power lines carrying current all over France. In stupid England we never have such fine power lines." Mrs. Churchill said, "I don't know, Winston, it seems to me that we have one or two like that," but by then he was on to something else. At Le Bourget there was an immense and enthusiastic crowd, and of course that pleased him too.

Ditchley Park
Enstone, Oxon, England
May 19, 1947

I am in bed with the flu, cursing my fate, while Bill and Odette are on their way to Chartwell to lunch with Mr. and Mrs. Winston Churchill. I could not be more comfortable, surrounded by beautiful things, and from my bed I look out through the tall sashed eighteenth-century windows at the Great Park of Ditchley. Deer move effortlessly in the far distance, the beech trees are a mile high, and I can see a little folly or temple on the horizon, Greek as Greek, but surely built for ladies and gentlemen out of Gainsborough portraits to take their tea in. This house and place seemed lovely in the February blizzard, now it is what I imagined England to be like in mid-May—sheer magic.

Ronnie is the kindest host imaginable, and the weekend house party was the greatest fun. The Lewis Douglasses (do you know them? I find it hard to imagine the U.S. being represented here by a nicer Ambassador, and she is charming too), Lord and Lady Salisbury, Sammy Hood, Marshall Field, Odette Pol Roger, Bill and me.[9] Lots of interesting people came for meals: the one I enjoyed

[9] Mr. Lewis Douglas was our postwar Ambassador to England. He and his wife Peggy were tactful, kind, and much beloved. When the Ambassador lost an eye

most was General Lord Ismay—Churchill's wartime chief of staff, who is one of the most engaging men I ever met. He was very gay and cheerful, although he had just returned from India that morning. You can imagine that I did *not* say "How was India?" It's a subject for foreigners to avoid, especially Americans. Men whisper about it at the end of drawing rooms. If you hear a muttered "Dickie says—" you know what their subject is and keep out.[10]

It seemed safer to ask Lord Ismay about the war and Churchill. He told me some fascinating stories, which I will put down although you may have heard them already, or some of them.

The stories of France in 1940 naturally interested me enormously. Ismay said that he would always remember Reynaud, the last Prime Minister of France, as a brave man. I said, "What about the Briare meeting, which has always seemed so incredible to me?" You will remember that by then the French government had fled to safety in this small town, refugees were beginning to jam the roads before the German advance, and General Weygand, in command of all French armies, seemed to have lost his nerve as indeed had

---

fishing for trout on the Test River in southern England, it was treated by the press as a disastrous accident to one of their own most popular statesmen would have been.

Lord Salisbury was the head of the Cecil family, and in the tradition of that remarkable family he served the state in many high offices. At the time at which I write he was out of power as there was a Socialist government. Before the war he had resigned from office as Undersecretary of Foreign Affairs in protest against the appeasement policy of Baldwin and Chamberlain which led to Munich. A man of infinite ability and charm, we always hoped that someday he would be Prine Minister but his chance never came. He was very kind and saw the best in people. Once, when we were having a ribald discussion about some aristocratic nymphomaniac of the period, he commented (he never could pronounce his *r*'s), "I would say that she has a vewy, vewy affectionate nature." His wife Betty, witty and very kind to us, became our loyal friend.

Viscount Hood was then serving as political counselor and head of chancery at the British Embassy in Paris. We had met him the year before and he instantly became a lifelong friend. My scrapbook is full of pictures of his elegant, elongated form lounging on the lawn at Senlis, or playing with the children, of whom he was very fond, or sightseeing with us in France or England. Sammy went on from Paris to other distinguished jobs, but retired early as the animosity of a British Labor Foreign Secretary arrested a brilliant career that should have taken him to the very top. His friends were furious but Sammy is philosophical and bitterness is not in his nature. He leads a happy bachelor life in London and is extremely busy both as a member of the House of Lords and on various important committees and boards.

[10] Dickie is Lord Mountbatten, who bore a heavy burden in India at the time of partition, pain, final independence.

Reynaud. Mr. Churchill flew out to see what he could do to help, and the French naturally begged for reinforcements. Ismay said that the staff sat paralyzed with fright, knowing Churchill's attachment to the French, knowing also England's total inability to provide reinforcements. "The Prime Minister hesitated a long time, then he said no. We left then, very conscious of the fact that the French were giving us a month or two to survive. In the car I didn't say a word, but the Prime Minister turned to me in a fury and said, 'No recriminations, Pug. I won't have it, don't you dare! Not against the French. No recriminations.'"

Tours, the last meeting, must have been the worst. The situation having deteriorated, there was no one to meet the small English party at the airport, which consisted of a grassy field with an elementary runway. The Foreign Secretary, Lord Halifax, as well as Lord Ismay were accompanying Churchill. Now I quote Ismay, who tells the story in the Prime Minister's voice, taking off his French perfectly:

"Je suis le Premier Ministre de Grande Bretagne. Un taxi il me faut. Ça existe, un taxi?"

In the taxi, Churchill speaking, "Well, the journey does not promise well. Do you not think that a good luncheon is in order? The hotel in Tours used to have some admirable Vouvray in its cellars."

After lunch a few members of the government were discovered, lurking, metaphorically, under their desks.

Lord Salisbury interrupted Pug Ismay's narration at this point, equally interesting. "Pug, just about then X[11] came to the Foreign Office, to tell me that we must no longer trust Reynaud, Prime Minister of France, as his courage and judgment had broken under his mistress's will."

Lord Ismay: "X was right. But he *had* had guts, Reynaud. And human feeling. At the end of this ghastly visit he said to Winston, with tears in his eyes, 'What will you do, when they come?' I think if he hadn't said *when*, but *if*, Winston wouldn't have minded so much. He replied, 'If they swim we will drown them, if they land we will hit them on the head, *frappez* them *sur la tête!*' Returning in the plane, 'Ismay, do you realize that we probably have a maximum of three months to live?' In a wonderful humor, enjoying himself."

[11] Important French diplomat, whom I knew well.

All these stories will be in the history books but it does send a chill down one's spine to hear them told by the actors in the drama. Bill and I had heard Lord Halifax in Washington describe that terrible French visit. He had said that he had walked in the garden, up and down, perfectly certain that Churchill would give in and send the last of the Royal Air Force over as reserves, which would have been the end of England.

Can you bear my going on? Odette and Bill won't be back from Chartwell for hours, Ronnie is busy, and as I can't see Churchill today it's comforting to repeat what I heard yesterday.

Battle of Britain—September 15, climax of this struggle in the air for Britain's survival. Scene: war room, below Whitehall's deep earth, watching all day the lights that flash on board as one squadron after another goes up. Girls like croupiers at Monte Carlo raking in the messages. At last every light on the big board is lit. (The board is a map of England and of northern France.) Churchill, "Air Marshal, pray, how many reserves are left?" "We have no reserves, sir." The day is over, they climb heavily and slowly up the stairs, for there is no elevator, and heavily get into the P.M.'s car. Churchill to Ismay, "Don't speak to me." Ismay to me: "As if I was going to say something about the weather." Then, Churchill, quietly, "Never, in the history of human events, have so many owed so much to so few."[12] Lord Ismay said that he had been so tired, so sad that he thought no words could stir him, but on hearing these he sat bolt upright and implored the Prime Minister to write them down, at once.

2 Buckingham Place
London, S.W. 1
May 25, 1947

Back in bed again with bronchitis, causing a lot of trouble to Gerry Koch de Gooreynd's[13] nice maid. He is in America. When will I learn to resist the English countryside, ducal homes, and

[12] There are other versions of how and when Churchill spoke these historic words, but this is what Lord Ismay told me.
[13] Gerard Koch de Gooreynd. Half Belgian, half English. He became our daughter Anne's godfather.

above all Ronnie's genius for giving pleasure? I last wrote on Monday from bed at Ditchley very jealous of Odette and Bill's day with the Winston Churchills. The next day we set off for Blenheim next door, Ronnie, Odette, and I, as Bill had had to return reluctantly to Paris. Lunching with the Duke of Marlborough is a mixed pleasure. His palace and his park are superb, as you know too well for me to bother to describe, but if you don't know him *watch it* as he is an arrogant, odious host who thinks he is a lady-killer and his leering glances at Odette and me were as conceited as his invitation to us to stay for the weekend—this on a Tuesday. "No, thank you, Duke," we said, and Ronnie hustled us off in the car to Compton Wynyates—that lovely rose-red Elizabethan many-chimneyed house where as Odette said, speaking of the owner, Lord Northampton, "This specimen of English nobleman is a lot more attractive than the last one." Then Chastleton House, built in Jacobean times and lived in by the same family who built it and, as they have always been poor, it is untouched and unspoiled by a rich Victorian grandfather. Mrs. Jones, the owner, is a tragic old lady, cameos her ornament, and the dress held up by rusty safety pins. She will not give in to the National Trust and as she doesn't have a servant she takes visitors around herself at fifty cents each. One longed to give her new shoes, for hers were split and her stockings had been darned so many times that they were of no one color, but she was a haughty, proud old soul and treated us as school children—"There is the Bible given by Charles I on his scaffold to Rupert Jones, kindly do not touch but you may look!"

On to Stratford-on-Avon for dinner and *The Tempest* in the Shakespeare theater. Such a drive—it was the English May that Shakespeare loved and which sings through the happiest of the sonnets, bluebells in the meadows, hedgerows of hawthorn; lilac and fruit trees in bloom, Warwick Castle bold above the river. And the names on the signposts, Chipping Norton, Stowe-on-the-Wold, Moreton-in-the-Marsh, Bourton-on-the-Water, Stratford-on-Avon. Worth a touch of bronchial flu, don't you think? I would love to spend a year exploring here, although Sacheverell Sitwell told me that he had spent a lifetime and still doesn't know England.

The next morning we visited the last house I will tire you with describing, but it and its owner moved me most of all. Ragley Hall, near Alcester, Warwickshire. This early Georgian house has a magnificent three-stories central hall molded in white plaster by James Gibb, and many other magnificent rooms of Ditchley-like elegance. We were received by one of the greatest ladies I have ever met, whose name is Lady Helen Seymour. Her poverty is extreme and, unlike the haughty Mrs. Jones, she is above pride. At the end of the morning she told us in the simplest possible way about her situation. Her husband is dead, she has a daughter my age who is now serving as lady in waiting to Princess Elizabeth, and a seventeen-year-old son. They haven't the money to endow the house for the National Trust (the Joneses could by selling things), and the son refuses to let her sell anything or move out. "It would be rather a bore to move, and he does so adore Ragley." But they can't go on much longer, so it will probably go to the "Teachers Association" who are sniffing around for a house.

We left Lady Helen to cook her lunch in a sad, small Kent bedroom made over into a kitchen, and moved on in uttermost depression to Oxford where Isaiah Berlin gave us lunch in the Fellows' Room of New College. This was charming, but I felt increasingly unwell, admitted this to Ronnie, and, with his usual sweetness and efficiency, presto and I was in this comfortable bed with the doctor here and antibiotics for a few tiresome days. At least Odette is able to fulfill our engagements and is the sensation of London, always finding time to come to see me, bless her. Bill sounds most cheerful and has been out every night, he is weekending at the Duff Coopers' and I should be able to travel in a few days. What beautiful things I have seen, and how grateful I am to Ronnie for that first spellbinding weekend.

Clos St. Nicholas
July 1947

Today Diana Cooper called up at dawn and said for heaven's sake do come to lunch at Chantilly to amuse Mr. Bevin,[14] who had suddenly decided that he would like a day of "nayce" country air. So I went and stayed until six on the terrace of St. Firmin listening to Bevin talk, except for half an hour when he went to sleep. I

[14] Ernest Bevin, Foreign Minister of Great Britain.

tiptoed over to put a pillow under his head, and he said, "Ta, my girl, no one ever thinks of doing that when I have a bit of lie down in the Foreign Office on my sofa."

I was vastly amused by his talk and impressed by him. Most of his stories are about himself, and many concern old trade union days: for instance, I being American, he is going to send me a photograph of the seal ring with which he seals all his treaties. This is a souvenir which he has treasured from the San Francisco convention of the A. F. of L in 1911 and is a picture of a Californian bathing beauty of the day, with diamonds around it. From early American labor politics we somehow came to Buckingham Palace. "For twenty years I got a card and I wouldn't go. This time I had to go. So Flo[15] dressed me up and off I went, and a more terrible two hours I never put in. I said to myself, 'Ernie, man, don't you just wish you were in Blackpool?'"[16] He is clearly in love with Diana, whom he addresses as Luff (Love in his language), and implored her to come to Durham for the great miners' convention at the end of the month, and to bring me. If we couldn't do that the next finest sight is Blackpool.

Of course you know that Bevin responded instantly to the Harvard speech of a few weeks ago, and saw at once the importance of Marshall's words.[17] He said of the U.S. today, "It's up to them, however you look at it, but we've got to make it possible for them to help us." He expressed great admiration for Marshall and asked

[15] Flo Bevin, his wife.

[16] Seaside resort, scene of Labor Party conferences.

[17] "1. Our policy is directed not against any country or doctrine but against hunger, poverty, desperation, and chaos. Its purpose should be the revival of a working economy in the world so as to permit the emergence of political and social conditions in which free institutions can exist.

"2. Such assistance, I am convinced, must not be on a piecemeal basis as various crises develop. Any assistance that this Government may render in the future should provide a cure rather than a mere palliative.

"3. Any government that is willing to assist in the task of recovery will find full cooperation, I am sure, on the part of the United States Government. Any government which maneuvers to block the recovery of other countries cannot expect help from us. Furthermore, governments, political parties, or groups which seek to perpetuate human misery in order to profit therefrom politically or otherwise will encounter the opposition of the United States."

The statement of purpose in the Harvard speech was designed to win over the critics at home of the brave Truman aid to Greece, and to confound the Soviet Union. The above three paragraphs rang around the world and England responded first, led by Ernest Bevin.

me how a soldier could be so imaginative. I said that I rather thought that a lot of people had put their ideas into the Marshall Plan speech but that of course Marshall was a great man and a brilliant one, that with forty Russian divisions in Central Europe, one hundred behind them, we with practically nothing, his training would naturally make him seize the ideas of the diplomats who were trying to recapture the balance. Bevin said sadly that it was a great pity that such a great people as the Americans do not understand socialism, and added, "One forgets Marxism when one has piles of work on one's desk." From there he spoke for some time with great pride of the practical accomplishments of the British Labor leaders of the past. He talks all the time as if the world was a great trades union, using union terms, and gives one the feeling that the U.S., France, and Great Britain are major A. F. of L. unions, with the Russians as an unpleasant C.I.O. infringing on their rights. That the whole thing is a Portsmouth dockside brawl, that he, Ernie Bevin, will stand no nonsense and is rather enjoying himself just as he did in those early trades union days about which he delighted in telling us.

This may not sound impressive but I can assure you that one feels confident that he will hit those dirty scabs over the eye and get away with it. Interesting to see him with Duff Cooper, who cannot be addressed as "Luff" and who calls Bevin "Secretary of State," yet they understand and like each other. Neither pretends to be what he isn't. Duff tells a story about Castlereagh and the Foreign Secretary says, "That's a good one, who did you say he was?" and follows up with a coarse and funny story about something that happened in Glasgow in 1917 and Duff adores it and laughs heartily and Diana, sitting between them, knits away, looking incredibly beautiful.

My chief contribution to the day was to leave—they must have been so tired—and promise that I would be at Durham if Diana went. "That's rich, Luff." Their departure for Paris was typical of them all, bless the English. Diana driving her Ford with the top down, Foreign Secretary beside her, the Ambassador and the detective in the back seat, the Rolls-Royce with the chef and other servants. The last thing I heard Mr. Bevin say was, "Please, Luff, drive a little slower than usual. You drive so well, but you frighten me more than the most 'ideous terrorists."

Senlis
August 1947

Yes, of course, there is an immense intense school of writing, and I should have told you about it before. I am sending over *The Plague* by Camus, who wrote *The Stranger*, which I did send you. He also writes in the newspaper *Combat*.

The Plague is terrifying as it's all about the moral crisis and decadence of our time, and is chillingly cold, as was *The Stranger*. There is no hero in the Camus-Sartre literature, everyone is a struggling mediocre character living as it might be in Forest Hills, Long Island, unable to make brave decisions, just standing on the platform waiting for the four-three to show up. But Camus is irresistible, you won't forget either book. You remember that my father always kept a Balzac by his bed and taught me to do the same; I still do and I love my Balzac heroes. He too was a satirist, an exposer of the corruption of Paris life at its very worst, but how gay compared to this. However, we must read Camus and we must see Genêt, the young playwright Jean Cocteau discovered in the war. Cocteau has always had an inner circle which seems to have dominated artistic Paris. Some people are unkind about his relations with the Germans during the war, others say that he protected French cinema actors and others due to his friendships with the enemy. Someday someone will write a life of him and all this will be sorted out.

In any case *Les Bonnes* by Jean Genet is shocking, brilliant, and has been the talk of the town. It concerns two female servants who plan to poison their employer, but one goes dotty and decides that she is the mistress of the house herself. This doesn't sound like much but I can assure you that it is the most interesting play that I have seen since we arrived in Paris.

Sartre's movement faded away in the fifties and if the existentialists are read today it is as classics. But it was very influential at the time, for the young French who had come out of the occupation disgusted by the bourgeois morality of the thirties were searching for a new creed. The immediate postwar period was a time of high aspiration, of high intellectual energy, which was canalized by Sartre and Camus. The two men split over the question of Marxist ideology, which Camus abandoned early on.

21 Square du Bois de Boulogne
Paris, August 4, 1947

We gave a singularly unenjoyable party yesterday at Senlis. It was a luncheon, for the Ambassador and Mrs. Caffery. We were fourteen, and everyone stayed until dinnertime. At six o'clock I felt like the *New Yorker* cartoon of the unhappy hostess passing hors d'oeuvres, with the caption "The house party that doesn't mix and thirty-six hours to go." The temperature was one hundred degrees. Someone brought her baby, who sat in its basket all afternoon in the middle of the drawing room, crying fitfully. Mrs. C's two nephews lay on the floor saying, "Gee, what sort of a country *is* this, without even one funny paper on Sundays?" Even with coats off the men dripped and of course we ran out of ice. The Ambassador wanted to go sightseeing, so off we set on foot to see the town and poor Mrs. Caffery became faint with the heat in the Château Royal, and we lost some of the French friends near the cathedral and they had a terrible time finding the house again, for the cobbled streets of Senlis are narrow and winding and they did not know the town. Dear me, I am sorry, as the Cafferys are kind to us and we longed to give them a good time. Bill always tries to cheer me up, and pointed out later that they didn't have to stay till nearly dinnertime. True.

The Marshall planners thrill me. They are working in the Grand Palais, one of the hottest buildings in town because of the immense amounts of glass. Of course no air conditioning, but I don't think the planners notice it much, for the sense of urgency is great and they don't even seem to mind their hours, 9 A.M. to midnight. Cripps came over from London last week and put the British situation in the blackest terms to Mr. Clayton.[18] It is nothing new, heaven knows, but it is new for anyone in the Labor government to admit it except

[18] Sir Stafford Cripps was minister of Economic Affairs and Chancellor of the Exchequer. Mr. Will Clayton was Undersecretary of State.

for Ernie Bevin. It is interesting to note how many of our old Washington friends have been dragged out of private life to help, Tommy Brand, Denny Marris, Eric Wyndham-White, and others, although they are Conservative to a man.

Brand, Marris, and Wyndham-White were Englishmen with top-flight minds. The first two were partners of Lazard Frères in London, and returned to private business after this emergency was over. Wyndham-White was a civil servant specializing in financial affairs. Many others came to join them. I write of Isaiah Berlin appearing like a bombshell, wrenched at twenty-four hours' notice from the tranquillity of Oxford to write the draft of the Marshall Plan report. One unbearably hot day Diana took us to picnic in the forest of Marly-le-Roi, an important day for me as I first met Pamela Berry, who became a great friend and will appear often in later letters as Marietta too became close to her. The wife of Michael Berry, now Lord Hartwell, Pam was a wonderfully loyal friend to us. She gave and gives the best parties in London: mixing politicians, men of letters, artists with great skill. How I wish that her dining room had been bugged all these years, for the historians would find the conversations that took place in it the richest of source material.
Sir Isaiah Berlin first came into our lives in Washington, where his wartime dispatches from the British Embassy were brought to the Prime Minister's attention for their brilliance. Brilliant is a banale and inadequate word for this remarkable humanist. Born of Russian parents, he was educated in England and has spent most of his life at Oxford, and it is to his inspiration and hard work that Oxford owes one of its newest colleges, Wolfson. His beautiful French-born wife Aline became a close friend of mine and Bill's and we often visited them.

21 Square du Bois de Boulogne
Paris, October 31, 1947

This morning Bill and I attended a most moving ceremony at the British Embassy to see our friend Jacques Allez receive a decoration for his work for the English during the war. Both our Embassies have these investitures now and then, but we do it at the Chancery, which is a fine office building but not as glamorous as the house that was built in the eighteenth century, lived in by Napoleon's beautiful sister Pauline, bought by Wellington. Lady Granville and other famous personages have left their aura in the walls. I am Japanese about this leaving of personality in brick and damask.

It makes one ashamed to realize how the cynicism in the air around one has affected one: all the stories debunking the resistance have affected me subliminally. If it hadn't been for Jacques I would not have gone. Once there I was ashamed. By luck I sat just opposite the door where the two hundred and fifty men and women were waiting to file through to be decorated by the Ambassador. This sounds as if it had been a long ceremony—but it went very fast and seemed not long enough as the citations were remarkably interesting . . . "King's Medal. Monsieur François Blanc, although the father of six children with a young wife dependent on him as were his parents, organized in 1941 a network in Passy-sur-Eure which assisted British Military Intelligence until 1943 when Monsieur Blanc was arrested and sent to Germany. Despite twelve days of torture by the Gestapo he refused to release information of any kind."

Up steps a tiny, sallow, stooping little man with the thickest kind of spectacles and a shiny blue suit. You wouldn't have picked him out of the crowd in a bus queue. But from my place of vantage I could see all the faces and study them as they waited and bus queue is the word. Nuns, chorus girls, old men and women, brisk café waiters, little boys of ten taking the decoration for a dead father, cripples on sticks, but these stood out, the majority were the middle-aged, the dull, the unimpressive.

What struck me most was how strong the women are and how tired the men. All the women looked as if they could do it again, the men didn't.

Afterwards the band played—oh, the smartness of those British bands—and we had a glass of champagne. This went to my head and I found myself holding hands with a policeman from Epernay, who said, "*Madame, c'est la France qui défile devant vous ce matin* [Madam, you are seeing France marching before you this morning]."

To Marietta from Paris

21 Square du Bois de Boulogne
Paris, November 22, 1947

Mother has sent me the Bar Harbor *Times* of November 6, describing the forest fire which devastated our part of the island, thank God not your side. Our house is all right, but so many things from our childhood are black and burned. Newport Mountain where we climbed and all the forest around it, the lovely Potter Palmer place and the Pulitzers' and many others. Mr. Rockefeller wrote a wonderful letter to Mother full of hope and encouragement for the people of Bar Harbor village, about whom she was naturally very worried. The hospital is all right, and the school, but there will be much unemployment this winter. Thank God for the Rockefellers and their endless quiet generosity. Isn't it hard to imagine our childhood summers and their memories made unrecognizable by a bitter uncontrolled October wind and someone's careless cigarette? Maine has been much in my thoughts, but you will have been following the French news. I loved your visit so much, and long for you to come over for the Duff Coopers' going-away ball next month, but I am beginning to wonder if you should. We have time to see.[19]

Paris is quiet but tense, our Embassy very worried over the labor situation. The Marshall Plan will save Europe, but it's too soon to expect results. The people are going to work quietly and there is strong opposition in the unions to the Communists who in several factories this week broke the machines so that work had to stop, but unquestionably wages are too low and many of the demands justified. General de Gaulle lurks in the wings, but despite Palewski's intelligent lectures to Bill and me we remain unconvinced.

[19] Marietta and Ronnie settled in England early that fall, and Bill and I spent several happy weekends at Ditchley. Ronnie's friends took to Marietta immediately and she ran that immense house with apparent ease. The transition from New York could not have been entirely as easy as she makes it sound, but she and Ronnie were much in love and she cared tremendously about keeping up the hospitable traditions of Ditchley. Also she took to England and the English at once. It was thrilling for me to have her there, and we persuaded them to stay with us in Paris in late October. I had looked forward to their December visit but as I suggest in this letter I didn't know if it was prudent. The Communist-dominated trade unions were threatening general strike, the government appeared to have lost its nerve, and we were clearly in for a dangerous time. Robert Schuman's new government came in and the tensions lifted for a time, but it was the most ominous winter we lived through during our years in France.

December 3, 1947

At last letters from home; the postmen are going back to work, protected by the police. Paris looks normal, except for the garbage standing about everywhere, and the long queues for bread. For lucky people like us there are the old minor inconveniences of electricity cuts; we have enough food and we don't have to travel. For our servants life is hell. Coming in by Métro, the train is jammed and often obliged to stop either by sabotage or by the women and children of the strikers lying down on the tracks. Yesterday was a particularly depressing day, bitterly cold, snow on the ground, no Métro, the Assembly sitting as it has been steadily for four days without result, no electricity anywhere after five o'clock, very few streets lights in the early evening, warnings over the radio to fill the bathtubs in view of no water today (so far plenty of water), what light there was on the street corners illuminated the tired faces of people waiting for the ever full busses. No excitement, the troops here and there looking calm and competent but as cold and drawn as everyone else, the incongruity of the rich cakes in pastry shop windows at absurd prices, the rumors and no one really knowing anything. Over and over the same refrain, the great majority of workers realize that they are being exploited by the Communists and don't want to strike. It is sad and instructive to see what can be done by a disciplined minority.

The terrible fact that this year wages have risen seventeen per cent and prices by fifty-one per cent makes one wonder that these recent angry strikes didn't happen earlier.

Saturday was Bill's thirty-eighth birthday, which we celebrated with a splendid cake made with American cake mix sent me by my mother, and the weekend was quiet and cozy. Diana Cooper is back full of descriptions of Princess Elizabeth's wedding, which apparently was very fine "in spite of the Labor government." Diana says that the evening party at Buckingham Palace was superb, but that the guests in Westminster Abbey looked pretty shabby in the gray morning light. However, the royal family's dresses were lovely and the Queen's fatness didn't matter because she looked so queenly and right, the King cried all through the ceremony, the Princess was a thousand times prettier than in her photographs, and everyone wished that she and Prince Philip could have been sent off on a cruiser to Jamaica and Bermuda, with possibly Canada later, instead of honeymooning drearily in a house that is half a hospital in Scotland.

Diana and Duff lunched with Mr. Churchill afterwards, who was in cheerful but bellicose form. He believes that next year, 1948, is the crucial year in which we must push the Russians behind the Curzon line[20] and if they won't stay there we must fight them. He believes that England will have a general election in '48 with a Conservative victory and stated that he expects to be Prime Minister again at the age of seventy-five, like Monsieur Léon Blum. This crack was directed at Anthony Eden, who turned pale and instead of saying something light and joky said solemnly that he was sure that that was what everyone there hoped too, which caused ribald laughter from Churchill, who said, "Oh, come off it, Anthony, and don't worry, I only plan to stay in for two years or so." No one else thinks that there is a ghost of a chance of a general election in Britain in the foreseeable future.

21 Square du Bois de Boulogne
Paris, December 18, 1947

Except for the deep sadness we both feel over Henri de Mouchy's death we are ending the year better than I could have believed possible. Brave Marie de Mouchy and the children make one feel that it is better, for he was too sad and miserable in these last months, but we shall remember him welcoming us to France nearly two years ago, the most charming and kind of men, a *grand seigneur* with infinite tolerance mingling with the cynicism, amused by life, surprised by nothing. How lucky we were to have become friends of the family. I am warmed and touched to find that Marie likes me to drop in frequently, and we are close to Philippe. It is a wonderfully tight-knit family.

You will have seen that the strikes have ended and the ominous tension has lifted, a triumph for the new Prime Minister, the magnificent Robert Schuman. This made the Duff Coopers' farewell ball the gala occasion it could not have been a week before. Mr.

[20] Line of demarcation between Russia and Poland.

Churchill flew over in the morning and by early afternoon the word had got about that he was at the British Embassy, so huge crowds gathered in the Rue du Faubourg St. Honoré howling for him. He went out to speak to them and was put in a wonderful humor by their enthusiasm. At the ball he looked well and young, wearing orders and decorations, with Odette in a superb red satin dress on his arm. He went to bed early as did most of the bigwigs, but Schuman stayed later talking to Duff, and we were all much impressed with him; the last big strike had broken that morning and he looked younger and less exhausted than French politicians usually do. He has a fine, sensitive face, the face of an intellectual, the first French statesman whose face has impressed me except old Herriot's. I was standing looking on in admiration when Henri Bernstein[21] lumbered up and said to me, "Well, thank God you Americans have at last declared yourselves for de Gaulle. Bravo for Mr. Dulles." I hope that Schuman didn't hear. This was the theme song of the Gaullistes that night, there was nothing we could say, but, privately, Dulles' statement to the press was insane. He seemed to imply that only General de Gaulle could save this unhappy country.

We stayed at the party till 5 A.M. and it seemed too soon to leave that beautiful house, every candle lighted, every piece of the historic gilt services gleaming on the tables, Diana in a pale blue dress of satin with lots of tulle the same color, making the most elegant young Frenchwoman look like nothing beside her. As you wrote, when you first met Diana, she is the only really glamorous woman one has ever met. She and Duff had been so beloved that the party was bittersweet as it meant farewell, but the guests outdid themselves to live up to the occasion. Every man who had an order or decoration wore it, even the most dismal prince appeared dazzling in the Saint-Esprit and the dimmest Spanish first secretary of the Embassy seemed like something out of the *Merry Widow.* The women's dresses were wonderful, all enormous except for a few short Dior ones which looked ridiculous on the dance floor. I wore a Schiaparelli dress made of stripes of mauve satin and heavy ivory grosgrain, with an enormous bustle, very *Lady Windermere's Fan.* Monsieur Christian Dior bowed to me and said, "That is one of the

[21] The famous playwright.

greatest dresses I have ever seen, and I wish it were mine," which made me feel badly, as he has been so generous to me.

We went to see the Coopers off at the station, as did about a thousand other admirers. Diana was in tears, we all were deeply moved, and the show was stolen by Louise de Vilmorin, the beautiful and talented poet and writer. Louise I have described elsewhere as the impatient lady who threw her butter ball to the ceiling of the British Embassy dining room one day when she was not the center of attention. On this occasion she flung herself onto the train, an arm around each of the Coopers, declaring that as they could not stay in France she, Frenchwoman though she was, must go to England. Which she did, briefly.

Everyone who had been lucky enough to know that romantic, brilliant Embassy felt gray and desolate at the loss. Thank God the French government continued to rent the lovely little château in the park of Chantilly to them, and they returned to settle there, Duff to write his last books and Diana to make life magical for the many friends who came to see them. It is with St. Firmin and its lake and its waterfall, its swans and its avenues of beeches, its daffodils and its bluebells, that I most associate Diana and Duff. Diana was a picnic genius, and the park of the great château of Chantilly was made for her. One Sunday we were led to a round glade in the middle of the park, undiscovered by all but her. It was decorated with busts of Roman emperors on tall pedestals, and the leafy circle was spread with rugs and wine coolers and delicious summer-day fare. The busts of the Roman emperors were dressed by Diana in fancy costumes—a hat with ostrich plumes made Julius Caesar look almost frivolous, and Marcus Aurelius became flirtatious in an opera cape and top hat. We had taken my charming cousin Charlie Whitehouse and his friend Obbie Filly to that particular picnic, and the boys were as bewitched as we were. It was a very hot day, and I remember that we all ended up swimming in the Oise River. Sometimes the picnics were at night, and we would find ourselves led (the surprise element was part of the charm) through the forest to a fairy tale building called the Pavilion of the White Queen which lies beside a lake. At water's edge a table was laid on a little landing stage, candlelit and formal with Diana's best china. As the moon came up over the towers of Chantilly Castle across the water someone, probably John Julius, began to play French ballads on the guitar. Every meal, even lunch with two guests, was a piece of theater for Diana, one never glimpsed the effort or machinery behind the scenes. Once I asked her for her secret and she replied simply, "Oh, just give them plenty of booze and hope it will go." The cocktails she made so generously, known as "the house poison," were a mixture of gin, fruit juice and mint, which she stirred in a tall glass pitcher; they smelled of the mint leaves and were not particularly strong, in no other house would they have produced the same conviviality.

The conversation at Duff's and Diana's table was the best I have ever known, and Duff the greatest master of the art. Looking at the pictures in my scrapbook, I feel again how lucky we were, Bill and I. Take a meal with Duff and Diana, Harold Nicolson, Desmond MacCarthy, Nancy Mitford, Bob Boothby, Raymond Mortimer.[22] The depth of erudition was never allowed to penetrate the surface, but without it could the talk have been so good? I think not. Very fast English conversation between friends of the Coopers was different, not better, but different from French conversation. This could be wonderfully amusing, stimulating, and brilliant, but sometimes one person was allowed to take the ball and run with it, pausing only for breath. This could be like watching fireworks but sometimes one shared the English impatience with monologues. English women are wonderfully gifted—knowing just when to put in the aside or the question that brings out the best in the men.

Bruges, Belgium
December 27, 1947

On Christmas Day I thought so much of you and Ronnie and Frankie and what a wonderful thing it must have been to celebrate

[22] Desmond MacCarthy was a famous English literary critic of the preceding generation. Once he said to me gently, "Your philosophy should be, my dear, that it is all right to do anything you like provided that you are absolutely sure that you are not hurting anyone." He died long ago, much mourned. Raymond Mortimer, another eminent critic who was a Cooper friend, is still writing admirably in London. Nancy Mitford will be described at length in a later chapter. Lord Boothby, a well-known Conservative politician and famous speaker, gave the eulogy at Duff Cooper's memorial service and those who heard it will not forget how fine it was.

your first Christmas in that marvelous house. I can picture the blazing fires and the holly and the Englishness of it all.

We decided not to stay in Paris, as unlike last year we didn't have my beloved cousin Charlie Whitehouse or any other guests staying in the house, and instead came to this beautiful little town with Bill Gibson, a colleague of Bill's and one of our closest friends. Besides looking at the Memlings and listening to the many bells of Bruges and walking by the misty, mysterious canals we have eaten and drunk as never before. Belgian prosperity comes as a shock as soon as one crosses the frontier, and although I don't like chocolates it's irresistible to see shops filled with real chocolates, delicatessens bursting with unrationed delicacies. The Belgians did this themselves, by adopting stern austerity measures with their currency right after the war, as Bill Patten among others hoped the French would. Holland, where we spent a day, is another story. We wanted to visit the famous island of Walcheren, which was totally submerged by sea water in order to thwart the Germans. Opening the dikes was indeed a brave thing to do, for the Dutch must have foreseen all too clearly what we have just visited, a starving bare island, the sea-soaked land desolate as nothing will grow there, the people struggling not just to bring back their soil but to survive themselves. It was grim, and we drove back guiltily to our luxury here.

May you have the happiest of New Years, dear, dear Trees and Frankie. I have written to Frankie but do reiterate to her that my favorite Christmas present was her gift to me. Did you see it? It's a notebook made and decorated by her, with pictures of ponies and "Happy Christmas to Mrs. Patten." I am so proud of it and of her. I sent her a hunting crop as I thought her well past the toy stage.

· 1948 ·

21 Square du Bois de Boulogne
Paris, February 3, 1948

I feel so very rich. Devaluation having taken place, I found Morgan's Bank like Christmas morning, strangers beaming at each other. I obtained over sixty thousand francs for two hundred dollars, imagine! The financial wizard, as Diana Cooper calls Bill, says that the decision was wise and bold on the part of the French government but that they are inwardly trembling as none of them knows what the effects will be. He has had some interesting talks with the man who compares to our Undersecretary of the Treasury, the title is head of the Offices des Changes. This man and his assistants were making up the rules of the market, which opened yesterday, based on theories learned at the School of Political Sciences thirty years ago, and hoping for the best.

Our friends are as lost as I am in the technicalities, the only real enthusiast I have talked to was one man who said, "Personally, I don't understand one thing, but as the English are against it, it is surely good for France."

We have had a most lovely weekend in Normandy with Tanis Dietz, who was Tanis Guinness. She lives in her father's manor near Deauville. The meadows are greener than Irish green and one can walk in the woods or go to play golf or sketch, like Cecil Beaton, who sets up his canvas on the lawn of a morning. There are always English guests and Tanis has the knack of combining the best of both sides of the Channel.

Last night Anne O'Hare McCormick and her husband and Duff Cooper came to us for drinks. If women are ever equal it will be due to the example of people like Ann. And she is so modest, no one would think that she was one of the most distinguished journalists in the world today. After they left, Bill and I went on to the Frank

Gileses'[1] for dinner in the Rue le Regrattier for Harold Nicolson. I don't think I have described the Gileses' apartment. The tiny street is a stone's throw from the Seine, on the Ile St. Louis—it's seventeenth-century Paris quite unchanged, and Kitty and Frank make every party fun. Harold Nicolson became converted to the Labor Party five months ago and is standing for North Croydon in three weeks' time as a Labor candidate. He said, "I am not going into the party because I want to, but because I can do good, and one can't do any good staying on the outside." This is highly understandable, and I hope he wins, but I wish he had got heated and tried to convince us on nationalization of industry or the House of Lords bill. He is the most attractive and brilliant of conversationalists, so asking for political strength too is unfair of me, and none of my business.

The French doctors are second to none in the world and I trusted and trust them completely. The doctor who was taking care of me during the autumn and winter of 1947–48 was a distinguished specialist of the liver. I had not been feeling well and Alix de Rothschild was able to get me an appointment with this man, who treated me for five months for my diseased liver until one fine day I happened to mention how tight my clothes were becoming, upon which he gave me a strange look, a pelvic examination, and an appointment with a gynecologist, who pronounced me pregnant, the baby due four months later. This saved a lot of trouble and was perfectly understandable. To the French there is no sympton which cannot be explained by the liver.

Bill and I were beside ourselves with joy, for we had waited for eight years for this moment, I had visited great doctors everywhere hoping for help, and had at last despaired. Bill always pretended that it didn't matter a bit—of course it mattered like hell, and his pleasure and mine were echoed by all the surprised and loving friends. In a flash arrived a lovely white lace tea gown from Marietta, huge boxes

[1] Frank Giles, the brilliant Paris correspondent of *The Times,* was, with his wife, Lady Katherine, among our closest friends then and always. She was Harold Nicolson's cousin by marriage, having been born Lady Katherine Sackville.

of baby clothes from my mother, and a wonderful trousseau for me of all Babe Paley's maternity clothes, made in New York, transforming my spring life, for in those days young French mothers didn't have modern maternity clothes and wore smockish things, whereas Babe sent me the lovely becoming dresses that she had just finished wearing and in which I felt less heavy and awkward.

During this gloriously short pregnancy (who else has ever been pregnant for four months—I bless that liver doctor) I was lazy and spent much time walking in the Bois de Boulogne with our boxer, Charlus, and lying on the sofa dreaming about the baby. Only two major political events return to me: the rape of Czechoslovakia in early spring by the Russians, and the beginning of the Berlin tension which was to lead to the siege. By late April I am writing that visitors from Berlin are grim, and wear an air of what I call "Custer's Last Stand."

William Samuel Patten, Jr., was born on July 4, 1948, in the American Hospital at Neuilly-sur-Seine, fulfilling all our hopes. By the next day I am typing away again to Marietta, his godmother.

American Hospital
Neuilly, France
July 5, 1948

Bless you for your dear telegram. Your godson is now twenty-four hours old, and although even the polite French have not yet said that he is beautiful, I find his comic, wrinkled face full of charm, character, ability, and am hugely proud of him. He gave me very little trouble for a first baby, and today I am sitting up.

About the baby's birth there was little to say. Marietta knew how stunningly happy I was and, as far as I know, only one writer has described the pain and the beauty of childbirth properly, Enid Bagnold in a little-remembered book called *The Squire*.

When I was in the hospital Bill brought me the exciting news that Tito of Yugoslavia had broken away from the Soviet bloc, and the grim news of the continuing tension in Berlin. The city had been fully blockaded by the Russians since June 24 as their counterattack to recent setbacks in Western Europe. The European Recovery Program, child of the Marshall Plan, was beginning to succeed and the Communist parties in Italy, France, and Finland showed signs of erosion. Abandonment of Berlin was out of the question, but we had to face the possibility that the Russians might deliberately have chosen Berlin as a pretext for war. It was a very, very dicey time.

Years later I heard about the argument in Washington concerning Berlin. James Forrestal, Secretary of Defense, had been bellicose at the beginning, his argument being that, as we had the bomb and the Russians didn't, we could afford to send in an armed convoy. Truman, more cautious, decided on an air lift instead. This was brave of the President, for the Chief of Staff for the Air Force foresaw heavy casualties from crashes at the airport near Berlin, as no one had ever attempted supplying a huge city by air before, and traffic was bound to be non-stop. Actually, there was almost no damage. The people Bill and I saw later who had been in Berlin in 1948–49 had tremendous esprit de corps; for them it would always be a memory that no one but they could share, like having been at the siege of Constantinople or at the Alamo.

The strain and the drama of occupied Berlin were well described to us by a friend who got out on leave that winter, Miss Rebecca Wellington, a Foreign Service officer in the days when there were not many women diplomats in critical posts. Rebecca told us about the short days, for night falls early in Berlin in the icy winters, and one never knew whether one would have electricity that night. Other essential services might at any moment be cut off by the Russians, and one lived from day to day; but the American and British airplanes never failed their steady task of supply and one sat up in the evening by candlelight with a bottle of wine and a few friends having, she said, a very good time, for the high spirits and courage of the besieged Berliners were infectious.

In the spring of 1949 the Russians backed down, due to the quiet, judicious diplomacy of Dean Acheson, who had become Secretary of State that January.

21 Square du Bois de Boulogne
Paris, September 24, 1948

We are back after the vacation in Biarritz. Ian Argyll lent us his house, which had been depleted of furniture by the Germans so it was camping out, which would have been fun but for the weather, day after day of cold and rain. The baby thrived, and on the few good days we embarked for the beach, which is called the "Chambre d'Amour" but is no love nest, rather a marvelous huge sandy stretch with unbelievably dangerous surf. Flags tell one if it is safe to put toe to water, and deck chairs and umbrellas provide comfort. Bill insisted on taking the baby and hiring a deck chair for him; he looked divinely happy and Charlus, the boxer, prowled around the tiny bundle to give added safety. Bill breathed so badly during this period that we went twice to Bordeaux, hours away, to see a new doctor of whom we had heard much. As usual, Bill is so brave and optimistic that the first treatment seemed to him "the cure" for which we are forever searching, the second time was a distinct setback, and on the way back to Paris in the car for the first time in our married life Bill spoke to me about how discouraged he really is. On this vacation, so looked-forward-to because it was our first with the baby, walking a few hundred yards was an effort for him despite the famous bracing air of Biarritz. He said how much shorter of breath he finds himself every year now and that he hated to realize that he is a near invalid at the age of forty and will never be able to teach his son games. Being a beautiful horseman and having a good eye and fast reflexes are probably gifts that the baby will inherit naturally from his father, but it broke my heart to hear Bill so discouraged.[2]

As you know, the United Nations are meeting in Paris and the night we got back we dined with Sammy Hood and went to the opening of the ballet. The Couve de Murvilles[3] were there for dinner, plus Hector MacNeill and Fred Warner of the Foreign Of-

[2] This was the first and last time in over twenty years of marriage that I heard Bill make a self-pitying remark.
[3] Maurice Couve de Murville, later Ambassador to the United States and Foreign Minister of France.

fice. Hector MacNeill is a bright and attractive person; like Chip Bohlen, he gives one a reassuring feeling of energy. They are all waiting for the Russian note on Berlin, and there is no new or encouraging gossip that I have heard.

21 Square du Bois de Boulogne
Paris, October 1, 1948

Berlin continues to make people extremely edgy. On Tuesday we lunched at our dear Gileses' for Gladwyn Jebb[4] and the foreign editor of *The Times,* Mr. MacDonald, who is Frank's boss and considered very brilliant. He and Frank both feel that we have no choice but to get out of Berlin; Gladwyn Jebb remained silent but one rather felt that he agreed as he didn't say a word in support of Bill, who took the American line. That night we dined at the David Bruces'[5] (oh, the heaven of having them in Paris) and I sat by Chip Bohlen, who spoke most violently about a London *Times* editorial of that morning which had hinted at the necessity for withdrawal. Chip said if there is one thing certain it is that President Truman will not go back on his word and that the United States would stay in Berlin come hell or high water, and damn the London *Times* and its Munich-like editorials. The strain of the summer siege is bound to tell on everyone's nerves, I don't think for a second that we should rat on the West Berliners, but I don't think that you could find a braver man than Frank Giles nor that *The Times* is the "appeasement at any price" paper that Chip seemed to feel it was.

We have seen a lot of the English press this week. The Rothermeres came here one night; he is the proprietor of the *Daily Mail* and other publications, she is my age and always so kind to me in London. Very clever and attractive, and very funny, is Ann Rothermere, and so is another of my English girl friends who came to the same dinner, Loelia Westminster.

[4] Gladwyn Jebb, now Lord Gladwyn, was a British diplomat whose distinguished career later brought him to Paris as British Ambassador. He was the first statesman to become a television star, during the dramatic U.N. debates on Korea in 1950.

[5] Chief of the Economic Cooperation Administration to France, May 1948–49; U. S. Ambassador to France, 1949–52.

Susan Mary Jay, 1936 Photo by Phyfe

Marietta Peabody, 1935

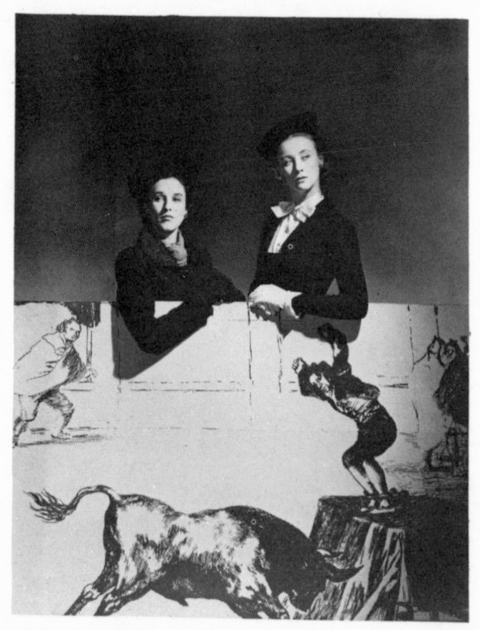

Babe Mortimer and Marietta FitzGerald, 1945

Horst

Bill Patten at wedding, 1939

Bal Masqué, Pré Catalan, 1946

David Bruce, Germany, 1959 Susan Mary Patten

Clos St. Nicolas, the house at Senlis, 1947–51

Susan Mary Patten

Frankie FitzGerald at Ditchley, 1948

Susan Mary Patten and Billy at christening, 1948

Aerial view of Ditchley

Ditchley

The Great Hall, Ditchley

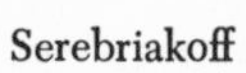

Serebriakoff

The Red Drawing Room, Ditchley

Bevin, Chantilly, 1947

The Raymond Arons (he is the best newspaperman in France) came and Freddie Reinhardt, who presently has the Eastern European desk in the Department. To this group Bill had added our new friend Hector MacNeill, Minister of State in England's present Labor government, and probably Foreign Minister should anything happen to Ernest Bevin.[6] We were not sure how he and the very Conservative publisher Esmond Rothermere would get on but it turned out all right. The men shouted politics at each other, the ladies remained silent but charming, and no one went home until 2:30 A.M.

Raymond Aron talked extremely gloomily. He predicts six months of strikes and misery and then the return of de Gaulle, possibly preceded by a very nasty week or two. MacNeill would interest you, if you don't know him already, and I do believe that he may be the most able man in the Labor Party, as people have told me he is. He has a strong Glasgow accent, is tremendously insistent on maintaining what he calls his simple working-class ways, "You'll pardon my paper collar, Mrs. Patten," but once he gets over pounding the table saying what a great thing nationalization is and talks about the subject in hand instead of in generalities he is mighty bright and impressive. We met him first through Fred Warner, one of his two assistants; the other, whom we saw at the Hotel Georges V, is called Guy Burgess. They are very different types. I should guess that Hector MacNeill is an innocent man in the ways of the world; he seemed like a child at a birthday party at one of the Duff Coopers' lunches last Sunday at Chantilly—it was fun to see someone so enthusiastic.

21 Square du Bois de Boulogne
Paris, October 11, 1948

Just back from thirty-six hours in the North of France. I feel as if I have been away for months, for it was the first time I have left the baby. How lucky we are to have an English nanny who takes better

[6] Hector MacNeill could not fulfill his promise, for he died young. Some said that his heart had been broken by the discovery that his protégé, Guy Burgess, had defected to the Russians. I have no way of knowing the true story, but he did seem as vulnerable as he was brilliant in those days, and the shock of discovery of the Burgess-McLean treason would have wounded him deeply.

care of him than I ever could, but I can hardly bear to leave him and look forward eagerly to her days out. He plays me up terribly sometimes, and has developed a malicious trick of pretending to be gravely ill when he wants attention. He draws up his little knees to his tummy and becomes rigid all over, accompanied by a scarlet face and fearful screams. These symptoms appear extremely dangerous to any Dr. Spock reader like myself, so I rush to him and pick him out of his crib, at which the symptoms disappear and he starts playing with my hair or my necklace in a contented, almost patronizing manner. Nanny's care is so good that we hardly ever need to visit the pediatrician, and he has the pinkest of cheeks and a huge appetite.

My brief trip was to the Lille-Tourcoing-Roubaix area, the industrial heart of France. It's as ugly as the Midlands of England and drearier than Gary, Indiana, but very interesting. Bill made friends with some of the people up there a couple of years ago and we have spent several weekends with them. The country and the plants took a terrible beating during the war but these are very strong people. On our first visit we stayed with one of the big textile families, the Prouvosts, and it impressed us to hear them talk of the future with confidence. They travel enormously, which is most un-French, and at dinner it was not unusual for one brother to say to another, "Oh, hello, I haven't seen you since Woonsocket" (Woonsocket, Rhode Island, is an important textile center) or "Well, I thought you were in Cairo, have a good trip?" Although the Germans have devastated their country three times in the last seventy-five years these people are too interested in the future to be interested in revenge and instead are full of ideas about German-French industrial co-operation. They are all owners of apartments or houses in Paris but Paris seems to interest them less than New Delhi; the ladies come down to buy their clothes and go to the theater but they don't belong to Paris society, by choice.

The last visit I was on my own, representing the U.S.A. at the opening of an impressive complex for mothers and children that we Americans have given. I had to make a speech to a huge audience, which nearly killed me. My French isn't up to it and I can't speak even in our own language. The Minister of Health went up on the train with me, he seemed very silent and austere until the next morning. We had both slept in the Prouvosts' guest cottage. My nervousness woke me up at six and I dressed and began practicing the speech over and over. Later, the Minister and I joined forces to motor to the stadium where the fatal event was to occur and to my surprise he beamed at me, saying, "Don't worry, your speech will do fine." I said, "Why do you think so?" "Because it woke me up at six this morning and I heard it a good many times. The walls in that guesthouse are paper thin. Good luck!" Such a nice man, he embraced me warmly when my ordeal was over. I spoke appallingly. Thank God that's over.

21 Square du Bois de Boulogne
Paris, October 1948

The French situation has been depressing people here more than Berlin, if possible, and there is once again talk of civil war. If this comes it will be short and snappy, but it probably won't come at all. The issues are much as in the period exactly a year ago before the big strikes; this time the miners are the most vociferous. As usual in time of labor unrest or national worry of any kind, one hears the name of General de Gaulle invoked. He is constantly with us, although bodily in Colombey-les-Deux-Eglises. Last night we dined with some of Bill's Gaulliste contacts, and I had a splendid time with "Colonel Passy," the former head of de Gaulle's secret service. As he is momentarily out of favor it was more fun to talk to him than to one of the devotees, and it was interesting to hear him say that he thinks the problem insoluble, as de Gaulle has learned nothing about choosing men and as he refuses to be a dictator, he will administer the country as badly as he did last time, yet there is no one else. Passy said that the General ought to begin by shooting several hundred people but unhappily "he hasn't got the stomach for it." Living with Madame de Gaulle, according to Passy, is mainly the cause for de Gaulle's inhumanity, as she is a bigoted, provincial garrison wife who is made physically sick by meeting a divorced person.

Now our great excitement is preparing for Billy's christening.

This great event took place on October 18 and was thoroughly happy except that I badly missed having the two grandmothers there and the godfathers, Joe Alsop and Charlie Devens, who were represented by Chip Bohlen. Marietta and Ronnie came over from England and we had a party at the house after the service at the American Pro-Cathedral. Billy wore a borrowed Mouchy christening robe of great beauty and was a cheerful, smiling figure. The Rougemonts, Odette, Marie de Mouchy (godmother with Marietta), the Bruces, and many of our other best friends came.
We were proud parents.

21 Square du Bois de Boulogne
Paris, November 8, 1948

We are still limp from celebrating Truman's victory over Dewey. I never thought, did you, that the polls could be so wrong? All hope seemed lost, and Bill and I felt condemned to four years at least of that smug Republican with his stuffy ways. If I was thrilled, you should have seen Bill, you will like a picture I am sending of him standing in the press attaché's office, looking at the ticker tape and grinning like a Cheshire cat.

I have never met President Truman but his humility in that terrible April after Roosevelt's death is spoken of by everyone who saw him then, and don't you agree that it is one of the most appealing things about him? To think how shocked we were only three years ago at the loss of F.D.R. and his replacement by a Vice-President who was perfectly unknown to the general public, and just look what has happened since. Greece saved, the Truman Doctrine, the Marshall Plan, and the defusing of the terrifying Berlin crisis this summer by the airlift. How very, very lucky we are.

I didn't know the half of it then. One has to read President Truman's own memoirs to appreciate him. Nothing is more moving than his letters to his mother and sister during the first weeks and months. Struggling day after day to master the overwhelming problems that were engulfing him daily, he found time to write regularly to "Mama and Mary." I particularly like his first letter after assuming office, which ends, "Soon as we get settled in the White House you'll both be here to visit with us. Lots of love from your very much worried son and bro. Harry."

21 Square du Bois de Boulogne
Paris, November 14, 1948

A couple of nights ago we had a pea-soup fog like London, so dense that to get to the Embassy for dinner I had to walk in front of the car with a flashlight. This would have been fine but for the fact that I had some sort of twenty-four-hour tummy flu so the foggy walk did me no good. Nothing would have prevented me from coming to the dinner as it was for General Marshall and I longed to meet him. He is most un-disappointing. Cool, shrewd, appraising eyes, speaking little, his tremendous impressiveness makes everyone else seem small around him. As I stood in a corner hero-worshiping, I realized that I didn't feel well at all but dinner was announced and sneaking out would have been a more unpopular gesture than tearing down the Stars and Stripes that flies over the Embassy. You know how terribly important seating arrangements are at embassies and we were twenty-four that night with four ambassadors, etc. Luckily I was at the very end of the table beside Brigadier General Carter, Marshall's charming aide. What an efficient training he had had. Halfway through I suddenly said, "General, I am going to be violently sick." "Right," he replied, and in two ticks had me out of the room and into the nearest bathroom, where he stuck by me. We thought that no one had noticed our absence, but later the Ambassadress said to me, "I looked down the table and said to myself, 'What can Susan Mary and that good-looking young man be up to?'" Dear Mrs. Caffery is always kind, never malicious, but oh dear, the ignominy of it.

21 Square du Bois de Boulogne
Paris, November 22, 1948

My only recent excitement is having had another fifteen minutes with General Marshall (this time I felt well), which would have thrilled me had not Charlie de Bestegui[7] made himself the third in the group and which made conversation a nightmare. Afterwards, Bestegui had the nerve to say to Bill, "*Est-ce qu'il est de bonne famille* [Is he of a good family]?" This was my second meeting with Marshall, who is frightening because I revere him so much that I am too shy to know how to talk to him. He exudes greatness and one's spine tingles.

Last night we went to Noël Coward's opening (*Present Laughter*) and squirmed with misery—like having a friend do a recitation at dinner which flops. The audience sat like frozen mutton, barely clapping, and by the end of the first act the word *catastrophique* was being freely and audibly used. Tonight we are going to the movies with the Windsors, then a blessed quiet weekend, followed by a party at Talleyrand's house to which we are taking the Walter Lippmanns. One is supposed to wear feathers. Helen is such a good sport, but dare I ask them to come covered in feathers? I haven't faced that one yet.

Paris
December 11, 1948

What a wonderful Ditchley weekend that was. Among all the brilliance and the fast English conversation one remark sticks in my mind, Franklin D. Roosevelt, Jr., looking at you at the center of a pretty high-powered group and looking your very best too, saying to me, "You and Marietta have certainly got around plenty since I was cutting in on you at the Kimball House in Northeast Harbor." He said practically the same thing a few days later at the Salisbury party for the Queen, and I could only humbly agree with our old friend. Incidentally, did you see me wretchedly trying to talk to Winston Churchill at that party? I was even more of a flop with him than usual; he was in a bad humor, chewing the cigar and glaring. Fortunately he associates me with Odette, so after a silence that seemed longer than ten Armistice Day pauses, he said, "And where is Madame Pol Roger?" And thank God she was right there and the sun came out.

[7] Carlos de Bestegui was a famous host of the period.

Ditchley was the best, Bill so loved the shooting and both of us the beauty of the house and the estate and we reveled in the company—Odette, the David Cecils,[8] Isaiah Berlin, the Salisburys, what could have been more fun? You and Ronnie will have had a note from me, but I can never thank you enough.

Bill worked hard in London and thinks the conversations[9] went well, he is maddeningly discreet about them. Pam[10] gave one of her brilliant political dinners for us and we returned happily to Paris, where I found Billy greatly changed in a week, beating his feet madly on the floor in an effort to turn himself over when laid on a rug and crowing and laughing more than ever. We return to find the French upset about David Bruce's careful and polite speech suggesting that they make more of an effort.

21 Square du Bois de Boulogne
Paris, December 30, 1948

We had the nicest possible Christmas, Billy Patten's first. Appropriately Godfather Joe Alsop and Cousin Charlie Whitehouse arrived on Christmas Eve, and Joe will be with us until the eighth. Christmas morning poor Joe, who had brought the flu with him from Berlin, still had it but he was cheery and we had a cozy morning gossiping in dressing gowns and opening our presents. Nanny Clark touched me very much, with an exquisite knitted bed jacket and an azalea with a card saying how grateful she was to have joined our family. She also made a superb plum pudding for our Christmas dinner, at which we were twelve, Billy the best dressed in white silk rompers with red smocking made by Nanny, and red shoes from London. He was showered with toys, all of which bored him, but he adored his shoes, which he thrust in every visitor's face, making arch crowing sounds.

[8] Lord David Cecil and his charming wife Rachel were frequent visitors to Ditchley. At that time he held the chair of English literature at Oxford. His books on Melbourne are his best-known works, but I love his book *The Cecils* (1973) about his own extraordinary family and their home, Hatfield House. He is one of the best talkers of our time.

[9] These conversations were technical and important discussions of the effect on European currencies of the Military Assistance Program.

[10] Lady Pamela Berry.

Today Joe is feeling horribly guilty as Bill is down with the flu, likewise Nanny and Edmond.[11] Luckily I feel fine but think it will be a quiet New Year's Eve.

[11] Edmond Rieffel was our butler for fifteen years and remains my devoted friend today. Without him I could not have managed our life in Paris for ten minutes, and when I go to France my first call is invariably to Edmond and his dear wife Madelaine. The Rieffels will appear in my story again.

• 1949 •

In February 1949 I returned to Washington for two weeks to help my mother with some business affairs. In those days one didn't think of flying unless it was an emergency, so I traveled both ways on the *Queen Mary*, taking an inside stateroom, one of the cheapest on the ship, which I noted cost four hundred dollars each way. It wasn't until the mid-fifties that flying became the easier and cheaper means of transatlantic transportation. It was hard to leave Bill and the baby, but I greatly enjoyed catching up with my family and friends. It had been four years since I left America.

1611 29th Street, N.W.
Washington, D.C., February 1949

Washington is thrilling. So was my brief stay in New York, in both places everyone asks for you and you are sorely missed. Ditchley is as famous at home as it is in Europe and those who haven't yet been to see you there are green with envy of those who have.

I am staying with Mama in Georgetown, which looks exactly the same as when I left it. I walk down the familiar streets and the identical black maids are sweeping the steps of the little brick houses and say their beaming "Good morning, how are you?" as if one had never been away, and the man behind the counter at Morgan's drugstore all but kissed me. The friends are infinitely welcoming and kind, and surprisingly interested in France. It's such a different world from before the war, when people might have said, "How's Paris?" and then gone on to talk domestic politics. Truman's stock is very high and it looks as if he would get the North Atlantic Treaty signed in a couple of months. If so, this will largely be because of Vandenberg's hard work in the Senate, swinging the Republicans behind the President's policy. When you think what an isolationist he used to be! I read that Truman spoke of "the inspired self-reversal of Senator Arthur Vandenberg," a fine line.

Washington is the coziest capital in the world, and it's nice to feel the optimism and the sense of controlled power. Everyone is very busy planning ahead and, unlike France, there isn't time to look back. Another thing, you know how we are always reading in Europe about how materialistic Americans are? The thing that strikes me is how unmaterialistic we are. Life is much less luxurious than when we were girls, but people give delightful dinner parties with next to no help in the kitchen and the meals are short but delicious and no one apologizes for their way of living. I love it all, and find that I have only changed in two very minor ways, both questions of manners. Four years in France have made it impossible for me to enter a room without shaking hands formally with everyone in it, and I can't get through a door at a dinner party, which comes from that tiresome habit of hanging back with all the other women saying, "*Passez, passez,*" to each other. This must come down from the manners at the court of Versailles.

My mother flourishes and sends you her best love, as does everyone else.

21 Square du Bois de Boulogne
March 23, 1949, Paris

Got back to the house at 8 P.M. last night. Billy had been kept up and was all dressed up on Nanny's knee. At seeing me he was overwhelmed with shyness and after giving me one of those long frowning looks of Papa's he buried his head in her shoulder, much to her chagrin, for she had trained him to say "Mama." He is eight months old now, and the strongest little boy you ever saw. He adores the boxer Charlus and speaks only to him. My mother-in-law is staying with us, and Bill and she both seem so well. To my delight everyone seems very glad to see me and you would think that I had abandoned them for a year. Tomorrow I am to take the baby and Nanny to a children's party at the Alain de Rothschilds'. Can you imagine anything more absurd than taking a baby to a party? But the English nannies of Paris are a formidable outfit, they like parties and rival each other in dressing up their children in exquisite clothes. There is nothing the mother of the host can do except smile, order up entertainment (a magician or a marionette show), and lay on a sumptuous repast.

We have the house again at Senlis, and I am already worrying about Billy's first birthday party, which will take place there in July!

The Berlin blockade was lifted and NATO formed in the spring of this year. France had emerged from the dramas of the immediate postwar years by 1948 and entered onto a sort of flat plain politically, which the French called *immobilisme*. It wasn't the dream of Servan-Schreiber of *Le Monde*: he wrote of the Europe that had emerged from the war as a Europe of "the tomorrows that sing," and deplored the bourgeois materialism of the present day, but if one vividly remembered the terrifying strikes of 1947 it seemed rather comforting to have the Communists snarling away in a sort of political ghetto and the governments that succeeded one another in the safe hands of a series of responsible Prime Ministers, none of whom except Blum, who was to die in 1950, and Robert Schuman, were outstanding personalities. This flat period in France went on until 1954.

In April we all went to England. First I went over to join my dear Aunt Martha[1] who was making her first trip to Europe since Uncle Eliot's death. Then Bill arrived to enter the London Clinic for another of Dr. Croxon Deller's treatments, which went much more easily this time. Nanny brought the baby over and took him to stay with her father in the country, near enough for them to come to London to visit Bill.

April had been a happy month in France. Maurice Petsche, Minister of Finance and Economic Affairs, took to the radio and actually thanked the United States for the coal and cotton and the wheat that had kept France going. This was the first anniversary of the European Recovery Program, the child of the Marshall Plan. Editorialists wrote that "France had turned the corner" and that the lucky French owed this to the generosity of the United States. At the

[1] Mrs. Eliot Cross.

time I rather took this for granted, perhaps we were smug, basking in the success of the Marshall Plan. One night Bill and I went to the Folies Bergères to see Josephine Baker, superb in her return to the Paris stage. Our companions were American newspapermen, who told us that they were bored to death with their assignments, for there was nothing dramatic to file from France. Janet Flanner wrote in *The New Yorker* that spring: "It is a remarkable tribute to France that she must now be credited with having in four years, amazingly, recovered from the war. It is a pity that she seems also to have recovered from the spirit of the Liberation."

Janet Flanner was the best reporter in Paris. We all read the "Letters from Paris" in the certainty that we would learn more about the city in which we lived than we could possibly pick up from observation and she never failed us. We admired her personally and her conversation was as worth listening to as her articles were to read.

Just before we left for England our friend Christian Bérard, France's greatest living stage designer, died. His death came suddenly, as he was working well after midnight in the Marigny theater. People regretted his absorption in the stage, for his studio canvases became fewer and fewer, but the theater was his love and no one who saw his sets and his costumes will forget them. He loved Molière and did *Les Fourberies de Scarpin* all in tones of gray and black, which sounds dreary but was in fact wonderful, and when twenty years later I saw the sets and costumes reconstituted for an exhibition they were as fresh and exciting as on the opening night. "Bébé" Bérard, who died at forty-six, seemed quite old to me, perhaps because of his beard and his rotundity. At parties his enthusiasm made one feel like a million dollars. Cocteau was a little scary, one knelt at his feet and listened breathlessly to the pyrotechnics of his talk. Bérard threw himself at one's feet as one entered a room, kissing one's hand and crying, "Oh, the beauty of it—Christian (Dior) has done it again." Very good for the morale.

The interplay of Paris life was half the fun. Politicians talked of art and the theater, a new exhibition was more of an event than the fall of a government. During the first years the great museums of Europe generously sent the best of their collections on loan. Berlin, Vienna, Munich, Amsterdam came to Paris, and the French for whom traveling was still difficult queued happily for hours. It is always touching to see the intensity of caring for beauty in the French of all classes. Mothers and fathers and children and babies in arms circled the Orangerie or the Grand Palais or the Louvre for half a day waiting to get in, the parents reading out loud to their children about the treasures they would see. There was a snob element about these great crowded exhibitions; the smart trick was to visit them with the curator in charge on the closed day. I remember visiting the Poussin exhibition at the Louvre in the fifties with the Gladwyn Jebbs—as he was then the British Ambassador, the director of European paintings of the Louvre, Monsieur Germain Bazin, who was our guide, naturally assumed that our party was English and I remember him waving a contemptuous hand at the Poussins on loan from the Metropolitan and saying, "Look at them, destroyed by the vulgar Americans, who don't know how to care for pictures. We consider that any picture that goes to America is lost to art." This made me furious, and I was not sorry later to hear that Monsieur Bazin had had difficulties with his career and is no longer in a high position at the Louvre.

But the great historic event of the spring of 1949 was the signing of the NATO treaty on April 4, the first peacetime military alliance concluded by the United States since the adoption of the Constitution. This was one more step in the evolution of our foreign policy and the Europeans liked the modesty with which Truman announced it.

Bakewell, Derbyshire, England
April 20, 1949

Aunt Martha is here staying with her old friends the Duke and Duchess of Devonshire. They were the parents-in-law of my dear Kathleen Kennedy Hartington, who died last year, and they kindly invited me to come over to join the party for a few days. I feel much farther away than the length of the trip warrants, as it is such a new part of England to me and the great rolling empty fields and steep hills are very different from the crowded counties in the south. It is dramatic, fine country, I can't get over the emptiness, as the industrial cities of Sheffield, Nottingham, etc., are so near—yet driving around here one feels that the Industrial Revolution hasn't arrived. I have been taken to visit the marvelous houses belonging to my host's family, Chatsworth and Hardwick Hall, and pray that there will be another chance to visit them as there is too much beauty to take in at once. Most romantic of all is Haddon Hall, belonging to Diana Cooper's family. Her sister-in-law, the Duchess of Rutland, is also staying here and so is the Duke of Portland. In the evening everyone compares notes about the daily take of visitors at the various ducal homes at two shillings and sixpence a head. Chatsworth had forty-five hundred visitors on Easter Sunday, for example, and every night the butler comes in to report the daily figures—"700 today; with 503 adults" (only adults count in this game). The Duke says, "Any gossip about tomorrow?" "Yes, Your Grace, three busloads from Sheffield in the morning, should be all adults as it's a men's club." I do think these people are wonderfully good sports, as until the war they lived in their own houses luxuriously and didn't have to open them to the public.

This is the first Easter that Chatsworth was open. In my vulgar way I wish that the hosts of these great houses could bear to exploit themselves too, for it would bring in so much more money if one could meet the duchess on her own turf. But this gentle, sensitive, and shy lot will never do it.

Later, British owners of historic houses did exploit themselves, very ably and successfully. The Marchioness of Bath used to sell picture postcards at Longleat and has written enchantingly about her experiences; the Duke of Bedford at Woburn is the master of the art today.

London Clinic, Devonshire Place
London, May 1, 1949

Bill's operation went brilliantly yesterday, there is a new anesthetist who has changed night to day, Bill is no longer sore and aching afterwards. In fact he will only have to stay in the clinic a few days this time, and Dr. Deller is delighted with the results. Nanny brought Billy up to London to see his father and Bill was not only up to a hilarious visit from the baby this morning but was so disappointed when I said that enough was enough that we kept the baby in town and took him back to see his father this afternoon. Aunt Martha lunched with the baby and me. What a comfort family are! I hate to have left Paris for another family reason: my beautiful young cousin Kitty Jay[2] is marrying Bob Bacon, a most attractive young man at our Embassy, and the wedding reception will take place at our house and Kitty will have worn my wedding dress.

Adare, County Limerick, Ireland
May 1949

We had a wonderful time staying with the George Garretts[3] at our Legation in Phoenix Park, Dublin. It's an eighteenth-century house which used to be "the Chief Secretary's Lodge" in the middle of a park of enormous trees which look even bigger and greener than the English oaks and chestnuts. The Garretts have great taste and although the house is luxuriously comfortable they have kept the spirit of the rather simple country house it must have been two hundred years ago. Unluckily I gave the kiss of death to it, I fear. One day while having a bath I narrowly escaped decapitation from huge chunks of plaster falling from the ceiling. As I had to inform the Garretts of this episode I am very much afraid that soon the residence will be full of State Department engineers who will declare the house about to fall down and will do it over and it will lose its style.[4] How lucky we are to have stayed in it before this happens. The Garretts are very popular and the house is full of interesting Irish; also we visited beautiful Georgian Dublin extensively. Then we hired a little car and drove down through the lush May coun-

[2] The offspring of this marriage, Kate Bacon, a girl as beautiful and good as her mother, was born in Paris the next year and later married our son Billy, the baby so much described in these letters.
[3] The Honorable George A. Garrett, Minister and then Ambassador to Ireland.
[4] I hear that exactly what we feared would happen did happen; efficient "refurbishing" by our government depersonalized that charming house.

tryside to this haven of peace and rest. Do you know the Adares?[5] It's one of the happiest transatlantic marriages I ever saw, she remains American in her speech and ways but is absorbed in local affairs and one feels how much she is loved. My view is that American women who marry abroad make a fatal mistake if they adopt the accent of their husband's country and become more native than the natives. The really popular ones like Nancy Adare and Kick Hartington are admired because they don't lose their American identities. Dicky Adare owns a property on the south coast of Ireland, Derrynane. We were loaned it and drove down via Bantry Bay and the island of Garinish, where the vegetation, Gulf Stream-warmed, is tropical and lush, camellias, magnolias, every sort of delicious southern flowering shrub. Derrynane is right on the sea. Bill and I felt like a honeymoon couple in the little house, he breathed beautifully and I was back in Maine, climbing over the rocks and slipping on seaweed as we used to do in all our childhood summers.

Paris
May 30, 1949

Stewart Alsop has been staying with us. Tish, alas, was dropped off to visit her mother so we haven't seen her, but he is interesting about their long Far Eastern trip. We had a picnic in the forest near Senlis, daffodil-strewn and the beeches putting out their first spring green, just Stew and Bill and me and dry martinis and chicken salad and hard-boiled eggs and white wine and bread and cheese. Stewart is exceptionally keen on the Thais. In Thailand they have their own government, are a gay people. Only in delicious Thailand were you not the enemy if you were white. And most importantly the Communists have identified themselves with the new sense of nationalism in Southeast Asia. This gave me the cold chills in the warm spring sunshine, as it is not what the French tell us about Indochina. Stewart's phrase about Saigon is that it is rancid-smelling. He feels that we should keep out, for it is not our concern, and stay out.

[5] Viscount Adare, later Earl of Dunraven, and Viscountess Adare.

We are sad to have him leave after only a week, he is the greatest fun to have in the house and we enjoy his wartime friends of the French resistance who are of every class and kind. They come to see Stewart and relive the dangerous days when he was parachuted into France; at the end there isn't a dry eye or a full bottle in the house. My tears come mainly from laughing, as Stew has a rare gift for telling very funny stories on himself. Yesterday, for a change of pace, we all lunched with Randolph Churchill on his birthday at that heavenly restaurant on the Seine, Les Fruits Défendus. One sits on the bank of the river and the scene is out of Monet or Renoir.

I know how happy you and Ronnie must have been at David Bruce's appointment as Ambassador. Bill has already called on him formally and we are to lunch there alone with the Achesons on Friday, which should be very pleasant. The Foreign Ministers' Conference is grinding away practically next door at the Palais Rose. Our delegation is full of good friends; it is particularly nice to see Paul Nitze again and he came to a big dinner we had for the Sheldon Whitehouses on Monday. But poor Evangeline sounds swamped, she hasn't even got a secretary yet, and besides the Foreign Ministers' Conference,[6] Paris is jammed with American tourists. Asked what help I could give her immediately, she said that it would be a big help if I could make her English nanny happy, so I am giving a children's party here next week where the Bruce nanny will, hopefully, make many a friend.

Avis Bohlen writes sounding thrilled about coming, they have one of the very nice houses that the government owns, on the Champ de Mars. Chip has asked me to help get servants so that it will be all set for her and the children's September arrival. *What an*

[6] Dean Acheson, Secretary of State, wrote later what he thought of these meetings: "To the Council of Foreign Ministers were referred all the questions which the Potsdam Conference could not decide, as well as insoluble ones which arose later. Up to January 21, 1953, unhappy Secretaries of State attended 218 sessions of this Council, which is no council at all. . . . All this would be a small price if it brought the world nearer to a stable, or even unstable peace. But it has not done so. . . . The futility and boredom of these meetings, amounting almost to physical pain, with their long, unresponsive speeches . . . this is obviously endurable. The evil of them is the distraction of so large a proportion of the top command of the Western foreign offices from positive action." *This Vast External Realm* (Norton, 1973).

Embassy. Our two very best and most attractive diplomatic couples as Ambassador and Minister, *Vive l'Amérique!*

The summer of 1949 was a gay time. There were no urgent political strains to spoil the fun and with the David Bruces in charge the American Embassy rapidly attained the distinction that no other embassy had had since the departure of the Duff Coopers in 1947. The Trees came to stay, and I reported to my mother that I had two ball dresses, price of both together a hundred dollars, and that one of them consisted of layers and layers of pink tulle interlaced with gray tulle, forty yards in the huge skirt. I wore this dress to a dance given by Sammy Hood for Princess Margaret. The Trees went with us, and it was a lovely party, marred for me only by an awkward moment after dinner when, our bachelor host having asked me to do so, I led Princess Margaret and the other ladies into Sammy's bedroom. After a few minutes the Princess, almost tapping her foot, said to me in her clear, low voice, every word distinct, "I don't enjoy the conversation of women much, do you?" I said rather nervously, "You won't have much more of it, but I did promise Sammy that we wouldn't join the men for twenty minutes." "I see." The minutes rather dragged.

English royalty came into our lives again in July when we went to England for Marietta's and Ronnie's farewell ball at Ditchley. The present Queen, still Princess Elizabeth, attended with her husband Prince Philip. It was a beautiful and historic party, but my heart ached for the Trees leaving the house they loved so much. Marietta had already written me in 1947 that she didn't think they could keep it up very long: for example, when she was brought there as Ronnie's bride there were thirty servants. They gave infinite pleasure to their friends for as long as it lasted, and carried their genius for hospitality with them to their New York home on 79th Street and to their Palladian rhapsody built of coral stone, Heron Bay, in Barbados, which is as beautiful as Ditchley. I missed Marietta terribly when she left England. The Channel is more easily crossed than the Atlantic, but whenever she could spare the time she wrote wonderful news-filled letters from New York, and our close friendship never faltered.

Paris
September 30, 1949

It's hard to write thanking you for having us to your last weekend party at Ditchley, tears risk staining the page. It was as beautiful a weekend as we have ever had, the September sun on the just-beginning-to-turn trees—don't you think the gentle European autumn is more moving than our showy display in America? And I loved the early morning mistiness when the men were going off to shoot, followed by our luncheons in the fields, the sun high by this time and everyone peeling off sweaters. And what a happy collection of people—Ronnie's boys, the Gages, Anthony and Dot Head, Duff Cooper, the fascinating Ann Cavendish.[7] I thought Ronnie and you perfectly extraordinary to be so cheerful and give us the usual gay time. Your hearts must be in your boots, for no one ever lived in so lovely a house, gave more pleasure, and were more a part of England. You are bound to be happy and useful wherever you live but it was warming to your old friend to hear everyone speak of you with deep admiration. Two years isn't very long, but Duff was saying on Sunday that he had never known an American woman who had fitted into English life as you have and that you are loved by all. Damn the financial situation and all taxes, it's sickening that you should go. I shall miss you horribly, our glorious Ditchley visits, your visits to Paris have been the best part of our Paris life since 1947. Thank you both from the bottom of my heart.

21 Square du Bois de Boulogne
October 1949

Bill has a really interesting job now, working as Chip Bohlen's assistant on the Military Assistance Program. He is delighted to have a rest from financial and economic affairs and has thrown himself into the job with great gusto. This is my favorite month in Paris, and we would be perfectly happy if I didn't have this

[7] The Viscount and Viscountess Gage and Lord Anthony and Lady Dorothy Head were old friends of Ronnie and Lord Head later became Secretary of State for War. Lady Ann Cavendish married Michael Tree, Ronnie's oldest son.

tiresome anemia,[8] which keeps me in bed most of the time, and if we didn't have to move. This house is to be rented to someone who can afford to pay a huge rent; we have been given until the spring to find something else, which is generous of my cousins, the owners, but it is maddening not to be on my feet house hunting. Housing is very, very short.

To occupy my time in the next months Evangeline Bruce has given me a beautiul edition of the *Journal d'une femme de cinquante ans* (*Diary of a Fifty-Year-Old Woman*) by Madame de la Tour du Pin and suggests that I translate it. It is one of the great French memoirs, about a lady who survived the Revolution and went to live up the Hudson River, returning later to France. It's more interesting than Madame de Sévigné and I long to do the English translation but I don't think I am up to it in either language. It's fun to have a try, but, my goodness, translating is difficult. Nancy [Mitford] has encouraged me as well as Evangeline, as the original French is as simple and clear as modern French.

Only the British aristocracy could have produced the Mitford sisters. There had been Unity, who had been Hitler's friend, and was now dead. There was Lady Mosley, wife of Sir Oswald Mosley, the leader of the British Fascist Party, who lived in France but was not received at the British Embassy during the Duff Coopers' time. There was Jessica, known as "Decca," who lived in California and was described by Nancy as "my Communist sister." Later she wrote *The American Way of Death*, a brilliant satire, and other books. The youngest, Deborah, known as "Debbo," married Lord Hartington, the younger brother of my friend Kick's husband, and became the Duchess of Devonshire.

Nancy was one of my earliest friends in Paris. Unhappily married to Peter Rodd, she left England for good as soon as the war had ended and lived alone in an apartment on the Rue Monsieur, one of the most attractive streets on the Left Bank of the Seine, and loved a Frenchman who is the hero of the best of her novels, *Pursuit of*

[8] I was expecting another baby in January. This time I did not consult a liver specialist and the diagnosis of pregnancy was made normally early. The anemia I speak of was serious, and I was in bed for months.

Love. She had a devoted maid called Marie, and her luncheons were never more than six at table; Bill and I met some of the most interesting people in Paris there. The talk was literary or theatrical rather than political, and the language was French-English, by which I do not mean a bastardized version of either but that if something was better said in French it was, if better in English, that tongue was used.

Nancy and I shared a passionate love for old Paris and competed with each other about our discoveries like children. "I found a doorway today in the Rue des Francs-Bourgeois by Pierre Lescot." "You couldn't have, the houses in that street were much later." "Well, someone could move a doorway—wait till I show you what I found at the Bibliothèque Nationale." We joined groups and societies of earnest French architectural buffs and the scene in one of her novels in which a guide opens the wrong door while showing a group around an aristocratic mansion, only to fall, horrified, upon the owner, in bed with someone who was not his wife, is a true story. Nancy and I were there, roaring with laughter. She was marvelous company, in love with French history, manners, and letters. I wish that I could have always been happy in our friendship but it cooled because of her violent anti-Americanism. As she had never set foot in the United States this seemed intolerable to me, and she generalized about Americans with little knowledge. We gave her lots of free material—Hector Dexter in one of her novels was a character compiled from many dinners at our house, she told me. As he was heavy and tedious beyond bearing, this made me cross, as I thought that our friends from home bore little or no resemblance to him. She caricatured me in *Don't Tell Alfred* (published by Hamish Hamilton) as the idiot American sentimentalist that I probably was and am. I didn't mind this, I did mind her blindness about my compatriots and my country, but I miss my witty, clever friend who died in France a few years ago, following a long illness which she bore gallantly.

I would like to quote Nancy's description of the British Embassy, a house which meant much to her as it did also to me. She is writing about the shy Oxford don's wife, Fanny Wincham, who had succeeded the most glamorous woman in the world, Diana Cooper, as the wife of the British Ambassador. The best-selling novel called *Don't Tell Alfred* contains the following passage:

> I shall never forget my first impression of the Embassy. After the hurly-burly of our reception at the Gare du Nord, after the drive through Paris traffic which always unnerves those not accustomed to it, the large beautiful, honey-coloured house, in its quiet courtyard, seemed a haven of delight. It has more the atmosphere of a country than a town house. For one thing, no town noises can be heard, only the rustle of leaves, the twittering of birds, an occasional mowing-machine, an owl. The french windows on the garden side fill the rooms with sunshine and air in amazing quantities. They open to a vista of trees; the only solid edifice in sight is the dome of the Invalides, a purple shadow on the horizon, hardly visible through summer leaves. Except for this and the Eiffel Tower, on the extreme right hand of the prospect, there is nothing to show that the house is situated in the centre of the most prosperous and busy capital on the continent of Europe. Philip took us straight up to the first floor. At the top of the fine staircase there is an antechamber leading to the yellow drawing-room, the white and gold drawing-room, the green drawing-room, and Pauline Borghese's bedroom. . . . These rooms all face south and open into each other.

I love this description of Nancy's for most great eighteenth-century houses in Paris are honey-colored, and their garden sides do make them feel more country than city houses. The British Embassy is one of the most beautiful examples.

I love less what happens next in the novel. The wretched new Ambassadress, Fanny Wincham, discovers that her peace is shattered and her sleep destroyed by the sound of merriment emanating from the left wing of the courtyard. It appears that Lady Diana Cooper, thinly disguised in the book as Lady Leone, couldn't bear to leave Paris so she got off the England-bound train at a suburban station and returned to the Embassy, where she is holed up in an unused suite of rooms entertaining the most amusing and fashionable people in Paris day and night. And who is providing the sustenance for these gatherings? Susan Mary Patten, whose name in the book is Mildred Jungfleisch.

The courtyard always seemed to be full of elegantly dressed people. I presumed they had come to write their names in our book. Why, then, were they so often grouped on the little outside staircase in the southwest corner of the courtyard? I could have sworn I saw the same ones over and over again, people with famous faces known even to me; a bejewelled dressmaker, a Field-Marshal; a pianist with a guilty look; an ex-king. A pretty young woman, vaguely familiar to me, seemed to live in the courtyard, constantly up and down the little staircase with flowers, books, records; sometimes she was carrying a huge picnic basket. Catching my eye one day she blushed and looked away.

Nancy read me part of the manuscript. "Nancy, you can't, it's too unfair." Mitford giggles, "You know you'd have done it, baskets of food and all. Wait, do admit that it gets funnier."

In the novel—Fanny:

"But Philip, this is very bad for Alfred." [Alfred was the dim-witted don Ambassador.] "That's what the Foreign Office thinks. They tell us to get her out—yes, but how? The Parisians have joined in the joke and it's the fashion to go and see her there. People are pouring back from their holidays so as not to be left out. The smart resorts are in despair—nobody left to be photographed on the beaches. So, of course, she's having the time of her life and quite honestly I don't see how we shall ever induce her to go. We're all at our wits' end."

"Can't we tell the servants not to feed her?"

"They don't. Mildred brings her food, like a raven."

"The one with the picnic basket? We could tell the concierge not to let her in."

"Very difficult, he's known her for years."

"Yes, I see, and of course we can't very well kidnap her. Then how could we bribe her? What does she like best in the world?"

"English top policy makers."

"Well, that's rather splendid. Surely these policy makers must be on our side? Why don't they lure her to England—luncheon at Downing Street or a place for the big debate on Thursday?"

"I see you don't understand the point of Mildred. They worship her in the House—they can hardly bear to have a debate at all until she's in her place there. As for luncheon at Downing Street, why she stays there when she's in London."

"Oh, bother—!"

In real life, me to Nancy: "*Come on!*" Nancy: "You'll adore the last scene."

The hall presented a picture of the Assumption: a mass of upturned faces goggling at the stairs down which, so slowly that she hardly seemed to be moving, came the most beautiful woman in the world. She was dressed in great folds of white satin; she sparkled with jewels; her huge pale eyes were fixed, as though upon some distant view, over the heads of the crowd. Following her, two of my footmen were carrying a large gramophone; then came Mrs. Jungfleisch, elegant in white linen, a basket on her arm. All the time, more guests were arriving. When Lady Leone got to the bottom of the stairs they divided into two lanes; she shook hands, like a royal person, with one here and there as she sailed out of the house forever.

November 30, 1949

My letters are so dull, but I do love your descriptions of your first New York fall since you moved back and I am a little homesick. There is nothing like walking down Madison Avenue on a crisp autumn afternoon, and I never feel that Paris understands Christmas although this year the French tell me it is just like a prewar holiday season. No rationed foods except coffee, everything one could possibly want to buy in the shops, and I have just read an article which says that the French family, no matter what class, spends forty per cent of its income on food. I don't believe this for a second, but they do spend a lot, and this year especially.

I have been allowed out by the doctor twice, once was to go with Bill to see Tennessee Williams' *Un Tramway Nommé Désir,* which is the hit of Paris, although the text by Jean Cocteau is very far away from the original, according to people who saw it in New York. We loved it—he evokes New Orleans curiously, with some pretty odd erotic Negro dances, but he hasn't lost it. As the curtain rises one hears crickets, which is forever to me the sound of the American South on hot evenings—the theater freezing but I threw off my coat at once, feeling as warm as if I were on a veranda anywhere south of the Mason-Dixon line, isn't it funny how sounds and smells do this to one?

My other outing was to de Gaulle's press conference. I couldn't resist it as I was given a ticket and it is always an occasion when he appears, extremely rarely, and never of course as a politician but as a savior. This time he was particularly contemptuous of "the Anglo-Saxons," and remarked of NATO that in case of trouble American aid for France would come along sometime "but we would be dead by then and such aid interests us little." The French was so beautiful that one wanted it to go on forever, averting one's mind from the substance. In an age of mediocrity de Gaulle is hypnotizing to the French, for he is so very grand.

The book of the moment, according to my doctor, who is a Communist, is *The God That Failed.* For his sake I have read it, and I am sending it as it will interest you, we both know some of the writers. Gide, Stephen Spender, Richard Wright, Arthur Koestler, Silone, all write essays describing how disillusioned they became with the Communist Party. Koestler is particularly good. My doctor is horrified and says that they are a bunch of rats but he is clever enough to want to argue about it. Don't worry—this isn't my obstetrician, who would die of horror if he knew about the political affiliations of the young resident he sends daily at 5 P.M. to transfuse blood and liver extract into my weary veins for the sake of the baby. At first I thought that this young man was a cruel sadist, giving me pain on purpose, then I saw that he was just bored sick with the job so we made friends and he no longer scorns Aunt Harriet's Louis XV paneling and takes it out on me, instead he does his work gently and we talk about Communism; it's very interesting.

Bill says that there are too many cars in Paris and one can hardly move. Isn't that fascinating? You will remember the fun I had bicycling down the empty avenues. He says that the new American cars are the worst, huge, with fins and things, I am sure that Nancy Mitford will enjoy telling me about them when I emerge into the light of common day. Don't worry about me, even the Communist M.D. who seems rather fond of me says that all will yet be well.

• 1950 •

American Hospital, Neuilly
January 21, 1950

As you know from Bill's cable our little daughter, whom we plan to call Anne, was born yesterday and is a beautiful baby. We feel so lucky as I had been so ill for months, but all those transfusions went into her and she is pink and sparkling and fat. No anesthesia this time except for a whiff of gas or two in the delivery room because of my anemia. Avis Bohlen got me through it, having so tactfully and unselfishly seen to it that Bill was out of the way during the last hours. I shall never forget her standing by my bed later, it must have been 3 A.M., still dressed in the big tulle ball dress she had been wearing early in the evening when she was summoned to my side, looking so happy and pretty and saying, "She's a *beautiful* baby, Susan Mary." I went to sleep at once, feeling deeply grateful and blessed.

21 Square de Bois de Boulogne
March 1950

We were lunching at the David Bruces' heavenly house at Versailles, which I shall describe in a minute, when René Mayer, who is presently Minister of the Interior, said apropos of the "Generals' scandal" (a complicated murky business concerning the high command in Indochina) that in France today everyone talks about scandals but no one really gives a damn. His wife said that this has always been true, at least in modern post-Dreyfus France. I do hope that this is still not true in the United States. We thought that Senator McCarthy (of whom by the way I have never heard, who is he?)[1] must be mad with his crusading speech last month against

[1] Senator Joseph McCarthy's speech took place at Wheeling, West Virginia, and was the opening salvo to his long campaign.

Communists in the State Department and that no one would pay any attention to his ranting generalizations, instead of which there is now the Tydings Committee to give him a platform and the press coverage he must long for, and to my horror I see that Senator Taft, who is a serious man, looks like backing him . . . this can't be true, for conservative support would make a national figure out of McCarthy. Surely he would disappear if he weren't taken up by the right wing of the Republican Party. One of the French papers yesterday said of him that he was a demagogue without support and would soon disappear from sight, I do hope that you can reassure me that this is true.

The Bruces have been lent by the French government a most enchanting little house in the park of Versailles, which originally was the home of the governor of Versailles. It's simple and plain and a marvelous escape hatch for them from the boiling Embassy in Paris. They picnic and try not to entertain, it's lovely for them and the children to have it.

Our housing situation is dramatic, nothing yet, and the French friends are so worried about us that if one ad appears in *Le Figaro* offering an apartment or house five people call us up. Goodness, the French are kind and loyal in time of trouble. Worry not, I have my strength back and something will turn up. You cannot imagine how adorable the baby is, she may, I think, turn into a great beauty.

21 Square du Bois de Boulogne
Paris, France
March 11, 1950

Your excellent, happy Barbados letter came yesterday with the lovely snapshot of you and the baby, which I adore and shall frame. Penelope is beautiful! I feel that one day people will climb on tables as she goes by, like those eighteenth-century Misses Gunning who all became duchesses, only she has an expression of kindly goodness which they lacked. As for your new house, 123 East 79th Street has always been my favorite house in all New York. I love the atmosphere of it, especially the library, and the big room will be much better without the paneling. I can't wait to see it, done by you.

Billy is heavenly, gay and affectionate, and, at last getting to like his new sister. He brings favorite toys and lays them in the bassinet and attempts to feed her cake from his tea. However, he needs a great deal of attention, for too much lavished on her produces terrible showing off, being sick, etc.

We didn't go to England for the elections after all. Piggy Warburg[2] describes the Camrose party as follows: he found himself next to a strange lady who was very excited and cried, "Charles is in by 500!" "Who was the opponent?" asked Piggy. "Oh, some Jew. I do hate Jews, don't you?" Piggy, in order not to embarrass his host, who was listening in frozen horror, said, "Well, I have some very good Jewish friends." "Everyone says that," said the lady, bitterly. Then, looking at him, "Oh, my God!" Duff describes sitting by Betty Salisbury at the state banquet at Buckingham Palace. She complained loudly about the number of Labor members present. "I tried to explain to her that the King's ministers are socialists, but it was no good—like trying to explain the hydrogen bomb to a Chinese of the Ming Dynasty."

The Cabrols[3] tell me that Paris is quiet; so it must be. Louise de Vilmorin has gone to Alsace to live alone in a tiny village and write. In more serious ways, Paris really does seem quiet. The strikes are a nuisance, but everyone goes peacefully about his business. So far, it looks like a flop for the C.P.[4]

4 Rue Weber, Paris
April 1950

Bill and I feel so very lucky to have found this house at the last moment. It's cheerful for us and the children, has a garage, and eventually our furniture from America will arrive. Until it does, I have hit on a solution that will sound absurd but I couldn't think of

[2] Paul Warburg, an especially witty member of the Warburg family of New York.
[3] Baron and Baronne de Cabrol, leading figures of Paris society.
[4] Communist Party.

anything else, i.e., to rent sets from a movie company. This is quite cheap and the results are very funny, although Nanny and even Edmond, our saintly butler, don't think so. We had hardly moved in before we gave a dinner party for Elise Mortimer[5] (my dear friend from childhood) and her husband Henry and the John Ameses from Boston. Just to tease I invited Charlie de Bestegui, the most fashionable bachelor in Paris, whose own houses are masterpieces of the decorating art; he didn't think it funny either, but you would. The dining room is from *The Three Musketeers,* the living room from *Madame de Pompadour* and so on. The vulgarity is only equaled by the shabbiness and, except for the children's rooms, for which I bought new and fresh things, everything is rather dirty. It doesn't matter, spring is here, the vans from Washington will soon roll up to the door, and we have a home.

In June Bill fell ill with pneumonia. His case was critical and, although his English doctor came flying from London to help our devoted Dr. Varay, it was a near thing. For the first time his strong heart faltered under the strain. I sent the children and Nanny to the United States in the charge of our close friends the Cy Sulzbergers (Cyrus L. Sulzberger, of the New York *Times,* and his brilliant Greek-born wife Marina) to be met by my mother and taken to her summer home in Bar Harbor, Maine. When Bill could travel we took the *Queen Mary* to New York and then proceeded to the Lahey Clinic in Boston, where Bill was hospitalized and became one of the early patients with respiratory disease to be helped by the steroids. Cortisone was administered in huge quantities and he continued to take this and other steroids, which prolonged his life and relieved the shortness of breath. There were unfortunate side effects which would not occur today as they understand the drugs so much better, but all that mattered then was being able to breathe again. As soon as Bill was discharged from the hospital, we joined the children at my mother's and spent a happy summer in Maine. It was the first time that television had come into our lives and we spent hours watching Gladwyn Jebb of England and Malik of Russia debate the Korean

[5] Mrs. Henry Mortimer later moved to Paris and became Madame Pierre Bordeaux-Groult.

war at the Security Council sessions in New York. Korea had burst upon us during those terrible days in June when Bill had been so ill in Paris. It took Duff Cooper to bring home the seriousness of the situation to me. A man of serenity of spirit such as I have known in no one else, he came one day to inquire about Bill and I noticed that he looked tired. He said, quietly, that he hadn't slept that night for the first time in years and that World War III was a real possibility. He then asked if he could offer us a present. Bill and I were to sail from Cherbourg, a tiring trip by train, and Duff suggested that he provide limousine and chauffeur to take us up, an offer that I accepted at once. It was typical of his and Diana's kindness to us.

4 Rue Weber
Paris, France
December 1950

Sat by a South American at old Charles Mendl's[6] last night who is said to be a financial genius. To make conversation, I asked him if he had any brilliant ideas for an American at the moment. Back came the answer like a whiplash—get out of dollars, get into Swiss francs, with something called a numbered account which I hadn't heard of before, if possible become a citizen of Lichtenstein. The dollar will soon be worthless; our recent catastrophic defeats in Korea, combined with our weakness in Europe and that of our allies, will provoke war with Russia within three months, as the Russians cannot resist moving into a vacuum. This cheery neighbor is not the only person who thinks war is quite imminent. Europe is badly shaken by recent events, and Joe Kennedy's and Hoover's speeches didn't help, but I believe in calm, wonderful David Bruce, whose line to the mission is that Europe will respond to leadership and action and that 1950 brought us the brilliantly conceived Schuman plan before it brought our reverses on the Yalu. How very lucky we are to have David and Evangeline representing us here at this ugly moment, plus the magnificent Bohlens.

[6] Sir Charles Mendl, famous British ex-diplomat and host, who lived in Paris in retirement. His wife, the late Elsie Mendl, was the first professional decorator of her day in New York.

The former letter to Marietta gives an idea of the sort of conversation we were subjected to at the period, not only from South Americans. The prestige of the United States was below the horizon following our Far Eastern reverses, and no one could understand General MacArthur with his manic communiqués and leaks to the press, at one moment euphorically talking about the troops being home by Christmas only to follow this with the most pessimistic views of the situation. The President made an ill-advised reference on November 1 to the atomic bomb which sent the French into a panic and Clement Attlee, the British Prime Minister, hurrying across the Atlantic to Washington. To the Europeans it seemed inevitable that the Russians would profit somehow, by attacking the undefended flanks, Berlin, or Iran or Yugoslavia, or that General MacArthur would start a world-wide conflagration by bombing Manchuria or mainland China. The situation remained extremely uneasy until the President relieved MacArthur in April 1951, and General Ridgway restored the situation in Korea, and General Eisenhower the same spring took over as Supreme Commander in Europe and formed the strong shield of NATO forces.

• 1951 •

4 Rue Weber, Paris
January 20, 1951

We really did have a happy New Year party for once. The Bohlens and we combined and it took place in their fine house. By great luck, Jacqueline François[1] was inveigled to sing for nothing. Both Chip and Bill are deeply in love with her, and, as Bill says, when she sings "La Vie en Rose," it makes one feel like a young Scott Fitzgerald character sopping up the romance of Paris instead of an asthmatic middle-aged civil servant, wondering how he is to avoid getting the flu. And well he may, as the children and I both had it. But Paris is such a wonderful place to recuperate in, even in January. Do you realize that any morning, I can drive myself out to the Parc de St. Cloud in ten minutes and walk up and down those wonderful Fragonard allées of beeches and oaks, and that the children and I have our choice of Marly and St. Germain and dozens of other magical places, and can be sure of no traffic and perfect peace?

It's a year for babies—Celestine Bohlen after Anne; now Evangeline Bruce is eight months' pregnant and despite it looked sensationally beautiful at Marie-Laure de Noailles'[2] the other night. It was one of her costume parties, and the Bruces, Marie Louise Bousquet and Christian Dior and the Carl Burkhardts[3] (Swiss Minister) made a superb entrée. It was a 1900 party, and they came as café keepers—Evangeline cast as a Toulouse-Lautrec bookkeeper, wearing a high red wig, a boned collar, and a voluminous black dress. As bookkeeper, she could sit down, tended by the men;

[1] A well-known night club singer of the day, specializing in sentimental songs about Paris.

[2] Vicomtesse de Noailles, patron of artists and writers, famous Parisian figure of the twenties and thirties, still a great hostess in the fifties.

[3] Carl Burkhardt was an admired diplomat of the period, who had served in Danzig during the dangerous Hitler days when that port was a bone of contention; now he was the Swiss Minister to France.

David, unrecognizable in a black wig and thickest black mustache. Mrs. Harrison Williams[4] was a black cat. I hope that when I am her age I will have half her courage, as she looked extremely well. There were side shows; in one, Daisy de Cabrol was the armless and legless woman, and there was a touching little beach scene in which Rede, Lopez,[5] and Daisy Fellowes[6] lolled in the sand eating caviar. Cocteau, Poulenc, and Février[7] did a cabaret. How strange and unreal these Paris parties are—not one deputy, not one member of the government or one newspaperman. Trade was represented by the Rothschilds and the dressmakers. I think that if it had been announced that the President and the whole Cabinet had been assassinated, not one man out of all those present would have turned around, except for the Rothschilds, David Bruce, Duff Cooper, Burkhardt, and Bill. And the pansies now outnumber the men at all parties. Is this happening everywhere? Arturo Lopez said to Bill, "Do you think it's safe for me to plant my herbaceous borders this year?" Bill said gravely that he personally didn't see imminent war, but of course knew nothing. Afterwards, Drian[8] said to me that

[4] Mrs. Harrison Williams, the legendary Mona Williams of New York, was one of the great international beauties of the day. Mr. Williams was a banker and they had houses in Palm Beach, Paris, and a famous one in Capri. After his death, she married Count Bismarck.

[5] Baron Alexis de Redé and Arturo Lopez were respectively of Austrian and Chilean birth. The former lives still in one of the most beautiful houses in Paris, the Hôtel Lambert, where he gives balls attended by the most glamorous people ever to come out of the pages of *Vogue*. He is said to be a shrewd and successful businessman. Lopez, now dead, was one of the kings of this same world of *Vogue*. His yacht, *Gaviana IV*, his house with its grottoed garden in Neuilly, his collection of furniture and objects were famous.

[6] Mrs. Reginald Fellowes, French born but married to an Englishman, frightened me more than any woman I ever met. I knew that she had broken hearts from London to Rio in the twenties but little more about her except that she was very rich and had a fine house in Paris, as well as an English country house. She had the effect on me of a snake with a rabbit; I was mesmerized and speechless in her presence. This was instinctive and based on nothing, for I hardly knew her and she never did anything or said anything unkind to me.

[7] Jean Cocteau, Francis Polenc, and Jacques Février were three bright stars of the stellar world of prewar Paris, which was then the cultural and artistic center of the world.

[8] Drian had made his name as an artist before the war but was still painting and we grew fond of this bitter, cynical man. Before we left Paris he did a drawing of my little daughter Anne, in three poses, which is one of my most cherished possessions.

Lopez had been disappointed, as he is eagerly looking forward to the new experience of being raped by the Russians.

You asked if we have plans for getting out in case of emergency. I wouldn't know but have faint hope that the children could be flown out. It isn't the sort of thing I like to bother Evangeline or Avis about; but I envision the good Colonel McClosky, our air attaché, heading for the U.S. flying the children, Evangeline (kicking and screaming) but if it's before March she really will have to go, accompanied by Dr. Maurice Mayer, our trusty obstetrician. Only I suggested this to Bill, and he rightly said that there are too many American children in the mission in Paris. I feel that New York is just as vulnerable anyway, don't you?

Anne is one today, crawling and cuddly, and her blue eyes are enormous. Avis's baby is another adorable one, and we only tremble lest Chip, presently in Washington, should be transferred there. We are so tremendously proud of our Embassy. Do you think there could be higher quality than David and Chip and their wives? Evangeline, despite her courageous appearance at parties, is not too well, but fraught with courage. She says that Eisenhower's visit was like having the Rock of Gibraltar walk into the house. He was only here for twenty-four hours but made everyone who saw him feel stronger and better, because he was full of calm optimism and incredibly well briefed on France. Our French friends were horrified by the riot against him on the Champs Elysées. I don't think any other foreigner retains such prestige in Europe.

Bill is up to his eyes working on the rearmament program under Chip; it's very interesting, and he seems so well.

P.S. Does Penelope stand up yet? I long for pictures when you have time.

The riots organized by the Communists against General Eisenhower, to which I refer in this letter, met him as he arrived as the first Supreme Commander of SHAPE, the offspring of the North Atlantic Treaty, the shield protecting Europe. He said sadly, "It doesn't matter about three thousand Communists demonstrating *against* me;

what *is* serious is that there shouldn't have been three thousand or even three hundred Frenchmen to demonstrate *for* me."

4 Rue Weber
Paris, January 27, 1951

One of my aunts has written gently but firmly that my letters to her make our lives sound very frivolous, and that anyone who didn't know me would think that I was fiddling while Rome burns. Our Paris life is many-sided, and I thought it was more fun to describe the gay moments, but it isn't all masked balls and delicious walks in the Parc de St. Cloud. Yesterday, I set off at eight in the morning for Les Halles, the great central market, to do my shopping. All the French friends have advised me against this but I persist. No Frenchwoman among my friends ever enters a market, on the theory that the cook is going to get his commission when he buys, and do his best to ruin one, but that if one tries to buy oneself one loses in the long run. They may be right. It took me half an hour to get there, another half hour to find a place to park, an hour to buy a roast of lamb and a roast of beef and some pork chops and vegetables and butter and cheese, all at wholesale prices, another half an hour to get home. The cook told me gleefully that I had been horribly cheated, as the meat is half fat. Of course I don't really understand the cuts in French. Maybe it's best to think of Les Halles as a place to go to at four in the morning to eat onion soup and watch the huge trucks come in from Normandy ten feet high in greenest artichokes and string beans, the flower trucks from the South, yellow Niagaras of mimosa, soft beds of pink and red carnations. After a disagreeable scene with the cook, Edmond was lying in wait with messages. Two American girls at the Sorbonne are in trouble and want to see me, soonest. I love the students, all eager and enthusiastic on arrival, but they can cause headaches. Bill has called, is bringing three men from the French Treasury for luncheon and can I collect a woman or two.[9] Also his great-aunt from Boston, Mrs.

[9] Mixed luncheons are greatly preferred by the French to segregation of the sexes.

Dexter, has arrived and can I pick her up at her hotel after lunch and take her to buy some shoes at a shop all Bostonians patronized before the war, unfortunately she has forgotten the name and address but no doubt I can find it. We have to go to cocktails at the Embassy for the delegation from the American Council of Churches, rush back to dress for dinner in ten minutes. Nanny says reproachfully, "The children were asking for Mummy." And added meaningfully, "If you have a moment off from your social schedule tomorrow I would be grateful for a little chat. Only if you have time, of course." Blast. The very tone was sinister. Laundry trouble again?

Dinner was a nightmare. Our host was a bachelor whom you know and like and so do I. It was a small party of eight, dominated by the Duc de Luynes. We had not before met this possessor of one of the greatest names in France. The conversation was of course general, the courses were of course five in number, each passed twice so dinner lasted a good two hours. When we rose from the table I had learned that the Duke had been in the French army during the retreat from Dunkirk, where the British in their usual barbaric way beat down French soldiers, hitting them in the head with the oars of the boats in which they were escaping like rats to the fleet of British warships lying outside the breakwater to take off only their own men. This astonishing tale was questioned, most politely, by Bill, and it emerged that perhaps the Duke hadn't been on the beaches of Dunkirk himself but he knew a lot of eyewitnesses who would vouch for his story. "*Parbleu!*"

Somehow we found ourselves discussing the Marshall Plan, which, as even the children in the Duc de Luynes's village know, is an anti-French conspiracy to put the French in debt to the Americans in order to serve the interests of American industry. "*Ah, le Wall Street, tout le monde le connaît.*" Our host was dreadfully embarrassed, but Bill handled the situation perfectly, changing the conversation with a light touch. This is the first time in our six years here that we have run into this kind of talk at a dinner and it doesn't matter at all except that it is rather a sign of the times: our defeats in Korea; McCarthy, who is more and more talked about here; the editorials in *Le Monde,* which is, as you know, the most influential newspaper in France, now advocating neutralism, which seems to mean the hell with everybody—let's be Sweden, only let's keep the American nuclear umbrella. It figures; but it was rather a long day.

4 Rue Weber, Paris
February 7, 1951

Rather an interesting dinner last night at the Walter Kerrs' (he is the editor of the Paris edition of the *Herald Tribune*) for the Prime Minister, Monsieur René Pleven, who had just returned from Washington. He is the author of the Pleven plan which followed last year's Schuman plan for the creation of an authority to pool French and German coal and steel. No one questions the brilliance of this first truly European conception, but the Pleven plan, which is a rather complicated scheme for rearming the Germans, has met a mixed reception. I rather gather that it was thought up last fall during the panic induced by our defeats in Korea, in some haste. Those French who are terrified by the idea of rearming the Germans even with bows and arrows are satisfied because the Pleven plan does not permit the Germans their own military organization or leaders, they will fight under French command as helots. The Germans have said, "No, thanks," and one has heard that the Prime Minister did not receive a warm reception in Washington. But if so, no one could guess it from dining in his company last night, he was ebullient, quoting André Siegfried, "Europe is moving in the right direction," waving his arms as he envisaged the industrial and military tapestry to be woven by the Schuman plan and his own. He had mentioned French neutralism in Washington but when asked about it last night he pooh-poohed it. I left unimpressed by Monsieur Pleven, it was a good public relations act and he is a pleasant man, but he will not join the gallery of my heroes.

Incidentally, the French in their cerebral logical way are having a lot of fun in the papers analyzing the word "neutralism." Experts on Thomas Aquinas from the Sorbonne have been called in. Neutralists claim that they are not defeatists but that another war would kill France and leave Russia and America, badly mauled, glaring at each other like wounded tomcats. It seems to me that this point of view is a touch defeatist?

The leader of the anti-neutralist party is Pierre Brisson, editor of *Figaro,* who doesn't often write editorials; so when he does it causes quite a stir. He has come out attacking the neutralists as desexed men. By this he is widely believed to be referring to his colleagues on *Le Monde,* especially the editor Beuve-Méry, whose articles cause intense pain to the United States Embassy. I'll quote one of Brisson's paragraphs because it is very French, very brave, and we hope that it expresses the views of the majority of the country.

"The passionate desire to avoid war makes no sense unless it is affirmed virilely, with readiness to make a supreme effort. Neutral France does not exist. There are neutral men, in the sense that they are *insexués* [asexuals]. They are few. It is not by them that the country will be saved."

Tough stuff, this, in the present climate. We naturally like Brisson, and see him now and then at parties given by the lady he loves, a romantic, charming person who lives in a beautiful house on the Left Bank. How Balzac would have enjoyed describing it: the thick yellow damask curtains, seventeen feet high, which exclude all noises from the busy Paris street outside; the hothouse flowers in winter; the discreet silent footmen in white gloves; the little groups of men standing about arguing, gesticulating; the languorous ladies on sofas in wide-skirted evening dresses.

4 Rue Weber
February 22, 1951

Barbados sounds more idyllic than ever this year, how dear you are to describe it all and to have urged us again to come out to you. That happy day will come, when the children are a little older and it's easier to leave them. But I do mind not sharing the growing up of our mutual children with you—I would so like to see brown Penelope on the beach and especially Frankie when she comes down.

We've had a nice week—lunched with the Alain de Rothschilds on Sunday at Chamant near Senlis. It was too early for it to be one of those wonderful spring days when the roads are crowded with bicyclers returning from days in the forests. First one sees them bent over their handlebars, which are mountains of wild daffodils, later it's great bouquets of lilies of the valley. But the sun was palely out and so were a few crocuses and we always have a good time with the Rothschild tribe. Also I admire the family enormously. When we first came to France the men our age—Guy, Elie, Alain—were just returning from the war to which they had gone immediately and courageously in 1939, only to face years in prison. Their parents and the wives scattered abroad, for it would have been suicidal to remain in German-occupied France. While they were gone their huge châteaux, which look like nineteenth-century châteaux on the Loire, all castellations and towers and roofs by Paxton, the architect of the Crystal Palace, were pretty well destroyed so most of them have built pretty little manors filled with chintz and sunlight. Only Guy plans to restore Ferrières, his château south of Paris; a few years ago he took Chip Bohlen, Bill, and me out there for the day to shoot and I will never forget the gloom of it. Alix and Guy took us around the immense house first and the smell of musty Victorian upholstery, tattered and torn, followed us down to the basement where in a more or less habitable room with a stove we had a huge meal in the middle of the morning, which is the sensible French custom before shooting, and the gamekeeper proudly showed us lists of the birds shot there a hundred years ago. "Emperor Napoleon III, 930 pheasants," and so on. At the end of the day we were presented with a card on which was beautifully written in the same script as the Emperor Napoleon cards, "Bag, Mr. Bohlen 4 pheasants, Mr. Patten 3 pheasants." This wasn't a reflection on Chip and Bill, both good shots, but in the immediate postwar years keeping up a shoot just wasn't possible. I remember Guy mentioning that each bedroom in the château had its own bathroom, which at the time it was built was considered rather ostentatious and vulgar. A Rothschild story of our epoch on which I must remember to check with one of them is that even the Germans were awed by the Rothschild possessions when they entered Paris in 1940, so, the better to enjoy the priceless objects themselves later, everything was packed with utmost care and sent to a salt mine in Germany. At the end of the war everything came back, still beautifully packed, so the whole family got on their bicycles and rushed to the storage warehouse to reclaim their possessions. As nothing was labeled the confusion was immense, for my friends had been young when the war began and it was hard to remember whose Rembrandt etching of *Descent from the Cross* was whose. Scratching of heads, then someone had the brilliant idea of telephoning to the old family butlers, who seized their bicycles and soon were at the scene like truffle hounds, accurately placing each object. "That's the Vermeer from the Baronne Edouard's dressing room," and so on. Alix told me once that she had never properly seen the Vermeer before the war—it's *The Astronomer,* one of the great pictures of the world—as there was so much in her mother-in-law's house and the dressing room was poorly lighted.

The Rothschilds do much quiet good for France, in many directions,[10] and although they appreciate and love their great collections which are kept in Paris, the house at Chamant at which we lunched on Sunday was typical of this generation's charming and modest tastes. The first course is usually, as at the Mouchy's, soft-boiled fresh eggs accompanied by fingers of buttered toast. When one sees this dish in France one knows one is in very grand company indeed. Then an old butler, one of the aforementioned bicyclers, leans over one murmuring, "Château Lafite, 1918," or something like that. If you are me, I am often so engaged in conversation with my neighbor that I don't hear the murmured evocation, so he has to repeat it. The third time he roars it, "CHÂTEAU LAFITE, 1918!" and I turn apologetically to accept the nectar.

The next night we dined with some people we hardly know, except that Bill has business contacts with the oldest son, a very bright young man in the Foreign Office. Curious evening, very interesting. Lovely apartment on the Ile St. Louis, the name and title of our hosts goes back to the Crusades, no other guests and a lot of interesting talk between Bill and the diplomatic son at dinner, the parents admiring and rather quiet. Too much food. I was getting sleepy when the door opened quietly and a blue-eyed young man in workman's clothes came in, who was introduced as the second son

[10] Years later Bill had to be rushed to the one hospital in Paris which had the artificial kidney. This was not the American Hospital, which had no such equipment, but the Hospital Necker, a big public hospital. Who had given the machine? I asked later, and was told it was the Rothschilds, of course.

of the house, Father Denis. His family looked surprised and not terribly pleased to see him, but I was absolutely delighted to see him as I guessed that we had fallen on that rare bird, a worker-priest, and even more pleased when a couple of sisters and their husbands showed up and I had a chance to talk to Father Denis alone. You have probably read about the movement, which was started after the war by some liberal members of the French Catholic Church. The idea was that, by infiltrating the Communist-dominated unions by sending priests into the factories dressed as workers and living as workers, a quiet missionary movement could accomplish more than a thousand sermons from the pulpit. One heard of the success the young priests achieved, and that Rome was delighted, then later there were vague reports to the effect that the Communist Party had converted the missionaries and that Rome had ordered the liberal French bishops to close the movement, causing a fearful row. It never became exactly clear what the end of the story was, but here was a very good-looking young man indeed who was both a priest and a factory worker and a Communist, no question about the last. He wasn't the sort to lecture one, but he talked quietly and confidently about the future of France when the Party comes to power and about how much he had learned by living with the masses. He only came home now and then for a bath, he said; his family thought he was a madman but one day they would understand when poverty had ceased to exist in France and everyone was lucky enough to be as happy as he was. I asked him if he had read a recent poll in one of the weekly magazines about the state of mind of the young French generation (the poll had showed, depressingly, that a large majority of the young feel that they are drifting towards some unknown catastrophe) and he said that he had but it only showed that he and his friends must work harder. Then he excused himself, with a charming smile. I don't suppose I will ever see him again, and I am sorry.

I forgot this conversation completely for twenty years but when I was in China in 1972 I found myself hurtling through the crowded streets of Canton the first night we arrived, horn going and the thin people in the ill-lit road scattering before our path. Because I was very tired I committed an unforgivable indiscretion, murmuring to our guide, "Oh no, oh no, it won't do." "It will do," he said. "You see, it's very hard for you to understand but I come from Shantung Province thousands of miles from here but I care about these people in the streets of Canton and want to help them and they care about me and want to help me. That could never have happened in the old China before liberation." That night I couldn't sleep because I was too tired and overexcited; I tossed under my mosquito net wondering where I had heard before that note of quiet confidence and faith. It came to me at last: on the Ile St. Louis, of course, sitting on a Louis XV chair talking to a blue-eyed young man dressed in the overalls of a worker in the Renault factory at Boulogne-Billancourt.

The anti-American feeling produced by *Collier's* Weekly's rather silly article purporting to be serious reporting of the far-off year 1955, long after the "Atomic War," produced some brilliant French journalism. The *Collier's* article depicted joy in the streets of ruined Moscow, with American fashion models delighting such Russians as remained alive. To our horror even some of the serious French newspapers took this as American softening-up propaganda for a preventive war. The wonderful satirical paper, *Le Canard Enchaîné*, produced the following skit. (Both Russia and America have been blown up.)

> It was a very short war. There was a Russian bang and an American bang almost at the very same moment. In the Rue des Petits-Pères we neither felt nor heard anything. One of our friends thought his glass gave a shiver, but since he was at his twelfth *pastis* we didn't take any notice. The papers did not begin to suspect anything for forty-eight hours. It was odd not to have had any news for so long of either Truman or Stalin. Then the rumor spread, "The war has started . . ." immediately followed by the rumor, "The war is over."
>
> It was a sensational bit of news. No more Russia! No more America! There was worry at the Treasury . . . "What about the next Marshal Aid installment?" In the boulevards Communist

> marchers were shouting, "To New York!" and in the Champs Elysées the cry was "To Moscow!" When they learned that neither place existed any more they joined in a single parade in the Place de la Concorde, sang the national French anthem, "La Marseillaise," and dispersed quietly to various bistros.
>
> After several months came the news that some gallant explorers had (unfortunately) rediscovered America, and that some Americans were still in existence. Others who had parachuted into Russia also found some Russians alive.

Then the *Canard* launched its "humanitarian appeal."

> These poor people must be re-educated, they must be taught to live, they must learn civilization, which they have never known in the days of their splendor.

From post-atom New York:

> Our first contacts with the tribes of North America warrant high hopes. Ten fishing clubs have already been set up. This peaceful sport has become very popular with the natives, who wish to have nothing to do with baseball or TV.
>
> French cooking has swept the country . . . the Brillat-Savarin Club already has 900,000 members . . . an anti-machine league has been created and the members are destroying all mechanical devices that can be found among the ruins. No more cars, no more radio or TV sets, nor refrigerators. People are learning to think for themselves. Charlie Chaplin has been proclaimed President of the United States. We are on our way to Hollywood, where we propose to establish a new magic-lantern industry.

From Moscow:

> We got here just in time. . . . The Russians were returning to their bad old tradition of eating newborn babies. We distributed instantly several million tins of pâté de foie gras and they left the babies alone. They have started a new kind of Communism, telling us that they want the good life for themselves, not for future generations, and have begun by locking up all policemen and all generals.

4 Rue Weber, Paris
April 1951

Two weeks of complete transportation strikes, no trains, few Métros, no busses, everybody very quiet and orderly but, oh, how hard on the French workers, whose days are terribly long at the best of times. They have to get up before dawn to get to work, walking sometimes right across Paris. All available bicycles are out on the streets again as in 1945, and the army helps out with trucks, but not enough. People driving private cars never seem to stop to give the weary pedestrians lifts; is this French, do you suppose, or would it be just the same in New York?

Bill and I have had two blustery weekends at the seashore looking for a cottage for the summer: once at Deauville and the next at Le Touquet. No luck, the villas for rent are too expensive or too bleak, but it was fun to walk on the empty beaches and make pigs of ourselves eating fish and drinking white wine in the evenings. Now Mama has promised to take the Carters' Senlis house for us again and to come over herself—this solves everything as you know how we love Senlis.

Thank you so much for the clipping of the Truman speech, which I thought excellent; and I am thrilled to see that Ronnie's effort to get Churchill over, about which you wrote me in confidence ages ago, looks like it's coming off. A speech from him is the one thing that might make sense of all this mess; everything seems to be coming apart and you can't imagine what effect MacArthur's huge ticker-tape welcome in New York had here. The French simply don't understand it. They were terribly impressed by President Truman's courage in firing him; now there is this general who by his insubordination and his arrogance, his inflammatory suggestion of carrying the war onto mainland China (which might have plunged all of us, including Western Europe, into World War III), is welcomed like Julius Caesar post-Rubicon. To the logical French it's intolerable, and although Bill and I are supposed to keep our mouths shut no matter what, it is equally intolerable to us. Plus the fact that this is the tourist season and we are constantly entertaining Republicans, members of the family, friends, friends of friends, children of friends, all of whom look at Bill as if he were a Communist when he points out that only the Taft-Wherry wing of the Republicans seem likely to profit from the mess and that the MacArthur row has done nothing but harm, for by discrediting the President and the Secretary of State only our enemies are given aid and comfort.

I am sick of running a travel agency. You do so many things of use and importance. I sit here and, except for an absorbing life with my two little children, the rest is meeting trains and making hotel reservations for the mothers of girls I didn't even like at school and taking them to the American Hospital when they have acute appendicitis, which turns out to be overeating half the time, and I am full of self-pity. The compensations are enormous however—last Sunday we took the Sacheverell Sitwells to Chartres for the day and it was thrilling to hear him tell about the history.

Spring, after a long hard winter, has come suddenly in a week, and for the sixth year in succession I pinch myself daily wondering how I can be lucky enough to be in Paris in April; the above-mentioned whines are shaming and selfish—for just to mail a letter I walk under chestnut trees in bud that are two hundred years old and the high sky, that I have mentioned before, never fails us in the Paris spring.

Joe Alsop and Charlie Adams have been exceptional visitors. Poor Joe fell down our stairs on his way to the Middle East and had to spend a week in what we laughingly call a guest room in this house, with a broken toe. He tottered off on crutches wearing a pair of cheap shoes bought by Edmond, one of them split and reinforced by metal. His last word was (with that laugh so alarming to babies Penelope and Anne): "I am doomed to be ridiculous." He had a very tough trip before him. Bill worries about Joe always, and we shall be glad to have him back in the house tonight.

Charles Francis Adams of Boston is an equally distinguished man.[11] I'd like to write about his visit at length and will later but it's time for me to stop tiring you.

[11] The Adams family of Boston has a record of continuous distinction unequaled by any other American family. From the war, Charlie returned to Boston and built a nearly bankrupt little firm, Raytheon, into one of the most important electronic firms in the United States. His many government contracts brought him to Europe often and it was interesting to hear him tell about his

4 Rue Weber, Paris
May 30, 1951

We have been to Rome for ten days' holiday, my first trip there since that curious experience of hitchhiking up the Italian peninsula to visit my ill sister-in-law in 1945 about which I wrote you. She is still not too well, so Bill wanted very much to see her. What a difference in traveling conditions. Instead of a bucket seat on an army transport plane it was the very elegant train, the Rome express, which slithers off from the Gare de Lyon on velvet paws so quietly that you hardly realize it is moving. Through the night, after a luxurious dinner, you hurtle through France and when you wake in the morning and pull up the blind it's the Mediterranean you see, cerulean blue on the right side of the train, and pink and white and yellow houses that couldn't be French on the left side, everywhere darkest green-black cypresses. The smiling attendant had become Italian overnight, although still wearing the brown uniform of the Wagons-Lits Company, that organization so much more international than NATO and much more polite. In a few years we will all be flying everywhere and as for Billy and Anne they will never know the luxury of a trip on an international express with coffee in bed and the slow unfolding of Tuscany through the morning and the arrival at the station in Rome and the dozens of beaming porters.

We stayed at a *pensione* near Jean's, to save money. Except for the lack of an elevator, which was distressing for Bill, it could not have been more comfortable, five dollars a day we paid for a huge room and bath. And the beauty, the wisteria and the flower vendors' stalls at every corner and the cheerfulness—it's so much much more cheerful than Paris. I won't describe the sightseeing, which you know by heart. We fell into three societies none of which seem to

---

negotiations with our NATO allies. A shy man, he nevertheless enjoyed what were really diplomatic dealings and did them skillfully; one could not but feel that this was the Adams blood. He occasionally talked about what complexes being the descendant of Presidents can cause you when young, and his shyness must have come at least partially from knowing what was expected of him. His ancestors must be proud of Charlie, for he has served the common cause in many ways.

interlock; in Paris everything interlocks and, as I have written to you before, the dentist is quite apt to quote Baudelaire, the grocer is an expert on proportional representation, the politician wants to talk about the Proust exhibition at the Bibliothèque Nationale, and the priest compliments you on your dress and says, knowledgeably, "*Dior, n'est-ce pas?*" (Of course this is a fashionable dining-out abbé, not a worker-priest or a country priest.) In Rome we of course saw most of Bill's sister Jean and her dear husband Peppino. He is of the Vatican, a member of the Guardia Nobile. His duties partly consist of dressing in a resplendent Renaissance uniform, armored breastplate and helmet with flowing plumes, and standing guard to protect the Pope. Thanks to him, we were permitted to see parts of the Vatican no one sees and were very lucky. Jean, a merry American woman, with all Bill's love for life, has been contained for twenty years in what is called Black Society, and very happy she seems to be in it. These people have nothing to do with politicians, diplomats, or the international aristocrats who travel about a lot. The children don't speak English or French, divorced people are anathema. Life centers around the family; luncheon, the main meal, may mean twenty people at table. I was so glad for Jean to see Bill, for although, as I have said, her large family is a very happy one, it is a limited life, healthier than the one I am about to describe, which consists of people with immensely grand names living in huge and very beautiful palaces. One's knees ache from climbing the stairs from the courtyard (I died for Bill, but he was game and amused) and then one goes from high-ceilinged room to high-ceilinged room, longing to pause to look at the frescoes on the walls, which are beautiful enough in the candlelight to be by Veronese, and no doubt sometimes are, but one is waved on by the white-gloved menservants to the final room where the party is assembled. As one enters one imagines a dead hush, but of course it's only a split-second pause because we are new and they haven't seen us before, then one is taken around and introduced to dozens of polite people who seem to speak only English and French, thank God. Our introductions to these circles came through my mother and the John Russells. John and Aliki are old friends now stationed in Rome, he a British Foreign Service Officer whom we knew well in Washington and she a Greek so beautiful that once, when as a joke she entered a beauty contest, she was acclaimed as "Miss Universe." The Russells gave a dinner for us of forty people which undid us, we weren't used to dining in a house above the Baths of Caracalla in full moonlight in May, the men in black ties and the ladies in ball dresses, it's all much more formal and bigger than Paris. Forty, the Russells explained casually, is the usual number for a Roman dinner party. The conversation is very gossipy and I should be terrified of staying here long, the men eye one as if they were looking apprais-ingly at a piece of meat they might or might not buy, in my case it's no sale. A gentleman who is supposed to be the lover of the famous Duchess of Sermonetta said to me in her house, in French, "Madam, everyone has been saying that with five kilos more you would have a tremendous success in Rome." Just too bad, my skinny frame. Politics are never touched upon nor literature nor the theater—music, yes, but mostly just if one has recently been to the Scala in Milan. Rome is everything, their country places a duty they have to bear, just as in the Henry James novels. But these are the observations of a ten-day tourist. I am ashamed to generalize, and there was the third world which we met through Mother's friend Princess Bassiano, an American lady who married into the great Caetani family and lives in a famous and romantic house outside Rome called Nimfa. She is an intellectual and is publishing a review in four languages which some people in Paris and London think is the best literary review in Europe. She told me that she genuinely believes in a renaissance of lyric poetry. The review is called *Botteghe Oscure,*[12] which is the name of the little street in which the Caetani palace stands.

4 Rue Weber, Paris
June 1951

We returned from Rome laden with delicious Italian toys for Billy and Anne; he will be two next month and she is eighteen months old. It's hard to leave them if only for ten days, but we are semi-established at Senlis where the linden trees are out, the house

[12] The next year *Botteghe Oscure* introduced Dylan Thomas to its readers. I will never forget the thrill of that autumn number.

is as welcoming as ever, and I come into Paris only to help Bill out with duties during the middle of the week and he joins us for every weekend and sometimes for several nights during the week. It is the two thousandth birthday of Paris, which means that every night all the historical monuments, squares, and bridges are lighted up instead of just now and then; this makes it immense fun for the visitors and for us who take them around. And there are new wonderful exhibitions in every museum of which perhaps the most exciting is the "Fauves," the name meaning wild beasts. They were led by Matisse into the violence of their colors, and the intensity, the almost savage shock, of the pictures makes one understand even today the sensation they caused fifty years ago. Vlaminck, Derain, Marquet, van Dongen, fifteen marvelous Matisses, and some fine Cézannes to start off the exhibition. The catalogue says that this was just one of the violent revolutions in French art and that the nature of the French is so essentially revolutionary that art will never stand still, which has been true up to now but some people think that this is a deadish period here in art and that the energy has moved westward to New York.

We went to the play that is the hit of the season and were depressed beyond words. It's Sartre's *The Devil and God,* which is a four-hour study of good versus evil placed in the time of Luther. The theater is jammed and no one seemed restless (one is given a break in the middle) but I really do think that it was only Sartre's fashionability which kept people glued to their hard seats. We were too cowardly to walk out on the interminable Manichaean dialogue (the Devil wins, by the way) but felt so guilty at having dragged my cousins the Aldriches to it. They are here accompanied by their very attractive daughter Mary Homans,[13] and tell us that Paris is back to what it was before the war, even more so as the new discovery of what is called *son et lumière* adds another dimension to the glamor of the city. This is a mixture of brilliant lighting, at which the French have always been good, with voices and music illustrating the history. It's only in its infancy, but will soon be everywhere, every night. For instance, that little jewel, the Gothic chapel called

[13] Mrs. Robert Homans, born Mary Aldrich. Having had no siblings since the early death of my sister Emily, I was and am dependent on the companionship of my many cousins.

Sainte Chapelle, is rather dark and gloomy if one wanders by it at night, but soon it will be lighted by subtle indirect means and visitors will hear the history of Paris recounted by the voices of some of the best actors in France accompanied by the appropriate sounds. Sainte Chapelle stands on the ancient island in the Seine where the inhabitants huddled for protection against the raiding Norman pirates in the ninth century; one will hear the sound of the cruel Norman oars and the story will be told of the successful first defense of Paris. A few minutes later the wonderful stained glass windows will fill with light and one will hear the story of Saint Louis, the philosopher king who so loved his little chapel that he prayed there all night before embarking on the Crusade to the Holy Land that led to his death. While his story is told one will have the background music of Gregorian chants, and the clear voices of thirteenth-century choirboys join in to complete the illusion. At least this is roughly how it has been described to me by the enthusiasts who plan to blanket France with sound and light, thereby stirring the imaginations of the dullest tourists. I know mine will be stirred—imagine Versailles, as they plan to do it, with Louis XIV crossing the palace, all one will hear and see will be the tap tap tap of his cane and a light going on in every room of that immensely long façade evoking the entrance of the "Sun King."

Senlis
August 1951

Since that lovely week at the end of last month when we had you and Ronnie in Paris, it has been even harder not to have you all the time. I miss talking over everything with you worse than ever, whether it's the children or world affairs. Of the latter I know very little, having spent the month here taking care of the former while Nanny was in England: early breakfast with them under the plane trees, walks around the ramparts of this cathedral town in the morning, Anne in her carriage, Billy sturdily beside me, stopping at the same baker's shop every morning at eleven for the pick-me-up which French children have loved forever, a cup of hot chocolate and a roll, back to the tranquillity we always find behind the high gates of this house, with my mother sitting on the lawn reading the *Herald Tribune;* rests in the afternoon followed by an expedition to the forest or, to please Billy, a drive to Chantilly station where we wait breathlessly for the Golden Arrow express to rush by on its way to Paris. The excitement is intense as the moment nears. Sometimes Billy buries his head in my shoulder, for it is too much to bear, yet the pleasure is intense when the signals flash and the roar approaches and the flashing shining blue cars filled with bored passengers from London go by us at seventy miles an hour. Do you think it normal for a three-year-old to adore noise so much? Evening is tranquil, stories and games and then, if we are lucky, Bill manages to come down for dinner and when the children are in bed he and my mother and I sit out on the lawn while he tells us about doings in the great world. Besides the peace treaty with Japan which will at last be signed, the main excitement is that the decision has been taken in Washington for us to back the European Army. Acheson drew up the memo and the President signed it. This means that in a couple of years, if all goes well, we will all be a lot safer and happier than we are now. The details are intricate, only David Bruce and the dedicated Tomlinson, his assistant from the Treasury, could explain them properly, but roughly it means that under a Supreme Commander, American at first, Germany will be properly incorporated in a European defense effort in a way that neither humiliates them nor gives them a degree of independence that would worry the other European partners, and this could lead to a truly strong and united Europe. It will be ages before we see this accomplished, but just hearing about it makes one believe, because the dedicated fervor of Jean Monnet and the other believers have found a practical instrument for their dreams.

Bill hasn't been well this summer. You saw him in July, but he seems better now despite working steadily through the summer without vacation except for our brief Italian foray in May. We are going to Italy again and I am a little worried about it. The first part of the trip will be heavenly, picture us bowling down the straight roads of France in a couple of weeks' time, guidebooks in hand, Sens, Auxerre, Avallon, Tonnere, Tanlay, Ancy-le-Franc (the last three are châteaux in Burgundy), eventually to arrive in Venice, for the ball given by Charlie de Bestegui which has been talked about in the papers as the most elaborate party given anywhere since before the war. Already when we were in Rome some of the principessas and comtessas were already worrying about their costumes, and I asked about the reaction of the mayor of Venice, who is a Communist, and of the poverty-stricken Venetian populace, only to be told that the Venetians will be simply delighted, being pleased by the publicity as well as the money the ball will bring to Venice, indirectly. But Bill and I are uncomfortable, torn between our Puritan consciences and our great curiosity to see the party. Curiosity wins, for we aren't likely to see anything like it again. Most great Venetian palaces are museums, or shuttered and quiet; for one night at least we shall be in eighteenth-century Venice.

Charlie de Bestegui is a very rich Spanish-Mexican whose genius is in decoration. Before the war he was famous in Paris as a bachelor whose taste ran to beautiful women and beautiful houses, but he outdid himself during the war which he spent, as a neutral with diplomatic status, restoring a large eighteenth-century château outside Paris, called Groussay. His nieces and cousins, all great friends of ours, tell us that without Charlie the upholsterers and painters and carpenters and carpet makers would have been sent to Germany as slave laborers: so that he did a great deal for the fine arts. The results are marvelous: I don't know a finer room than the library at Groussay, which is three floors high.

I'll write about the party—Odette and I are going in similar costumes made by our little dressmaker. We hope we will look like eighteenth-century ladies but if we don't our masks, which come from Reboux and are much more expensive (velvet with ostrich plumes) than the dresses, will hide and shelter us.

San Vigilio, Lake Garda, Italy
September 8, 1951

Well, I feel like Stendhal's young hussar in *Le Rouge et le Noir* trying to describe the Battle of Waterloo. We first encountered the party in the courtyard of the Beau Rivage Hotel in Lausanne, where we spent the night. At 9 A.M. it was full of chauffeurs, strapping and restrapping Dior boxes to the tops of basketwork Rolls-Royces in preparation for the Simplon Pass, which we crossed in what I can only describe as a human chain of Reboux hatboxes.

With some relish, we lost the cavalcade about Stresa in order to come to this delicious place, but the arrival at that huge Fiat garage where you leave the car at Venice was something—you know how big it is—four thousand cars, isn't it? But Bill couldn't even get the Chevrolet a place on the roof; he and Berry Berenson tossed up for the last corner of a sort of appendage. We arrived at the Europa Hotel to find a huge crowd all down the Grand Canal waiting for a regatta which was about to take place. As my things were taken out of the motor launch (I was carrying all of Odette's as well as my own), a cry of "Bestegui, Bestegui" went up from the crowd and everyone laughed. You can imagine we trembled with shame and horror, but most surprisingly, the tone was friendly then and the next night. I shall return to this subject later.

That night we dined with Diana and Duff and the von Hoffs,[14] and then all the people who were making entrées went to a rehearsal which lasted till 2 A.M., and at which Aliki found that she was expected to curtsy to Paul Louis Weiller,[15] as he was part of Diana's Antony and Cleopatra tableau before which everyone bowed on entering the room. She wouldn't do it, and there was considerable tension.

The next morning broke gray with black clouds—no one dared to call up the Palazzo Labia, but word came that Charlie was taking his tapestries in and out of the courtyard as the clouds got blacker or lightened, and that he was *très courageux*. About midday there was a thunderstorm, and Charlie retired to a room in the Grand Hotel without a telephone. No one could get through to him, but Cora Caetani[16] reached Ode de Mun[17] and got her to ask him if she

[14] Lady Elizabeth von Hoffmannsthal is Diana's niece. She is as beautiful as her aunt, dark as Diana is fair, with thick black hair and a marvelous white camellia skin. She and her husband Raimund, who was the Austrian-born son of the composer Hugo von Hoffmannsthal, added much to the lives of those who saw them. Raimund died in 1974, and I know few today who have the vitality and warmth that radiated from him. He worked in London for Time-Life Publications.

[15] Her former husband.

[16] Donna Cora Caetani was a Florentine, so beautiful that when she came out of the church on her husband's arm on her wedding day the traffic stopped and the crowds forgot their errands, cries of "*Bella, bella!*" resounded through the streets.

[17] The Comtesse de Mun was a great friend of de Bestegui's who could handle him during even his most difficult moods.

could bring some Italian friend to the party who was an old friend of both but, for some reason, hadn't received her invitation, and the reply came back, "*La réponse est non, non, non.*"

The day was a kaleidoscope of strange and wonderful sights—Diana being dressed by both Oliver Messel and Cecil Beaton and at the same time stitching away at a sack for Duff to tie around his waist to hold a flask, as he discovered that he had no pocket in his domino and was taking no chances at a Bestegui party. Harry's Bar at lunch filled with people saying to each other triumphantly, "they say they have some spirit gum left at a shop near the Rialto." David Herbert in the piazza carrying a broken drum, looking as if he was going to cry, saying, "Does anyone know where one can get a skin for a red Indian drum?" Monsieur Antonio and Monsieur Alexander and all the other good Paris hairdressers running through the streets like Paul Reveres, carrying gold lacquer and white powder from hotel to hotel. Three men from Time-Life leaving our hotel in masques and dominos cunningly concealed their camera. Oh, so many funny sights and, of course, every dressmaker and pansy in the world, but they somehow seemed submerged, and this is true of the whole week, by the genial friends who were there too, and we all had such fun laughing, and everyone was in such a good humor, that it wasn't a bit like the horrible atmosphere the newspapers have described. Pat Wilson, the entire Rothschild tribe, Devonshires, Michael and Ann, Judy, Liz and Raimund, Odette and Pierre, Johnny Walker, Baba—dozens of us all living in adjoining hotels and meeting constantly made the week like a huge house party.

But to return to the party—Bill and I went with Duff in a gondola, after a hurried dinner in powdered hair à la Louis XV and a tennis dress, where we saw Jean Larivière, who said that Loli hadn't come because she had taken a vow a year ago that if their son passed his baccalaureate in June she wouldn't come to Charlie's party—this being what she cared most about in life. He *had*, so she couldn't go and neither could Daisy de Cabrol, as on their way to Venice a cousin she hardly knew died, and so she was in mourning. Poor Daisy, it was tough, as Fred was Antony to Diana's Cleopatra and was able to go, not being, as Daisy explained to me, in *le même degré de parenté.*

All the way to the Palazzo Labia, and you remember how far it is, the bridges and the sides of the canals were jammed with people, clapping each gondola as it went by and shouting how beautiful and have a good time! At the piazza by the palace, there were grandstands and four thousand people standing. We arrived just as Diana did, and it was an unforgettable sight, fifty or more gondolas circling for the landing stage, filled with people in beautiful costumes—Diana's gondola coming through them, and she stepping out assisted by her Negro pages. She turned on the landing wharf to look down at the scene, and I don't think I ever saw anything more beautiful than that—the light from the palace windows falling on her face and the pearls and the blonde hair (a wig just the color of her own hair but done like the Tiepolo picture). Her dress was blue brocade, very decolletée and in shape just like the picture, which you will remember is roughly Queen Elizabeth shape or a bit later, very becoming to her. We then went upstairs and watched the entrées come in—you have seen the palace, so I won't describe it, and you will see pictures of the clothes. I was most impressed by the Italian women—the French clothes were perhaps better, but the Italians more beautiful; the four seasons done by four very young Italian princesses was a sensational entrée.

The only bad costumes were Marie Laure de Noailles'—monstrous as the Lion of St. Mark—and the Jacques Faths, all glittering gold, white, and like an oversweet dessert. Barbara Hutton, referred to in the papers as having spent fifteen thousand on her costume, was identical with Tony Pawson—in fact, everyone got them mixed up all evening. It couldn't have cost fifteen thousand. The Lopez entrée was the most magnificent, next the Turkish Embassy in which were John and Aliki—she in a white dancing girl's costume looking very beautiful and John in red velvet and gold as a pasha, both still not bowing to P. L. Weiller, who was crouching behind Diana and Fred as a mysterious oriental figure. Funniest entrée was the Chachavadze[18]—Elizabeth as Catherine the Great, stupendous in black velvet, preceded by what was said to be her lovers, but looked a

[18] Princess Chachavadze was a powerful Parisian hostess of American blood. She seemed ageless to me, and must have weighed over two hundred pounds. Catherine the Great was just the role for her.

motley group to me. Besides Potemkin, there were Chips Channon and P. Coats as Bonnie Prince Charlie and the British Ambassador, and there was old Baroness Lomonaco as the Irish patriarch and lots of unidentifiable figures. There had been a placement row about Elizabeth's dinner, as someone said that Bonnie Prince Charlie and the British Ambassador couldn't sit together at the Empress of Russia's table or couldn't sit ahead of each other, or something. This had been referred to Duff, who said that the Empress would never have asked them together anyway and to leave him alone with the *Times* crossword, for God's sake.

Our own friends came out very well, I thought. Mary de Rothschild very pretty as a Tiepolo peasant girl or rather Christian Dior's idea of a Tiepolo peasant girl. Pat's costume, about which she had complained, was very becoming and she looked almost prettier than anyone, in fact. Debo as Georgina, Duchess of Devonshire, in a big white dress—lovely. Alix de Rothschild in a superb pink brocaded costume of the period. Odette and I, in feathered coiffures and pink and blue velvet masks, were, we felt, *convenable*—by which I mean that we got by—I certainly hadn't expected to cause cries and sharp intakes of breath and was grateful to feel that it could have been worse. After the entrées were over, one wandered about, and most of all I noticed how very many authentic costumes were there—some of the people owned them, such as Charles de Gramont and Charles d'Haremberg, and some of the Spaniards—the rest, I suppose, bought them or had them made of old stuffs, but it gave the most lovely, rich effect to see so many old velvets and satins and damasks glittering away instead of artificial sateen from Brooks Costume, Inc. Also, nearly everyone seemed to have on real eighteenth-century shoes. I couldn't take my eyes off the buckles.

Because of Charlie's beastliness about invitations, the house was not crowded nor hot—in fact, it was a splendid party entirely apart from the spectacles. Lots of the best kind of supper and lots of anything one wanted to drink—everyone in a good humor, two good jazz orchestras. I had never expected to enjoy myself but really did. Every time one went to a balcony, the crowd roared applause, and I never saw one policeman or heard one hiss—on the contrary, cries for Don Carlos, which is what the Venetians call Charlie! Don

Carlos himself was eight feet high. I never made out why—it must have been uncomfortable, as he changed into a more normal costume later.

About three o'clock, my feet hurt so that I had to go home. I bitterly regret this now, as I missed the best part of the party. Odette stayed till six, dancing on the piazza with the populace.

The next day, coming back from the Lido, we saw a huge crowd in the Piazza San Marco and stopped to see what had happened—believe it or not, it was Charlie and Ode de Mun having a lemonade together. I can't understand Italian very well, but I could see that professional guides had led their troupes from San Marco itself to observe this more interesting spectacle. "Don Carlos, Don Carlos, himself," they were saying. I saw many friends who swear to have seen poor women stop Charlie in the street and kiss his hand to thank him for what he had done for Venice—but I didn't see this myself, and all I am writing is strictly eyewitness!

Bill, I am enchanted to say, enjoyed Venice as much as I did—the heat was not great and after his wretched summer and my qualms about his not being up to the trip, he stayed up far later than I did every night. I think he got home at 6:30 A.M. from the Volpi ball. This was a beautiful party, but your correspondent had gotten up at 9 A.M. to do some sightseeing with Johnny Walker, and my feet, to which I am sorry to keep referring like some old housemaid, hurt so that night that I got the Marriotts to take me home early, or at 3:30 A.M. Bill seems untired and looks wonderful—he liked the Lido and this place, where we know nobody, is bliss, as you remember. How wonderful are Verona, Vicenza, and Padua, aren't they? Tomorrow we do Mantua and then start for home via Bavaria, which Bill has never seen. I loathe leaving Italy and dread the return to Paris, which is said to be cold and rainy, and the children are at Deauville in a pension with Nanny Clark, who writes dreary letters about the weather and says that she is very lonely but consoles herself reading about the Bestegui ball in the papers and hopes we enjoyed ourselves.

Mr. Churchill was such a strange figure to be mixed up in all this—he didn't go to the Bestegui ball but did to the Volpis' and one kept meeting him everywhere, Table Mountain, at a Dior collection—very unexpected but giving one a reassuring feeling of reality.

The Grand Canal of Venice, on which lies the Palazzo Labia, where the ball took place, is lined with palaces of most confusing and mixed architecture. Byzantine, Gothic, Palladian Renaissance façades on the canal side, behind them are dozens of tiny streets with shops and little courtyards; approaching on foot from the back, one cannot imagine that the modest little doorway in front of you leads into palatial splendor. On the grand entrance side are gaily colored poles to which visiting gondoliers tie their craft, and the owner of the house, if he can afford it, has his own gondolas and gondoliers to pole him, wearing the livery of the family. We could afford a hired gondola only once or twice in Venice, and took the steam boat, which serves as a bus, everywhere, or walked. However, the visitor arriving by gondola finds that the ground floor of the palace is the entrance hall and boatyard, for in the winter the gondolas used to be laid up there. Also it was a warehouse, for the original builders of these palaces were merchant princes, and bales of silk from the East, myrrh, frankincense, and ivory were brought there for safekeeping. From this rather dark and somber entrance hall one goes up a severe staircase to the second floor, correctly known as the noble floor, for it is very noble indeed. Charlie's palace was famous for its central room, which is of tremendous height, decorated with a brilliantly colored series of frescoes by Tiepolo representing Antony and Cleopatra. Then came a series of rooms nearly as fine, leading one into another. One is automatically drawn to the windows, for the waters of the Grand Canal lap the stones of the palace and one is never out of the bustle and color of Venetian life. Above this floor are floors of surprisingly small and stuffy bedrooms, at least there are in the other palaces I have visited—I never penetrated upstairs at Palazzo Labia, and on the very top is a little wooden platform designed for the ladies to sit on in privacy in order to bleach their hair in the sun in order to achieve the tint we know from Titian's portraits. Nowadays I imagine that the ladies go to the hairdresser's to obtain the tint from a bottle. The noise must be intense on the back, where the little narrow streets are never empty, but the high voices, the laughter, and the curses are part of Venetian life. In Florence the palaces are fortresses, here they are warm, alive. I visited Palazzo Labia many years later. By that time it was empty. Charlie was dead, Bill Patten and others who had been there that legendary night were dead. I dreaded the visit but wanted my little Anne to see it. We both found it full of enchantment: the sun fell full on Cleopatra's blue and gold robes; Antony was still the handsome passionate lover; and empty as it was, it wasn't hard to hear the long-ago violins.

4 Rue Weber, Paris
November 1951

We haven't been away since we came back from Italy. Bill was very well on our return and he hasn't missed a day at the office, but is too tired after a bronchial attack a few weeks ago to go out much and weekends he must rest. We made an exception for Thanksgiving luncheon at the Harrimans', and for a party given by Diana and Duff at Chantilly for Princess Margaret, who had terrified me when I met her before but seemed entirely different under the spell of the Duff Cooper magic. We were twenty-four for dinner. Bill had Greta Garbo as his neighbor to make him happy; she looked exactly as she did in *Anna Karenina* and was talkative and gay so he fell more in love with her than ever. I had Cecil Beaton, which was great fun, and one of Princess Margaret's young swains. Afterwards the Princess sang and played the piano for an hour, better than most night club professionals; her feature was American hillbilly songs sung with a twanging accent and a deadpan face. Then from "Mountain Girl" and "Old 97" she went into Scotch ballads and French ones with equal skill and grace. I never saw such poise, or a stronger personality, but I still think that I might be frightened if I knew her at all. In any case that night she was enchanting. John Julius,[19] who plays the guitar like a dream, followed her act, as did two very good American blacks from a Paris night club, then suddenly the park of Chantilly was floodlighted and we went out to eat

[19] John Julius Cooper, 2nd Lord Norwich. Only child of Duff and Diana. His radiant, cheerful disposition survived being the single, late-born offspring of that brilliant pair and he had a successful career in the Foreign Office, from which he retired to return to his first love, history and the arts. His books on the Normans in Sicily brought him scholarly and popular attention; he has done many fine documentary films for the B.B.C. His attainments are multiple and various.

roasted chestnuts, standing around a brazier on the terrace. The view was of the waterfall and the lake, very mysterious and shimmering, the trees very white. The French guests seemed to love it all and so did the Princess, it was after five when we got back to Paris, but well worth it and Bill was none the worse.

Our only new friends are some of the SHAPE officers. The more I see of the latter organization the more I admire it. Everyone you meet is introduced as "the most brilliant young officer in the War Department" and at first I was very leery, as I didn't think that even our elite could be as good as advertised, but I am eating my words as we seem to be producing so many quiet soldier-statesman types. The ones I have met are sold on the European army conception, admire the French, appreciate the British, and are humble about our own capacities. We dined with a Colonel Black this week ("the most brilliant young man in the War Department") and he was dying of humiliation over a lecture given that day before all the nationalities by one of our hottest Air Force generals fresh from the U.S. who had patronized every one of the foreign colleagues and boasted about American superiority. The modesty of the Colonel Blacks must stem from Eisenhower himself, what a loss he will be if he runs for President as I suppose he will.

We are beginning to prepare for Christmas, Billy very much aware of it and Anne very much alive to something in the air that is extremely exciting. She is talking like anything and loves to do errands with me, has learned to pay for things and flushes with excitement as she brings out her simple phrases, "A bottle of ink, please." Soon she will be answering the telephone. I shall be thinking of you and yours with so much love, and always wishing we could spend the holiday together.

• 1952 •

Domaine de Migran, Biarritz
January 23, 1952

I am here on my annual pursuit of looking for a seaside home for next summer. Thank God, I am staying with my English friends the Teddy Phillipses in their lovely house in which they live all the year around. Biarritz, which in summer is a large international resort, becomes in winter an English enclave centering around the golf club and the English club, which are full of quiet people who have sought retirement far from their cold, still postwar austere country. I imagine that there must be enclaves like this all over the world, surely in your West Indies and I even imagine in more remote India? The London papers come, and the *Tatler* and the *Sketch*, and they talk about "home" but this is really home, greener grass than England, even in January camellias are out. The Atlantic surf rolls in on the deserted beaches and the huge turreted villas which were old when King Edward VII and Mrs. Keppel sought retreat and privacy here are closed and shuttered, but it isn't dreary, I can quite see Bill and me retiring here one day, with dozens of books and a fire lighted at teatime and a game of gentle bridge to look forward to. As the small inexpensive villa for next summer doesn't exist we have crossed the frontier and looked at the Spanish resorts, but they don't appeal to me. The beaches are black sand, the mountains crowd menacingly close, and one can picture the Spanish families huddled under their beach umbrellas and the difficulties of finding friends for Billy and Anne with whom to share their sand castles.

Just before I left Paris came the arresting day and night of the funeral services for General de Lattre de Tassigny. Last summer Marshal Pétain died and hardly anyone seemed to notice his passing. General de Lattre's death caused national mourning and produced the most impressive ceremonies since the war. He was of course, with General Leclerc, the great Free French leader who gave the army a new confidence, he had a personal dash that made him as controversial a figure as our General Patton and as much disliked by some people, but his death obliterated the controversy and it is thought that he stabilized the Indochina war last year. His death came as a shock, very few people knew that he had cancer although he himself had known it was hopeless, and indeed the *mauvaises langues* (wicked tongues) had been spreading the rumor that he was lingering in a Paris clinic in order to avoid having to go back to Indochina. The night they moved the coffin from the Arc de Triomphe to Notre Dame there were huge crowds, quite silent, waiting for hours on the long route, and the torchlight procession accompanying the gun carriage had that special splendor that the French give to great occasions. When the procession reached the cathedral the bells of every church in Paris tolled together for ten minutes, and the whole city seemed to stop moving. I had never heard or felt anything like this before, and it was all the more impressive for being at night—a bitterly cold one. General Eisenhower and most of the ambassadors caught colds. David Bruce came down with a terrible one and Evangeline said he came home trembling with cold and fever and much depressed by having had some old Frenchman say to him that the last time he had walked with an American Ambassador on a night like that it had been the much-loved Ambassador Herrick, who died of pneumonia immediately afterwards.

4 Rue Weber, Paris
February 1952

The Bruces are leaving and will be terribly missed. All Paris reveres David and is in love with Evangeline, who is a most romantic and beautiful person. She has not got much self-confidence and her modesty is remarkable, as she has only to enter a room to cause a sensation. The United States' position in France has been difficult since the autumn of 1950. Looking back, 1949 seems a honeymoon period and it was the one in which the Bruces arrived. Thanks to them holding their heads high, we survived Korea and McCarthy and the rows about Tunisia and Morocco. Personally I owe Evangeline a great deal, her thoughtfulness and kindness are non-stop, and *how* hard an Ambassador's wife has to work if she is doing her job. Out every night or entertaining, and French evenings are long as no dinner invitation is for earlier than eight-thirty and often it's 9 P.M. on the card, now that they have taken like mad to *le cocktail*, and dinner is a very long meal, it's impossible to get home early even if one is an Ambassador and so is supposed to be the first to leave the party. Then it's up at eight and to the desk and the telephone handling the days of the many guests who actually stay at the residence and the many more who come there, plus the American charities, the churches, and the American library and so on, then there are those Embassy wives who have the right to come for comfort and advice to Evangeline in case of domestic or other trouble, the household to keep going, and above all the three little children. Evangeline is a model mother and I know that it weighs on her if the three cocktail parties she is quite likely to have to attend of an evening prevent her from the storytelling hour before they go to bed, but she manages it all somehow without great physical strength. I know that David is one of Ronnie's greatest friends and he would be proud of him if he could see how Paris is practically in mourning, although the Jimmy Dunns who are to succeed them have the highest of reputations.

One of the Bruces' great strengths was their closeness to each other: they made the same wonderfully close team in Paris, Washington, Bonn, London, and Peking. Once David told me how he had met Evangeline. It was during the war in London, where he was running the O.S.S., the precursor of the C.I.A. He needed a secretary, and was rather annoyed when some colleague insisted on his interviewing a Miss Evangeline Bell. He didn't want a secretary foisted on him by this man but agreed to interview her. To this day he remembers that she wore a little black veil. Determined to put her off, he began by saying, "I take it that you speak French?" "Yes, not as well as I would like but I do broadcast to occupied France twice a week." This was rather putting-off but David rallied by saying that of course there were lots of young women who spoke perfect French, he was more interested in the Central European languages. "Would Hungarian do?" (This, of course, is the hardest of all Middle European tongues.) Thinking wildly, he said that one must be looking ahead to the occupation of Japan. "Oh, my family lived there for several years, we had a governess every day." At the end of his rope, "And the Scandinavian languages?" "I'm afraid that my Swedish is a little rusty, but I could brush it up." David said that he collapsed, and did the one thing possible, which was first to hire her and then to take her out to dinner.

(continuation of February 1952)

Your friend, Mrs. Franklin Roosevelt, has just done me a great favor, and I am deeply grateful. Hearing that she was going to tour the mining areas of northern France, I wrote to her, hardly knowing her, to tell about the little children's center near Lille in which I am interested. She went way out of her way, changing her schedule, to visit it, which thrilled the people up there. Then she sent me the nicest message by Bill Tyler, who accompanied her, to the effect that she had been impressed with it and that my speech opening it was still remembered, also that the mayors of Lille and Roubaix look on me as an old buddy. What a wonderful woman she is.

I met another woman I admire a couple of days ago. Standing in the Post Exchange at St. Cloud drearily regarding a sale of army towels at thirty-five cents each, and wondering if Nanny would think them worthy of Billy and Anne, I suddenly ran into Mrs. Eisenhower. Having heard that she had been in bed for two weeks with gastric flu, I was much surprised to see her there. It was a Saturday afternoon, the place was jammed and appallingly hot. She explained to me that she was up for the first time and to celebrate had come to buy Ike's favorite food, pickled pig's feet. No one recognized her and we stood in line for hours before the canned goods, "stateside prices," waiting to be served. I am very grateful for our PX privileges, which save us a lot of money, but had I been Mrs. Eisenhower with a large staff at my disposal I would not have spent my first convalescent afternoon struggling away in 90-degree temperature. She said that Ike had the afternoon off and was painting, preparatory to stuffing the fish. I got away before she did, reflecting on what a really nice, quick-minded, unpretentious woman she is. The SHAPE people at the lower levels, who are the ones we know, lead rather insular lives which is a great pity as the French would be much impressed with them if they knew them better, but perhaps they prefer it and are homesick—this may even be true of the Supreme Commander and his wife.

We are due to go to England to see Bill's doctor. It will be three years since our last Ditchley visit and I never can cross the Channel without missing you and Ronnie horribly, it can never be the same.

The French are mourning King George VI with deep feeling, people go about streets with sad faces carrying the newspapers with that classic picture of the new Queen coming down the steps of the airplane. Duff telephoned Diana that the meeting of the Privy Council yesterday was terribly moving, all the old boys including himself looked wicked and lined and the Queen very young, white-faced and pure. She was red-eyed but composed. They say that Prince Philip is very much in love with her and she with him and that their relationship is perfect.

We lunched today with the Bruces at the Embassy, a meal consumed under the beady eye of the packers, who couldn't wait for us to finish. The atmosphere was gloomy, for the European Defense Community plan is running into serious political opposition.

London
February 20, 1952

Last week in Paris was exciting but mighty depressing for those of us who follow that very inspiring man, David Bruce. The European Defense Community plan which had seemed hopeful in December ran into snags, and on Saturday it looked like a defeat for the government in the Assembly. Bidault made a fine speech, and there was only one outburst of emotion, a deputy who rose on two canes to say that his grandfather had died for France in 1870, his father in 1914, and he, himself, had been a prisoner of the Germans in the last war and had only a year to live—must we go through it again? This was not popular, but in the debate, one caught again and again the same old themes—distrust of the U.S., distrust of England, and fear of being isolated on the Continent with a dominant, armed Germany. We sat up nearly all night at the Ben Welleses', with Teddy White, some other reporters, and some people from SHAPE. Jock Lawrence said that Ike's reaction is patience and more patience, and if the French and the Germans don't get together this time, some other formula must be tried. How fine he is when one remembers that he used to be against the E.D.C. until sold on it by Jean Monnet.

This is my first time in London since you left England, and I can't bear not having you here. Everyone is in deep mourning for the King, although giving dinners right and left. And they cared terribly—last week must have been intensely moving, especially the lying in state. It was such a relief to find Ann Tree at her mother's yesterday in a bright red blouse, having just left Liz and Virginia Sykes in deepest unrelieved black, looking beautiful but naturally a bit sad. Ann told me about passing a candy shop which had a window full of the blackest caramels and all the other candies, even the white peppermints, wrapped in black paper. Next door was a lingerie shop, its window a waving black forest of brassieres.

Sammy Hood and Fred Warner[1] took me to the theater last night. Fred was just back from Russia for good. He managed to travel extensively and says the Russians he met in remote places are convinced that they are the finest, kindest, most peace-loving of peoples, who only want to be let alone to lead a happy life, which means to them six children, a new suit every five years, and maybe part of a communal tractor.

Today, I lingered in Westminster Abbey, then walked on to lunch

[1] Sir Frederick Warner is presently British Ambassador to Japan. He has been a close friend since we first met him as a young assistant to the Minister of State at the Paris "peace" conference in 1946. Very tall, with thick shaggy black hair, he is one of those people whose many friends delight in discussing him. "Did you hear that Fred is inseparable from a perfectly horrible otter? It bites people, but Joe Alsop was made to exercise it daily in the swimming pool of the British Embassy residence while Fred was at the office." (This was in Laos, where Fred did a brilliant job.) "Did you hear about Fred in Crete? He's been living in a monastery. Some people think he may become a monk." He did not become a monk, instead married late his lovely wife Simone and is the father of two adored sons. A man of controlled passion, bordering on the eccentric but never overstepping the line, a fine letter writer and a superb raconteur, he is one of the most interesting men I have ever met.

at Pam's,[2] to find the Walter Moncktons, Fitzroy McLeans, Malcolm Bullock, and Henry Hopkinson.[3] Very gay, despite the somber black of the ladies. Bill is arriving and we go to Hatfield[4] for the weekend, which is great fun.

4 Rue Weber, Paris
February 1952

Just to report that we are back from England infinitely cheered up as Bill's doctor found him so well that no treatment was necessary. Despite the real sorrow for the King, about which I wrote before, they are enjoying speculating on the new reign and who will influence the Queen. It is sincerely hoped that it will not be the Mountbattens but rather her mother, who is admired by all. I hope it will be Lord Salisbury. Our weekend at Hatfield was two days of sheer pleasure, just the Salisburys, their three enchanting little grandsons who are five, three, and two, and Sammy Hood. The house must have been an awful mess after the war when it was a hospital, and I think Betty has done it over wonderfully. They live in a few rooms—Bill and I had Queen Victoria's suite, which looks exactly as if she had just stepped out of it. The state rooms are open to the public but look just as if they were living in them, full of flowers and family photographs and magazines. Nothing is gloomy, and they were so kind taking us all over the immense house and explaining the history of everything, Bobbety spent two hours in the cellar with us showing us family papers which include thrilling things like Lord Burghley's diary. I thought it so good of him as he is tired and worried and told us that the chances of England avoiding bankruptcy by July are fifty-fifty. Once more one marvels over the English courage. In London there are still no big houses open and I don't suppose there ever will be again, but in the small ones

[2] Lady Pamela Berry.
[3] The guests at Pam's were distinguished politicians of the day. Fitzroy McLean was also a famous traveler and writer. He had fought courageously in Yugoslavia on Tito's side during the war and his tales of his adventures were told as well in his books as in his conversation at the Berry table.
[4] Hatfield House is the historic home of the Cecil family.

such as Pam and Michael Berry's in Westminster the conversation is as good as ever. The food situation isn't much better, never meat but delicious fish or chicken and fresh vegetables at meals. They are worried about us and asked a good many questions about the United States, especially why doesn't Eisenhower turn over his command in France to someone else as his organization, or rather the Republican organization, is said to be disappointing. Curiously, there was not much questioning about Democratic possibilities for the nomination, I suppose it is too soon for that and they assume that Eisenhower will sail in. His reputation is still enormous in Europe.

Terrific arguing over the European army scheme, which Bill hotly defended as the only way to political union. The present Secretary of War, and Hore-Belisha, a former Secretary of War, and the very articulate and clever politician Bob Boothby argued the question at Pam's dinner table and all but Boothby thought it would never work. I didn't hear a good word for France in London, but this was mostly because of the ghastly debate in the Chambre des Députés in Paris last week which I described in my last letter.

Speaking of debates, I got a horrible impression of the Labor Party one afternoon in the House of Commons. They were after Mr. Churchill about the petty thing of his travel expenses to the United States and whether he should have allowed the Cunard Line to pay for him. The faces were ugly, like our dogs after an old fox. They will surely stop at nothing to get in again.

Just before leaving I went to say good-by to Betty Salisbury with Bill; while we were there a letter from the Queen arrived which she showed to us. The writing was young but the style of the first paragraph was as formal and cold as possible, Betty said it was like a letter from Queen Mary. Then suddenly she broke down and the second paragraph read, "Oh, Betty, this is so awful for Mummy and Margaret. I have Philip and the children and the future but what are they to do?" Then the third paragraph was Queen Mary style again, and the signature very grand and big, like a child writing to show off, "Elizabeth R."

I am bewildered by the general gloom over Mummy and Margaret. The former is only fifty-one and is very attractive and clever and can surely make herself extremely useful, and the Princess can get married, can't she? Not one person mentioned the Duke of Windsor, although he came for the service.

4 Rue Weber, Paris
March 4, 1952

The children have returned from a Swiss vacation, which is really mandatory in this climate and everyone who can afford it takes to the mountains annually. I sent them with Nanny, for Bill couldn't get away, and they look like Swiss peasant children, solid and strong with pink cheeks under the sunburn. I have been in bed with a cold and they are both so nice to me. Billy said to Bill, "I tell you what, Mummy's cold is a bore!" He sits outside my door and when I asked him why he stayed there the reply was, "I stay in case you want something." Anne is equally affectionate, bringing me bouquets of grass from the Bois de Boulogne, carefully tied with neat rubber bands, and today it was *Life* magazine open to a horrendous display of NATO forces and tanks. "You like soldiers—I found lots of soldiers for you." Why does she think I like soldiers? But there is nothing like small children's affection to cheer one up. I can't resist sending you a snapshot of them taken by Alec Guinness when he lunched here one day. What a wonderful actor's face he has—almost no face, for although it is charming when one meets him I imagine that people don't turn around in the streets when they encounter him, yet it can become King Lear or a clown in ten seconds. Invisibility is a fascinating quality, Momo Marriott has it. She is the last really luxurious woman I know and a personage in Paris. When I came back from New York on the *Queen Mary* with her a few years ago it was a revelation to me to see how the really rich and non-ostentatious travel. She invited me to drive down from Cherbourg to Paris, so I joined her in her suite on the *Queen Mary* as we entered Cherbourg Harbor, passport and customs declaration in hand. She said gently that I wouldn't need any of that, and I didn't. A polite little man appeared, bowing, to say that any time Lady Marriott felt like disembarking the boat was ready. We went on deck, and in front of the gaping passengers who were lined up awaiting the formalities we descended to a sort of tugboat which was already carrying ten Louis Vuitton trunks, marked M.M., Momo's maid, the polite little man, my meager luggage, and a customs official from Cherbourg who said he had come out just to welcome Lady Marriott back to France. At the customs we never saw the luggage—Momo walked through, with me three steps behind her, just to wave at the customs inspectors, who gave me a beaming, "*Bonjour, milady.*" The Cadillac was waiting, with Paul the faithful chauffeur, who handed her a fresh pair of pale beige gloves and a package of *biscottes* in a cellophane wrapper. As you know, no lady who wants to keep her figure eats bread in France; *biscottes* are gritty dry rusklike objects, just the thing to nibble at on a long drive, for even Momo could not stop the *Queen Mary* from docking at 6 A.M. No money is ever seen to change hands, everything must be organized from some obscure little office in New York or Paris.

In Paris Momo has the same room every year at the Ritz, the same table at the restaurant downstairs at which she eats puréed carrots and minced chicken and drinks Evian water herself, while dispensing the finest of food and drink to the clever and varied people of every nationality whom she invites to meals and who delight in coming, for she is marvelous company, very political and probably as intelligent as her famous father Otto Kahn. Her clothes are so discreet that they are invisible, one never can remember exactly what she wore but only that she is invariably the best-dressed woman in the room. To achieve this, she goes to fittings at Dior that can last six hours, and how her tiny frame can stand this is a wonder to us all. I get faint after half an hour in one of those hot little fitting rooms, but Momo is a true perfectionist. I am very fond of her and wish I could describe her without making her sound purely frivolous, for she is much more than that.

4 Rue Weber, Paris
May 1952

I am so delighted for Bill as Jimmy Dunn, the new Ambassador, seems to appreciate him as much as David Bruce did and he has an interesting job working as assistant to Ted Achilles, the Minister or number two. He is not only a very nice man to work for but French politics is always fascinating, although I don't write to you about it often as I feel that only we who live here can be absorbed in the labyrinth of this extraordinary multi-party system. Do you know that if this government falls, as it probably will one of these days, it will be the eighteenth since we have lived in France? The French retain their calm by pointing out how remarkably efficient the permanent civil service is, all those thousands of quiet men all over France going about their business of running the country no matter what. They are badly paid, seldom rewarded. The top ones are often very impressive like Wilfred Baumgartner, governor of the Bank of France, with whom we lunched the other day in his glamorous dining room at the bank, which is decorated by Fragonard.

The Jimmy Dunns could not be nicer, but I have the feeling that they miss Rome where they served so long and with great distinction. They brought a whole staff of Italian servants with them who seem marvelous to me but this has not gone over with the French. "What, don't they like our food?" We went to a dinner there recently where the food could not have been better, but the evening was ruined for me by a curious episode. After dinner I was sitting on a sofa talking to one of the most important and admired foreign ambassadors here—Duff Cooper thinks he is the cleverest of them all—when he leaned forward and said he wanted to tell me something important and confidential. He has the habit of getting so close that he spits in your face and I withdrew as far as the sofa would permit me. What he wanted to tell me was that Jean Monnet was a member of the Communist Party and that our American confidence in him was naïve to a degree. Monsieur Monnet was sitting about fifteen feet away on the other side of the room, talking to Mary Dunn. I was really furious. Monnet of the Monnet plan that started France back on the road to recovery after the war, Monnet the brains of the Schuman plan and the European Defense Community, the two most original and imaginative ideas of our time, Monnet who works day and night for a strong and safe future for Europe and for us. And I wasn't hearing this libel from some fellow-traveling troublemaker, but from the Ambassador of a major NATO power. I asked him coldly why he didn't inform Mr. James Dunn of this astonishing assertion instead of me and he just laughed and tried to squeeze my hand. This trick always irritates me. These mischief-makers don't dare to try it on with our Ambassador but by telling their story to someone lowly they are pretty sure it will get back to the Ambassador, which of course it did the next morning when Bill reported it at the morning meeting. Naturally the reaction was the same as my own and I wouldn't think the story worth repeating to you except that it left me with a bad taste in my mouth. Do ordinarily intelligent people think that we are so undone by McCarthy that we are prepared to suspect practically anyone once the word "Communist" is used? I cannot say how strongly I feel about the harm McCarthy has done to us abroad. Of course, except in the cases of the few personal friends who have been badly hurt in the State Department, we don't live it day to day as you do, but the poison blows across the Atlantic like some horrible prevailing wind.

To be more cheerful, we have had a personally happy and varied spring. One weekend we went up to Noirmoutiers with the Alain de Rothschilds. This is Brittany, and the island in early spring is battered by gales. We staggered from end to end of this bleak and rocky spot for two days looking at houses for rent for the summer, entirely because we all are dominated by our children's nannies and they believe in sea air for the little one's pink cheeks. No one can exaggerate the force of an English nurse in Paris, imagine four perfectly sensible people wasting forty-eight hours in a grim and inaccessible place nine hours from Paris which we knew would be hopeless before we started. At least the Muscadet was delicious and helped us to put up with the damp sheets and the gloom.

For Easter we took my mother-in-law to Holland and had four happy tulip-filled days. It's an ideal country for Bill, who walked easily down the flat pretty streets of The Hague, and we ate plovers' eggs and looked at the wonderful pictures and had a perfect tourist time.

Last weekend we took the children to Chantilly and on Sunday Diana and Duff gave one of their wonderfully funny mixed-up lunch parties after which I picked wild lilies of the valley in the forest with Lord Ismay and Orson Welles. We could not be luckier to have Lord Ismay as Secretary-General of NATO, he has all the tact one used to hear that Eisenhower had in dealing with the Allies and to me he is a bigger man.

And our cultural life is intense due to the festival put on by the

Congress for Cultural Freedom, paid for by American benefactors and the director is our old friend Nicolas Nabokov. The Boston Symphony got the biggest reception but the greatest excitement for the real music lovers was the Stravinsky opera *Oedipus Rex* conducted by Stravinsky, narrated by Jean Cocteau, sung by Patricia Neway. I was out of my depth and confused by the narration but much too much of a snob to say so at a supper party for the cast afterwards given by Hervé Dugardin, director of the Théâtre des Champs Elysées at his beautiful house on the Rue de l'Université.

But our real news is that Bill's job is so good and he is in on everything. They want him to take a short holiday now and to stay here all summer, which is fine. We are going to England again, where we have some lovely invitations, but I hear that things are less well even than in February, so I am stocking up on food to take over as presents. We shall spend the summer at Chantilly, reading every word about the presidential campaigns and thinking of you.

4 Rue Weber,
Paris, France
June 14, 1952

We are just back from a fortnight's holiday in England, and I am emotionally exhausted and very depressed. How ever are they to get out of the economic mess they are in? But I have felt this so often, and they always manage somehow. In 1947, that horrible coalless freezing winter, I used to sit in Bill's room at the hospital wearing my fur coat and fleece-lined boots and gloves (and he a lung patient just postoperative) listening to our gallant friends talking about the effort that had to be made. I hear Tommy Brand saying calmly, "Exports must be raised this year, not by a hundred per cent but by a hundred and twenty per cent," and thinking that darling Tommy had been driven mad by overwork; but I know they did it or came very close. How I admire them and love them; so does Bill, who also feels strongly that they are indispensable to us for their brains and their leadership, and I note that he is increasingly a believer in the "special relationship" no matter how unequal the power balance.

We stayed partly with the Salisburys, who were wonderfully

kind, both at Cranborne and in London. Bobbety seems to think it is touch and go and is desperately worried, according to Betty. On the surface, he is as serene and charming as ever, although I should think he was killing himself. Twice we came in at 2 A.M. and found him still sitting up over his red boxes.[5]

Naturally, being the season, there were lots of parties. Mereworth you will have heard about from Ann,[6] who turned that glorious house into a Palladian paradise. Pat Wilson was lent the Spanish Embassy for a debutante party for her daughter, Caroline Villiers, and I never had a better time in my life. The only debutante I saw was Caroline, who looked lovely. I expect there were many other young girls, but the stars were our middle-aged friends, Odette and Mary de Rothschild from Paris, Liz, and Pat herself. What do you think we would have done as girls in New York if the debutante parties had been taken over by our mothers and their friends? Mutiny, don't you agree? I am more or less used to it in Europe by now, and Winthrop Aldrich tells me that no woman is at her best until she is thirty-five. (I wonder if he changes this date every year, bless his heart, as I shall be thirty-five next year.)

Bill and I walked out into Belgrave Square at 5 A.M., in full sunlight, feeling like characters from "The White Cliffs of Dover." And that afternoon Mr. Winston Churchill took Odette to Brighton to the races. I haven't heard a report yet, as Bill and I took the car for a week's sightseeing in the west of England. I have never done anything lovelier than to walk with David Herbert and Bill after dinner in the Arcadian park of Wilton, nightingales and Sir Philip Sidney accompanied us.

But hospitable and effortless as they all make it seem, the shortages I caught glimpses of reminded me of 1946. I went to the PX as soon as I got back to London, but I couldn't get everything I wanted. Would you be a saint and do some shopping for me for the people on the list I enclose? Canned butter, canned bacon, sugar, rice, tongue.

[5] These beautiful red leather boxes were traditionally used by members of the British Cabinet to carry their papers.

[6] Lady Ann Tree, Marietta's daughter-in-law, lived at beautiful Mereworth Castle with her husband Michael Tree.

Château de St. Firmin, Chantilly
France, August 8, 1952

Your description of the convention is marvelous. I have been reading it to every close American friend who has come to see us here, and Kitty Herrick,[7] a good judge, agrees with me that *The New Yorker* deserves you when you give up politics. Your touches are so vivid . . . the log cabin on the seventh floor of the Hilton, the ladies' luncheon heavy with orchids. Stevenson sounds better every day; is it, by the way, true that he is in love with Judy Montagu?[8] This is just English gossip. She would be an executive wife at the White House rather like Dolly Madison at times of fire and theft, but we are not always in a state of emergency and I should have thought that he could do better.

The French press have been too stupid and slow about catching on to Stevenson's quality, but now they are fascinated by him and write that he is cerebral and complex as a personality, nothing could be higher praise coming from them.

We feel as always so serene in this lovely house. The children and I punt on the lake and fish with nets, Bill manages to commute nearly every night and we sit on the terrace looking at the waterfall and feel how lucky we are. The weekend usually brings guests. We have just had the Vincent Astors, Bill Paleys, and Christopher Sykes[9] for a couple of days, which was great fun. Christopher much admired Minnie Astor[10] and Babe and said that they as well as you and I are like Henry James's American women. I have heard this before, haven't you? It always rather depresses me as I remember

[7] Mrs. Parmely Herrick, a close American friend living in Paris.

[8] Judy Montagu, later Mrs. Milton Gendel, was a brilliant young Englishwoman who much loved America but there was nothing in the rumored romance.

[9] Christopher Sykes, talented British essayist and historian. *Four Studies in Loyalty* is the one of his books that I prefer. A great traveler, he had been at Oxford in the early twenties with Robert Byron, whose books on Persia are still classics, Evelyn Waugh, Freddie Birkenhead, and others who formed a brilliant coterie.

[10] Mrs. Vincent Astor, now Mrs. James Fosburgh, was born Minnie Cushing, sister to Babe Paley. Frail, elegant, possessed of great taste and a huge heart, she shares the famous charm of her two sisters. The other is Mrs. John Hay Whitney.

Henry James's women as donkeys without a sense of humor, but Christopher insists that to him there is no higher praise, using such words as fresh, gay, beautiful, yet high-minded. I must reread Henry James.

4 Rue Weber, Paris
October 1952

Watching the campaign from Europe is misery. I have to take Bellargil (soothing drug recommended by Joe Alsop—get it from him sometime) thinking of Eisenhower knuckling down to the McCarthy implications that General Marshall is a Communist and eliminating the praise of him that he was going to make in the Wisconsin speech. The only speech that I have really liked is the Flint one about Vandenberg's heritage to the party. I admire Stevenson more and more, especially his courage in appealing to the eggheads. It seems to me that the American public will respond to being treated as eggheads, or won't it?

The French took great offense at Eisenhower's casual remark referring to them as morally debilitated and atheistic people and grow increasingly pro-Stevenson, there is immense interest in the outcome of the election. I hope that you are not totally exhausted. My mother can't stop talking about how pretty and attractive Frankie was this summer . . . tall, thin, and lovely. I never thought that she would stay fat as none of your family is, but what fun to have her looks blossom so young.

I see much of Odette Pol Roger and Louise de Rougemont, the latter a bit nostalgic for the U.S. and struggling under the weight of French family life, although, being Louise, she never complains. I never get over what she and my other friends go through. She gets up at six o'clock to cook a decent breakfast for thirteen-year-old François, who takes a seven o'clock bus to school. He returns at 7:30 P.M. having had no exercise and little lunch; after dinner he does homework until 11 P.M. or midnight. This is typical of the French schoolboy's schedule, which includes Saturdays. They do get Thursday afternoon off but often spend it trying to catch up on their work. No wonder so many of them break down at the moment of the critical examinations later, and one never sees a relaxed schoolboy. To return to Louise, after the departure of the children she makes the mandatory daily telephone calls to all the family, checking up on Aunt Jeanne's sprained ankle or Cousin Berthe's problems with the children; the closeness of French families is a permanent source of wonder to me. Then she goes downstairs for the daily morning visit with her mother-in-law, who lives in a perfectly huge flat quite alone except for servants one floor below the cramped Rougemont apartment in which the seven Rougemonts live practically in cupboards, which everyone thinks quite normal. By the end of the day Louise, if I catch her on the telephone, will not tell me about the family problems or various good works which she has fitted into her schedule, but she will discuss a new and controversial play we have both seen this week, a leading article by Aron in *Figaro* or an Alsop piece in the *Herald Tribune*, and tell me a good political story she has picked up at luncheon. How do Frenchwomen do so much? They also read everything, not just the reviews, and don't miss an interesting exhibition. I never get over the modesty of someone like Louise de Rougemont.

It is lovely for me to have Elise[11] in Paris, installed with the children in a little apartment on the Rue de 29 Juillet. She is happy and likes being here, but is exhausted by all the admirers in hot pursuit. They want her to sit up all night at Monseigneur listening to the romantic violins, but she says that she has had enough of night club life and is bored by all the desperate gentlemen who wish to jump into the Seine for love of her. So far these are Englishmen and Americans; she had just the same effect on gentlemen when we were eighteen (and so did you) and now that she is unattached again the locale has simply changed from the Triborough Bridge to the Pont Neuf.

[11] Elise Mortimer (later Madame Pierre Bordeaux-Groult), like Marietta, was a childhood friend and my relationship with her was that of a sister. She had devastating charm combined with a brilliant mind and immense courage and loyalty. After an unhappy marriage was terminated I persuaded her to leave New York and bring her small children to live in Paris. Soon after this she met a fascinating young French bachelor, Pierre, and married him from our house a few months later. Her coming to Paris and the life we shared was very important to me. Her untimely death in 1973 left those of us who loved her desolate.

To Marietta from Paris

Excelsior Hotel
Florence, October 12, 1952

My mother brought us here, giving us a luxurious week at this deluxe hotel, and we have been lucky enough to have a series of golden days for our sightseeing. As you went to school here and know it all by heart I won't weary you with a description of our eager days looking at the wonders of this city, but I have fallen in love with it in quite a different way from my love affair with Venice—the latter is open and welcoming and this is mysterious and closed; I should love to have been a nineteenth-century lady, neighbor to the Robert Brownings, taking my carriage to see the sunset from San Miniato and going on to a musical evening in one of the tall palaces that seem so shrouded from the street. It is only our second visit, and surely to know Florence would take years.

Bernard Berenson, whom Mama knew in Rome, gave us lunch at famous I Tatti the day after we got here. We were shown into a little antechamber to await the great man in company with Harold Acton, the English writer whose beautiful Villa Pietra we visited later. Mr. Berenson came in, the little figure huddled in shawls of whom I had heard so much, vitality itself, luncheon was delicious and we stayed till four as he didn't seem to want us to leave but seldom have I been so disappointed. I had not expected him to ask our opinion of Mantegna or Cimabue or to discourse on Correggio, but I had not expected three hours of gossip of the level of a Paris tea party. He was avid for news of Paris, parties and scandals and who was having an affair with whom, he seems to know everyone and keep up with all the doings of French aristocracy. At last he fastened on to Bill with some extremely shrewd political questions and this was much more fun, Bill gave as good as he got and amused Berenson. But I left sadly, you know how I love to add to my gallery of heroes and I had been longing to meet the legendary Berenson. We had tea with Harold Acton, which was much more fun, his house and garden infinitely more beautiful than I Tatti and the talk was better. His particular subject at the moment is the Bourbons of Naples but he knows about everything. We were received by his mother, a lady originally from Chicago, wearing a black velvet tea gown trimmed with Valenciennes lace. In spite of a lifetime abroad she retains a strong whiff of Lake Shore Drive in the days when Mrs. Potter Palmer was discovering the Impressionists and one took one's private railroad car to New York and the steamer to Paris annually. We were warned by both Mr. Berenson and Mr. Acton not to go near Violet Trefusis, with whom they are feuding. The small expatriate colony in Florence is evidently full of malice—like most expatriate colonies.

On return to the hotel there was a note from Mrs. Trefusis—God knows how she heard that we are here—asking us to lunch in a couple of days' time, which we instantly accepted. She is a very strange woman, but she has been kind to us in Paris where her house is always fun, so we had no qualms. She is Mrs. Keppel's daughter, and lets it be known that she is therefore the illegitimate child of King Edward VII, but Diana Cooper says that this is not so, that she is the child of a respectable man called Keppel.

Violet Trefusis's lunch was very like her Paris parties. The villa is rather empty, the view beautiful, the other guests pleasant Florentines and a couple of hanger-on beaux from Paris—she is very mysterious about her money and sometimes the rumor goes about that she is ruined, sometimes that she will leave a huge fortune. She warned us seriously about Berenson and Harold Acton—at no cost must we go near them. I decided that I did not like her.[12]

How silly this trivia must sound to you, working so hard, but I thought to distract you perhaps for a moment.

4 Rue Weber, Paris
November 1952

Naturally I thought of you the moment we heard the election results. They are heartbreaking, and as I know how hard you

[12] Nigel Nicolson in *Portrait of a Marriage* vividly describes the tremendous love affair between his mother, Vita Sackville-West, and Violet Trefusis. Reading the moving love letters in 1973, one could not imagine that the woman we knew could have inspired such passion. Sitting on the terrace of her mother's Florentine villa, in a Parisian drawing room, or at her country house outside Paris, she seemed to us quirky, spoiled, and a bit of a fraud. A physical detail was what most put me off. She wore flowing, full skirts and was a messy eater, so when she rose majestically at the end of a meal a cascade of crumbs and odd bits of food would fall to the floor. I was revolted. We were rather ashamed of going there, and didn't very often. Reading *Portrait of a Marriage,* I feel an obtuse fool; there must have been poetry and fascination there.

worked for Stevenson I can imagine your state of physical as well as moral exhaustion. I am so sorry. Please don't despair for Stevenson comes over even to us here as a man of such vigor and youth that I feel certain that he will try again and win. But this is small comfort now.

The French turned sharply against Eisenhower after his harsh remarks about their decadence and are deeply disappointed that he won. They are also already worrying about John Foster Dulles as Secretary of State as he has the reputation here based on what I don't know, of being bellicose and anti-colonialist. *Paris-Match,* the very popular weekly magazine, has published a list of the causes for the present anti-Americanism here. They are pretty obvious. There are too many Americans living in Paris working for the various government agencies. Their fat cars take up too much room, their families take up too much housing, and they drink too much and talk too much. We are moralistic about anti-colonialism and, having hurt the English and the Dutch by encouraging the loss of their empires, we are now hoping that the French will lose their vital North African possessions. Above all we are clumsy and might well plunge France into another world war. The Marshall Plan was fine but what they want now here is trade, not aid. *Paris-Match*'s conclusion is "No country was worse prepared than America for the world leader role she had to play. The Americans are leaders through the force of events but without having the desirable first-rate qualities like sure judgment and a cool head."

Our frequent weekends at Chantilly with Diana and Duff do a lot to cheer us up. He is writing his memoirs and has shown us part of them. It will be a beautifully written and moving book. I particularly like the description of their early days, when he had left the Foreign Office to stand for Parliament and Diana was working her head off playing in *The Miracle* to keep them afloat financially. They always had such fun, no matter what their problems. Of all Duff's jobs, representing England in Algiers with the Free French must have been the trickiest, as de Gaulle was suspicious to the point of paranoia; Duff had a terrible time even persuading him to go to England for the Allied landings in June 1944. Yet despite the difficulties and frustrations Duff saw de Gaulle's bigness far more clearly than Churchill did, and was marvelously patient. Bill and I were much impressed with a dispatch to the Foreign Office written in Algiers well before the end of the war. It is long, and Duff calls it his political testament. The essence of it is that the Western European countries should form an alliance leading to federation. This was a new and radical proposal in those days and the Foreign Office replied that such an alliance would increase the danger of Soviet expansion and also offend the United States. Duff writes, "It was the old familiar attitude, rather than risk offending anybody, do nothing."

What gives the educated English such wonderful memories for poetry? Start Duff on a line from Horace or Browning or Shakespeare and he is capable of reciting the whole poem, and it's the same with Mallarmé, that most difficult of the French symbolists, and many others. He mentioned that he knew all but seven of Shakespeare's sonnets by heart, for instance.

Diana is nearly as good, especially at Shakespeare. Another thing I envy the English is the pleasure that generation takes from reading out loud. The Duff Coopers do this most unself-consciously, he doing the reading while she stitches away at some sort of sewing.

I don't know which of them writes the best letters. We were amused by a recent one from Duff, who had been in London to make a speech with which Churchill did not agree. They met the next night at the men's club which is called, mysteriously, "The Other Club." "Winston kept off the subject of my speech for a long time and I thought he didn't wish to discuss it, but of course we got down to it in the end and went at it hammer and tongs for about half an hour. When he finally had to leave the table to speak to Anthony Eden in New York he said, 'Never have I heard so much intelligence, such learning, so many gifts, such eloquence squandered on talking such nonsense as you have.' I replied, 'That's just a smoke screen to cover your retreat.' Neither of us lost our temper for a moment and it was all very happy and great fun."

· 1953 ·

4 Rue Weber, Paris
January 1953

We have had a month of fog, the gray Paris streets wear a ghostly air. With this came the flu in epidemic proportions, but it is a very light variety. Bill caught it at Strasbourg where he was sent to observe the European Constitutional Assembly. He said that the meeting was so interesting that it was quite worth a touch of flu. Representatives from the parliaments of six European countries met to discuss "a political community, supernational and indissoluble." The French delegation was very mixed, old Paul Reynaud, Michel Debré, who is a Gaullist, and Guy Mollet, the Socialist. Surprisingly they backed the plan with enthusiasm. Of course this is all words, the Strasbourg assembly has no power, but the papers wrote it up as an historic occasion.

Anne has had her third birthday, celebrated by a large party here with movies. She is adorable when Bill is ill, "Daddy, me run upstairs for your aureomycin." I dined at the Embassy while Bill was in bed and was congratulated by the Ambassador for giving Marshal Juin such a good time that he stayed until after midnight; two days later he made a viciously anti-American speech so I don't feel very proud of myself. One wonders about Embassy entertaining. The big dinners and receptions are very expensive, just the Fourth of July party alone costs all one year's entertainment allowance and ambassadors have to dip into their own pockets and often leave Paris practically ruined, but people like to be asked and I suppose that once in ten times some substantive good is done.

We went to the Diplomatic Reception last night at the Elysée Palace, which could not have been grander: the President and Madame Auriol spared neither expense nor trouble and the hothouse flowers in huge vases, the orchestra playing Offenbach waltzes, the candles everywhere made everyone feel that it was an occasion from another and more romantic century than this one. Only the

Russians looked gloomy; as usual they kept to themselves in a tight little group, not a smile on any of their faces. The Japanese ladies in kimonos were the most decorative of the women at the party; the Arabs the most decorative of the men. We dined beforehand with some friends from the Quai d'Orsay, the men wore such sparklingly becoming orders and decorations that I had a moment of regretting our simple American ways, for dressing up is such fun.

I must leave you to obey Billy's order to read to him. *Kings and Queens of England* by Farjeon is his favorite book, but he likes Lear's nonsense rhymes and *Hiawatha.*

4 Rue Weber, Paris
March 1953

This has been an exciting month. First our dear friend Elise married Pierre Bordeaux-Groult and the reception was here at our house. Pierre is most attractive, good-looking, clever, and Paris' most eligible bachelor. Elise will live in a huge house containing Pierre's father's remarkable collection. The eccentricity of the collector begins at the door, where one is greeted by an ancient, balding, very vocal parrot. One continues through room after room, forty Turners hang on the wall as well as several hundred other fine pictures, on tables lying as casually as newspapers and books do on our tables are drawings by Fragonard and Watteau and Boucher (I believe that this is the most important collection of eighteenth-century drawings in private hands in France). Cases carry priceless china and ancient snuffboxes, also souvenirs from Monsieur Groult's trips, sea shells marked "Welcome to Brighton" and a small replica of the leaning tower of Pisa jostle priceless miniatures. He was no snob, old Monsieur Groult. Everything is slightly dusty, dark, and mysterious. There is a large garden containing an ornamental pond on which float swans—this on the Avenue Foch is comparable to having a large garden on Park Avenue at 72nd Street. Elise has a job on her hands running this vast establishment but I know that she will bring light and gaiety to it without losing the style and character that makes it so special in this city which contains many great houses but none as unconventional as this.

Pierre and she are madly in love and I rejoice in the marriage as does Bill.

Today was springlike after weeks of gray cold. I crossed the bridge at the Place de la Concorde slowly, on foot, the better to enjoy the view of the spires of Notre Dame. There seemed to be a lot of police about but I paid no attention until I got to the Chambre des Députés, which was ringed with steel-helmeted figures, bayonets drawn. This sent me back to pick up the car at the Embassy and go home. Later I learned that they feared serious riots demonstrating against the Algerian war, which is much, much worse and more real to the French than the faraway struggle in Indochina.

We were sent up to Le Havre to meet our new Ambassador and his wife, the Douglas Dillons, on their arrival from the United States. The appointment came as a surprise and the papers have written up his banking career, but Bill, who has known him since schooldays, says that banking is just one thing that Douglas would be good at, he has a first-class mind capable of grasping any subject and that in three months he will know as much about France as the oldest Foreign Service officers who have served here for years. I hardly knew them, but already my admiration for them both is considerable. She looks about twenty although they have two nearly grown-up daughters, and is very shy, but has a strong character, adores her husband, and is determined to do well for his sake. Even on the train coming down to Paris from Le Havre she had a French teacher beside her and was working away. She is so pretty and full of charm it won't matter if her French isn't perfect, but I admire her for taking it so seriously.

Bill was quite right about Douglas Dillon's brilliant mind. Within a very short time he was at home in France and he and Phyllis became widely respected and liked by the French. We were very proud to serve under them.

Nothing annoys me more than the cliché that because of the rapidity of modern communications ambassadors are nothing more than messenger boys. Of course American ambassadors respond instantly and loyally to the orders of the Secretary of State, received by cable or by telephone, and deliver their instructions personally, if the issue is very important, to the Foreign Minister of the country to which they are accredited, however much they agree or disagree with the instructions from Washington. But then come the nuances. If an ambassador has the standing, the confidence in himself, the prestige that accrues only from incident after incident during which the government of the country to which he is accredited has learned to trust him, black and white orders from Washington become issues which can be talked about between friends, softened from cold cable words that, without the ambassador, might lead to very ugly headlines. A good example is Douglas Dillon's handling of the crisis of the spring of 1954, over Indochina. I come to that in a later letter, but my point is that Douglas, who then had to deal with a situation that might easily have led to World War III, had the confidence of such very different and volatile men as Bidault of France, of Eisenhower and of Dulles in America, of Anthony Eden of Britain. A shy man, he never could have attained his position without Phyllis, who had smoothed the path, deferring always to her husband, but made the friends.

Stalin's death on March 5 had of course been the major event of that spring. Since the defection of his daughter Svetlana we have learned how it happened but at the time there was talk that he had been murdered and a good deal of speculation about what was called "the thaw." There were many gestures of détente, the release of British prisoners in Korea, the amnesty of Russian political prisoners condemned to less than five years of prison, the reopening of the Korean peace negotiations, followed by the cessation of hostilities in Korea, the Russian agreement to Dag Hammarskjöld's appointment at the U.N. which they had held up for months. These gestures persuaded many people in the West that the time had come to seek an accord with Russia, even Winston Churchill said in a public speech that the U.S.S.R. had changed enormously.

4 Ru Weber, Paris
April 10, 1953

The Bohlens arrived at last, after two airplane engine failures, they were twenty-six hours late and the children were exhausted but Avis and Chip remarkably fresh and gay. We saw them off for Moscow yesterday after celebrating for three evenings with them at the Bruces', Reinhardts', and here. These astonishing Russian gestures of the last weeks make it a fascinating assignment for Chip instead of the sterile post it has been for the last few years, and hearing them all talk about it is like reading a detective story which never comes to an end. The theories are endless and the repercussions in Europe, especially what will happen in Germany, are question marks.[1]

My pet theory of Stalin having been murdered is the one thing the experts think unlikely. Otherwise anything could have happened and Chip goes out there with the frank admission that he hasn't the faintest idea what has really taken place and the impression that we won't know for some time. It is heartening to see someone so alert mentally and physically, with a fresh and elastic mind, taking on the job of Ambassador to Russia. Every day comes some new sign of détente: yesterday a Russian ship tied up at Rouen and the sailors came down to Paris on leave and wandered about just like G.I.s, an unprecedented occurrence.

I haven't described Easter. It has become our habit to celebrate the holiday with the Cy Sulzbergers, which means celebrating it twice as she is Greek and their Easter comes later. This year we took all the children to Chantilly where we stayed for our Easter, picking daffodils in the forest with icy fingers, for the weather was rotten. The Greek Easter was a beautiful day and we picnicked, this time in the forest near Senlis, eating the traditional roast lamb. Marina is a Greek from the golden age of Greece, her erudition is as great as her charm, when she tells a story everyone from six to sixty is mesmerized. Her children, Marina and David, are to be envied by all other children, for she makes life such fun for them and at the same time casually implants an astonishing amount of information, historical and literary, in their minds. When Cy does big trips for the New York *Times* Marina goes along and must be a great asset to him. Her politics, she says, are Extreme Center. Her letters, full of hopeless mistakes in spelling, are awaited eagerly by all her friends. Whether she is describing dinner with the Prime Minister

[1] What happened in Germany was that the Berliners overestimated the signs of détente and thought it safe to demonstrate for freedom, scaring the Russian occupiers to death and causing savage reprisals.

of Japan or picking wild flowers in Nepal, she conveys the atmosphere as no other letter writer of our age can do, she is unquestionably the best of our generation, which is high praise as there are many brilliant letter writers today—you for one.

4 Rue Weber, Paris
April 1953

Each year the Paris spring comes as a surprise to me, for the gray winter can seem long. Now after four days of sun the chestnut blossoms have rushed into bloom and young lovers stroll hand in hand through the gardens of the Luxembourg. I am glad that our destiny is so uncertain and each year may be our last year in Paris, otherwise I might take it for granted.

Events of the week—a visit from Lew Douglas' brother and wife, who were taken by our rented house and think of buying it. Thank God I think we have frightened them off. The children have learned to point dumbly and sadly to the roof and I say apologetically that I hadn't meant to mention it but the constant leaks are rather disturbing.

We gave a dinner for the Dillons and sat up till very late listening to our new friend, the head of the Sûreté Nationale. I don't know how to translate his position in our terms, he is more than the chief of police, more than J. Edgar Hoover. Young, tough, attractive, and a good talker; one rather forgets that he is considered expert at putting needles under toenails to extract information. He was instructive and hopeful describing the confusion and disorder of the Communist Party in France. The return of Thorez, who is old and very ill, hasn't helped and they are leaderless and fighting badly among themselves. After the Ambassador and Phyllis had left and the other guests had followed their example our new friend accepted a nightcap and interrogated Bill and me about McCarthy. The theme was the familiar one we hear so much this spring: "What are you going to do about him?" Not easy to answer.

By the way, speaking of McCarthy, our friendship with the Windsors is finished. The other night, at the British Embassy, the Duke announced to all and sundry at a formal dinner given in his honor that General Marshall was unquestionably a Communist so the President had been quite right not to speak in his favor. This sent Bill into one of his very rare rages and he took on the Duke, asking for proof of his statement about General Marshall, and a real row ensued between them. At the end of it I happened to look at the Duchess. She was tight-lipped and cobra-eyed. I think we will not be invited to the Windsors' again.[2]

It is thought that the government will soon fall, and that isn't news as I have written the same phrase to you several times a year since we first came here and it is always true of the Fourth Republic, but this time is interesting in view of the soft, friendly gestures from Russia since Stalin's death, and the disintegration of public support for the war in Indochina. Paul Reynaud may well be Prime Minister. We lunched in his company at the Frank Gileses' the other day, the only other guest was Kitty Giles's father, Lord De La Warr, who is in the present British Cabinet. Reynaud returned to the war and told us some extraordinary tales of June 1940, the terrible month in which France fell. He said that at the fatal Cabinet meeting in Bordeaux at which the vote was taken against going to North Africa in order to establish a government in exile, and fighting it out from there, there was still hope as the Cabinet was undecided, so he, Reynaud, telephoned de Gaulle in London asking him to get in touch with the British and ask them for naval and air support. De Gaulle not only obtained this but came back with Churchill's magnificent offer of common citizenship for the French and the English. The trembling Cabinet would have been reassured by this but for General Weygand, the Supreme Commander of all French armies, who had tapped the telephone calls to London and spent the afternoon rushing around lobbying against Reynaud's appeal to go to North Africa and convincing the politicians that England's offer to help was inadequate. The vote then went against Reynaud and we know the rest of the story. I asked him if he had ever seen General Weygand again; he said that they had ended up at the same German prison camp several years later and caused some trouble to the dining-room staff as they insisted on separate tables.

On the next night after this lunch I was lucky enough to be able

[2] We never were.

to ask Lord Ismay about the accuracy of this story; he blew it sky high. I would think that one should distrust Reynaud totally when he returns to the past, but he is so astonishingly alert and timeless in appearance that I can quite see why he is being considered for Prime Minister.[3]

4 Rue Weber, Paris
May 15, 1953

We are getting excited, Bill and I, at the thought of coming over for the coronation next month, and above all spending a couple of days with you just before it. Your rented house is said to be a dream. We hear here that the mood of England is that of a second Elizabethan age, full of hope and confidence in the future. If true, how very wonderful that the advent of a young Queen to the throne should produce this, or if it is a coincidence and England is in an upbeat mood for reasons that have nothing to do with the coronation, how very nice that the pageant of the coronation should focus the optimism.

Here things are not so hot, and I remember Dean Acheson saying a couple of years ago that we would soon reach the end of phase one of Soviet policy (constant pressure, intimidation, ceaseless violent propaganda, hammer blows at our weak spots). He thought that if we pulled off a series of Allied successes which God knows we have—Greece and Turkey saved by the Truman doctrine, followed by the Marshall Plan, NATO, etc.—Soviet policy would enter phase two, seemingly one of détente, to lull our fears and assure the splitting up of the Allied coalition. For the moment the Rosenberg case is a convenient stick with which to beat us. Not only *Humanité*, the Communist newspaper, headlines the story of the trial of the Rosenbergs; the whole press has taken up the cause, and it's a bitter business. What was originally an anti-American Communist stunt has caught on everywhere, the argument being that, whether they are innocent or not and their innocence is taken for granted

[3] Paul Reynaud was offered the premiership a month later but turned it down, his argument being that the postwar average of French governments in tenure had been five months, and the Constitution must be reformed to assure eighteen months of governing.

generally, it has been a fearful miscarriage of justice to have "tortured them with hope" for two years. If they are convicted we are told to expect vicious anti-American riots.

The Dillions are becoming very popular and now I am convinced that Embassy entertaining is worth it, despite what I wrote to you earlier. Douglas when he first arrived talked to us about stag lunches and the occasional dinner party, but someone has persuaded them that showing the flag in Latin countries pays off, and the Dillions have thrown away their shyness. On Monday they had a reception for two hundred, last night a supper and dance in honor of the American ballet, four hundred people, today luncheon for twenty people, and tomorrow a dinner for thirty. Then they go off on an exhausting tour of the provinces. The ballet party was particularly successful. The American ballerinas arrived looking so young and fresh, dressed by Dior for the occasion, and due to the attractiveness of the Dillions, the gaiety of the orchestra (a discovery of Bill's), and the warm spring night, everyone stayed up very late. Phyllis looked lovely, although she and her two daughters and I had spent five hours that day on our feet doing the flowers, and her back must have been aching, as mine was; I had been at the residence all day, arriving home with eight minutes to dress for a pre-ballet dinner party of sixteen at our own house.

Please don't imagine that I harbor any illusions, nobody has his mind changed about the Rosenberg trial as a result of an Embassy party, but it is truly important that the Dillions should be known personally and appreciated for their tact and charm.

The coronation of Queen Elizabeth II was marred for me by the absence of Bill, who wasn't well enough to go to England and insisted that I should go alone. I thought of him all the time with an aching heart, for he would have so enjoyed the pageantry. However, coronation day was bitterly cold with heavy rain; it would have been dangerous for Bill. I wrote to him:

"At the last moment Isaiah Berlin gave me his ticket, which was much better than the ones we had. Everyone had been so alarming about the difficulties of moving about London that I got up at five and walked to the War Office in Whitehall. It had been raining intermittently all night and the people who had slept on the sidewalks must have been sodden and their blankets also, but they were smiling and cheerful, here and there one smelt frying bacon, delicious and surely illegal. My seat was in a window on the second floor of the War Office, the procession was to pass directly below us. It was a long wait, but Marietta and Ronnie were with me and our excitement and anticipation kept us going. You saw it all on television but what I minded your missing was the almost electric sense of joy that exuded from the millions of people massed along the route and reached us in our second-story window. After all these long dreary postwar years the English had something to cheer about and for several hours they made the most of the glamor and the colors and the romantic coaches, the bands and the scarlet-coated outriders. Westminster Abbey we saw only on television, as you did, but I felt tears in my eyes several times.

"That night I went to a big party at the French Embassy, the ladies in their finest dresses and diamond crowns and the men covered in orders and decorations. Despite the long day euphoria was still with us and except for the constant misery of missing you it was great fun. This afternoon I go to stay with the Evelyn Waughs but have cut the visit to one night and a day and will be back with you soonest."

Evelyn Waugh had become our friend through the Duff Coopers, whom he visited in France fairly frequently. As a writer I admired him enormously, as a man we had only seen him charming and very good company. I was now to see the eccentric side. The day after the coronation I took the train down to Gloucestershire where I was met by Evelyn in a large Rolls-Royce with a chauffeur, clearly hired for the occasion. For reasons that I could not fathom he had been so bitterly anti-coronation that he hadn't come up to London for the occasion or permitted his children or his wife to do so, nor were they allowed to look at television. So my surprise was great when we turned a corner and saw a huge arch with "God Save the Queen" written across it, and Evelyn said, "Welcome to Pier's Court, and do you like my arch?" I said that the arch was beautiful but had I misunderstood Evelyn's sentiments? He said that I had not, but he preferred to celebrate the coronation in his own way, the next day, so the arch had gone up that morning.

In the drawing room of the very pleasant house we found Laura, Evelyn's wife, lying on a sofa with a leg in a cast, looking most unhappy. It appeared that she had broken the leg fairly recently. "Don't worry, I'll be all right for the party tonight," she said to her husband in the tones one might employ on the steps up to the scaffold. Horrified, for I had been told that I would be alone with family, I said, "What party?" Evelyn reassured me by saying that it would in fact be just the family, and not to worry. I went up to dress in the very simple long-sleeved evening dress I had brought with me and came down to the most extraordinary scene. All the children were lined up in their best clothes, faces shining in anticipation. Laura was wearing a ball dress and a tiara, Evelyn a white tie and decorations. It could have been Buckingham Palace. I felt underdressed and a fool. Poor Laura struggled to the kitchen, crutches, ball dress, and all, and in a few minutes a gong rang and Evelyn offered me his arm to go in to dinner. As I never saw a servant presumably Laura did it all, most ably, the food was delicious. At the end Evelyn, who was evidently casting himself as Lord Curzon or any other great proconsular figure, made a speech about Queen, country, and Empire straight out of Kipling. The children looked astonished. One of them said, "But you wouldn't even let us look at television yesterday!" Then came the warning of my downfall. Evelyn announced that I would give a speech describing the coronation. ("Mrs. Patten was in Westminster Abbey watching the Queen's liege lords drop to one knee as they rendered homage to her.") Oh, the fiend. Of course I had been nowhere near the Abbey, but with all those eager children's eyes turning to me I could do only one thing, which was to describe the glorious scene as I had viewed it on television. I did it very badly, but they were a spellbound audience. I shall never know what the point of all this was. Perhaps Evelyn had felt sorry for his children, who had missed a great event, and just used me because I was at hand. Or perhaps it was a joke to make fun of me. He was a strange man. The last time I saw him he was carrying a huge old-fashioned ear trumpet, into which one was asked to shout. I don't know if he were really deaf or not.

The next morning another Evelyn emerged: Evelyn Waugh the country squire. He appeared wearing heavy tweeds and carrying a shooting stick and we climbed into the Rolls. Laura with her poor leg in its plaster cast sat in the back with me beside her, Evelyn sat in front with the chauffeur. The object of the drive was to show me the countryside, which is very lovely, and at the end to stop at Stanway, one of the most beautiful houses in England. Throughout the morning Evelyn carried on a monologue about the farms we passed. As I don't know oats from rye I couldn't judge the accuracy of his views, but I suspected that Laura, sitting silently beside me, knew a lot more about agriculture than he does, as she loves the country and really lives in it, and suits it, and it her, whereas Evelyn wears an urban air, despite the tweeds. They dropped me at the station and I proceeded to London and then immediately to Paris, where my coronation souvenirs made a hit with the children, especially a tiny replica of the Queen's coach.

The summer of 1953 was a sad time, as Bill's mother was dying of cancer in Lenox, Massachusetts. We divided our time between her and my mother in Maine. In September we had to go to Washington, trembling as there were rumors of cuts in the Paris Embassy staff and we feared for Bill's job. Fortunately the State Department was merciful and he was safe for a year or two more. The children and we spent our last night at Marietta's and Ronnie's lovely house in New York and then flew back to Paris.

4 Rue Weber, Paris
October 10, 1953

Paris is coming to life again—cooler days, cars crashing around the Etoile, Schiaparelli clipping into crisp bolts of satin, the state of the nation blacker than ever, everything in fact as usual.

Nanny has left and we have a new governess for the children, Mademoiselle Oger. She is sweet and the children got through the trauma of change remarkably easily. They love the stories she tells them and she reads to them a great deal, also is helping Billy learn

Winston Churchill and
Odette Pol Roger, Chantilly, 1947

Duff Cooper, Chantilly, 1948

Susan Mary Patten

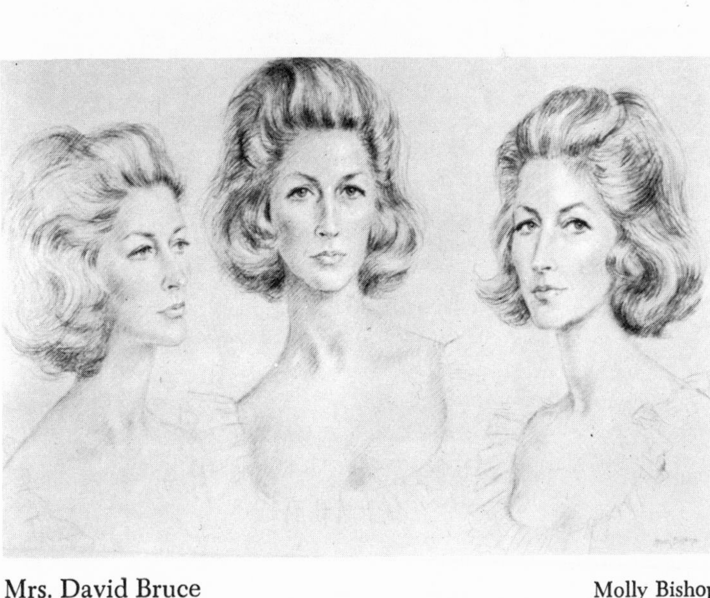

Mrs. David Bruce

Molly Bishop

Mr. and Mrs. C. Douglas Dillon, Paris, 1953

Lady Diana Cooper, Chantilly

Sir Cecil Bea

Lady Diana Cooper as Cleopatra, Bestegui ball, Venice, 1951

Susan Mary Patten

Duff Cooper and Susan Mary Patten,
Volpi ball, Venice, 1951

Salon, Palazzo Labia, Venice, 1951

Marietta Tree, 1967

Patrick Litchfield

Mother and Billy, Senlis, 1949

Billy and Anne, Beaulieu, 1955

Billy and Anne, overlooking the Seine, 1954

Bill Patten and Billy, Senlis, 1959

Billy, Britanny, 1956

Bill Patten, Bar Harbor, Maine, 1950

Susan Mary Patten

Anne, Paris, 1959

Drian

Anne, Billy, Lyndon Baines Johnson,
Washington, D.C., 1961

Joseph Alsop, Washington, D.C., 1961

Ollie Atkins

to read himself. He practically can read now, both in French and English.

We lunched today with the new Supreme Commander and his wife. General Norstad is about fifty and looks about twenty-five, one can hardly believe the four stars. She is an attractive San Franciscan, and they live in a hideous modern villa at St. Cloud, furnished richly in the inevitable boring style. One of our Air Force privates was on duty at the gate, the servants are men from the French Air Force, except the cook, who I should think was German, from the food, which was excellent but not French. General Norstad is immensely international in his outlook and so popular with our Allies that I should think he risks getting into trouble with our own military establishment. General Gruenther had made an optimistic statement in America about the NATO defenses despite the Russians having the hydrogen bomb; Norstad said that every word of the statement was true, which was encouraging to hear from him, as one cannot imagine not believing what he says, he has a quiet but impressive personality.

Duff and Diana are very excited about the publication of his autobiography, *Old Men Forget*. The other day Duff read to us some of the things he didn't put in for lack of room. The following is an excerpt from a dispatch written when he was Ambassador. It's such beautiful English that I cannot resist copying it for you.

> The French mind, shaped by tradition yet contemptuous of authority, tenacious of history yet avid of novelty, easily inflammable and coldly logical, capable of the loftiest idealism and the most cynical materialism, ever changing, yet in some respects unchangeable, is not easy to portray and impossible to photograph.

4 Rue Weber, Paris
November 2, 1953

You and Ronnie must have been as saddened as we were by Gerry's death.[4] He was a wonderful friend, and I have never known

[4] Gerard Koch de Gooreynd.

anyone more brave. The funeral was a short requiem mass in the Farm Street church, filled with truly grieving faces. I shall miss him always.

We spent Sunday at Randolph Churchill's. He, too, had loved Gerry. He took us to tea at Chequers with his father and mother. Sir Winston looked very frail and very, very old but his mind was alert and quick. Lady Churchill put me beside him at tea and I trembled as I have always been such a failure with him, but this time was much easier as he was in a very good humor. We talked of *Quentin Durward*, by Walter Scott, which he had been reading all day for the first time, with great pleasure, then of his horse, Pol Roger, named for my friend Odette. This led to France. He said that people are too impatient with modern France, forgetting her losses of 1914–18, which had been greater than England's, and that she has not recovered, so the younger generation should not judge her harshly. That Paul Reynaud did the best he knew how during the summer of 1940 at the time of the fall of France but made some deplorable mistakes; however he liked Reynaud and would like to see him in power again. That de Gaulle was a tragedy, he had such very good points and such possibilities. Then he spoke about the Continent today and said that he had never meant that Europe should be a federal state, no matter what people pretended he had meant. He wanted a united Europe but not a federal state. (I suppose he meant a grand alliance, not the "one Parliament-one government" Europe of Jean Monnet's dreams.) Then he went back to his affection for France, and I only wished that Odette could have been there. I think that from the talk one hears in London he must be the only Englishman left who believes in France. Fred Warner was saying here last night that while the British have always thought themselves superior to the French in every other way (character, ability to govern, etc.) they have considered the French cleverer than they are and that this continued until about last year, when the poverty of modern French literature, painting, architecture, philosophy has been realized across the Channel (see the depressed reviews of the pro-French critics—Connolly, Raymond Mortimer, Nicolson). So, now, the English think that they are more clever than the French, as well as better people; and there is no holding their impatience with France and their self-satisfaction. I don't know if this is true—or a good thing.

I long to see the result of the New York elections tomorrow. Don't write till later, for you must be exhausted; but I would love to hear your observations.

In Paris, we talk only of the two British diplomats who seem to have defected to the Soviet Union. Did you know them? Bill and I feel very lowly not even to have heard of them. It appears that Joe Alsop kicked Burgess, if not McLean too, out of his house in Washington ages ago.[5] The story fascinates me and varies every time I hear it. Did Mrs. McLean join him because she could not face returning to England for the sake of the children (of course to be known at school as the traitor's sons), or could she simply have felt that life in Switzerland was too dreary because of her mother-in-law, an American dipsomaniac, and that anything would be better? All is theory, no facts yet; but for the moment I am hypnotized by the case, partly as Bill's wife and anything may happen any time in the Foreign Service, and partly because of the human interest. Do you know the Lees Mayalls in the British Embassy here? He had his leg broken in Cairo by Donald McLean and now has a corner on him like Hugh Trevor Roper had on Hitler, if you remember 1947. I suppose the Mayalls can talk of something else, but I haven't heard it yet; and this is my fault, for I lead them on. They now recognize me as an old fan, not lightly put off with old stories, such as the one about the Egyptian lover of Mrs. McLean. So, every time we meet, they come up with something new. I think it has quite gone to their heads—and why not—for on Tuesday the Lees Mayalls led into the Frank Gileses' dinner McLean's brother! I was there, and it was as if the president of the Women's Poetry Club of Des Moines, Iowa, had produced T. S. Eliot.

He was half drunk, rather charming, and so neurotic that the Gileses' lovely mahogany table shook with his twitching, and he had even slammed the door of Lees Mayall's own Jaguar on its owner's leg, just not breaking the bone. So Lees was able to say laughingly, "I just might have had my leg broken twice by

[5] This caused a great sensation. Both Burgess and McLean were well known in Washington.

McLeans." The brother left the table before dessert, mumbling excuses. The Mayalls, taking their second helpings of chocolate profiteroles, explained that no wonder the poor man was nervous, as he had to meet Mrs. Dunbar (Donald McLean's mother-in-law), who was arriving from Switzerland to accuse the McLean family of having forced her daughter to go behind the Iron Curtain by ghastly cruel behavior to her.

Bill and I are fascinated by the case and will keep you in touch with the gossip here if it interests you. Tony Rumbold[6] really knew and loved McLean; he is haunted by it and extracts no juicy relish.

Burgess died in Moscow about three or four years ago in rather sordid, sad circumstances. Donald McLean still lives there and has a small job in the Institute of World Economics and International Affairs, as an expert on Britain. His son Fergus returned to England and is a student at London University. His wife Melinda left him and married Philby, the British-born spy who defected to Russia a few years after Burgess and McLean. Donald McLean is listed in the Moscow telephone book and is delighted to see English visitors; they find him rather sad and lonely. It is established that he was recruited into the Communist Party during his student days at Cambridge.

Château de St. Firmin
Chantilly, France
December 27, 1953

We have had the happiest Christmas ever. Diana and Duff lent us this house, and we had the dear Bob Joyces[7] and Cy and Marina and the Sulzberger children, plus our own (Billy so excited over his two-wheeled bicycle), then Joe Alsop joining us just back from Indochina. Jane and I came down ahead with Nicholas, our old chef, who loved shopping with Jane and me for our Christmas fare in the

[6] Sir Anthony Rumbold appeared to be a British diplomat out of a Broadway play. The adjectives "languid," "tall," "handsome" spring to mind. Using few words, he is in fact sharp as a fox and very funny. Bill and I were devoted to him.

[7] Robert P. Joyce was political counselor at the Embassy.

local market. I think of this usually as a summer house, but it's even more beautiful full of holly and pine, with every fireplace blazing and the view across the lake to the beech forest diamond clear. We played parlor games and walked miles down the long allées of the forest, empty but for the ghosts of the Condés and the very live and active race horses working out, for it wasn't cold enough to freeze the ground. The Chantilly dialect always amuses me, for the trainers and boys still speak a sort of English which goes on from generation to generation. "Morning, madam, fine day to be out." They couldn't possibly carry on if one engaged in conversation.

Joe was interesting about Indochina. Our people in Paris do not agree, but he considers a place called Dien Bien Phu crucially important. I had not heard the name of the fortress or seen it in the press—French or American. Joe says that it is considered impregnable by the chief French planners, but he has his doubts and for the first time I began to wonder if we are going to run the risk of becoming involved. Up to now, the French have emphatically resisted such a thought.

We return to Paris for a big dinner at the Bruces' but will be back here, the same happy party, for New Year's. Diana and Duff, Christmasing with her family in Wales, sail for Jamaica next week. They telephoned, sounding so pleased by our euphoric descriptions. Diana for some reason doesn't want to go; he is looking forward to it. I pray that your holiday went as beautifully as ours did.

P.S. from 4 Rue Weber, Paris, France

I forgot to mail this, so before returning to dear Chantilly for our New Year's party, I thought it worth adding a curious and worrying political episode the day after the Bruce dinner, which was candlelight and happiness. Joe came in to say good-by late in the afternoon to find me reading to the children. Usually the best of godfathers, he seemed abstracted and rather eager to get rid of Billy and Anne. On their retreat, he asked me if I would take notes and report a conversation he had just had with Bidault to the Embassy, as he did not feel he could publish his piece without informing the State Department.

The gist of the piece was that the Indochinese situation is far worse than the public knows. If the facts were out, the government would fall and Bidault himself would be stoned in the Place de la

Concorde. Despite the optimistic denials of the French government, they will soon lose the war without American help, and he didn't mean just economic help. The army has lost confidence in its generals and its government at home, and there is not much time to lose.

Joe then left; I rang up Bill and said that I had what I feared sounded like an "Eyes Only" telegram for the Secretary which ought to go out to Washington tonight. He got hold of Bob Joyce, who is in charge in the Ambassador's absence, and the message went out. Mr. Dulles will be very cross indeed, and Joe's column will make a sensation, and there will be one hell of a row in the Chambre followed by a denial by Bidault, and everyone will say that Joe's French wasn't up to the interview, and it will be forgotten; but I feel sick. Joe is an absolutely first-class reporter and would make no mistake on anything as crucial as this. His French is quite up to following the Foreign Minister. A trial balloon like this is a dangerous sign, it seems to me. That place, Dien Bien Phu, that Joe was talking about over Christmas is never mentioned here, but I don't like the sound of it, nor do I like the fact that not so long ago Bill and I were at a political luncheon, at which I sat by Michel Debré,[8] who is said to be a coming man, who told me that American help was the very last thing the French wanted or needed. You see, when the war started, class after class of the St. Cyriens were wiped out, as our elite regulars from West Point had been decimated at the beginning of Korea, and the war is so unpopular that the present poor wretches who are fighting it feel bitter and abandoned by Paris, and the present government isn't strong enough to ask the country for the national effort of support they need, yet too proud and too influenced by the rubber lobbies, etc., to admit that they might have to pull out. Hanoi, Hue, Danang, Bien Hoa, Saigon, the Mekong Delta, and many other names have been imprinted in one's mind if one lives here for what seems an interminable time, and while you know I am no isolationist, I feel queasy at the thought of us getting involved. Well, probably this is just depression caused by overdoing at Evangeline's and David's party. I am so looking forward to our lovely New Year's, walking under the beeches in the forest of Chantilly.

[8] Later Premier.

• 1954 •

Château de St. Firmin
Chantilly, France
January 3, 1954

I know how desperately sad you and Ronnie will be feeling, for you were so close to Duff. We got the first bad news here on New Year's Eve, as we and our house party were preparing for a sort of dinner dance that night to be held here. Diana radioed me that Duff was desperately ill and that the ship was turning back for Spain. She wanted Dr. Varay to meet them, with an air ambulance. This was arranged, heroically, by Bill, who somehow got Dr. Varay in Florence on holiday and the British Ambassador in Madrid. But at 8 P.M., John Julius called us from London that the Foreign Office had received news that his father had died, following severe hemorrhaging. The Royal Air Force is sending a plane to Vigo, the inaccessible port they are in, to bring Diana and Duff's body to London. One felt so terribly sorry for Norah Fahey, the dear secretary, who is with us, and brave as a lion. We went on with our party; the guests besides the house party were close friends and neighbors, Mary and Alain de Rothschild, etc.

The next day we were all preparing to disband and return to Paris, when we heard that England was fogged in, and that Diana, after a seven-hour flight, would be landing at Le Bourget, and wished to sleep here at Chantilly. The Frank Gileses and Bill and I met the plane. It was a cold, cold night, and the airfield seemed large and lonely as the tiny plane circled and landed. Diana came down the steps looking like an angel from Chartres cathedral, very beautiful, very calm. She introduced us to the English crew, who were nearly as numb with cold as she, for they had been flying at twelve thousand feet without heat. We started for the cars, flashlights and newspapermen a bore, but Kitty handled that so well, by flinging herself against Diana, arms outstretched, and walking backwards to our car. Frank stayed behind to speak to the Embassy men about the guard of honor and the Union Jack on the plane's small surface, then we all returned to this house, and Diana stayed up for dinner with us. The Gileses and the Joyces were the greatest help. We talked brightly of Oscar Wilde and whether there is still fox hunting on the Rock of Gibraltar and of the Knights of Malta. Bill was just perfect; she clung to his light but loving touch. She was particularly disturbed about the trouble she had caused Norah's holiday and our party. Norah and I waited with her by her bed until the sleeping pills began to work, which was, mercifully, very soon. About seven, she sent for me and asked me to remind her of a quotation, which I couldn't do, so I got the book and read it to her. I wish I could remember it, for it was lovely—about being very cold and alone but not mattering because the Elysian fields are warm. Then she said, sitting up, practical as always, "This is no good, Susan Mary, you and I reading poetry, it would be better to have breakfast."

The weather being clear, they got off to London later that day.

4 Rue Weber, Paris
January 10, 1954

I moved out of Chantilly a couple of days after my last letter to you, having helped Norah Fahey a little bit with her heavy task of handling the mail, the telephone, and the press. The press, by the way, has been magnificent about Duff both in France and in England, with the exception of *The Times,* which published an obituary that I haven't seen, but which seems to have annoyed everyone. Frank and Kitty Giles had to entertain the editor of *The Times,* for which Frank is the Paris correspondent, and I am told that Kitty said to him at a dinner party that Duff's friends had no intention of bothering to defend him to *The Times,* but that it had given them pleasure that the newspaper he had so despised in his life should be despicable at his death. The next day Frank Giles filed a news story from Paris stating simply and accurately that Paris was stunned by Duff Cooper's death and quoting some of the French press tributes. At the end he remarked that no French statesman's loss would have been more profoundly felt, and that the news from Paris today was the grief of the French for the loss of their friend. *The Times* published this article in full and prominently, and a week later Frank still has his job, thank goodness.

We took the Golden Arrow to England with Norah and were met with a message from John Julius asking us to come around at once. We found him in bed with the flu and Diana sitting cross-legged before the fire exactly like herself, and the little flat full of people. The train for Belvoir where the funeral would take place was to start at twelve noon the next day. John Julius paid me the great compliment of asking me to come over to the flat early in the morning, Evelyn Waugh to be the other companion. I found Diana still incredibly under control, and Evelyn was delightful. Bill and Kitty Giles picked me up and off we went to Belvoir in two special cars attached to a fast express to Grantham. The party was like a Chantilly party, utterly ill assorted, our only link our mutual affection for Duff and Diana. Lunch on the train, arrival at Grantham in a blinding snowstorm, and a bus to meet us. It seemed so odd to see so many top hats bouncing up and down in a bus driving through remotest Rutlandshire. At Belvoir it was impossible to see the castle, Diana's home, with its towers and battlements, and the bus got hopelessly stuck on the drive. Diana's nephews, two extremely handsome young men with white faces and black hair, the Duke of Rutland and Lord John Manners, then took over and the elderly and the frail were put into cars. Thank God, Bill, about whom I had been frantic, was forced into one of them. The rest of us walked. It was impossible to tell where one was—Valhalla? Great pine trees laden with snow, and the only noise our footsteps. At last a tiny building in the park which they call the Mausoleum, a sort of chapel. On either side of the walk leading to the open door were masses of spring flowers, casually distributed, half covered with snow. The service was short and very beautiful, afterwards we watched the burial, in the snow, just outside the little building. Then we walked to the castle, only two hundred yards, I suppose, but one couldn't see it until one was just under the battlements, when it loomed, immense and dramatic, in what was by now twilight. Inside, the Duke of Rutland, who ordinarily lives in a corner, had done wonders. Big rooms open, fires blazing, tea and drinks. After a while we hoped that someone would announce that it was time to leave for the southbound train, instead of which the Duke announced with amazing calm that the train was very late and might not get through the snowstorm at all, if so he would be charmed to put us up for as long as we cared to stay, that it was no trouble to open forty bedrooms. Everyone murmured "How kind," with the look of trapped rats, except for one very snobbish gentleman from Paris who looked delighted. I had noticed him on the train, having the time of his life making friends with Cabinet ministers and duchesses. We eventually did get back to London that night, exhausted and sad.

In the morning we picked up Odette Pol Roger, who had come over from Paris, and went together to the memorial service at St. Margaret's, Westminster. It was an icy, clear day with sun, which came through the windows just as Big Ben struck twelve and the service began, and sun seemed to fill the church at the end when the organ played the March of the Grenadier Guards. The big church was full of people who cared, once again as varied as one of Diana's parties. Near us I recognized Vivien Leigh, Isaiah Berlin, the purser from one of the Golden Arrow boats, and the Duchesses of Devonshire and Buccleugh. Later, before returning to Paris, we went to see Diana and found her breaking down fast, which is probably healthier than the composure she had shown till then, but I cannot bear to think of the sadness of her lonely future. Thank goodness the book is selling like hot cakes and should make real money—the English press is making a lot out of the last paragraph. . . .

> Life has been good to me and I am grateful. My delight in it is as keen as ever and I will thankfully accept as many more years as may be granted. But I am fond of change and have welcomed it even when uncertain whether it would be for the better; so, although I am very glad to be where I am, I shall not be too distressed when the summons comes to go away. Autumn has always been my favorite season, and evening has been for me the pleasantest time of day. I love the sunlight but I cannot fear the coming of the dark.[1]

[1] From *Old Men Forget* by Duff Cooper.

4 Rue Weber, Paris
February 14, 1954

We saw Bidault last night at a dinner at the Embassy. He was very cheerful because of Dulles' speech comparing him to Abraham Lincoln. Goodness, how heavy-handed Mr. Dulles is. It is only a few months since he talked of "agonizing reappraisal," in other words hinting that we would get out of Europe if the Europeans wouldn't cooperate. The last time I saw Duff Cooper was just before Christmas when he asked me to help him with his Christmas shopping. We came out of Dior's triumphantly carrying a beautiful green velvet bag for Diana that we thought she would love and stopped at a café opposite to have a drink before he left for London. Duff, pro-American and seldom critical of us, was very worried about Dulles. He said that blackmailing the French is the height of stupidity, it never works, and gave me some examples of what has happened in history when people have tried the Dulles technique. Now here we have Dulles swinging like a massive pendulum the other way, giving the cartoonists great pleasure as they draw Dulles and Eden presenting France as the linchpin of Europe and Bidault saying modestly that he has malice towards none.

Do my letters sometimes sound hysterical? Perhaps it would be better if I didn't care so passionately about so many things. Diana and Kitty Giles tease me about my morning telephone calls, claiming that in exactly the same tone of agony I wail, "Oh, Diana, there are posters[2] all over Paris of Eisenhower with every tooth an electric chair, and Spaak told Bill that even he is worried about Europe, and Nanny is so cross to me again and I can't placate her, what am I to do?"

Here comes a morale-building story instead of a wail—it concerns little Abbé Pierre, the priest who has persuaded the Parisians to give and give during the recent weeks of bitter cold. Being an avid newspaper reader, I had been following Abbé Pierre for some time and on Monday morning I read such a desperate little story in *Le Figaro* about his tent on Mont St. Geneviève in the Latin Quarter

[2] The posters reflected the vicious anti-American feeling during the Rosenberg case described in an earlier letter.

that I nipped over. It was an impressive but pathetic little effort at this early stage, the tent tiny and overcrowded, no heating, and the tired volunteers were shoveling straw over the bundled rags that were people. It must have been about twelve degrees Fahrenheit. There seemed little that I could do there so I came home and did a lot of telephoning to friends, which was quite unnecessary as the evening papers carried the story and Abbé Pierre himself went on the air appealing for more tents, and for volunteers with private cars who could carry people to shelters. In the middle of my telephoning Mademoiselle appeared asking me if I could spare a moment to consider the problems of 4 Rue Weber. The pipes on the nursery floor were frozen, Anne had a pain in her ear and a temperature, and Billy didn't look too well either. This dashed my spirit considerably, as you know how much easier it is to do good away from one's own home. On account of my poor children I didn't leave the house that night, but Elise and Pierre Bordeaux-Groult describe it vividly.

They drove to the Place du Panthéon in the Latin Quarter, laden with blankets, only to find that the scene, so deserted when I had been there in the morning, now resembled the Place de la Concorde at rush hour. So many cars had responded to the appeal that the police were turning away the latecomers like Elise and Pierre. Returning along the Seine, they saw a man lying on the sidewalk, over one of those vents through which the tepid air from the subway below escapes.[3] He turned out to be a professional *clochard* or tramp, who lived all the year round under bridges, and he said that he didn't want to be taken to a shelter. Pierre argued with him, pointing out that he would die if he lay there all night, the tramp became lyrical (he was a little drunk) and quoted Ronsard to the effect that the earth was his bed, the skies his cover, and that while he appreciated the kindness of the Bordeaux-Groults he wished they would go away. They drove off, feeling very foolish, and after a few hundred yards they decided to go back to give him some money. The tramp said wearily, "What is it now?" but accepted

[3] The tramps, or *clochards,* of Paris were a special tribe in the fifties. The police estimated that there were three thousand or so of them, generally rather proud and often poetic. About twice a year they were dragged in for a bath and delousing, but they were considered harmless and the police seldom interfered with them.

some money, giving back change as he found Pierre's gift too generous. The only result of this evening was that the next day Pierre himself was in bed with a high fever.

4 Rue Weber, Paris
February 1954

This week the French Academy voted to put *le bluff* in the dictionary. Another word that will shortly join it is *drive*, used as a noun. Today at lunch I overheard René Mayer, the former Prime Minister, tell Bill in French that the present government hasn't got the *drive* to force the Assembly to vote for E.D.C., adding that Monsieur Laniel, the present Prime Minister, lacks guts (*manque le guts*).

We dined last night with an American friend who is at NATO and I sat between two Germans, the first time that has happened. It's absurd, but I felt a slight chill although they were both nice. One was Von Walther, a diplomat, the other was General Speidel, who had been Rommel's chief of staff. The latter looks like a very mild-mannered history teacher and has the reputation of being extremely tough. It is he who will make the new German army if there is one. We got off to a poor start as he began the conversation by complaining about the French. I soon changed the subject, thinking that I simply could not sit in Paris moaning about the French lack of *drive* with a German. He talks like a European and said he dreamed of a European army as no nation can afford to rearm unilaterally again because of the cost of the new weapons. Later he told the whole table a fascinating story about Hitler in June 1940. The flower of the British army was cut off at Dunkirk and could easily have been decimated by the Germans. Speidel and the other generals were waiting for the order from Berlin. It never came, in spite of frantic telephone calls to Hitler, and the frustrated Germans had to watch the evacuation of British and French troops from the beaches. The explanation is that Hitler still thought that he could make a negotiated peace with England and had the loony idea that the best of the British army would understand Hitler's genius and be delighted to make friends. It hardly seems possible but that is what General Speidel said.

Then everyone talked about the Indochina war. One never sees pessimistic stories in the newspapers but there are rumors that General Navarre[4] is very worried and that he informs Paris that the French ought to negotiate peace and get out.

We are going to Rome for the wedding of Bill's niece, Flaminia, dreading it as apparently no one in the fiancé's family speaks a word of English or French, and it will be a struggle to be warm and gay during the festivities.

Athens
March 3, 1954

Bill's niece was successfully married in Rome; we were poor guests due to our lack of Italian, but it delighted Bill to see his niece looking so pretty and happy. He returned to Paris and I decided to join Diana Cooper as her traveling companion. We took the train to Brindisi and then a cheerful little Greek ship which stopped at Corfu. Diana, who had been so tired and sad in Rome, revived under the excitement of the journey, learning how to cope with drachmas and the language and above all teaching me a little about classical Greece. She knows the gods and goddesses and the myths as well as she knows her own family and is appalled by my ignorance. Coming back to our ship in the late afternoon after a drive around Corfu, she said happily, "How wonderful, I forgot myself for nearly an hour."

We were met here by Sir Charles Peake, the British Ambassador, who is a combination of all the Englishmen we like the most: the charming kind ugliness of Pug Ismay, the distinction of Lord Halifax, the sense of humor of Duff, and the latter's memory for poetry. She is equally nice and the atmosphere of their Embassy is the warmest of any I have ever visited. They seem busy enough, but it is always possible to drop everything for a day's picnic if someone describes some new wildflowers out near Delphi; one runs into the

[4] In fact we now know that, as early as January 1, General Navarre reported that he could no longer guarantee success, owing to the masses of arms China was sending to the enemy, and the whole tenor of his message was so discouraging that a strong government in Paris would have evacuated Dien Bien Phu at once. The weak government then in power did not dare to do so.

Ambassador in the hall, a volume of Keats in his hand. (Diana said, "The only nice embassies are the ones in which the Ambassador is always hanging about in the hall.") The staff seems to largely consist of attractive young bachelor attachés; I said to the Ambassador, "Who is that?" "Oh, that's one of my best men, there isn't a better helmsman in the whole Aegean and he paints remarkably well." Even the New York *Times* correspondent is an eccentric, charming character, most unlike the tense *Times* correspondents one knows in Western Europe. I said to him, "Do tell me, is there any news yet about the President's press conference on Zwicker-McCarthy?" "Oh," he said, "I believe there was something but I didn't read it. Have you been to see the church at Daphne yet?" Yet he is said to be a very good correspondent, just as Charles Peake is an exceptional diplomat. How attractive the slow, civilized tempo is . . . I never want to return to Paris or Washington and would give anything to move Bill and the children here.

Diana is a wonderful companion. Naturally a few bad moments when some unexpected view, word, or association with the past will break down her courage—at Olympia it was the intensely romantic beauty of the ruins in the sunset; they were covered with wild blue iris and red anemones and there was no one but us there, no guide, no signs, no turnstiles. Diana walked along sobbing piteously, I read the guidebook out loud, and she got better under my dreary monotonous voice. The next morning she looked badly but brightened at once on discovering that there was a hitch about our return to Athens; instead of the Peake Rolls-Royce we must return on our own by bus and train, eleven hours over appalling roads, and what was more a fearful storm was obviously about to break out. Diana was in her element, "Now we shall really travel." She got the hotelkeeper to write on a large card in Greek, "We do not speak, understand, or read Greek, and we must get to Athens, can you help us?" and stashed the card into the basket she always carries her most essential things in. By showing the card to everyone we did get back, Diana particularly pleased because the bus was jammed and every time it stopped the engine failed. At first cranking it worked but it became quicker to get it started by everyone getting out and pushing. The rain and wind were intense. Much to my relief at Patras, five hours later, we caught up with the Peakes again, who took us back to Athens, Diana and Sir Charles doing word games with immense enthusiasm, fresh as daisies. I was exhausted but I have never seen a place so lovely as Olympia, with its wild iris and red anemones. No one had prepared me for the delicious smells in Greece, especially thyme, which seems to grow wild everywhere.

A day or two later Diana's passion for doing things on the cheap combined with her pleasure in the bizarre got us into trouble. We returned to the British Embassy before lunch to find the Ambassador in the hall, as usual, but far from his usual equable self. "Diana, you can't do it." "What can't I do?" "You cannot go to Delphi with that terrible Frenchman; he is vicious and notorious and no one in Athens speaks to him." "But, Charles, it's his friend I know and like, she is charming." There was a row, which Diana won, and we went off to Delphi with the Frenchman and his girl friend, who was a lovely White Russian. The Frenchman may have been vicious, for all I know, but if so he makes up for it as a traveling companion by his wide knowledge of classical Greece. He was a splendid guide, and Delphi overwhelms one so that anything on a human scale seems insect-small and unimportant. We were forgiven by the Ambassador for our two days in bad company, and spent the last weekend cruising in cold, clear weather among the magical Cycladic Islands. Today, the last day in Athens, I woke with a terrible fear that I might not come back to Greece again, and the thought was unbearable, so I took a taxi to the harbor and there, with the help of our yachting companions, I took a caïque, a sort of ketch, sleeping five people, for this September. The price, with two in crew, is a million drachmas a day, or about thirty dollars. Oh, I do hope Bill will approve.

Twenty years later Diana and I were reminiscing about this trip and she reminded me of a facet of Sir Charles Peake that I had forgotten. He was unself-consciously, deeply religious—high Anglican—and during our long motor trips would interrupt the word games or the gossip to say gently, "Sorry, it's time for my meddies." So we sat in silence for half an hour or so while the Ambassador conducted his meditations, prayer book in hand, then he would return to us, smiling and refreshed. The Frenchman we went to Delphi with was Roger Peyrefitte, whose novel, *Les Ambassades,* about an orgy at the French Embassy in Athens had caused a tremendous scandal; since then he has written many another best-selling, scandalous novel. Diana thinks that indeed she should have thought twice about accepting his invitation to us but it did save the expense of a car to Delphi and even Diana had lost her passion for Greek busses. Diana had been brought up to be extremely economical; she has described in her own wonderful autobiography what it was like to be the daughter of the Duke of Rutland. One's feet ached doing the sights of Florence by tram and bus and one was very sparing of what one ordered for lunch; meanwhile her adored mother was buying columns, statues, whole pavilions of marble to be sent back to Belvoir Castle to embellish the park, and this order of priorities seemed natural to everyone concerned. Diana's grandfather was one of the first British noblemen to open his estate to the public on certain days; he greatly enjoyed this and didn't object to the litter afterwards or anything we would object to nowadays—preservation of the environment is not a Victorian phrase. What he did mind, terribly, was seeing ladies in the park who had let down their hair. How interesting this phrase is—to us today it means President Nixon letting it all hang out; to me since girlhood it means being frank. To Diana's grandfather it meant that the great hairpins that held up Victorian chignons (in the case of the rich the hairpins would have been made of tortoise shell, but surely black tin for the poor?) released masses and masses of falling beautiful hair (one's mind's eye swings with delight from Rossetti to Manet, from Burne-Jones to the girls on Madison Avenue and the Left Bank of Paris today) and to the Duke this was intolerably vulgar. Not sexually arousing, just vulgar.

4 Rue Weber, Paris
March 20, 1954

Leaving Athens, I was still immensely pleased with myself about the caïque for our vacation, but by Zurich the cold gray light of northern Europe had brought me to my senses and I felt that I had been very rash. Orly, where Bill met me, was freezing but he looked exceptionally well and was nearly as enthusiastic as I about the boat. It seems to him, as to me, the perfect vacation for him, no dust at sea, perfect weather, they say, and donkeys at all ports for the expeditions.

Billy has had the mumps, of which I knew nothing, but it was a light case and both children are flourishing. Billy, at six, loves having poetry read to him; the *Lays of Ancient Rome* go down well and so does *The Charge of the Light Brigade;* he doesn't understand much of it but the meter appeals to him.

The Battle of Dien Bien Phu gives a warlike atmosphere to Paris today; there are crowds at the newsstands and the papers carry black headlines, "Forteresse Isolée [Fortress Isolated]." How extraordinary to think that just three months ago we had never heard of the place until Joe Alsop told us about it.

4 Rue Weber, Paris
April 27, 1954

Such a strange week: each day the news is worse and each day Paris is more entrancing. The spring came late after a cold winter but last week the chestnut trees came out, the sun shone every day, and the green of the Avenue Roch looks exaggerated, theatrical as it always does. The siege of Dien Bien Phu, like childbirth, seems worse than you expected although you had been preparing for the pain. It isn't like the war, one doesn't rush for the latest news on the radio and sometimes a whole luncheon or dinner goes by without anyone mentioning it, but I think it is in everyone's mind all the time. What the public reaction will be to the fall of the fortress, no one knows. Of course General Navarre will be kicked out as scapegoat. The people really responsible are his intelligence, who predicted that the big guns could not be brought up through the jungle. Louise de Rougemont read me a letter today from one of her friends in Tonkin. He had gone out last week to be General de Castries'[5] chief of staff but arrived too late to be parachuted in. The

[5] General de Castries was in command at Dien Bien Phu. Later I met him at a dinner at the Bordeaux-Groults' and summoned up my courage to ask him what would have been the outcome if we Americans had intervened. He said to feel

letter was only three days old. He said that the Rougemonts would be very proud of the way the French are fighting, "our young men are hanging on with unimaginable courage . . ." but spoke sadly of the fact that the only passion left is in the French and Ho Chi Minh's troops. Of course the worry here is that the Vietnamese from the south, fed up and discouraged, will turn against the French and cut off escape routes to the sea if things get worse. Twice since 1945 they have risen against French outposts. Louise also knows the nineteen-year-old nurse who is cut off in Dien Bien Phu, the only woman there, who is said to possess unusual courage and unselfishness.

Bad as the nightmare is here, I am almost sorrier for those men at Geneva who have to make the decisions. Last week was overwhelmingly busy. Lots of the people with Dulles were old friends so we had two dinner parties in succession here and were a good deal at the Embassy. Mr. Dulles is apple-cheeked and fresh, his assistants gray-faced and lined. On the whole Foreign Ministers seem to bear up best; on Saturday we saw Eden and he looked young and well.

This was a strange and frustrating evening. The Jebbs had very kindly asked us to dine to meet the Edens quietly on Saturday; there were just to be some of the staff and the John Hopes (he is a very nice young M.P. and she is a friend of mine—Liza Maugham, daughter of Somerset Maugham). We arrived to find Eden explaining to Lady Jebb that he couldn't stay for dinner after all as he had to fly to England at once to see Churchill. This bombshell was treated with appropriate casualness, as if it was the most ordinary thing in the world, and dinner was provided for him and his two private secretaries on a card table while we had cocktails. Someone—I think it was his wife—asked if he would be back in the morning. He said no, that he probably would "ask the colleagues to come round, so as to keep them au courant," and everyone said, "Of course," "What a pity," and "Poor Anthony," even more casually than before. Lady Jebb had meanwhile summoned three grisly characters from the Foreign Office underworld to act as replace-

no guilt about this as intervention by bombers from the Philippines, as was suggested at the time, would have done no good to the besieged and quite possibly have started World War III.

ments for dinner, and in we went, smooth as the hollandaise sauce on the asparagus. I sat by Gladwyn talking about the French theater, imagine my frustration, but I don't know him well and dared not ask any questions. Bill had a pretty good idea and so did I why Mr. Eden had rushed to Chequers in the middle of the night and called two Cabinet meetings for an April Sunday, but it was not our place to notice as the English were treating it as an ordinary occurrence.

You may have seen Cy Sulzberger's piece of yesterday about the French asking for Allied help in their desperate situation. It is accurate, but God knows what will happen at Geneva. The French attitude is that the Nixon speech and other Administration statements of the last few weeks had led them to believe that we would intervene if things got worse. The English do not want to become involved. Forgive a long, badly written letter.

The feverish weekend above described as seen by Bill and me was the climax of a feverish month. Admiral Radford, chairman of the Joint Chiefs of Staff, was eager for direct intervention in Indochina using bombers. This plan was known as Operation Vulture. It never came off as collective action was essential and the British had been against it from the start. The reason for Eden's dash to England that Saturday night was to have the British Cabinet confirm his policy of nonintervention. In a way it was a relief to the President and the congressional leaders to be able to blame the British when Dien Bien Phu fell, for they were more prudent than Radford and Dulles. It was said at the time, and it has been published since, that Dulles offered the French two atom bombs to use themselves, to which Bidault replied that if the bombs were dropped in the Dien Bien Phu area the besieged would be as badly hurt as the attackers, and their use elsewhere might provoke general war. I don't know whether the above is true; one difficulty was that Dulles would break into French when talking to Bidault and his French wasn't up to conversation with the harassed, exhausted Foreign Minister. It worried the staff badly when occasionally the Secretary of State would lead Bidault off for a quiet chat on the sofa, without interpreters. More disturbing and more important than the Dulles-Bidault relationship was the

Dulles-Eden disharmony. Both were brilliant men, both spoke English, but Dulles thought that Eden was frivolous about important things, and Eden found Dulles moralistic about the same things. This lack of harmony between the two men became dangerous two years later, at the time of the Suez crisis.

As for Indochina, a sort of peace was established that same summer at Geneva, known as the Geneva Accords. The French Parliament approved the accords by 569 votes to 9, grateful for the end of an unpopular war.

4 Rue Weber, Paris
May 10, 1954

Such a wonderful green sweater for Billy—we are very grateful and the contents of the box surrounding the sweater provided endless excitement, the coloring books, the crayons and paper doll book and paper hats. The children think of you as a magician. "How did she get so many presents in one box?" And I wonder myself how you did. I wish you could see them as they are so much better company than last summer. Billy's reading is coming at last and Anne is fast on his heels—in the car he begins to spell out "ESSO" and Anne says, "Oh, say ESSO, I know it's that." I was told the other day by an older child that Anne was a famous conversationalist; they hang on her words. Her latest story was that she had been to America and Indochina, that her clothes came from Schiaparelli, and that her father fought the Mau-Maus in Kenya.

Bill seems well and hasn't taken cortisone for a couple of weeks, which is marvelous as he hates the bloating and other side effects of the drug. We heard the news of the fall of Dien Bien Phu three days ago just as we were preparing to go to dine with Elise and Pierre Bordeaux-Groult. There was nothing to do but go, the dinner had been planned weeks before for the Bill Paleys, who were as miserable as the rest of us. Strange that we foreigners should feel so shaken by the fall of a little French fortress in the jungle thousands of miles away. It was a quiet evening, as you can imagine, without political argument. Since I last wrote dinner tables have become battlefields. The most recent arrivals from the United States seem to think that public opinion at home would have supported intervention in Indochina with or without the English and I see that there is a lot of talk in the press about England having let us down. The English say, "How could we have supported Dulles in intervention when congressional approval was so uncertain, why did Dulles take the risk of threatening the Chinese Communists without being sure that he could get united action, why do Americans talk so much when every newspaper carries reports of the disagreements among their own chiefs of staff?" I change my mind three times a day, depending on whom I have last talked to. General Norstad is literally the last one, dining with him and his charming wife last night. His argument will, I think, be my final point of view on the sad subject. He thinks that the English were right and that we shouldn't be in Indochina. That we can't save it without general war, which American public opinion is not prepared for, that further aid and above all sending troops would only land us in an indefinite extension of the present tragic mess. He, incidentally, has been running the emergency transport service of the last month; you have probably read about how much we are doing carrying French troops in our Globemasters which have to do fifteen hundred or two thousand miles extra on account of that tiresome Nehru not allowing passage over India. Norstad, like everyone else in government service here, has been imploring Washington to make up its mind about Indochina in order to avoid an atmosphere of uncertainty and emergency when the crisis came. But, admittedly, no one thought that anything as dramatic and ghastly as Dien Bien Phu would happen. It is all awful, and one can hardly face the evening newspapers. The Dillons are superb. He looks white with fatigue at the end of the day and, although he is absorbed in his job and loves it, one wishes he had a little extra strength. They do all the official entertaining and going out that is necessary and are first rate at both, but I wish that they had a little energy left for fun, which hasn't been the case since his back trouble.

De Gaulle sounds not just difficult but rather mad. He told Cy Sulzberger, off the record, that if the E.D.C. passes he will make a revolution, and at his last press conference he said, "*Je suis la France* [I am France]" with such a demoniacal gleam in his eye that our friends who were there wondered if the next step might not be a kind doctor in a white coat appearing on the platform to lead him off quietly.

Did I write that we took the children to Chantilly to a little hotel for Easter and had a lovely time? Anne is a natural hotel child, making friends with everyone. We went to St. Peter's, the English church in Chantilly, for morning service, then to Diana, who had a brave house party of young people for John Julius and Anne, plus a splendid Easter egg hunt for all the children, Sulzbergers, Rumbolds, our own, etc. Prizes, great excitement, blue skies, daffodils and wild narcissi on the lawn and in the woods.

4 Rue Weber, Paris
June 1954

We have had two such lovely weekends, for come what may the French celebrate several holidays in May, which gives us long weekends, one spent fishing in Normandy, the river full of trout and Bill so happy to have one sport that he can still do; another weekend we drove down to Burgundy to stay with a friend with the improbable name of Chou-chou de Magenta, who lives in a very fine Louis XIV castle called Sully. Then we have had several successful family picnics. Billy's favorite book at the moment is *Treasure Island*, which I read aloud during the postprandial naps. Anne doesn't understand a word but anything that Billy admires she admires so she sits upright looking absorbed and watching his face to see when to laugh or be frightened.

Of course you will have followed the fall of the government. Mendès-France is young and dynamic, he doesn't speak well but his ideas are diamond hard and clear and although he is equivocal on E.D.C. he has promised to obtain a cease-fire in Indochina within a month and, if he does this, he will be a national hero.[6] You must be tired of my talking about E.D.C. but we will know one way or another, in a couple of months, whether the French will accept it and then I shall try not to mention it again. We are encouraged by the recent polls, probably partly a result of the blow of the fall of

[6] Pierre Mendès-France pulled off his promise to obtain the longed-for cease-fire and did become a national hero, following the Geneva Accords.

Dien Bien Phu, which left the French feeling sadly weak and isolated; most of the young certainly seem to want a European Defense Community and are fed up with chauvinism. It will be very interesting indeed to see what Mendès-France does; for some reason our people have never trusted him much, for despite his brilliance he is suspected of a lack of guts.

I am sending you a new novel by an eighteen-year-old writer, Françoise Sagan, unknown until this spring. She is said to have run it off during a month in which she had little to do, having failed her Sorbonne exams. *Bonjour Tristesse* is the name; it is remarkable in its almost eighteenth-century sparseness of language and yet rich in feeling, hauntingly so. She is possibly a great writer.

4 Rue Weber, Paris
July 15, 1954

Last night we went to a party at Eve Curie's to watch the fireworks from her marvelous apartment above the Seine. Newspapermen of all nationalities, people from NATO, diplomats from the Quai d'Orsay, everyone cock-a-hoop over Mendès-France's success at Geneva.[7] His feat of capturing the imagination of the French people in three weeks, his energy and ability are enormous. He is surrounded by a tight little group of able young men called "le Brains Trust" like the New Dealers around Franklin Roosevelt, and is beginning to be known popularly as P.M.F., like F.D.R. I asked the governor of the Bank of France what he thought about his character; he hesitated, then said, "*Je commence de croire qu'il y a tout de même de la pureté dans son cynisme politique* [I am beginning to believe that, all the same, there is a quality of sincerity in his political cynicism]."

Loelia Westminster gave us a splendid English weekend, with the main feature a ball of nine hundred people at Petworth, which many people think the most beautiful house in England. You remember the Turners of the interiors and the glorious golden misty ones of the park with the deer under the oaks? It was bitterly, bit-

[7] Conference of 1954 on terminating the Indochina war.

terly cold but at last I have got the solution for England in summer. I just took some heavy ski underwear to Balmain and had them fit my dress, which was of white organdy covered with roses, over the dear woolly underwear so that for once I wasn't quivering with goose flesh and screaming for warming whiskies. I spent a quiet evening with the Aldriches before Bill came over; Harriet is moving into the new residence in Regent's Park and is delighted with it. She is adored by the English, her kindness and her simplicity and her directness appeal to them no end and she is the only person I ever saw who can get away with wearing horn-rimmed spectacles with a tiara. She is a great Ambassadress.

How I hate the French mania for the summer holidays. Paris is so lovely in the summer, but even the nicest French, like our Mademoiselle, become like maniacs come July. Our trip to Dinard was typical. Gay departure from happy, cool Rue Weber at 8 A.M. with servants smiling and waving and crying, "Good holidays." The station a nightmare of families and children, Boy Scouts, nuns with orphans, nuns without orphans, orphans without nuns. Great heat, for the first time this year, and not a porter. Mademoiselle found the one porter, eventually, and as she is so much more distinguished-looking than I am, I, by remaining silent, was able to follow along and watch her tip him a sum which I would have been knocked down for offering and he went off smiling. Instant worry about lunch—it appears that I forgot to get tickets in advance for the dining car and now there are no more. I humbly suggest that I hop out at Le Mans, where we have twenty minutes, and buy sandwiches and fruit; Mademoiselle, shaken out of her usual perfect politeness: "Really, Mrs. Patten, we must nourish your little children on this long voyage." And dashes off, delighted, having bribed our way into the wagon-restaurant. The bribe was a hundred francs; I would have had to offer a thousand, at least, but I would willingly have paid two thousand not to have to sit down at 10:45 A.M. in a broiling-hot dining car to hors d'oeuvres, roast beef, potatoes, peas, assorted cheeses, then that terrifying weapon of the French, *la bombe glacée* with little cakes, followed by fruits, coffee, and of course washed down with claret. Dinard mercifully at three fifteen, hideous scene at the station as Mademoiselle disputes fare with taxi driver, who she says is a cheating Breton and all Bretons are cheats.

Who wanted to come to Brittany? The hotel is ideal, thank God, huge sand beach directly below our attractive and simple rooms, other guests all families with children. The weather is just like our Northeast Harbor, Maine, deep fog and very chilly. However, the children and I left Mademoiselle to unpack and went at once onto the beach, which was lovely; people with nets catching shrimp, fishing boats at anchor in the fog, dim and distant Maine-like islands. Suddenly Anne disappears, I am frantic for fifteen minutes—see her, at last, being led down the beach kicking and screaming by a policeman; her story was that she had seen a crab and followed it, only to lose us in the fog. Poor little Anne—she was much alarmed. Billy said coldly, "*Petite idiote.*" Back at the hotel I argue with the director about getting dinner early, earliest possible eight o'clock, at which hour we are alone in the huge dining room except for another American family, which includes attractive grandmother wearing print dress who says sadly that she would never have brought it had she known what the weather was like in Brittany. Billy and Anne very hungry but quite untired, sitting up as if they dined in hotel dining rooms every night. I do hope that we can make friends on the beach; then I can leave and commute between them here and Bill in Paris.

Bayreuth, Germany
August 29, 1954

Dinard is the greatest success, the children are brown, happy and surrounded by friends. On rainy days they take walks and collect shells. Anne is particularly popular in the beach events, and won a hundred francs the other day in a gymkhana, excelling in the potato race. I hated to leave them but Bill terribly needs this Greek holiday towards which we are heading. The last week in Paris was extremely tense; I shall never forget sitting on a bench in the Avenue Marigny with Evangeline Bruce reading the midday extra of one of the papers reporting how badly the debate was going in the Chambre des Députés. Her face was as calm as usual but she looked very tired—this battle is personal to the Bruces as well as an international issue. The weekend was full of drama, Bill happened to be duty officer as the telegrams and telephone calls flowed in. What a moment when old Adenauer[8] went down on his knees to Mendès-France, pleading that France should realize that if she refuses E.D.C. the chance to make Europe may never come again.

It was hard to leave Paris before the vote, but we continued with our plans. The end of the dream caught up with us sightseeing in the Hohenlohe Valley. This family had possessed two hundred castles in the beautiful wooded countryside; they now have three and we were to stay in one of them. We arrived about teatime to be greeted at the drawbridge by the housekeeper. She had been crying, she told us apologetically, because the news had just come over the radio from Paris that the Chamber of Deputies had turned down the treaty. Her despair was echoed by the other servants, some very young, and by Prince Constantin Hohenlohe, who is not young. They all felt the same bone-chilling apprehension about the future, i.e., nationalism could again become a force in Germany that might lead to war, and they told us that their bitter disappointment was shared by every generation but was particularly strong among the young.

Well, this will relieve you of my endless letters about the subject, I have been a bore going on and on about it, but you know what it's like to get caught up in a crusade.

Our German sightseeing is immense fun. We are well away from the cities and the sprawl of the Ruhr and lunched yesterday at Pommersfelden, a gigantic baroque schloss untouched by the war. The owner asked us if we were related to General Patton, and was disappointed when we weren't, because they owe him a great deal. When he arrived to occupy the schloss, he sent for the owners, told them that he absolutely hated the castle and everything in it, but that this was his personal taste, and as he could see that it was a sort of Versailles and that some people must think it very beautiful, he was issuing the strictest orders that nothing should be touched or looted. Nothing was, so they have twenty house guests staying right now and there isn't a chip off the gilding. I sat by the son of the house, young Prince Schönborn, whose principal interest it is to keep the place going, to have an American deep freeze in every farmer's house and two motorcycles and a car in every garage; his

[8] Konrad Adenauer, Chancellor of Germany.

logic is that Germany has been let down by France and ideology is out the window, so material success is what matters and Germans can outdo France economically given a bit of time. Too bad about the E.D.C. but now it's every man for himself.

I forgot to write that I drove the car from Paris to Frankfurt alone, in order to save time for the vacation—Bill took the plane and joined me there. En route I stopped at Cologne and stayed two nights with the Charles Ritchies. He is Canadian Ambassador to Germany and he and Sylvia are capable of making anything fun, but, oh, that Rhineland valley is depressing. The climate makes everyone feel tired all the time, in winter it's fog and smog, in summer it's smog. It also makes people neurotic, I think—Bill and I have had some rather odd conversations in Bonn and Bad Godesberg. But, as I say, it takes a lot to get the Ritchies down. One night I sat by an attractive man called Axel Vanderbusch, he is now at the Reichschancellery with Adenauer, has one leg, and had been one of the July 20 anti-Hitler plotters but told me about a very special plot of his own. Knowing Hitler's love of uniforms, he arranged to go to see him with a model of the newest uniform for the S.S.—with a bomb in its pocket. At the appropriate moment, he and Hitler were to be blown up together. All the arrangements were perfect, then the Allies bombed the storehouse containing all the new model uniforms and Hitler canceled the appointment. This sounds like a Japanese story from a bad film, but I believed it.

To my children

You and your children will find it difficult to understand our enthusiasm for that failed crusade, the European Defence Community, but at the time Bill and I thought it the last, best hope for the United States and Europe. I have described the gloom of 1946, 1947, 1948 when one really felt that the weakness of Europe might lead to an unraveling of every seam of civilization as we knew it. And I have written of our pride in the taking up of the challenge by the United States with the Marshall Plan, of NATO and of other successes. But the follow-up had to come from the Europeans themselves, Germany brought into the community, and the E.D.C. seemed a thrilling conception.

The Cold War seemed to us something that might become a hot war at any moment. It must sound simplistic to you, but the third world didn't matter very much then, Japan and Germany were recovering ex-enemies whom we hoped eventually to bind to us, China was a remote country, ravaged by civil war. We were obsessed with Russia, and at least wise enough to know that we alone could not contain Russia, so it was all-important to have a strong Europe. I don't want to give you the impression that as I went to fit a ball gown at Balmain's I wondered as the fitter stuck the pins in whether I would have a chance to dance in my new dress, but now and then that sort of thought did cross one's mind.

I'll quote a letter from a friend in Washington, that same year, to try to give you some sense of that long-ago time of tensions.

"This is to report that the U. S. Fleet is being gradually liquidated to raise a few million drachmas for the Patten caïque. It sounds like the precise remedy for the last year in the Pentagon, which I would happily trade for Piraeus right now.

"There is something about this spot that eclipses tomorrow's problems and magnifies yesterday's to such an extent that all of our time is spent trying to make what is already history *look* better.

"Topic A domestically continues to seethe with McCarthy, successful because he, alone, speaks for his side while there is no single St. George to do the job which is now spread amongst many with resultant varieties of pressure, conflicts of purpose, etc. It is a task of such proportions that it cannot be delegated and I hope the Boss will realize this.

"Internationally, your home continues to hold the spotlight. Certainly the next couple of weeks will be the important test of our relationship with France, as well as a test of whether you can make friends through diplomacy or must impose your will by A-bombs. Fortunately, we are reasonably well prepared militarily to do anything."

My correspondent, no Dr. Strangelove, was certainly not talking about using the bomb on France; the letter is undated but must correspond to the anguish of the spring of 1954, when many people felt that we must go to the aid of the French in Indochina.

You cannot imagine a war in Europe, conventional or nuclear, nor can you picture a Russian invasion of Western Europe. We could and did, and the smallest drama in Berlin sent shivers down our spines. The last time I was really frightened about Berlin was in 1961. Joe Alsop had attended the Vienna conference and I was in London to meet him; we went together to the christening of Princess Radziwill's baby and at a small party afterwards President Kennedy took Joe aside and told him privately just how tough Khrushchev had been. "It will be a very cold winter." Weeks later we were back in Washington dining at the Australian Embassy; after dinner I sat on the sofa by Robert McNamara, the Secretary of Defense, whom I had not met before. He kept looking at his watch and my heart sank, I felt I was boring this charming man to death, but it wasn't up to me to make the move to go, the room was full of grand people. At last I said, "I'm so sorry, Mr. Secretary—I know how tired you must be but Joe and I can't leave before all these ambassadors." He smiled—and no one has a more attractive smile than McNamara—and said, "It's not that—it's just that forty minutes ago a small contingent of American troops were to cross into Berlin via Checkpoint Charlie. If they hadn't made it without trouble I should have heard by now. Forgive me for being so distrait." This was very familiar language to me, the Cold War lingo, may it never come back.

At sea, aboard *Argo*
September 9, 1954

On Tuesday, Bill, Bill Gibson, and I flew to Athens from Milan, and the Gileses joined us in the evening from London; we had a smashing dinner on the eve of the cruise at a romantic harborside restaurant looking at the lights of Athens on one side and, on the other, the lights of the giant yachts in the harbor. Little *Argo* looks so small and shabby and pathetic next to Niarchos' *Creole*, Onassis' *Christina*, which carries an airplane on the deck, the Lopez yacht, and several others. Happily my group are wonderfully kind to me—if this trip is a flop it will be my fault as you will remember that I went mad in the early spring when I fell in love with Greece on my trip with Diana and engaged *Argo*, knowing nothing about boats. Much will depend on the Greek naval hero, Costa Tsallis, who accompanies us. So far so good. We have stocked the boat, and made friends with the three members of the crew, and should set sail tomorrow. Athens Harbor is like a cocktail party; we ran into Harry Brooks and Fulke Warwick, who took us aboard *Creole,* a beautiful three-masted black schooner furnished in Renoirs and Van Goghs. But one could hardly look at the pictures because of the frenetic excitement about a dinner that they were giving for the King and Queen that night. Fearful agonies about who would sit where and the atmosphere of high drama that precedes major Paris social events. The ship-to-shore telephones were buzzing from yacht to yacht, "My dear, I shall cut my throat. Dior forgot my black velvet belt. Have you got one?" Elsa Maxwell[9] seemed to be everywhere at once, and was the last person we saw as we sailed out to sea, looming down from the high stern of the Lopez yacht. She did wave, rather contemptuously. We don't look very grand in our dear, fat, lumbering caïque, deck piled high with cans of corned beef hash, whisky, Gibbon, Agatha Christie, Scrabble board, rubber mattresses.

Then, with fair favoring winds, we sped in our black ship across the wine-dark seas to Cape Sounion, where we rested below the Temple of Poseidon. (Forgive me, I read the *Odyssey* three times this summer. Frank Giles also knows it by heart, and the rest of the party have already told us that if we must speak Homer to each other we can jolly well go and sit together up in the bow; it's too much when we talk about honey-sweet wine when we mean a dry martini.) Enough wingèd words—we are off Cape Sounion, anchored below the glorious ruined temple, arguing hotly about our route just as we have been doing since March. The argument continued politely but with some increase of tension, until a vote was taken, and we are now buzzing along at eight knots an hour (sails and auxiliary) with W. Patten at the wheel, heading for the Cyclades. Bill is in a rage with me because I voted against Skyros, on which he is hell bent for some reason, although it is miles out of the way and Rupert Brooke's grave is five dusty hours by donkey. Except for this, he is utterly happy, hasn't coughed once, and adores the lazy life and the sun. It is neither too hot nor too cold, we lie on mattresses or deck chairs watching the sea and the headlands. At the moment we are passing Marathon and Frank and I have just been told that if we wish to lecture about what happened there we

[9] Elsa Maxwell was a tough old war horse who gave famous parties all over the world.

will be sent to the bow again. The naval hero seems not only competent but charming, and the cook is surprisingly good. Sleeping conditions are pretty terrible but what can one expect at thirty-three dollars a day, and the boat is immaculately clean. We shall be sublimely happy if it goes on like this.

In the air, between Athens
and Milan
September 23, 1954

We sailed into Athens Harbor last night, sunburned, healthy, and very happy. We wandered from island to island, anchoring each night in a different enchanting cove. Sometimes near a village to take on supplies, usually in a remote little bay where the only sound at night would be a shepherd playing his flute in the moonlight. The white island villages are inhabited by the kindest and most welcoming people; if one stops to admire a grape arbor the owner of the house comes out and insists on cutting off a bunch as a gift. Shopping was always an excitement—would there be eggs, or fish, oh, look, here comes Frank Giles with an octopus, good for him. If there was nothing we lived on American cans from the Athens PX and there never was a bad meal. Occasionally, we would go ashore to wash our clothes at a well in a biblical setting. For expeditions there were donkeys, so Bill never had to walk. We saw many beautiful things, had only three days of storm out of fifteen, and had only one row, which is remarkable if you could see the size of the boat. But I won't go on about it, we are landing and also other people's vacations are often a bore to hear about. My great happiness is Bill's look of health; we all swam three times a day yet he never seemed tired.

4 Rue Weber, Paris
November 9, 1954

You must forgive me for not having answered your fascinating letter, now nearly a month old. We did so enjoy having Ronnie here for a week, not only because we adore his company but it was lovely to hear about you and Frankie and Penelope. Frankie riding at Madison Square Garden!! I can hardly believe it, and feel nearly as proud of her as I do of you. Ronnie is also immensely proud of you and told everyone about your campaign job and when I said that several people had told me that you have never looked as beautiful as this year he said, so simply and nicely, that it was true.

I am enraged about some of the aspects of the election, but from what we can make out there was a liberal, anti-McCarthy swing and very few major disappointments? How interesting Joe Alsop's article is about this being a real success for Stevenson, but Stevenson, himself, is fed up with the sordid side of politics and unenthusiastic about running in 1956. True? I hope it's only temporary discouragement.

Bill has been riffed (State Department language for fired), and this time it is final. I have never admired him more. Of course, he hates it, as he doesn't want to retire yet, but not a word of self-pity. He will leave the Embassy on January 10, exactly ten years from the day he entered it, and what a ten years, with four ambassadors fighting with the State Department to keep him despite the wretched health reports. We think of staying here for a while, as there is more likely to be a niche for Bill here than at home. The doctor thinks that it would be much better for him to work and hopes, as I do, that the interval should not be too long. Just for a moment, he lost all of his old resilience and pep, but there is no one with such courage, and the morale will be restored once confidence in himself returns. The friends here are wonderful, and the World Bank might be a possibility.

Hôtel de l'Etoile
Chablis, France
November 28, 1954

You will be surprised by this address—Bill Gibson and Bill are guests of honor at a celebration of Chablis growers, it's a merry weekend, although hard on the liver.

You and Ronnie wrote me such wonderful letters, full of wise advice and encouragement. How blessed we are to have such friends.

The invitation to Barbados is wildly tempting but we feel that we shouldn't leave the children for too long this winter; Billy is having a rough time at school where the work and the hours are very stiff for a six-year-old, and my mother is coming for Christmas and very generously proposes to take us all to the South of France on a vacation immediately afterwards. Bill's morale is much better. Lord Ismay is mainly responsible for this as he seems so genuinely anxious to find a job for Bill at NATO and is taking the most infinite trouble about it. It looks discouraging, as the other thirteen members are already enraged because there are so many Americans attached to the international secretariat and there is great pressure from the small countries for any job that comes up. However, it is awfully nice to be wanted and Bill really cares about NATO as a cause and would love to work for it.

My morale is also good; the Balmain clothes strain at the seams and my face, though lined, is round like a harvest moon. Paris is quiet and delicious, politically the extraordinary Mendès-France is still as unknown and as fascinating a quantity as before. His American trip did him harm because he was so popular there; the French Assembly hates their leaders to get on well with other countries' leaders and loathes success in a Prime Minister; bets are now that he will get through the winter but be out in the spring for a lot of reasons.

Social Paris revolves around the annual Cabrol fête next week, this time a ball in a skating rink; the theme is sables and diamonds and Baron Alexis de Redé will be drawn in on a sled, wearing both, as Ludwig II of Bavaria. He went to Munich twice to see about the details of his costume, and the six ladies who will draw him in, dressed as swans, are minor figures in the act compared to him. We are not going, thank God, instead we are asked to go to Berlin with Fred Warner to stay with the British High Commissioner, Derek Hoyar-Millar and his wife,[10] old friends from Washington days. We will travel aboard Derek's train and will see as much of the East Zone as is allowed; it will be very interesting. Then Mother's arrival, Christmas, and the South of France. Having a glorious holiday and thank you again for your loving letters.

[10] Now Lord and Lady Inchira.

· 1955 ·

On January 1, 1955, Bill left the Paris Embassy, ten years after entering it. It was a remarkable tribute to him that, despite his poor health, Ambassador after Ambassador fought to keep him for such an unprecedented tour of duty, but at last the State Department machinery caught up with this irregular procedure. He, the doctor, and I all felt that he would be happier working at some not too taxing job than retiring, and as the World Bank was about to open an office in Paris, all of our friends threw themselves into the task of getting him a job there. I particularly remember the kind and beautifully expressed letters of David Bruce, Winthrop Aldrich, Bob Joyce to Eugene Black, then president of the World Bank. On January 22, my cousin Harriet Aldrich and her husband, then representing us in London, were to give a ball for the Queen to which the Blacks were coming, so they summoned us to come over from Paris.

2 Swan Walk
London, England
January 21, 1955

We arrived last night in dense snow and bitter cold. Never mind, the housemaid is an old friend and slips me hot water bottles like insulin to a diabetic. Sammy Hood met us at the station, and we went at once to the Aldriches' to see them and all the cousins. It was warm and cozy, Winthrop floating on a pink cloud of happiness like a Boucher cupid in a pin-striped suit, reveling in the intricacies of seating the dinner guests. Harriet, relaxed and genial as always, and both so hopeful, worried, and excited about us and the World Bank job. They are putting Mr. Black by the Queen Mother at dinner, as she is said to be so charming that she would put anyone in a good humor. Lots of family talk about whether I wear a tiara or not. This is decided in the affirmative, as everyone, even the Americans, are wearing them. Betty Sallisbury rushed to the bank today to get one for me to borrow. She even offered me her own, which I turned down—too big—but very gratefully accepted a very small band of diamonds usually worn by Molly Cranborne,[1] who is too pregnant to come. Boucheron is lending me a superb diamond necklace, five rows of very plain, very white square-cut diamonds, and earrings to match. This sounds like a Christmas tree display, but I think it will be okay, as the jewels are so plain and so is my dress, which has a huge white tulle skirt and black lace top, from Balmain.

London is as welcoming as ever. We dine with Pam Berry before the ball. I have never written enough about Pam because you know her as well as I do, but aren't we lucky in having such a friend? Since I first met her years ago, she had never let me down once. Each visit to London is treated by her as if she were getting a huge Christmas present, and the people at her house are always the most interesting in England. Pray for Bill and me at the ball, for we are very, very frightened of meeting Mr. Eugene Black.

4 Rue Weber
Paris, France
January 24, 1955

The Aldrich ball was a sparkling success. Knights of the Garter in knee breeches, English beauties wearing their tiaras like crowns, and my own cousins looking smashing. I was especially proud of Cousin Mary Whitehouse's elegance. For Bill and me personally, it was a disaster, as Winthrop told us as soon as we arrived that Mr. Eugene Black had arrived unwell and left immediately after dinner, so we never met him, which may be as well, as he had time to tell Winthrop that he was sick to death of the name Patten and could find his own employees for the bank. Apparently other eager volunteers had written to him recommending Bill, not just the three I mentioned in my last letter, and he was fed up with hearing about us. However, Bill is wonderful, and when we got back to Swan Walk we sat up having a drink and laughing about my borrowed finery and our high hopes and discussed how much we had to be

[1] Viscountess Cranborne, now Marchioness of Salisbury.

thankful for, not only our own happiness but our marvelous children. It had been Anne's birthday the day before we left for London. She had fifteen fellow five-year-olds to a party and looked delicious in a white dress with a blue sash to match her eyes, sitting by her great friend, Sarah Giles, who was the prettiest child there, blonde with a lovely English complexion, sparkling brown eyes with long lashes, cheeks pink with excitement, and an enchanting dress, white with a red velvet sash. Kitty probably made it herself. The Gileses do more and give more pleasure with less money than any couple in Paris. I have never had a dull moment there nor left Kitty and Frank without feeling the better for having been with them. Speaking of them made Bill and me realize once more how lucky we are in having made such friends as we have in these eleven years. If we have to struggle to live jobless on our small income, our friends won't let us down.

The children made our return home gay instead of dreary. Billy is quite himself again. He was so good about having the scarlet fever over Christmas and Anne was never out of her nurse's costume from F. A. O. Schwarz, wiping his fevered brow.

I won't go on as my own brow has been fevered; flu struck on the Golden Arrow channel steamer. Christian Dior was sitting next to us, and we began to sneeze at the same time. Like all French dressmakers, he can't speak French any more, only American with somewhat outdated slang. "Oh, baby," he said, "there we go. Gosh, can't wait to hike myself aboard that good old French train at Calais. Think of the heated cars—KERCHOO!" I like Dior very much, but it was too late to be saved by the French, nice as the heated cars were.

Mr. Eugene Black relented later, after being persuaded to give Bill an interview, which so impressed him that Bill went to work for the World Bank in Paris almost at once, remaining there until his health forced him to retire.

In March 1955, I flew unexpectedly to Boston to see my mother through a dreadful operation. She survived it and in April I was able to take her back to Washington where I stayed with her and wrote to Bill every day. I quote one or two letters because they give a little flavor of the time. Scott McLeod was in the administrative section of the State Department during the McCarthy years, and was loathed and hated by all our Foreign Service friends. We knew men who considered that their careers had been ruined by him and I was anxious to see what he was like, this security-scourge of the State Department.

1611 29th Street
Washington, D.C.
April 15, 1955

To Bill,

I wish I could compete with your letter of this morning but I can't, it was much too good. Maybe I can try tomorrow as I am waiting to be picked up by Marietta to go to a party given by some brilliant young Democrat who lives in Georgetown, where I shall at last meet Mr. Stevenson.

Today I went to the Senate by myself. The hearing was on a man called Cossi, not especially interesting but I wanted to see Scott McLeod, who was testifying. He is astonishing physically, large, crew-cut, ex-captain of Yale football team type of appearance, slow, pleasant smile. He explained in simple, straightforward, homely terms what a splendid job the State Department has done on the refugee question, illustrating with the aid of diagrams and a ruler the happy, Cinderella-like path of an immigrant to the United States from the moment he decides to leave his homeland to the job in the U.S., always under the watchful yet paternal eye of Mr. Scott McLeod. This was as soothing as a lullaby and went on for so long that I feared that the senators would fall asleep. But when he had finished McClellan and Hennings sprang like serpents; and Senator McClellan, with his still cellophane-wrapped cigar in his mouth, thanked Mr. McLeod for his exposition and said that, interesting as it had been, it was still mysterious to him why, if the program was at halfway point and the law was to allow 206,000 immigrants into the country, had only 1000 been admitted? McLeod then did very badly, I thought, first attempting to lose the scent in a mass of technical trivia, then putting all the blame on this man Cossi, whom he said, sanctimoniously, he pitied, rather than blamed, for his mutinous incompetence. Nothing very interesting about this story, except that, if McLeod is irritating the senators as much as he did today, eventually Dulles will be given the moral courage which he has so conspicuously lacked up to now, and will fire him. The tweediness of the man is offensive, I would have preferred him to look and talk like Himmler.

Georgetown is delicious, dogwood-filled; I lunched with Dottie Kidder[2] and heard fascinating tales of her life in Saigon; ran into Stew Alsop skulking along in the shadow on Dumbarton Avenue—he said that a process server was expected at the Alsop office with a suit for half a million dollars. Miss Cosden, their secretary, was on the steps looking both ways up and down the street and gave him the signal to come in and land. Both were taking this very lightly, apparently a normal morning at 2720 Dumbarton Avenue.

Mama is doing beautifully, but I think I will have to spend the summer at Northeast Harbor. This is an unbearable thought if you can't come, but it's too soon to make plans. She is a combination of guts and good manners such as I never saw, but I can't bear to see her so old and frail.

April 16

My evening last night began at 11:30 P.M. with the arrival of a tiny car containing Marietta, Evangeline, Kay Halle, and Archie Alexander, hot from the Jackson Day dinner at which three thousand people had paid a hundred dollars each to be poisoned (Evangeline dealt out digestive tablets) and to hear Truman, Rayburn, Mrs. Roosevelt, Stevenson. A rapid drive through the warm Georgetown night to a charming house on Prospect Avenue with a big room filled with thirty or forty people, the inner circle of the Stevenson group. I knew only Averell Harriman, whom I was very

[2] Mrs. Randolph A. Kidder, an intimate friend since childhood. Witty, gifted, elegant, she has been admired all over the world during her husband's diplomatic career, and afterwards.

glad to see, especially as he seems so happy. His face is Santa Claus round, his eyes light up with enthusiasm in argument, he springs into discussions with passion. Clinging to my cousin Archie Alexander, I was introduced; a senator said warmly, "Gosh, haven't seen you since New Orleans, what a night that was!" Someone else asked me what the news was in the Ninth District these days, I said it was splendid. There were decorative blondes, there were two real beauties, Marietta and Evangeline, who seemed automatically to be expected to play the role of senior duchesses in this realm. While waiting for the king to arrive, they sat on either side of Averell, I sat nearby between Archie and Senator Fulbright, to whom I would have liked to talk but just then the king arrived. Electric atmosphere, everybody carefully casual, subtle sinuous slidings of position in order to be ready to slip into place at his feet when he decided where to sit down, except on the part of the senior duchesses, who don't need to jockey for position wherever they go. He chose to sit on a coffee table in front of Archie and me, and was instantly engaged by Doris Fleeson, a woman columnist of considerable fire, energy, and eloquence. She said that she was appalled by the weakness of the speeches at the Jackson Day dinner, that no one had had the courage to attack the President, that it is not enough to attack the Administration, that Eisenhower is a weak, lazy, superficial man who through his refusal to face hard decisions has twice let us drift nearly into war. That she is sick of the Democratic Party acting like gentlemen. That it is much too late for that. Stevenson looked undisturbed, amused, said that he would like a drink, and attempted to engage Archie in light conversation. But the fiery Miss Fleeson was at him again. "And how long must we endure Senator George as spokesman of the party, silly, vain old man? Who should do something about this? Bill Fulbright, sitting right there." Fulbright looked uncomfortable, but nothing would stop Miss Fleeson, egged on by Averell, "You're dead right, Doris, George has got to go." Mr. Stevenson very gently got up and without a word walked over to the end of the room and stayed there with another group. I thought that he was quite right, but I felt that everyone in the room agreed with Doris Fleeson and applauded her courage.

Stevenson left and I never talked to him, but I am grateful to have had an impression. He is truly charming, with an amused, quizzical gleam in his eye, an attractive smile, and complete lack of pretension or professional political charm. Or perhaps it is so smoothly professional that one doesn't realize it isn't natural. My instinct is that it is natural, and that he is highly undisappointing.

The party drifted away, but for a hard core including me who remained until 3:30 A.M. Marietta, Bill Blair, Clayton Fritchey, and our host plus a beautiful young Kansas committeewoman in white organdy and camellias. As you see, the new Democratic Party is not too afraid of public opinion to be dressed by Mainbocher, and very nice too. I loved the vitality—God knows our old New Deal gatherings in Georgetown had vitality but this isn't at all similar. No theories, no orations on social security, all rather pragmatic and tough in the right way. Wasn't that an interesting evening for me?

April 17

To Bill,

I am getting so excited about the departure of PAA Flight 62 and your face at Orly, the children, that it's hardly worth writing to you, but I did want to say that I am bringing you a rather special present—I hope—it's a brand-new kind of cortisone that prevents your horrible enemy, insomnia. I'll explain all about it when I arrive, and I have cleared it with the Lahey Clinic and all your doctors here, and they think it's the greatest refinement yet on the steroids. I suppose with our passports I will have no trouble at Orly? I'll declare medicine. I thought that I would keep it as a surprise, but I can't resist letting you know that you should have a good night's sleep on Monday and also breathe better than you have in ages. Someone is taking this scrawl over to Paris tonight. I am happy over my visit here. Mama is really better. And the strength and excitement of this country—it isn't the drab, McCarthy-dominated flabbiness we had worried about and heard so much about that remains with me as I leave. Of course there is that—but in the opposition there is real fire. I'll describe my last engagements, a dinner at the Bruces', a very interesting cocktail party at Sylvia

Whitehouse's full of Stevensonites, an evening at Tish and Stewart's. Until Monday.

4 Rue Weber
Paris, France
April 20, 1955

Bill and the children met me, all longing to hear about dear Granny, and Bill had filled the house with my favorite spring flowers. Billy is on the honor roll, and Anne is happy at school but shows less sign of scholarly success. Bill has invented an amusement for her which is to copy printing, which she does with infinite pleasure, accuracy, and skill. While Bill reads to Billy or tells him a story, he gives Anne a newpaper story to copy. She gave me with great pride, saying "This is for you," a letter from The *Times* beginning, "Sir, the modifications in the income tax proposed by the Chancellor of the Exchequer may please a certain illiterate proportion of the public, but as one who has since 1903 been familiar with inflationary trends, I feel it my duty to lay before . . ." You wouldn't believe the Japanese-like accuracy. When she finishes, Bill and Billy cut out something else for her. They claim that she greatly prefers this to books and stories. Diana Cooper, who is staying here, says that Anne gives her articles copied in manuscript hand on the Bandung conference. The poor baby can't read "Daddy" or "Paris." I feel that there may be something wrong with this system, as she is only five, but everyone seems happy. On my pillow tonight is a note from Billy, almost illegible, saying, "We are glad you are home, dearest Mummy," and one from Anne, in beautiful writing, saying, "Smoke King Edward cigars."

I spent the summer of 1955 partly in Boston with my mother, who was once more hospitalized, the rest of it in Maine with her and the children. Bill wrote cheerful letters from Paris, describing his weekends at Chantilly with Diana and the many visitors he entertained at the house in Paris. Stewart Alsop spent a week, not in his role as the distinguished correspondent, but as Captain Alsop of the wartime

French resistance, holding a reunion with his old friends of the Maquis who came from all over France to greet him. Bill saw much of the Ismays and described Lord Ismay's rather pathetic description of Sir Winston Churchill, who is suddenly very, very old; "I can no longer clothe my thoughts in words," he said sadly. Lord Ismay replied that by that one beautiful phrase he had proved himself wrong, but told Bill that his visits left him very blue.

The summit at Geneva took place and Bill saw a good many of the people who had attended. "The Spirit of Geneva" was the headline in every paper in the world that July and it wasn't all synthetic cordiality. Eisenhower inspired a sense of trust that impressed even *Le Monde*, the important, anti-American Paris paper, and emerged as a man of peace. His Open Skies policy was excellent public relations—he offered the Russians an opportunity which they could not accept but the world was struck with the contrast between the President and his bellicose Secretary of State, Dulles. Macmillan[3]

[3] Mr. Harold Macmillan, then Foreign Secretary, later Chancellor of the Exchequer and Prime Minister of England, is famous for his ability, his charm, and his conversation. The latter is romantic and he was considered to be something of an actor, capable of bringing tears to his own eyes and certainly to those of his audience. In the summer of 1974, Diana Cooper gave a luncheon for me at her house in London, which he attended and made the party of eight shout with laughter over a story about a visit to the Vatican. He gave a ride home in his car to Evangeline Bruce and myself and the mood changed as in the heavy traffic he observed the new ugly buildings that deface London in some areas. "Do you suppose," he asked us, "that any period in history can have seen such changes as the one in which I have lived?" Waving his gold-headed cane in the direction of an ungraceful block of flats—"In July 1914 there was a particularly gay summer season. I remember that my sister-in-law was brought down from Chatsworth for it. She was a bit of a tomboy and one day she was caught walking up St. James's Street before lunch without a maid or a footman accompanying her! Quite unheard of in those days. A scandal. The family immediately closed the house and returned to Derbyshire. In any case one went to a ball every night, carrying a supply of collars which one handed to the butler as one arrived, and every now and then one went off to put on a fresh one. We danced so hard, you see. And fresh white gloves, of course, one went through several pairs of white kid gloves in an evening of waltzing. What a waltzer Bobbety was—the best of them all." (Evangeline and I strained to imagine the late Marquess of Salisbury as a frenetic waltzer.) "One night the Salisburys gave a ball in Arlington Street for Moucher and when I left the newsboys were on the streets with a new edition, in those days the papers came out every few hours. It carried the news of the murder of an archduke at Sarajevo, I didn't bother with it. A few weeks later everyone I knew was in uniform. Most of them were killed. Well, here we are."

expressed the view, later, that this conference had been a milestone because all the great nations now accepted the fact that nuclear weapons precluded war, which could only lead to mutual destruction. This was certainly not spelled out at Geneva, but was widely felt. One of the British participants said to Bill, with whom he was staying, discussing the Foreign Ministers' conference planned to follow up the Geneva summit, "It is painfully clear that we shall not succeed in doing serious business, and we shall have long, frustrating battles with little to show for our pains. However, it is much better to talk than to do other things."

The children, Mademoiselle, and I returned to Paris in early September.

Château de St. Firmin
Chantilly, France
October 9, 1955

We have had such a happy month since we returned from America—the first joy being Ronnie's arrival. Then, Bill is extraordinarily well; the new perfected cortisone called metacortone suits him, and he has been breathing beautifully, so he has a continual twinkle in his eye—the old Bill. Then, Paris is intoxicating. Every October, I think of a man I met ten years ago, shortly after he had been released from a German concentration camp. Awkwardly, I asked him what he had missed the most, and he replied, "Walking up the Rue Mouffetard to the Place de la Contrescarpe in October. I thought that perhaps I might not do that again." I try to do his walk nowadays sometimes. These are little streets in the 5th arrondissement which haven't changed since the seventeenth century.

The children have started school—a new one which I chose hoping it might be less of a strain than the last one; but oh dear, here we go again—tiny classrooms (windows never opened), packed like sardines and, on return, brows furrowed, circles under the eyes. To keep them up to the standard, Mademoiselle and I have to do a good deal of coaching. I am humiliated to find how bad I am at it. Teaching Anne a recitation yesterday, I was horrified to hear my own voice which I was controlling tensely. The shrill screams that I really wanted to give would have been more natural and better for the child. I hope to acquire patience, and it is interesting to follow the French system of education from the ground up.

You will have been following the bleaker-than-ever political picture, and I have great sympathy for the French position in North Africa (not for the die-hard *colons* or the generals but for the reformers who are the majority of the people we see). There continues to be a strong current of anti-Americanism. For example, at the Guy de Rothschilds' the other night, I got a laugh by telling a joke about Gladwyn Jebb (as described to me by a mutual French friend) playing golf with the head of British intelligence, who is Nancy Mitford's maid, Marie. Marie is, in fact, a man, and on Sunday mornings she puts on plus fours and meets Gladwyn; while they pretend to search for balls in the rough, she whispers secrets to him. And what they are up to is fomenting the recent labor troubles here because of fear of British competition. I added that, when I reported this unlikely story to Gladwyn, he told me in return laughable stories about what American "interests" are doing to egg on the nationalists in Morocco. This went over like a lead balloon—instead of a laugh, dead silence, eyes on plates, a hasty change of subject.

I wonder why it is that I remain so happy in France. Partly that I can walk up to the Place de la Contrescarpe in October; mostly, it is the friends and their loyal affection. We are very, very lucky.

Momo is here and says that Dior has lost his touch, so has Antoine; Lucienne of Reboux is losing hers, and that this is symptomatic of the decadence of the nation; nevertheless, she would rather be here than anywhere and that Morocco will be all right. Bless Momo.

4 Rue Weber
Paris, France
October 1955

A golden weekend, Sammy Hood here staying with us and a lovely long sightseeing châteaux day, you would think by now that we knew the environs of Paris, but we don't at all; from the guidebooks we found four or five châteaux we had never heard of before, all looking like tapestries from the Cluny. Golden leaves, men out of the tapestries shooting pheasant and partridge in the fields as they have since time began, the children with us hanging on to Bill's wonderful stories which he invents to make motor trips easier. Dinner at the Ismays', he for once a little less patient than usual with the vagaries of the partners in NATO as he had had a bad Sunday with lots of upsetting news, mainly caused by one of the never ending Greek-Turkish rows. And since General Gruenther has been told by his doctors to take a complete rest there is no one left to run anything on the military side except Monty,[4] "who is never around, always off getting the freedom of some city or other," or Maréchal Juin—this last a horrible thought, as he is supposed to have political ambitions.

On Monday we lunched with Nancy Mitford to meet her publisher and his wife, both delightful (Mr. and Mrs. Hamish Hamilton), and a young man called Adrian Secker from the *Daily Telegraph.* Lots of teasing of Nancy about her article on British aristocracy in *Encounter.* As in *Pursuit of Love* she remarked that to say mantelpiece instead of chimneypiece is common, so in the article she expands her list of things that one can't say (for example, never "glasses," always "spectacles") so much that, as we told her, none of us can open our mouths in her presence. The *Daily Telegraph* man was very funny describing how he had spent the morning trying to get the article (*Encounter* is out of print because of it) before coming to lunch with Nancy, whom he hardly knows, miserably certain of making some irrevocable faux pas within the first five minutes. Nancy takes teasing in very good part and doesn't mind an angry fan mail. She is making lots of money—averaged ten thousand pounds a year these last three years. And the man she has loved so long is really a very important figure in the present French government, so she seems very happy.

That night, following a dullish diplomatic dinner, we stayed up late at the Café des Deux Magots with Ben Bradlee,[5] a brilliant

[4] Field Marshal Lord Montgomery of Alamein.
[5] Benjamin C. Bradlee, now executive editor, Washington *Post.*

young man who is a great friend of Bill's. He had just been in Morocco and Algeria for *Newsweek* and had much to say. Faure, the present Prime Minister, who had been fairly competent under hideous difficulties until about a week ago, now seems to be floundering and to have given in to the military, which means of course Juin, who is a stupid, difficult man. The army is still loyal to the state and so far shows no signs of fomenting a take-over but they are the last people to handle the politically delicate task ahead. Morocco will somehow come out all right, but Algeria seems insoluble. Thank goodness, no incidents involving our troops; the air bases are kept isolated with very strict curfews and no passes to the Arab quarters. What a long, tragic story it is. My friends, when they talk about North Africa, are unanimous in criticizing the younger generation, who, they say, have lost their sense of empire. Many have sons or nephews in the army who have gone off bravely but *contre-coeur* (unwillingly). And the friends of every party, except the left, are fiercely determined not to lose North Africa and are far more united than they ever were over Indochina.

Our remaining years in France were overshadowed by the struggle for independence of the Moroccans, Tunisians, Algerians. Algeria was legally part of metropolitan France and the French there were in many cases the descendants of settlers who had lived there for over a hundred years. Thus the bitterness was deep, and Algeria was to be the bloodiest and most difficult of the French postwar problems. Foreign advice was most unwelcome. We were asked to have to dinner Congressman John F. Kennedy, whom we didn't know, and I still remember beautiful Odette Pol Roger's face when he told her and the other French guests that independence for the North African territories was long overdue. I thought Odette would hit him. It must be remembered that the French felt that, without them, North Africa would have remained a poor, underdeveloped area ruled by tribal chiefs, and it was the French who had pacified the tribes, built the roads, the hospitals, the schools and had brought those students who wished to come to France to continue their higher education to French universities. Thus, to be considered guilty of what they regarded as a superb missionary effort was intolerable.

To Marietta from Paris

4 Rue Weber
Paris, France
October 24, 1955

Where but in France could there be a state school for roofers? There is one at Angers, and the Elie de Rothschilds are employing some of the former students, putting a roof on their new house that will last a hundred and fifty years. By new house I mean the eighteenth-century Etienne de Beaumont house on the Rue Masseran, not far from the Invalides. It's thrilling for the workmen on the roof to be using their textbook knowledge, and the young men are as excited as the old. Perhaps this is the last house of our time to be done over, top to bottom, by a private family and I admire Lilianne and Elie hugely; their problems have been so unexpected—for instance, the house wasn't linked to the Paris sewage system, so imagine the horror of discovering two hundred years of muck in the basement. Economy on the part of the Beaumonts, I suppose. Did you ever go to one of their parties? I remember him as a creepy white-haired figure, hung about with tarnished tinsel from the past, and Bill complaining of the lack of drinks. But I believe that in the twenties it was an exciting and glamorous house and Etienne de Beaumont a famous host. Now it will live again, this time with a far happier atmosphere and the hosts an enthusiastic warm couple who adore their children. Lilianne is a scholar and, while she doesn't show off her knowledge, I learn much when I talk to her. This summer's great Marie Antoinette exhibition at Versailles was due not only to Gerald van der Kemp,[6] who deserves immense credit, but to Lilianne and other non-professionals. Its catalogue is one I shall keep always. Just reading it makes the period come alive: a serious letter from Maria Theresa of Austria begging her daughter, the Queen of France, to be less frivolous; the Queen's dog kennel, velvet-lined; the little waistcoat embroidered by her in prison in the Temple destined for the Dauphin; the portraits from youth to old age which came so young and was caught forever by David as she rode to her execution. The exhibition has focused the Marie Antoinette cult which has always existed in France, for they have long forgotten her failings and remember the youth and beauty of the *ancien*

[6] Gerald van der Kemp was and is the distinguished curator of Versailles.

régime. Nancy Mitford, who has written critically of her, tells me that she would be stoned in the streets if she dared to leave the Rue Monsieur.

Our only festivity this week has been a dinner for the Walter Lippmanns.[7] Helen had written that the only person Walter really wanted to see was Frank Giles, so we collected and added the Servan-Schreibers, Perkinses (he is our Ambassador to NATO), Sammy Hood, and Cécile de Rothschild. I thought it went pleasantly, although the topics were rather threadbare: how do we keep Russia from making further headway in the Middle East; how do we keep the Israelis and Arabs from starting another war; the status of the Saar. Walter is so kind and affectionate and wise. He is always worth listening to and I am devoted to both Helen and him.

4 Rue Weber
Paris, France
November 1955

It is a Thursday, so Billy is out of school, and as it was summer-day warm we celebrated by taking a row on the lake in the Bois, stopping at the little island where we tied up at the chalet at the water's edge. This chalet is full of lovers, winter and summer, Strauss waltzes coming out of a wheezy machine their background music. Billy, Anne, and I have our own routine. We eat a huge tea, no matter what hour of the day it happens to be, play nine holes of miniature golf rather solemnly, and re-embark to make a tour of the lake, Anne with me at the oars and Billy trailing his sailboat on a string from the stern. Anne and I talked clothes. She has a new party dress, pink organdy with a stiff crinoline skirt; I have a new

[7] Walter Lippmann was considered in France the most eminent American columnist of our time. His arrivals were news items in themselves, the red carpet was rolled out wherever he went and he deserved the homage. But I feel sad reading my letter about the little dinner party we gave that particular fall, for the Saar—thank heaven—has fallen, leaden heavy like its own resources, from dinner-table conversation. Yet, as I write now, in 1974, the other two topics mentioned above, which I call threadbare in 1955, were the topics discussed at a dinner I attended the other night. Walter, older and infinitely cleverer than I, would not be surprised. He always took a long view of history and was not impatient.

party dress, skin-tight black velvet with an ostrich-feather hem, and we both wonder what parties we will be asked to. Tying up the boat for good, we ran into one of the Vogués, an old friend and a cousin of the remarkable couple who created such a stir in Paris this summer by marrying off the last of their five children and then quietly entering a convent and a monastery. They will not see each other or their children again, as each entered a very severe order. I am told that they were a most devoted couple, this Marquis and Marquise de Vogüé, who had kept their religious vocations to themselves, so their departure from the life of the world was an immense shock to their family and friends.

I went to England last week to see my old nurse, who lives in an old ladies' home near Birmingham. These biannual excursions are too painful to talk about, dark in Birmingham comes right after lunch and I cannot bear to leave Nurse, nearly blind and very feeble, holding the albums with pictures of my sister and me as if they were diamonds, and the coal fire in the grate very low indeed. Fortunately, she has never been sentimental; her last observation was on my table manners. "Your appetite has improved but you handle your knife and fork in a funny foreign way, comes from living in France, I suppose."

The Paris autumn lingers on while winter has come to England. Pam Berry is staying with us, and we had a lunch for her of a most French kind—the entire conversation was about silver, although the guests were French politicians or diplomats. I don't mean silver like silver dollar, I mean old silver such as the important collection which the shipowning Greek, Stavros Niarchos, has just presented to the French nation. It is superb, but very dirty; you know how surprising it is to see the dinginess of antique French silver if one is accustomed to the high shine of English or American silver. Gaston Palewski claimed that this is quite unnecessary, and that French silver could be just as white as ours if anyone took any trouble, but the French are lazy and fall back on the false excuse that French silver has a less high silver content than English and can't take the polish. This led him into saying that the Hall of Mirrors at Versailles must have been perfectly hideous with all its silver furniture under Louis XIV, for the furniture would have been boardinghouse dingy. This produced an uproar you wouldn't believe, for it was heresy not to deplore the loss of the silver furniture of Versailles. Our guests shouted at each other until three o'clock and then dashed off, crying to us what a brilliant success lunch had been; perhaps it was but I would have liked some politics for Pam, to thank her for her wonderful political parties for us in London. However, she is interested in everything and knows the French passion for debate on every subject connected with their culture and history.

Of course, being French, the conversation about silver had many a diverting side trip. I always think of a great highway, say the road from Paris to the south, N6, along which race high-powered cars at high speed. Then one darts off on a secondary smaller road to see some minor château or minor village of interest, or just to have a drink, returning to the great N6 to crash on at eighty miles an hour. Lunch today was similar. If N6 was silver, the secondary roads were: (1) for what would the French fight today as they fought under Louis XIV? (nothing, we were told); (2) would any of us have been able to stand life at Versailles? (certainly not—lack of plumbing and tedium of ceremony); (3) will France ever have another revolution? (certainly—French history is a series of zigzags, swinging from dictatorship to anarchy, up and down).

Perhaps it wasn't as dull as I feared.

· 1956 ·

In early January, Bill went back to the United States for the World Bank and found Washington stunned by Secretary of State Dulles' article for *Life*. This was known as the brinkmanship article, and it frightened the whole world. "You have to take chances for peace, just as you must take chances in war. The ability to get to the verge without getting into war is the necessary art. If you cannot master it, if you are scared to go to the brink, if you try to run away from it, you are lost. We walked to the brink and we looked it in the face." Only months before, President Eisenhower had come to the summit meeting in Geneva as a man of peace; one wondered what he thought of Dulles' bellicose article. Bill reported Dean Acheson saying purrily, that his taxi driver had commented, "I wouldn't mind so much if the United States weren't involved!"
In New York, Bill was entertained by Marietta, who was going into an intensely exciting year working on Adlai Stevenson's second presidential campaign.

4 Rue Weber
Paris, France
January 1956

What a five-ring circus you run. Bill admires the way you run it enormously and gives a description of you looking more beautiful than you ever have and never tired, while with one hand you arrange a brilliant dinner for Isaiah Berlin; with the other remove unsuitable pictures from the room in preparation for your father, the Bishop's, visit, and still have lots of time for the children and Bill himself. You read everything and write letters, this on top of your big job. I shall not lecture you again about getting overtired, but I know that you must be a lot of the time and I do so admire you for not showing it.

Frankie has been writing such interesting, funny letters from boarding school. In her last one, she says that the *Democratic Digest* was not in the school reading room, despite a free subscription from Clayton Fritchey. She suspects censorship. Foxcroft was heavily Republican even in my day.

Here, the French are in a state of shock over the success of the extremes at their elections. Pierre de Montesquiou[1] was heavily defeated, running on an extreme left-wing ticket, which is unusual for a duke. Odette is delighted and calls his effort an exercise in futile demagoguery. Louise sees crisis, the end of the Republic, dictatorship. Our Embassy is less gloomy, mainly because there aren't any effective dictators around. It was curious being in Paris alone, with Bill away. I couldn't wait for him to come back from America. There are so few extra women in Paris that one is asked out a lot, and at first it is great fun. I found myself sitting up until 4 A.M. in cafés with post-Existentialists discussing literature, thin stuff this, although all Frenchmen make magical cobwebs if they speak their beautiful language well, and it does seem to me that ninety-nine per cent do speak it well. In the morning the cobwebs seem truer than the magic. I cannot feel that this is an age of literature, but I hope I am wrong. On nights at home I read the Bible, which I am determined to do, cover to cover, at last. I find the Old Testament horrifying, although instructive in many ways. For political evenings there is fun to be found at the Servan-Schreibers', sitting on the

[1] The Duc de Fezensac-Montesquiou was an old beau of Odette Pol Roger's and a cousin of Louise de Rougemont's. It was politically wise of him to vote for the extreme left, for he was running in the Gers, a department in the southwest of France that in those days was poor and full of underprivileged voters who would have never sent a duke to Parliament unless he was left-wing. Aristocrats in the French Parliament, or Assembly, were unusual but not extraordinary. Normally they worked at the local level as mayors or members of municipal councils. I cannot remember one aristocrat reaching Cabinet level during our sixteen years in France but I may be wrong. This has changed. In the Giscard d'Estaing government of 1974 the toughest job in the Cabinet is held by Prince Michel Poniatowski, the able Minister of the Interior. This seems to me to show a new sense of security in the French. A generation ago it would have been unthinkable to appoint a prince, let alone one whose name echoes royal Polish connotations, to this difficult job. Jules Moch, a hardened, able Socialist, was the prototype of the French Minister of Interior during the Cold War years. During the dangerous strike-ridden winter of 1947–48 his handling of the unions was thought to have saved France from a Communist take-over. It would have been grotesque to imagine a Prince Poniatowski in those days, but the French are less caste-conscious every day.

floor until 3 A.M., and I enjoyed dining with the Spaak and Monnet brain-trusters. The café society Bestegui-Lopez world is a great change from the above; I ventured into it occasionally and it's fun to see the clothes and the jewels and the houses. But having no one to talk it over with spoils all fun.

4 Rue Weber
Paris XVI, France
February 23, 1956

Thank you for your good letter from Barbados. I delight in thinking of you there after such a winter, only I think that, as usual, you are much too kind and hospitable and, diverting as your delightful house guests are, please don't fuss about making the food extra good. This should be a holiday for you, and if anyone complains of flour in the hollandaise, tell him to have his flown in from Maxim's.

Isn't it a strain waiting for the President's decision? Paul Nitze dined here a couple of nights ago and swore he wouldn't run—not on health grounds, but because he doesn't know the answers and quoted Reston's views about his being a "genuine phony," with accent on the genuine. But others speak of the President's confidence and calm. We are terrified by reports of Nixon's growing popularity. Is this true? Stevenson's stand on segregation went over well here; his courage in the West Coast speeches understood and appreciated.

As for France, the endless, cruel cold is trying. We will run out of coal next week, but it's not serious for lucky people like us, who can always move to a hotel. The only heat here has been generated by two very different people—the rightist politician Poujade and Marie-Laure de Noailles. I had a Poujadist to dinner, Bourbon-Busset, which I found out by saying to him that I suspected lots of our friends admired Poujade but none of them dared admit it, to which he answered, "*Madame, je suis Poujadiste et j'en suis fier:* [Madame, I am a Poujadiste and proud of it]!" I admit to what the Victorians called the agreeable thrill of horror, for we all had been wondering when we would catch a declared member of the party among our friends. Was Berlin like this in the thirties? As soon as I could, I turned to Gladwyn Jebb to whisper the news that I had trapped a real live Poujadiste. He replied in the trenchant tones of British diplomacy, "So what!" and turned back swiftly to the pretty girl on his other side. Gladwyn is very clever; we at our Embassy may be taking the smell of Fascism too seriously.

Before I turn to the other source of heat—Marie-Laure's costume ball—I hear that there has never been a better party than yours for the Russells. Evangeline wrote at length about it, describing the wonderful mixture of people and the warmth and gaiety. How I wish I had been there instead of at 11 Place des Etats Unis.

This entertainment had been the talk of Paris for months—opinion, as usual, divided between those who found it the worst of taste to give a ball in view of Algeria and those who said that if the French had waited for stability there wouldn't have been a party since 1792. One had to go as an artist or writer of one's own country or someone from a book or painting between 1400 and 1900. I went as Annabelle Lee, taking with me, at the last moment, your young cousin, Chauncey Parker, as my dear Bill was in bed. C.G., as you probably call him, was a very good sport about putting on a hired Edgar Allan Poe costume, and I took him to dinner at Pam Churchill's[2] where we found the English contingent. Bindy Lambton was the best as Lady Windermere, all black velvet and wasp waist and smooth sloping shoulders; Ann Fleming[3] as Harriet Wilson, Judy Montagu a handsome George Eliot, Diana Cooper as Lady Blessington, red velvet and romantic yellow ringlets, Pam herself an ethereal pale blue Titania, Kitty Giles as Mrs. Patrick Campbell, with Frank an excellent George Bernard Shaw in red beard and Norfolk jacket, Paddy Leigh-Fermor as Byron, Tony Pawson exquisite as the miniaturist Nicholas Hilliard, black velvet and ruff. The other men were Paul Louis Weiller as François I after the Titian portrait, amazingly successful, as their profiles are just alike, and the other gentlemen, French, Italian, Brazilian, etc., were as richly damasked and satined and velveted and pearl-hung as any guests at a Veronese banquet. C.G. was dazzled and

[2] Pam Churchill is now Mrs. W. Averell Harriman.

[3] Mrs. Ian Fleming appeared earlier in the letters as Lady Rothermere, the wife of the owner of the *Daily Mail* and other important English papers. She left Lord Rothermere, his fine houses, and his riches to marry for love Ian Fleming. It was a very happy marriage, and his death left her desolate.

asked me to give him a two-minute sketch of each guest. I said, "Some other time," as we were off for the ball after some pretty frantic minutes in Pam's dressing room where one and all were fighting for the assistance of Monsieur Guillaume and two assistants. ("Oh, Tony, do get out of my way, he can touch up your eye shadow next." *"Vraiment, Paul Louis, il me faut quand même un petit coin de la glâce* [Really, Paul-Louis, I *do* need a tiny corner of the mirror].") In the car, C.G. was very gay until we reached that great extraordinary house, at the entrance to which a crowd of poorly dressed people were standing in the icy cold to watch the guests arrive. This not unnaturally, brought out every Puritanical instinct from your family, and he was undone, talking of decadence, Algeria, Abbé Pierre, Poujade, until I was obliged to hit him sharply over the head with a stuffed raven, which I had hired for the evening, at some expense, to be worn on his shoulder, and carry him into the house. You will think me brutal, but as I wrote you from Venice after Charlie de Bestegui's ball in 1951, it seemed insane and shocking to be clapped by the ragged crowds as one swept up to the Palazzo Labia in one's gondola dressed as a lady from a Tiepolo; but I confess to a strong Lambert Struthers side—you will remember him from Henry James's *The Ambassadors*—one comes to Europe to see the sights. In the hall, I revived your cousin, and we queued for our entrées—a terrifying business. You had to mount a flight of stairs with hundreds of people leaning over to see you, to be announced as the characters you impersonated, followed by the flourish of trumpets from Aïda, then ascend a few steps more to be welcomed by our hostess, who was dressed as a large green bush, a mixture of Archimboldo and Graham Sutherland, said to impersonate some Renaissance figure too arcane for me to follow. Our ascension was an obstacle course, for preceding us up the stairs was a beautiful, young Countess Ruspoli, as the Boldini portrait of Countess Morosini, tall and dark and wearing the original Worth dress. Her companion, the famous greyhound, must certainly have been the original greyhound from the portrait, his age and fatigue obliged him to lie down suddenly as he approached the top, causing us to stop abruptly and poor C.G. to put his foot squarely through my white organdy crinoline.

Then, we were free to wander from room to room, and the sights were wonderful. On the whole, the women were less good than the men, although Cora Caetani, as a Ghirlandaio portrait in a plain quattrocento dress by Dior, headband around her beautiful forehead, and Maria de Maud'huy, as the Duchess of Alba from the Goya portrait, dress by Lanvin, were superb. The men were extraordinary—every portrait in the Louvre was there—Chardin in his turban and glasses, all the Clouets, Voltaire, and the Encyclopaedists and perhaps the most memorable, a young Englishman, Granville, as Byron just out of the Hellespont, all wet and romantic, sea shells and seaweed. I took your cousin to the bar, where he was instantly picked up by Oscar Wilde and Toulouse-Lautrec, both, in real life, actors from the Comédie Française; and I lost him for a moment but saw him later dancing merrily; and he told me the next day he had forgotten all about decadence and had had a very good time. As for me, I danced till dawn, realizing quite clearly in my mind that I would probably never have a good time at a ball again. One is getting old.

Forgive a much too long letter; the cold makes it impossible to go out, and I have been at my desk with a rug over my knees all afternoon.

4 Rue Weber
Paris, France
March 4, 1956

We are just back from a gastronomic weekend in Burgundy with the Frank Gileses and Joe Alsop. I have written you too many letters about our life in Paris—too few about the glorious weekends, of which this was typical. We pooled a month's gasoline tickets with the Gileses and set off in the early spring sunshine down the long, nostalgic road to the south, N6, which is my favorite road in all the world. Fontainebleau, Sens, Auxerre, Avallon, Vézelay—stopping now and then for Frank's sake to look at battlefields of the Hundred Years' War, that struggle so satisfactory for the English to read about, as there always seems to have been a hundred thousand well-armed French facing a handful of brave English archers; yet the English always seem to win, at least according to the books we have with us. We slept at the Moulin des Ruarts below Vézelay and dined so well that the ordinarily prudent Frank fell into the Cousin, the little trout stream outside the Moulin. It was terribly expensive; I should think dinner must have cost twenty-five dollars each, and we rarely go to places like this, but Joe was giving the party and planning to sell an article to the *Saturday Evening Post* about Monsieur Dumaine's restaurant at Saulieu, whither we were bound the next day, and which some people think is the best in France.

We set off, a touch liverish but still elated by the sunshine on the poplars and the excitement of the open road, stopped to see two lovely churches, arriving in time for the exquisite luncheon ordered by telephone ahead by Joe. The food was as fine as reported, the bill only about three times the price of Maxim's, as is often the way with these little country inns, and the proprietor so grand that he didn't want to be written up in the *Saturday Evening Post*. Joe took the blow well, and we returned to Paris.

4 Rue Weber
Paris, France
March 6, 1956

Today we had a lunch party which was made spectacularly successful by Ben Bradlee of *Newsweek*. In the morning paper I had read that he had been arrested and ordered to leave the country within twenty-four hours, and thought, "Oh dear, poor Benny languishing in jail, what can we do for him?" But, to our amazement, he showed up right on time for lunch, with a policeman. They had let him out because he had a luncheon engagement, in their civilized French way. The policeman sat in the hall at first so as to keep an eye on his charge, but then was persuaded to go down to the kitchen for a proper meal with our household, which took hours so we had Benny until three-thirty and he was such a success with our French guests that they stayed too. He had been picked up a couple of days ago and looked tired and drawn. It was Algeria, of course. He had been out there and made contact with the F.L.N. (the rebels) which will make an excellent story and was a brave thing to do, but I wonder if he will be allowed back to Paris on his next trip.

To Marietta from Paris

No one talks of anything but Algeria. We dined with Loli Larivière this week and after dinner I sat in a corner of her beautiful drawing room listening to Elie de Rothschild, out of his mind with worry, cross-examine the Minister of the Army. He asked if it was going to be like 1939 again, when he and his brother Alain had been obliged to take three of their polo ponies into war with them because their mechanized equipment wasn't there. The Minister said that Algeria was all right from the point of view of equipment. Elie said that the equipment was just the trouble, American tanks and airplanes would be no use in a guerrilla war and what was needed was tiny helicopters and light arms, and what the hell was the matter with the War Department, was France as decadent as some people say or simply mismanaged? The Minister replied calmly that, in 1951 in Lisbon, France had promised to fulfill its part in the Atlantic alliance by providing five divisions for Germany, to be used in case of Russian invasion, and they had been equipped for that contingency, which at the time seemed likely. They could not have afforded to prepare for the mobile war they are now fighting in Algeria as well as the above, anyway no one had foreseen it. Why no one had foreseen it led them into the usual depressing conversation about too little and too late and the failure of French colonial policy. I came away sad, as always after hearing two sincere, honest Frenchmen talk about their country, bitterly.

In June 1956, Stavros Niarchos, the Greek shipowner, lent his beautiful yacht *Eros* to Ronnie for a fortnight's cruise around Sicily. Marietta was deep in Stevenson's presidential campaign and Bill couldn't get away from the office, so the party consisted of Odette Pol Roger, her lovely sister Jacqueline Vernes, Guy Dumur, a new friend who became and remains a dear friend, Ronnie, and myself. It was a far cry from our cruise of three years before on the little *Argo* in Greece. The crew was numerous; I recall two chefs, two deck stewards, and a cabin for me big enough to hold the large double bed in which I slept; we carried a Chris-Craft speedboat on the deck for water skiing and our entry into any harbor caused a sensation. Again, it was a wonderful trip, not more wonderful than the earlier one but very happy. I needed it, for once again we had had to move, and although I open the letter to Marietta with a phrase about "the minor worries like house hunting" they still were not minor in Paris in the fifties, even for relatively prosperous people like ourselves. The reason is sociologically not uninteresting.

Between 1914 and 1954 almost no new dwellings were built in Paris; even by 1958 a census showed that seventy per cent had been built before 1914, forty-five without inside toilets. After the war, unlike Germany and Britain, priority was given to industrial recovery, perhaps wisely, and as there were no new satellite towns and a rising postwar population, the congestion in Paris was appalling. This has all changed, greatly for the better, and one of the most exciting things about modern France is the decentralization which makes towns like Grenoble, Toulouse, Rennes, Nancy, Montpellier, and many others exciting centers to which many harassed Parisians move with relief. Twenty years ago, the provinces were dead, and every energetic young man or woman lived only to get out and move to Paris. When I was house hunting I despaired over the prices and above all the dreariness of apartments and houses in the affluent quarters. There were always several reception rooms which gave on the front. Then a long musty corridor led to the dark bedrooms whose only air and light came from an inner courtyard, the kitchens were medieval and worse still were the maids' rooms in the attic. These never had a bathroom, one was lucky to have one toilet which served the needs of all the servants in a big apartment house, and central heating was very rare on their floor. We loved our three faithful servants and nothing would have induced us to put them in such quarters. Happily, we found the most beautiful apartment I have ever lived in, in a building belonging to my dear friend Aline Berlin's mother, so I could leave for Sicily with my mind at rest.

Aboard *Eros*
Agrigento
June 10, 1956

Paris and the minor worries like house hunting seem a million miles away. I have never been happier, but "if only Marietta were here," Ronnie, Odette, and I say ten times a day. Ronnie is the best host I ever saw; smooth behind-the-scenes organization makes every day a delight. He says that he has described the sightseeing to you, which I have enjoyed even more than Greece, as Sicily is so unexpectedly varied. Yesterday we visited a Norman castle in the morning, shrouded in fog on top of a mountain. We shivered on the romantic battlements as if we were at Haddon Hall in Derbyshire. Even the vegetation was English, wallflowers and box. Two hours later by Sicilian taxi, we were peeling off our sweaters to climb in hot midday sun up to the Greek (Doric) temple of Segesta, lying in an arid amphitheater under the bluest of Mediterranean skies. One felt that the homesick Greeks and Normans had gone far indeed on this Italian island of orange groves and almond orchards to find their own landscapes in which to build.

Palermo is a city that grows on you, when you get used to its weird, sprawling mixture of Byzantine, Norman, Arab, Spanish baroque, Mussolini's Italy, and Brooklyn's slums. We found the *Eros* stretching her elegant greyhound length on oily scum in a harbor that might have been Liverpool, and surely added to the Communist vote by lying about on deck our first night, eating caviar with our martinis before a crowd of miserable characters, straight out of the cast of *On the Waterfront.*

The next night we crashed high society, thanks to Fulco di Verdura[4] whose friends gave a party for us in a very fine palace. Ronnie was pursued by a lady in a black satin garden party dress and a huge flowered hat with the wonderful name of Principessa della Ciccela della Carriore del Campo Reale (we have her card) who talked to him of the dukes of England, getting their names slightly wrong. Odette and Jacqueline are too beautiful and charming to fail to have success wherever they go, but Guy Dumur had even more success with the flower of Palermo's aristocracy, as he is so young and good-looking. The young nobles are still writing him notes, asking him to come back. Guy, by the way, is going over well with the sisters. I am much relieved, as they didn't know him (I met him through Pauline de Rothschild). After one awkward conversation about Algeria, we have kept off politics. He is a former

[4] Duc di Verdura. Maker of Cellini-like jewels and a shrewd, wise man.

Combat reporter, friend of Camus, brilliant, young theatrical critic, politically much further to the left than anyone else these teakwood decks are accustomed to bearing.

Good-by for the moment—we are off on an expedition, so I leave you to continue soon.

Ile de Bailleron
Brittany
July 23, 1956

I hope that Ronnie got back safe and sound and has persuaded you to come abroad this fall if only for a short holiday. Perhaps you can't take even that, but I cannot bear to think of this long, hot, struggling summer for you with no letup. For fascinating and exciting as the work is, you must be taking a physical beating.

We adore the new apartment—54 Avenue d'Iéna 16 is the address. The ceilings are eighteen feet high, and we look over a forest of chestnut trees. As all the workmen leave Paris for the summer, we can only picnic, so I have brought the children for ten days to stay with Elise on this remote and beautiful island. We are alone but for the fisherman who runs the boats. The weather could be Maine; but unlike Maine, it is haunted—for me, by pleasant Celtic ghosts; for Elise, by Celtic *fiends* who resent her occupancy and direct their considerable powers towards making life untenable. The cook left at once; the fisherman on whom our life depends has turned from a jolly Breton sailor friend into a disagreeable drunk who disappears daily for the mainland bars, forgetting to take the laundry. Elise has only to step into the house for the water pump to break down or the generator to snarl to a stop. It rains and rains, but we are frightfully busy cleaning and washing and organizing charades for the big boys, treasure hunts for the small children, keeping up the spirits of the two nurses, and telling each other how well we look in this wonderful air. We also have a young Jesuit who tutors Richard in math. He is brilliant on explaining the parables and fascinating on the history of Palestine, but he looks remote and weary if one asks him to help repair the outboard motor. Brought up as you and I are to a climate of damp towels and raincoats, I feel completely happy, and today we have awakened to a beautiful day, so I must leave you to go shrimping.

We left the Ile de Bailleron on a rare, sparkling afternoon, Billy and Anne and I hating to say good-by to that magic island and return to Paris. Elise and the children and even the reserved Jesuit priest-tutor waved us off. Our shrimp nets were full of shrimps for Daddy and the jolly Breton sailor who was to take us into the port from which we would catch the night train to Paris was not only sober but jaunty. All went well until we arrived in harbor. The sailor deposited us at the railroad station, we were assured that we had only an hour to wait for the express train, and we settled down comfortably. It then emerged that the Paris express was not running that night, so my tickets were no good. I was informed that with a bit of luck we could catch a slow train leaving at 1 A.M., it was then 6 P.M. Rain, as is inevitable in Britanny, had begun to fall, suddenly but remorselessly, and our raincoats were packed in our suitcases, checked in at the station. That was the night I learned to appreciate my children. Anne, aged six, had never been up later than eight o'clock at night, or occasionally nine if Daddy was very late from the office. I expected enthusiasm for the adventure, followed by fatigue and the inevitable whines which would have been my addition to the party at her age. Billy, two years older, I counted on to be game, and he was, but it was Anne who got us through the night. "We go to a bar," she said, and we did, dripping and pathetic, the children still carrying the shrimp nets. At the bar, which she chose, Billy and I watched with amazement as she snapped her small fingers at the waiter and ordered for us in her admirable French. "Cassis," she said, "for my brother and myself, and for my mother, who is very tired." "*Oui, mademoiselle.*" We then made friends in the bar, entirely thanks to Anne, and they invited us to join them for a seafood dinner in a bistro on the harbor. Billy, shocked, said, "We don't know them, Anne." I rather shared his view as they did look like Brittany's branch of The Family. But it was too late—we were soon on the harborside square, engulfed by and enjoying the local Mafioso. The rain cleared, we passed a merry evening, a glass of the local wine, Muscadet, was never out of my hand. Anne soon fell asleep in my lap but roused instantly when it was time to make the 1 A.M. train, cheerful and smiling. I had had so much Muscadet that Billy had to handle the tickets and the luggage. We traveled for nine hours in two third-class seats, the children taking turns on my lap, emerging at last at the station in Paris, shrimp nets still in dirty paws. Never a whine or a grumble.

After a weekend in Ireland which I describe in the next letter Bill and I went off to Bavaria so that he could take a "cure" in a quiet place in the hills. This was a disaster, and I was very glad that the children had gone to Cornwall with Mademoiselle to stay with a wonderful friend of hers, a teacher called Dorothy. My chief problem during those years was how much I should share my desperate concern about Bill's health with the children. It was hard for them to understand how their gay, fun-loving father could change overnight into a gasping, suffering figure, smiling heroically through an oxygen mask. Anne bore the brunt of the strain, for Billy soon went off to boarding school. She was marvelous with Bill; I hope we did not ask too much of her.

August 1, 1956

Bill and I spent last weekend at Russborough in Ireland. I thought the house most beautiful and the Beits' beaming pleasure in it touching. Instead of the rustic Irish neighbors we had expected to meet, our surprise was great at finding the Lopez yacht in the harbor carrying *tout Paris*—Cabrols, Redé, Chips Channon, Ghislaine de Polignac, etc.—so I sat by Arturo Lopez three times at meals and didn't learn much about Ireland. The house party of von Hoffs and Alan Pryce-Jones was highly congenial, and Alfred Beit the best-organized host I ever saw. If I quote his pre-dinner Saturday evening speech, please don't think it is malicious of me, for I am devoted to him. Picture us assembled around the fire in evening dress, great masters in gilt frames above us, and a cocktail in our hands.

"We are, as you know, leaving shortly for Aileen Plunkett's dinner dance. The drive is about forty-five minutes; in this rain, we shall allow an hour. We shall proceed in two cars—one, driven by the chauffeur, will leave between 1:30 and 2 A.M. to return home; the second, driven by me, will leave between 4 and 5 A.M. Hands up now for those wishing to return in the first car." All hands went up, except for the loyal Clem's. "In the morning, our plans will be a little more complicated. I really must have silence—Raimund, *please!* One car, for Alan and Laurence, will leave for mass at 10:25 A.M. Another car, for Susan Mary, who is visiting Carton, will leave at 10:30 A.M. The rest of the party will visit Liz's birthplace in Phoenix Park, leaving at 11 A.M. Susan Mary, if she stays twenty-five minutes at Carton, can rejoin us at 12:15 P.M. We will then drive to the harbor—a drive of about an hour, to lunch with Arturo Lopez aboard *Gaviana IV*. Both cars will then continue on to Castletown for tea with Lord Carew, and we hope to be back by 6 P.M., as Chips Channon is bringing some guests for drinks and to see the house. In the evening, as you know, we have the Lopez party to dine. Now, shall we go?"

I feared for Bill's health; but he loved it all, and it was extremely nice to see two people so happy as the Beits are. I like her so very much, don't you? Both are wonderfully kind.

This great house became front-page news in 1974 when the owners, Sir Alfred and Lady Beit, now much older people who had done nothing but good for their adopted country, Ireland, were rudely disturbed as they sat alone after dinner, by the entrance of a masked band of I.R.A. who proceeded to tie up the Beits at gunpoint and make off with some of the greatest pictures, including the famous Vermeer. The Beits survived and made light of their horrifying experience when I saw them later in London, and the pictures were recaptured. I suppose the reason I wrote to Marietta in detail about the visit was that it was so surprising. One didn't expect to fall on Parisian café society in the Irish countryside, and I had never met such a well-organized host as Alfred. English and Irish country house visits were generally casual in atmosphere. Our fellow guests were Liz and Raimund von Hofmannsthal, she the niece of Diana Cooper, whose beauty was nearly as famous as her aunt's, he a charming man of Austrian birth whose warmth and friendship meant much to me until his death, and Alan Pryce-Jones, the writer and critic. The people on the yacht were well-known members of international society.

It was several months before I started writing letters again. In

August, as I have said, Bill and I went to Bavaria to a quiet hotel for our vacation. It was a miserable time, as he fell ill and instead of returning to Paris, instantly, for medical care, we stayed on, hoping that he would feel better in the good air of the Bavarian hills. Eventually he had a heart attack and for a day or two his condition was critical. We limped back to Paris and during September and October his amazing resilience reasserted itself and he was able to return to normal life.

Marietta had been knocking herself out working for Adlai Stevenson and my next letter is addressed to her immediately after hearing the election returns which announced Stevenson's defeat and Eisenhower's victory. We were shaken by three events that week: the presidential election; the invasion of Hungary by the Russians; and the Suez operation. At the time I wrote I had no knowledge of the background of the Anglo-French "police action" and, as the letter will show, my judgment was extremely poor. The operation was, in fact, a bungled effort by the British, French, and Israelis to throw over Nasser and install a more accommodating leader in Egypt. I was suspicious of Dulles, our Secretary of State, for many reasons, and thought that his peace-making efforts, especially a plan devised by him called the Suez Canal Users Association, was hypocritical. Always pro-English, I thought it brave and right that Eden should attack the Egyptians, and it never occurred to me that the plan hadn't been thought out and would collapse within forty-eight hours of the landings in the face of opposition from the Labor Party in the House of Commons, world opinion, and above all the deterioration of the pound. In retrospect it seems to me that everyone went wrong over Suez. Eisenhower felt betrayed but he had allowed John Foster Dulles to dominate our foreign policy and in an election year the President greatly preferred not to have to make unpleasant decisions.

54 Avenue d'Iéna
Paris, France
November 7, 1956

I hate to think how tired and depressed you must be today. I never felt more blue, but I didn't lift a finger for the campaign and I know how terribly hard you worked and how much it meant to you and Ronnie. Although it is too soon for us to know more than the barest outline I write at once as my first thought was of you, Marietta.

These have been the worst eight days I can remember. Hungary overshadows Suez here, rightly, and the French flag is flying at half mast today over the Hôtel de Ville (Town Hall of Paris) in honor of the Hungarian dead. But we talk Suez constantly and NATO is in pieces. Pug Ismay I haven't seen, but Dary Ismay says that she has never seen him so sad—for he faces the representatives of twelve enraged countries daily. Our English friends are miserable. Diana is staunchly pro-Eden, the Gileses feel that no end could justify such means. The French are jubilant, don't care two pins for U.N. or world opinion, and are united in applauding the landings. Bill and I are for Eden and disgusted by the smugness of the Administration. Who forced Nasser to nationalize the canal? Dulles, of course.

P.S. I am continuing this the next day, November 8. It's been rather a horrid day—rumors of Soviet aid to the Egyptians and of American fleet movements. The latter are surely only to counter the former, but are assumed by the press here tonight to be preparatory to our entering the fracas against the English and French. Can you believe that I am writing such words? I can't, and of course it won't come to that.

Pauline[5] came in and is as sick as I am at the election results. She says that the French intellectuals are still solid behind Mollet and Eden. Fulco di Verdura joined us and described being in London. He was astonished to have Clarissa Eden call him up to thank him for the verbal support he had given the Prime Minister at some party the night before. Fulco said, "My God, if they care about the opinion of a bloody little Italian like me things must be bad." Oh dear, I hope my next letter will be more cheerful.

American Embassy
London, England
Thanksgiving Day, 1956

Thank you for your kind, sympathetic cables. It was such a stupid accident. After dining in Swan Walk alone with the Salis-

[5] Baroness Philippe de Rothschild.

burys and Buck De la Warr, I tripped at the head of those beautiful, shining, uncarpeted stairs. It was such a nuisance for everyone. I lay on the floor covered with rugs and remember Buck saying, "If only she had been drunk," as apparently, when relaxed, one doesn't break bones. The doctor soon came and drove me back here where I was and am staying. He wanted to get up Harriet Aldrich, but this I refused to do. Everyone has been under such strain since the Suez crisis began. We went up to my bedroom, and the doctor said that he would cut me out of my dress, adding that he had often done it for the Queen and the Queen Mother. Do they fall downstairs all the time, do you suppose? I said he would cut me out of my dress only if my body was dead, which it wasn't, as it was a French dress from Balmain, so he undid the hooks and eyes, said he couldn't tell a thing without Xrays, but that it looked like a fractured collarbone, elbow, and arm, gave me a blessed shot of morphine, and left. Next morning, feeling terribly contrite, I had to inform the Aldriches, who came racing and were adorable, efficient, and affectionate. After an operation on the elbow, I returned here and could not be more comfortable, and should be able to get back to Paris soon. I am worried about Bill in the fuel rationing.

The English friends are angels of mercy. Sammy Hood comes every day from the Foreign Office, and although Harriet has had to return to America, I get great pleasure from Winthrop's company. He has had a very difficult time but is happier than he has been for weeks, as, at last, the President has regained his temper and is taking over personally. It's something to have Dulles out of the way, if only for two weeks. Please, God, let them decide soon and affirmatively about the economic help England needs. We are horribly unpopular, of course, and the Chancellor of the Exchequer uses the service stairs when he comes to ask for help, and Winthrop receives him in the sitting room down the hall, which we use *en famille*. Personally, I think we deserve to be unpopular and so does Winthrop, for all that sneaky phony Suez Canal Users Association of Dulles' in the summer which misled the British. But I am utterly horrified that Eden should have permitted himself to be so misled. I thought he had hated Dulles since that dramatic post-Dien Bien Phu confrontation in Paris two springs ago and had got his number then. Also, I am confused and wretched because of two conversations—God knows I must have heard two hundred, but these two were special.

One was in Paris at a small dinner at Pauline de Rothschild's during which Bourgès-Manoury[6] told us the French side of the story, the gist of which was that during all the secret planning the British took the leading role; Mr. Eden made a lot of sense, and the French were delighted with his courage, and although dismayed as time went on by the lumbering British execution of the plans, they still thought all would be well if they were permitted to make a spirited dash for Cairo. Then Eden went to pieces under pressure, according to Bourgès-Manoury, who was very nice about him, seemed genuinely fond of him, and felt that he was dealing with an ill man. It was a terrible story, with details which I will not put in an open letter.

The other conversation was at the Salisburys', the night of my stupid accident. Bobbety, trusting my discretion, told his wife and Buck what it had been like from the British side. You remember that he had been ill and at Hatfield during the crucial period. If he hadn't, I think it might have been different. In any case, he felt that he fully shared the responsibility and was totally loyal. But what he didn't say was worse than what he said, and I reeled out of that drawing room. I was so tense that it's a wonder that I only broke four bones on those shining stairs.

And this brings me back to the subject we have discussed before—Americans like you and me, Marietta, have been the most deep-dyed of Anglophiles since childhood. Guy Mollet is a brilliant and likable man, but Lord Salisbury is a great man, and this time he and the whole British Cabinet were wrong, and the result will be years and years of bitterness, not just the traditional French-English rows, but rows between all of us because British self-confidence is eroding, fast. And, surely, the history books will write that this was Britain's last hurrah as an independent great power. Perhaps it doesn't matter, and Britain in Europe, which eventually will be the outcome, will be healthier, but I feel sad.

To cheer me, a lovely tray with Thanksgiving turkey and cranberry sauce is arriving, with strengthening wine and hottest mince pie.

[6] Minister of Defense in the Guy Mollet government.

American Embassy
London, England
December 27, 1956

Our family Christmas here with the dear Aldriches has been the greatest success. Harriet thought of everything, from taking the children and me to the pantomime, to service at Westminster Abbey on Christmas morning with seats in the choir, to a huge children's party. For Bill, she provided gay evening parties and oxygen by his bed. I feel so lucky to have such a warm, American holiday for all of us, and the children have behaved beautifully. Anne flirts madly with Winthrop, who adores her and says that she will be a great beauty. The nicest thing about this sad and difficult year has been the children's progress. At last, I pulled myself together in the spring to teach Billy to read in English. He was an easy pupil. And did I write that when I went over to London in September to pick up the children, who had been in Cornwall with Mademoiselle, while Bill and I had been in that horrible German cure where he fell so ill, I found Billy hotly political. Between visits to Rowe's to buy his gray flannel shorts and cap and blazer and Liberty's to buy Anne's flowered dresses, with which she insists on wearing a stiff taffeta petticoat to make them stick out like a crinoline—she does look enchanting in them—and I do hope you like the photo this summer of her in her straw hat from Harrods trimmed in cornflowers, which made her big blue eyes sapphire-colored, Billy lectured me fiercely on Suez. He feels very gunboaty and is extremely worried lest this be another Munich. He is suspicious of Dulles and very pro-Eden. I cannot think how he picked all this up at eight years old staying with Mademoiselle's friend, an ex-governess who lives in a small Cornish seaside village. It is too soon to tell what their characters will be like, but Anne at six has been a real help to me this year. On her birthday, she had scarlet fever and never complained once. During the moving, she was so efficient that I found her toys done up by her and labeled. I particularly liked a Dior hatbox marked "*Affaires de la poupée Isabelle, propriété de Mademoiselle Anne Patten, 54 Avenue d'Iéna, Paris 16.*" And the headmistress tells me that she is no longer *dissipée* (all over the place); in other words, she is concentrating and has been first in her class several times. Billy is a rock of Gibraltar. Everyone loves him, and I don't think that his rows with Anne mean much. When Bill asked him what he wanted to be given for Christmas, he replied, "A bow and arrow to shoot Anne," but this is par for the course.

Hungary and Suez made this a cruel autumn. The French, with their usual instinct for what is important and what is less so, have minded the Russian invasion of Hungary more than the Suez disaster. Still close to the memory of occupation themselves, they felt the barbaric savagery of the efficient Russian machine bitterly and from bus driver to cabinet minister shook with rage over our Allied impotence. It still makes one sick to think about it. In Paris, of course, we saw many people who had been to the frontier to do what they could for the refugees. The Austrians must have behaved splendidly.

Here in London, the Aldriches and I talk of the happy things that have happened in the family this year, such as my cousin Sylvia's marriage to Robert Blake, a young Foreign Service officer whose reputation is high, and everyone likes him enormously in the family. We talk privately and sadly of the floundering ineptitude of the Eisenhower Administration, except in economic policy. Winthrop said solemnly that if Dulles died before he did he would not attend his funeral. Quite a statement, as Winthrop is a punctilious funeral-goer.[7]

[7] When John Foster Dulles died in 1959 Winthrop Aldrich did not attend the funeral.

· 1957 ·

54 Avenue d'Iéna
Paris, France
February 18, 1957

Bill and I went to London at the beginning of the month, he on World Bank business and both of us anxious to see off the Aldriches, who had been so very kind to us while Winthrop was Ambassador. There was a huge crowd at Waterloo Station to say good-by to them and they must have been very pleased by the affectionate letters and messages from their English friends during the last days. Bill dined as Winthrop's guest the night before among the highest in the land, and heard him make a speech which Bill thought excellent. As it was a men's dinner, Harriet took me to dine with Mrs. Brown of the American Embassy to listen to Winthrop on the radio. It was all women and I sat by Lady Alexander, wife of the Field Marshal. She was funny about a recent visit to the Queen at Sandringham. In the morning the men leave for shooting; if you get dressed and go downstairs early, in case the Queen wants you, she stays in bed till lunchtime. If you thankfully stay in bed, reading, you get a message at nine-thirty that the Queen would like you downstairs at nine forty-five. For tea, one changes into a printed silk dress (this in January) and, after tea, play games with the royal children. The favorite involves turning off all the lights and hiding in cupboards. Then the children disappear and rock and roll music is put on the victrola, everyone dances until eight-twenty when one is released to change into full evening dress for dinner at eight-thirty, and, believe me, one is on time.

Bill went on from his dinner to White's Club and stayed up late talking politics. I was delighted as it has been a year since he has felt like sitting up late; he came in with a sparkle in his eye and still didn't feel like going to bed so we sat up chatting and comparing notes. We agree that the post-Suez mood in London is distressing. They talk of little but the failed intervention last autumn and the reasons for it, and over and over again the cease-fire, whether they could have gone on to Cairo, should have gone on, and similar questions are brought up. It's bitter stuff. Our friends divide into three groups. One group blames the disaster on us and feel that, with our support, the operation would have been a roaring success. These are the happiest people, for their anti-Americanism absolves any possible guilt or doubt they might have felt. Group two, the majority, see clearly that they were quite wrong to have been for intervention at the time, that their judgment was at fault, and ask only to make a fresh start. Bill and I would have fallen into this group if we were English, for, as I wrote to you, our judgment was hopelessly pro-Eden at the time. These friends are miserable, but most miserable seem to be the friends (mostly intellectuals) who were farsighted enough to be against intervention from the start, on moral and practical grounds. They dislike their popularity with left-wing politicians, whose opportunism is showing more and more, and no one feels like crowing. It will be very long before the pain and hurt are over.

Paris seems so restful and cheerful, in comparison, no inhibitions about their role in the landings, and lots of pleasant things going on. Loelia Westminster is staying with us and we spent an afternoon visiting the theater at Versailles, built by the great architect Gabriel, messed up by Louis Philippe, abandoned since his day. It has taken five years to restore it and it will be inaugurated by a performance for the Queen of England in April. The restoration is a breath-taking success. The colors are blue and gold, all shades of blue from pale aquamarine to deep celestial blue, with touches of palest pink in the false marble columns. The velvets, taffetas, and moirés are of superb quality and nothing is pompous, the effect light and gay. Gerald van der Kemp, the charming young curator of Versailles, took us around and told us of recent gifts to the palace. Kress has given a hundred and fifty thousand dollars which will be spent on a bedspread in the Queen's bedchamber, the Chilean, Lopez, is doing the King's bed and also donating the material for the walls of the room. This costs just under three thousand dollars a yard. Van der Kemp was interesting about using his money—the theater was paid for by donations from the French public. He feels that it is worth spending these huge sums on hangings and embroidered materials in order to have a few rooms exactly as they were. With new treatments of cleaning and spraying, they should last for five hundred years, and in twenty years there will be no one left willing to make them. Even today only one house in Paris and one in Lyons can provide the workmen, as modern employees refuse to work in gold thread, doing the eye-straining embroidery, except at wages that no factory can afford to pay. Last week all the employees of Versailles struck and they had to close the palace for a day. It was a struggle to get them back, for they are badly underpaid. A guard gets fifty dollars a month and his tips. Van der Kemp, in charge of the most important collection in France, except for the Louvre, makes a miserable three hundred dollars a month. He got his employees back to work by appealing to their love of the palace, which really exists and is genuine, according to him, although one third, at least, are Communists.

54 Avenue d'Iéna
Paris, France
March 1957

Diana is back and we went to Chantilly for the weekend. Instead of one maidservant and her faithful secretary, Norah Fahey, we were greeted by a stylish Italian manservant called Carlo, a charming young French maid called Jacqueline, and the glowing Norah, who said that there was an equally nice cook in the kitchen. This was like the old days, and we were delighted for Diana, especially as the Prime Minister, Harold Macmillan (an old friend and admirer), had invited himself to stay. The next morning was less gay. Carlo appeared and said that the maid Jacqueline had been taken off in the night by three policemen. Diana said that that was impossible, as no one could be arrested without a charge and a warrant. Carlo said that if one had lived in Italy in the days of the Duce, as he had, one knew that anything was possible. Diana rang up the Chantilly police, who denied all knowledge of the abduction, and then the Paris police through Lady Jebb, who also knew nothing about it. Then Carlo appeared again, looking mournful, and announced that he had received a letter informing him that he must return at once to Milan to be tried for the murder of his former employer. Diana is wonderful in emergencies, summoned us all into her bedroom with Carlo and conducted a sort of trial, she lying in her big bed in the sunny room looking about thirty years old and very beautiful. The case was fascinating, we all became absorbed and decided eventually that Carlo was innocent, and that the murderess was probably the Marchesa di Caserta, wife of the victim, and a very nasty-sounding piece of goods. Diana thoroughly enjoyed her role as Lord High Chancellor but then remembered about the Prime Minister's arrival and leapt from her bed like a young girl in order to go to search for Jacqueline, the maid, in which task she was assisted by John Julius and Anne. They had the address of her house, forty kilometers away, and Bill and I left them to pick up our children and Mademoiselle at the station. When we all rejoined the search party was downcast. They had found an empty house, on which was written in French, "Abandon Hope All Ye That Enter Here," and on the door hung a bone, held by a string. They swear that this is true.

The Prime Minister canceled his visit at the last moment, and we had a lovely quiet weekend after that, but I do feel sorry for Diana. She doesn't deserve to have such servant problems, and Chantilly is one of the loveliest houses in the world to live in when it is running smoothly. Even when it isn't, like now, you can see that there is never a dull moment.

One thing that flatters Bill and me a lot is that Diana, who is normally shy with children, seems genuinely devoted to ours so we don't feel that it is a strain for her when we take them to Chantilly. Anne hangs on her words and follows her in from the garden helping to carry the great heaps of flowers, and stands adoringly passing them up as Diana creates one of her magical arrangements. "Four delphiniums now, Anne, mix the paler blues with the darker. Thank you. Now a big bunch of roses. That's it. Always remember when doing a mixed bouquet to have clumps of the same flower together. Not one here, one there, that makes for an arty bouquet. Arty things are common, don't you agree?" "Yes, Lady Diana." "Now, what shall we put on the luncheon table?" "Is it a party, Lady Diana?" "No, it isn't, and that is why we must take a lot of trouble. Parties are easy, but family lunch with just your parents and my children needs a little effort to make it gay for them. Suppose we put the white china unicorn on the middle of the table and make a wreath of white flowers for him to wear around his neck. Shall we go to pick the wild flowers?" "Oh yes, Lady Diana, can Billy come too?" "Of course he shall come"—and off they go, small figures skipping behind the beautiful tall one in her slacks and her huge straw hat, which Cecil Beaton calls Diana's uniform.

The above is a summer memory but, no matter what time of year, the children were always welcomed and loved by Diana, whom you once rightly called the only really glamorous woman in the world.

54 Avenue d'Iéna
Paris, France
April 11, 1957

The Queen of England has been in Paris and the fever of excitement has been like nothing we have seen since V-E Day in 1945. The papers relegated Algiers to the back pages and wrote about the golden toilet that had been brought to Versailles for her use (the suite will only have pinewood ones) and the arrangements for her trip down the Seine in a specially built boat, by night, with the whole city lighted up, and the evening at the Louvre which has been rehung so that in three rooms she can enjoy the gems of the collection and there doesn't seem to be a word of criticism anywhere. France is bankrupt. *Vive la Reine d'Angleterre!*

Joining fully in the fever, I took the children out of school the day she arrived and watched the procession from the balcony of the Rougemonts' apartment, which is ideally situated on the corner of the Boulevard des Invalides, down which she was to come. Being on the corner, we could see the Esplanade des Invalides, the huge space thronged with crowds waving flags and laughing and talking as they waited. It was a beautiful morning, cold but clear with brilliant sunshine, a sparkling light with the chestnut trees vivid, vivid green, their flowers slender candles. Louise de Rougemont had crowded her balconies with children, there must have been twenty or thirty small voices ready to shout as we heard the cannons sounding the salute far away across Paris as she entered the city. Then, at last, one caught the gleam of the burnished helmets of the escort, the Garde Républicaine, and the flash of the Napoleonic uniforms, which are scarlet and gold and blue. First came a squadron of chestnut horses, then bays, then grays, then an open car with the President of France, the Queen, and the Duke of Edinburgh. They had to slow down for our corner, and by chance the President looked up, drew the Queen's attention to all the children, and she glanced up at the waving, shouting little figures and gave them a huge smile. She looked lovely, in beige and white. Then they disappeared to thunders of "*Vive la Reine*" across the Seine to the Elysée Palace. The children will never forget this, and I must have been an English nanny in another life, for I was as excited as they. The next night we went to the Louvre reception, owing our invitation to the kind Jebbs. The guests, dressed in ball dresses and tiaras, and the men in white ties and decorations, lined the hall on both sides all the way from the Victory of Samothrace on the lighted staircase to the main entrance, and the Queen and her party walked down the middle between the curtsying ladies and the bowing men. The river trip the next evening brought several million cheering Parisians into the streets, and now that the visit is over the city seems as flat as a morning hangover.

Cy Sulzberger says that only the royal excitement this week has kept the British White Paper from causing a public outcry. There has been much gnashing of teeth in the NATO command here, as no one had been informed of how extensive the English defense cuts would be, and most of all they mind the sentence saying that the British Isles are no longer defensible, as this is going to sow defeatism and panic in France and Germany. I gather that, as of next December, Europe will be defended entirely by three very reluctant German divisions, only half prepared, four American divisions, three English, and one French. This is a long way from the Lisbon goal of thirty Allied divisions, but I feel that it was very sensible of the English to face facts. The bitter lesson of Suez sinking in, I suppose.

Today we are to picnic in the forest near Senlis, where years ago the Sulzberger children and our children built an Indian camp. It has become traditional to go out there every spring to see how it has fared through the winter. We will pick wild daffodils and primroses and Marina will cook Greek lamb over a wood fire and make it magical as she makes all occasions. My girl friends here are remarkable in their different ways. Elise Bordeaux-Groult, with her fragile body and her huge blue eyes, has been conducting a brilliant campaign against the important newspaper *Figaro* because of some vicious articles called "Letters to the Americans" that they have been publishing. She can be very fierce when she is aroused. And this spring she had another baby and moved Pierre, the family, and their great collection of art into their new home, a most lovely eighteenth-century house in the Rue du Bac. Bill thinks that she has more charm than any woman in Paris, and I would agree.

We are coming home this summer. I pray that you and Ronnie will be there as letter writing isn't enough and I can arrange our dates and plans any way that suits you. My poor mother is having a wretched time, as her youngest sister, my dear Aunt Harriet, is fatally ill and Aunt Martha not too well either. So our summer will be built around Mama, and perhaps you could join us in Maine? If not, we'll work out something else.

54 Avenue d'Iéna
Paris, France
May 18, 1957

Forgive me for not having written since before Easter, but I am so worried about my poor aunt and my mother that I write to them nearly every day. We spent the holidays at a very cheerful *pension de famille* in Chantilly, full of children for ours to play with, and visited Diana for the odd meal. She had a highbrow houseful over Easter—Patrick Kinross, who writes books about Turkey, Paddy Leigh-Fermor, who writes books about Greece today, Maurice Bowra, who writes books about ancient Greece and the French symbolists and is Warden of All Souls, Peter Quennell, who writes books about the eighteenth century. All these lions roaring away made for the gayest of dinner tables, but much the gayest experience we have had this spring has just taken place. I can only call it twenty-four hours with Adlai Stevenson. It began yesterday with breakfast at the Cy Sulzbergers'. The invitation was a typical piece of Cy's kindness, for he knew that Bill longed to meet Stevenson and I had only met him once when you took me to that party in Washington. The only other guests were Bill Blair and the New York *Times* man in Berlin. Stevenson impressed Bill Patten and me, enormously. In two hours of political conversation, he didn't drop a hint or a word of criticism of the President, his retentive mind was anxious to learn all Cy, the Berlin man, and Bill could tell him about Algeria, the Common Market, France vis-à-vis Germany, vis-à-vis England. He undoubtedly was highly informed before arriving but gave the impression of wanting to learn the maximum before going off to see the Foreign Minister and Spaak. The day before he had seen the Prime Minister at length and his comments were perceptive. I can't judge what kind of a President he would have made but it was refreshing to meet a distinguished American with a mind and a grasp like his, who instead of telling one his own views wanted to listen. I envy you deeply for working closely with him and knowing him so well.

We said good-by and did not expect to see him again but that night when we were in bed and nearly asleep, exhausted by a cocktail party we had given for World Bank types and others, the telephone rang and it was Bill Blair from the British Embassy where a dinner party was just breaking up, with an invitation to join Stevenson and him at the Lido in half an hour. The flattery hardly ballanced the fatigue, but we felt that it would be too middle-aged and dreary not to go so we dressed and set off for the horrible Lido, with its screaming endless floor show and its questionable champagne. It was quite worth it, as Stevenson was in splendid form and after the night club we returned here for another hour. The conversation was political, and he did the talking. We were enthralled and were sorry when at 4 A.M. Bill Blair took Stevenson home, still apparently quite fresh. How I love the quickness of his wit. The next day the British Ambassador said, "Didn't that four-hour Lido floor show cost you fifty quid?" Stevenson replied, "Gladwyn, don't you sometimes find that it is well worth fifty quid not to hear the sound of your own voice for four hours?"

Today I lunched at Marne la Coquette, which is the ridiculous name of the quarters of the Supreme Commander Larry Norstad and his pretty Isabel. It's Fort Benning done by Hollywood. The garden was full of flowers, the lake full of trout, the tennis court beautifully rolled, and a delicious lunch was served by smart Negro gentlemen, I suppose Air Force privates. As I looked around I hoped that the luxury makes up for some of the ghastly responsibility of the job, and thought of a story I heard last year of a flight of ducks crossing a radar screen in Central Europe. As they looked on the screen like Russian planes there was a frightful flap, but the Supreme Commander personally and fortunately decided that they were ducks and not planes. It can't be much fun.

The Algerian war is costing a billion francs a day and gasoline is nearly a dollar a gallon. Raymond Aron tells us that he is preparing a brochure which will make him extremely unpopular with the government. He plans to open with the line from Montesquieu, "Every citizen is obliged to die for his country but not to lie for it." He thinks that there is a lot of lying going on, and that Algeria must be given her independence. You would like Aron. Besides being the most respected political commentator in France, he is also a full professor at the Sorbonne and his lectures on government and history are so popular that the students attend the lecture ahead no matter what the subject, in order to be sure of a seat for the Aron class. He is tiny, birdlike, electric, with a thin big nose and tense long fingers, which he curls and uncurls when someone else is talking, not because he doesn't want to hear what they have to say but because his quick mind has caught the other's thought from the first words and he wants him to get on with it. His wife is just as bright as he is but, like all good wives, she knows when to shut up. I wish I did.

The children and I spent the summer of 1957 in Maine with my brave mother, who was mourning the loss of her beloved youngest sister, and facing the grave illness of her only remaining sister, my Aunt Martha Cross. Bill joined us briefly and we all returned to Paris in September. It had been and would continue to be an immobile year in international politics. The Eisenhower Administration seemed frozen on the defensive. I remember a Herblock cartoon of a woman in a supermarket with her cart carrying packages marked "Frozen attitudes," "Frozen platitudes," turning her worried gaze towards a sleepy John Foster Dulles at his desk. The caption was "Don't you ever have anything fresh?" The Russian artificial satellite, Sputnik, launched in early October shocked Americans into a crisis of self-doubt. As for France, the Fourth Republic was mortally ill, but the crisis and the drama were for the following spring. It was a dull, uneasy time.

54 Avenue d'Iéna
Paris, France
October 10, 1957

Billy picked up Sputnik the first morning it was heard, and came in swinging his little radio, which was going beep-beep. He explained it to me and, like all modern children, was quite undisturbed but very interested. The next morning we were all out with field glasses to catch it from the balcony but failed to see it. The French are taking it calmly and the papers are full of surprisingly pro-American articles pointing out that the Russian lead can be overtaken by our intelligent, industrial people now that they are warned. They go on to say that this is the time to draw closer to the United States and help in every way possible. This attitude is in sharp contrast to the auto-critical articles in the *Herald Tribune.* Russian pride is rampant in the kitchen. Old Nicolas, our White Russian chef, wounded veteran of Wrangel's army of the First World War, loather of Red Russia and all its works, is now so proud of his country's triumph that he buys every edition of every newspaper and sits gloatingly by his oven reading them.

It is now definitely decided that Billy will start school in England after the Christmas vacation. I feel sick, but we see no other way of preparing him for his later education in America. The school is near Oxford, and the atmosphere seems warm and kind. Aline Berlin's[1] boy, Peter, is starting there too and David Sulzberger is already a student, so he will start off with two friends. But nine years old! I

[1] I have already written of Sir Isaiah Berlin, our friend since wartime Washington. Surrounded by admirers, he nonetheless seemed to me a little lonely sometimes, and I rejoiced when in 1956 he married Aline, whose beauty and distinction come from her mixed French and Russian blood. It has been a truly harmonious marriage.

hope you won't think me brutal. Besides the importance of getting an Anglo-Saxon education, it also might be well to get Billy out of this apartment, for although both children are perfectly accustomed to the three oxygen tanks permanently in the hall and Bill is extraordinary in the way he rises above his illness, there is tension, and Mademoiselle thinks that Billy worries in private. It isn't a good atmosphere for Anne either, but I feel that girls are stronger when it comes to illness. The school is called Beachborough.

Another advantage is that I will be able to concentrate on helping Anne with her problems at school. I wrote to you before that the teachers complain that she is what they call *dissipée,* or unable to concentrate. In France this is already a problem to worry about, for they feel that a child of seven should be able to apply herself. They are probably right, and I got so worried myself at the teachers' reports that I took her to a child psychologist for an assessment. The tests show that she is well above average, in fact, near brilliant. What the block is remains to be determined. She is extremely popular at school, so it isn't that. We could put her in the American School, where the standards are extremely low, but it seems a pity. In any case, with Billy away she will get Mademoiselle's full attention as well as mine. Her father is the best of us with her, and her return from school each day will be even more of an event for him than it is now when he is dividing his strength between the two children he loves so much.

54 Avenue d'Iéna
Paris, France
November 27, 1957

Thank you for your beautiful letter about dear Aunt Martha. She liked and admired you enormously. Did anyone ever have such a talent for friendship? I owe her so, so much and shall miss her all my life.

This has been a gloomy month, hasn't it? Is the President's stroke as minor as they say? The French press are assuming that it is serious and are grinding out articles about Nixon, who is little known here. The sense of them is that anything would be better than Eisenhower. The French are in a vile humor. First there was no government at all for thirty-seven days, and the prestige of the Parliament is so low that if a deputy, any deputy, appears on a newsreel in a cinema everyone boos. Then we gave arms to the Tunisians and the entire country seems to think that we did it deliberately in order to hurt the French army in Algeria, as the Tunisians are suspected of running arms across the border to the rebels in Algeria. Our nice new Ambassador, Amory Houghton, is having a rough time. At dinner the other night, all French guests, except two, canceled out at the last minute; hearing of this, I put on a reasonably dressy red satin Balmain and felt like a fool, as the other women wore short black dresses, mainly wool. The front door was protected by helmeted Gardes Mobiles and there was some sort of minor riot outside during the fish course. The English are just as unpopular as we are. "Down with the English" is written in huge yellow letters on the Rougemonts' apartment house. A very English story was given me by Eddie Tomkins[2] about the Macmillan-French talks yesterday. Scene—the Matignon (Prime Minister's beautiful eighteenth-century house), the English party hours late on account of fog, the French biting their nails and tapping their pencils on the conference table. Mr. Macmillan, at last arriving, makes a moving speech about the failure of the Greek city-states to band together against Philip of Macedon. The moral is obvious, but the British Prime Minister, carried away by his subject, begins to speak in ancient Greek, and the other members of the British delegation outdo each other in quotations from Demosthenes about disastrous disaccords of the Achaean and Delian leagues. At last Gladwyn, who had been one of the best performers, caught the outraged eye of Monsieur Pineau[3] and recalled the meeting to the dreary subject of Tunisian arms.

Christian Dior is dead and I went to his funeral. He was very kind to me in the early days and I shall miss him. They say that a young man called Yves Saint Laurent is his chosen successor. It is an important business, for fifty per cent of the much-needed dollars France gets from the fashion industry came from Dior alone.

[2] Sir Edward Tomkins, then a young secretary, is now British Ambassador to France.

[3] Christian Pineau, Prime Minister of France, 1957.

54 Avenue d'Iéna
Paris, France
December 19, 1957

Your descriptions of New York and Washington are very interesting. No wonder you came back from Joe Alsop's feeling triple doomed, his recent articles send icicle shudders down one's spine and leave no hope. Knowing his convictions and courage, I sometimes wonder if he thinks out the effect on his readers, which is enough to turn us all into isolationists. I am much interested in what you say about the trend towards conformity in America. Have you read *The Twenty-fifth Hour*, which was a best seller here last year? It is discouraging reading, representing the widespread view in Europe that, while the Russians are barbarians, our values are as crushing to the individual as theirs are; and that, while more comfortable physically to be dominated by the United States, there is not much to choose spiritually.

The NATO conference here started with a sense of frustration and gloom. Paris was apathetic. Political meetings were banned, which was thought to be efficient of the French police, and there were no incidents on the route from Orly airport when President Eisenhower arrived. The White House people, who had been here for a week, seemed like men from Mars, our Embassy friends told us, as they were worrying about large enthusiastic crowds on the route. They were surprised to be told that this would not be a concern, as the President is hissed every time there is a picture of him on the screen of a movie house, as is the Queen of England. (The boring Tunisian arms business I wrote about before.) I took the children to church on Sunday and to my huge surprise saw a man, who I had thought from his pictures was old and withdrawn and ill-looking, pink and energetic and vital. As his stroke was so very recent, I could hardly believe it, but the French are very quick at appreciating courage and quality and within forty-eight hours the word had got around that the President was putting up an extraordinary performance and people began talking about Ike the Liberator, which was the name they called him long ago, and the press changed its tune as did the crowds, which really did applaud him as he passed through the streets in his car. Perhaps the enormous piece of window dressing which is this conference will not lead to any real achievements, but as it ends one rather gathers that the dangerous atmosphere of everyone for himself and Devil take the hindmost, of the last few months, is less prevalent. I have no idea how much Eisenhower affected the meetings, but perhaps one phrase was said, one chord was struck that will make it worth his having come, and I would like to think so.

We are saving your Christmas presents with our usual eagerness, you are much too generous to your godson Billy and to me. He is eager to be off to school in England, which makes it less bad for us, and after Christmas we go to Switzerland with Aline Berlin and her boys for a skiing holiday before the dread day.

· 1958 ·

7 Park Place
London, England
February 21, 1958

I write from my new discovery, a small, comfortable London hotel where, for two pounds a day and the shillings one drops into the gas fire, I have a view over the Green Park, a bathroom with boiling water, and Piccadilly around the corner. Nothing could be more cheering, and I did rather need it as Billy's departure for school a month ago was traumatic for us. He was courageous, so was Bill, I was a mess and even fell ill with flu, so Bill had to take him to England alone. He and Aline Berlin drove the boys to school, and Billy wrote the next week that all was well and that the older boys and the masters had both told him that homesickness would be perfectly natural and that he should cry if he felt like crying, because everyone would understand. It must be a kind school, and I was further relieved when Billy wrote that he hadn't felt homesick yet. This last weekend I stayed with the Berlins and Billy has never looked so well, pink-cheeked, fatter, eyes sparkling, his first words, "Oh, Mummy, I adore school!" It will make the most tremendous difference to have Aline nearby at Oxford, she is as kind as if she were Billy's aunt and he feels totally at home in her house. It was lovely to spend the last afternoon in the Berlins' nursery, with the boys playing with toy trains, and not feel that Billy was tight-tummied with anguish as the hour grew near for return to Beachborough. Peter, Aline's son, was miserably unhappy, and I felt all the horrors of homesickness again as I watched his brave efforts to down tea. Sunday afternoon is the cruelest time.

It is now definite that Bill will leave the World Bank, probably on May 1; they have been wonderful to him as for them it is the worst of luck that his health should have deteriorated so much since they took him on. He feels that any tough organization would have fired him long ago, and looks back on his two and a half years there with pleasure. We debated coming back to America to live, but Bill dreads being a retired semi-invalid of forty-eight in the United States, where we have no home. In Paris we have a beautiful apartment, our devoted servants, and enough money to live very pleasantly. Already we are planning the trips we will take and morale is excellent. My wonderful mother is coming over and is renting Diana's house at Chantilly for the month of April so that we can enjoy the childrens' holidays in the country. Then we have the glorious summer plans to look forward to with you and Ronnie in Portugal. So don't worry about us.

I am going back to Paris tonight, after a fascinating unexpected visit to Yorkshire with Marina Sulzberger. We stayed at Nostell Priory, which belongs to the Winn family. The title is St. Oswald, and Marina knew the present owner in Cairo in the war. Marina is so Greek and Mediterranean that even Paris seems too northern a climate for her, and although she adapts chameleonlike to any ambiance in which she finds herself, it did seem odd to be on a train in England in February with her, heading five hours north into the heart of the black country. Nostell is one of the most famous houses in England; Chippendale was the house carpenter, so most of the furniture, the picture frames, the fireplaces and fire implements, the billiard table, practically the kitchen table are by his hand, or that of his friend, Robert Adam, who came up from London to work with him. Best of all is a doll's house, the completely furnished model of a London town house in 1740. Lord and Lady St. Oswald are young and brave and poor, due to some trust arrangement they can't sell a doorknob from the house, if they could they would be millionaires. We walked in a park which was full of deceptively beautiful trees; by deceptive I mean that if one reaches out to touch one the bark is so black that one's fingers look like a chimney sweep's. The coal mines are very near, and dark comes down by midafternoon. Inside was nearly as cold as out, but I slept in a room decorated with emerald-green eighteenth-century Chinese wallpaper about which red and blue parrots swooped, and the furniture, of course by Chippendale, was of the brightest green lacquer. It is a marvelous house, and I so admired the courage of the owners.

It will be fun to get back to Paris with so much to tell Bill and Anne. I have had a letter from Anne, saying that she had a rich week with Ronnie's piggy bank.

I had rather forgotten the piggy bank, so in 1974, sixteen years later, I asked Anne, now Mrs. George Crile, to write down for me what she could remember about it: "The piggy bank was one of the most exciting things in Paris. No one had a piggy bank like it. It was a present from Mr. Ronald Tree and was gilt-covered in fake diamonds and rhinestones and pearls. It had huge blue eyes, and long eyelashes that blinked when money dropped in. When you put in a centime it would not tip its hat but anything over five hundred francs and it would lift its crown of diamonds in thanks. I would be allowed into the library while drinks were on and I would curtsy to the guests and then make an immediate demand for money. I kept a list of chief suckers. Mr. Joyce, Uncle Joe Alsop, the Duchess of Westminster, Guy Dumur, Sammy Hood. There were many other suckers, mostly people who came from far away. Lady Diana was not a sucker."

In May of 1958 the tottering Fourth Republic of France fell. The first dramatic event was the insurrection of the Algerian settlers against Paris. On May 13 the chief government building in Algiers was sacked and two generals came into power, Salan and Massu, invoking the name of de Gaulle. Mendès-France called this sedition, and at first there was little popular demand for the return of General de Gaulle. But fear of civil war grew daily, and by the end of the month de Gaulle's return was greeted with relief. The irony of it was that no one knew what his position really was on Algeria. The military junta took for granted that he would never give independence, in which they proved quite wrong, for he later led France out of North Africa with skill and courage, ending the horrible long war. Those two weeks in May were extraordinary.

54 Avenue d'Iéna
Paris, France
May 15, 1958

Paris, since the riots in Algeria two days ago, has been quiet as a May morn. It is eerie, as except for the vast numbers of police thrown about one wouldn't know that anything was happening. What this means is that the center of power has passed or is passing to Generals Salan and Massu in Algiers and the Republican government here is floundering like a stranded whale. One listens to the radio, talks to one's friends, and prepares nightly for the occupation of Paris by Massu's paratroopers. It has occurred to us to send Anne to England, but we rather feel that there will not be civil war and that by the time you get this you will be reading of an uneasy compromise between the government and the military. But it is too soon to know much. Raymond Aron sounds nervous. He rang up Bill today and suggested that, as a friend of Joe Alsop's, Bill should ring him in Washington and tell him not to wait but to fly here tonight "as the situation is getting more serious hour by hour." Cy Sulzberger dined here and thinks that it is that bad or worse. While we debated about ringing Joe, he called up himself to announce that he was on his way soonest.

I'll write again as soon as possible, and don't worry about us. Marina Sulzberger, Elise Bordeaux-Groult, and I have taken to lunching at Chez Marius, near the Chambre, where the deputies lunch, and we agreed today, over our Charolais melons, that it's too awful, but one does rather enjoy having adrenalin running through one's veins.

54 Avenue d'Iéna
Paris, France
May 30, 1958

I hadn't thought that anything could have been more exciting than last week but this week was. Joe has been a tower of strength, so calm and sensible. Monday night was all rumors and uncertainty, Tuesday Joe could find out nothing about the mysterious meeting of Pflimlin[1] and de Gaulle known to have taken place at St. Cloud during the night, this was most frustrating, and the atmosphere in Paris was heavy and uneasy. People went about their business as they have throughout this. I had had my nails done and remarked to the manicurist that she looked tired, she sighed and said she wasn't tired but the days of agonizing worry seemed interminable; I think everyone felt like this, although the streets seemed quiet and rather empty, except for the queues at the newspaper kiosks. The *Tribune*

[1] Pflimlin was the last Prime Minister of the Fourth Republic of France.

was taken off the stands that day, for an article about the navy, and there were more and more blank spaces in the French press. Joe and I decided to go antiquing, and spent the afternoon on the Left Bank; we found the antique dealers delightfully unpolitical and had a very good time, buying nothing. Stopped at the *Tribune* office to find that the atmosphere was worsening as the General had returned to Colombey as the Socialists unexpectedly had refused to support him, in spite of their leader, Guy Mollet. Joe went off to see some useful contacts and returned to the Avenue d'Iéna with the news, new to us, that the reason for the Prime Minister's appeal to de Gaulle had been that paratroopers from Algiers were now covering all the military airports and the high command had told the government that they couldn't hold them much longer, Paris was encircled. He then left for the Chambre. Bill was in bed, I told him little of this and dined alone. Cy Sulzberger then rang me up and told me not to repeat his opinion but he thought things were very bad indeed and that he hoped I had money in the house and to fill the bathtubs. Joe rang up a few minutes later from the Chambre, said that he still felt in his bones that there would be no civil war but he might well be wrong, and that he was sending along a black markety sort of man he had got hold of who would take a dollar check and give us francs. This type appeared about 11 P.M. and was rather agreeable; we had a little political chat and he said that de Gaulle would get in, after a blood bath, and go straight off to Moscow; he had it on the best authority. Maria de Maud'huy rang up to gossip and exchange news; she had heard that General Salan depends for his comfort on opium or heroin, I forget which, had for some reason run out of it, and had lost all his will power and Massu was in complete control. This is typical of the kind of unlikely conversation one has with one's friends these days, one believes little but can no longer be surprised by anything. Mademoiselle rang up from Normandy and said that tension was rising in the provinces and would I rather she kept Anne out of Paris or that they stayed there? I said to wait and see, I would let her know. At midnight or so I went into the kitchen to find Nicolas and Janine listening to the radio. I told them that, while I didn't want to alarm them, Mr. Alsop had heard some worrying news about the paras being all around Paris, and in the morning we must see about our stocks. Old

Nicolas said gently that he had known for two days about the paras, but not to worry, there would be no civil war. Joe came back very late; he said that the Chambre in its death agonies had been rather impressive, the Prime Minister had been moving and there had been other good speeches, that Jules Moch had joined the others in pleading to de Gaulle (Moch is the tough, excellent Minister of the Interior who saved the situation in the riots of 1947) and he hates de Gaulle, but the prefects' reports from the provinces were very alarming.

In the morning, Wednesday, the first telephone call was from Kitty Giles, in a towering rage, to say that Joe had insulted Frank in the bar of the Chambre that night and that if he didn't call up to apologize she would never speak to him again. I mention this only because it was typical of the many tiny unexpected things that happen when nerves are on edge. As Kitty is due to have a baby next week and sounded in a most frightful state, I went in to Joe at breakfast and made him call up and apologize, which he did with grace. He had no idea what he could have said to annoy Frank; it turned out that he had merely said that Frank was writing the story all wrong and knew nothing about history! Bill was better and got up for lunch. We saw Joe off to the Communist demonstration very nervously; it turned out to be as disciplined and unexciting as a Sunday school picnic. Another evening of rumors, radio, conjecture. I mustn't wear you out, but last night is worth describing. We all three dined at the Eddie Tomkinses' on the Avenue Gabriel, to meet Eddie's stepfather, a French banker who was interesting as he had been in Algiers on the thirteenth of May. After dinner we sat about, the radio on low, as it always is nowadays, Gladwyn Jebb telephoning nervously to hear what news anyone had (this was after Coty's[2] speech threatening resignation unless the Socialists and the MRP gave in and accepted the General). It was the first hot summer night, the Tomkins apartment is high over the chestnut trees of the Avenue Gabriel and it was very pretty. I remember Eddie's stepfather had just commented on the heat and remarked that the thirteenth of May would never have taken place had not the temperature that day been thirty-five degrees centigrade and a sirocco blowing, when suddenly through the open windows we

[2] René Coty was the last President of the Fourth Republic.

heard the unmistakable sound of a crowd coming down the Champs Elysées, singing the *Marseillaise*. We jumped up, and I am not proud of the next part of the story as it sounds so selfish, in fact it was. Gill Tomkins is having a baby and can't move off her sofa, Bill clearly can't move much, and Eddie was obliged to stick with his wife. The stepfather turned rather puce, the butler ran in in hysterics crying, "*Fermez les volets* [Close the shutters]," the spaniels began to howl—I didn't even take my bag, I just grabbed Joe and we ran downstairs and out to the Champs Elysées, so fast that Joe forgot his glasses, which was important later. I wouldn't let him go back, also Joe had cold feet about my being with him and I felt if I let him hesitate we were lost. At the corner of the Avenue Gabriel and the Avenue Matignon, by Reboux, we were momentarily cut off by the police, who for two weeks had been lounging about under the chestnut trees playing belotte and smoking, but now became very efficient. In a second, two great trucks were thrown across the road to the Elysée Palace[3] with a great many tough-looking types lined in front of them, whistles were blown and Gauloises cigarettes were discarded in favor of submachine guns which came from nowhere. Joe began to curse himself up and down for having me there, and it all seemed very exciting. Only for five minutes, then the word was passed that the demonstrators were innocuous young students, the paras were not out, and everything relaxed so that we could proceed to the Champs Elysées. This looked exactly like V-E night, cars covered with girls and boys, horns blowing gayly, a cheerful crowd walking, shouting "*Vive de Gaulle*," many had torn off branches from the chestnut trees and swung them. We joined the procession and walked to the Etoile; on the way we passed the Mouchy family, who had just come out of the movies and were standing with their mouths open on the corner—they opened wider at seeing Joe and me in the middle of a Gaulliste demonstration. We turned down and walked to the Place de la Concorde, the gaiety, shouting, honking by now indescribable, and at one moment Joe was arm in arm with a large fat blonde who was singing one of the old liberation songs that I hadn't heard for ages. At Fouquet's we peeled off to telephone to our loved ones at the Tomkinses' that everything was like the Fourteenth of July, and not to worry. Joe, however, was still un-

[3] The President's residence.

certain, he thought this might well be a cover. Then an unpleasant thing happened. We stepped out of the crowd at the Franklin D. Roosevelt Métro station to have a moment's rest and regard the scene, and, looking down, we both saw five armed paratroopers at the bottom of the stairs. Only for a second, then they disappeared. Joe without his glasses was frantic. At the Place de la Concorde we met a *France Soir* man who advised us not to go to the Chambre, which had been my idea, as nothing was going on there, but to the Elysée Palace, so we went there–nothing there but more gay crowds. Still worrying about our paras, we returned to the Tomkinses', picked up Bill, and drove easily in our own car to the bar of the California on the Rue de Berri, where we found the staff of the *Tribune* comparing notes. Frank Kelley, who is a good, serious correspondent, had also seen a couple of paras, so we felt better. Home to bed for Bill and me; Joe went to the Place de la République but nothing was happening.

Today has been quiet, de Gaulle should have his government and be in before the weekend is over.

54 Avenue d'Iéna
Paris XVI, France
June 3, 1958

Postrevolution is terribly dreary, and don't let anyone tell you it isn't. Hangover after three weeks of intense excitement is both physical and moral, and yesterday, our first normal day, I found everyone cross. First, Bill, to whom I made the above remark about dreary old normality, to which he replied, no doubt rightly, that I had been making a Roman holiday out of a sad affair and an intellectual word game out of a near tragedy. Cross, I went in to Joe, who has been divine and a calm, optimistic, wise support throughout, and found him cross, so soon I was crosser.

Then I went to have a drink with Guy Dumur, a member of the non-Communist left, at the Café Flore. I hadn't seen him since the fourteenth of May, the day after this all began, when he had lunched here with Marina and me and had been excited and happy. He said then that this would show that if France was not rotten—and he didn't think it was—the extreme right had gone too far, and these events would enable the non-Communist left to show leadership, regain control of the Republic, and finish the Algerian war.

Yesterday, he greeted me sourly, saying, "And where have you been all this time, demonstrating in the Place de la Bastille, I suppose?" This crack was because the left-wing demonstrations have been a failure, and there have been things in the papers about ladies in Balmain dresses demonstrating.

Guy's view is that Guy Mollet is a villain, betraying the Socialist Party; but he admits, sadly, that there was little to betray, for there was no real fight in any party of the left. He feels that the de Gaulle Cabinet is a horrid mess. I tried to cheer him with André Malraux, and he said what sort of a Cabinet was it that had Michel Debré (right-wing nationalist) balanced by Malraux, that this compromise would merely paper over the cracks, and that the "system" remained unchanged. I left him with the impression that he would have greatly preferred a proper civil war last week.

He, at least, told me a funny story. Perhaps you will have heard it, but I liked it. De Pen, notorious Poujadiste deputy, hired himself an airplane and went to Algiers ten days ago. Instead of being met by enthusiastic supporters, he was met by some soldiers who told him they didn't want him in Algiers and to get back on his airplane. Astounded, for, like all the right wing, he had misjudged the army and thought them to be as Fascist as the civilians involved in the various plots, he got sadly back, and was taken aloft, only to be briskly called to earth again. Alighting, full of hope that there had been a mistake, he was told that they had merely forgotten to kick him in the pants and planned to rectify that mistake now; at which he burst into the *Marseillaise*, causing them to have to go into the *garde-à-vous*.[4] When he had finished intoning the last bars, which as you can imagine, he dragged out as long as possible, they fell on him and he returned to his airplane beaten and mauled. Even Guy liked this story and, as he said, for all their faults, the French army is sane.

I left Guy to return to the Rougemonts, whom I found none too cheerful either. What, they said, can you do with a government con-

[4] Attention—position automatically assumed if the national anthem is played.

taining both Malraux and Michel Debré (simply reverse the point of view) and the "system" remains unaltered. I left them also with the impression that they wished that things had gone further last week although, like Guy, they have a horror and loathing of coups d'état. I forgot to say that, to cheer up Guy, I had said what about the rebirth of France, demographically and economically, which has been evident to anyone who knows anything about the country for the last couple of years; to which he replied that economic renaissance without an ideology is a false, dead thing. I didn't put this to the Rougemonts, but I think they might not have disagreed. Please don't quote any of this, for I know that Jean Louis and Louise really did not want blood shed, and they both stated categorically that, from the international point of view, what did happen was better. Their only question was whether France might not have emerged a stronger country without this compromise. In my own view, this is the only possible way it could have worked out. I personally loathe it and cannot swallow it without feeling sick. This greasy legality—there I am with Guy—de Gaulle got in because the whole of France was terrified of the parachutists, and I find it very sad that there was no one to fight for the Republic. There is, however, a very good chance, as Joe and Bill believe, that with the reform of the Constitution this new energy above mentioned will be canalized.

After this, Bill and I went to do some errands. We met Hoytie,[5] who was garrulous about her troubles, which were that she has a tame taxi driver. Hoytie had forced him to carry a gun during the past few weeks, indeed arming him herself with a blunderbuss dating from the Civil War, which was all she could put her hands on. The poor man has now been arrested by the police for carrying a weapon without a license and put in jail, and Hoytie is very cross because she can't get the taxi driver to take her to parties, which will now blossom again with the end of the crisis, and the taxi driver's wife is very cross, and it is all most unhappy.

Home to say good-by to Joe, with whom I had a last splendid tease, as General Ely had sent for him to thank him for his articles and to say that the whole French army consider him its spokesman! This really seems going a bit far, relieved as we are that the French

[5] Miss Mary Hoyt Wiborg, aged American expatriate, sister of Mrs. Gerald Murphy, survivor of Scott Fitzgerald's Paris of the twenties.

army are not the Fascist beasts we thought they might have become. We had a lovely dinner, toasting the new "spokesman" in champagne. It doesn't seem possible that Joe can avoid the Légion d'Honneur, although he swears that he will never accept it. He left for Algiers at midnight and Mary Whitehouse arrived from Italy and is with us now for a week.

Forgive this letter, badly written, but loving.

Bill and Anne have been having such a funny time since things quieted down. We are worried about her math and Bill has taken on the job of tutoring her for her exams. To teach her the multiplication tables he sent out for crates of oranges. His system worked well, but Edmond has lost his sense of humor about the demonstrations. Ten by ten oranges is bearable, but when they got to twelve by twelve, oranges were rolling all over the apartment. No one gives his children more care or more fun than Bill. Have I ever written about the Saturday expeditions to eat oysters? Since they were very small Bill, who adores oysters, has been taking them to a place near the Gare St. Lazare where they sit on the sidewalk eating their fill. Bill has a glass of white wine and the children water with a drop of wine in it. Everyone loves these expeditions, and since Billy went to school in January Anne was allowed to accompany her father until the oyster season closed. But I am sure she will tell you all about it herself during our lovely summer vacation together in Portugal, to which we are all looking forward intensely.

I have written in early letters of how impressed I was by the independence of spirit and courage of Frenchwomen. Legally they were in those days anything but liberated, and those of us who have struggled through the endless pages of Simone de Beauvoir know the hard side of the story. But my last tale of the Algerian war, which took years to terminate, is about the spring of 1961, when there was another revolt, this time on the part of the military, who felt that they had been let down and tricked by de Gaulle. Once more, three springs later, parachutists menaced the Parisian skies. One of my best friends, a glamorous creature whom we shall call the Comtesse de X, rang me up casually and said that it was believed that Orly airport would be overrun the following morning. She said that her car, a little Renault, was already in position, backed into the garage and ready to go. I said, "But where will you go?" "To blockade the road from Orly to Paris, of course. They say that we should be in position by 5 A.M. when we get the word." "Are there enough of you? And what do the husbands say?" "There are lots of us, and the husbands will be asleep in bed because they know nothing about it. You must realize, Susan Mary, that this will be the Foreign Legion we are dealing with. Nothing but Germans these days, too sad, it used to be so chic." Happily for the Foreign Legion, the parachute landings never came.

We had wonderful plans for the summer of 1958. As usual, Marietta and Ronnie were responsible for the pleasure in store. Ronnie had discovered that a beautiful old house near Cintra in Portugal had been made into a hotel. It was called the Setais, and perhaps appealed to him because its classical eighteenth-century façade had a look of Ditchley, the house in England which he and Marietta had left so regretfully nine years before. As the hotel was new, small, and not well known, we were able to take most of the rooms for the summer vacation. Elise and Pierre Bordeaux-Groult, their children, our children, as well as the Trees with Penelope and her nurse Mabel, our Mademoiselle Oger, and Bill and I was the party we planned. The beaches on the Atlantic were not far away, the forests are perfect for picnics, the hotel had a huge garden, and for the grownups the sightseeing possibilities from Cintra were endless and rich. However, Bill fell acutely ill and there could be no question of our leaving Paris. Typically, the Trees and the Bordeaux-Groults took Billy and Anne and Mademoiselle with them and gave them a glorious summer. It was the most terrible time in both our lives. I owe a debt to France for his care which I can never discharge. The next letter describes what happened.

54 Avenue d'Iéna
Paris, France
July 10, 1958

"Letter to Mother"

It seems to me a great privilege to live among people whose minds work quickly and who cut red tape. We had a lovely weekend in England taking out Billy from his school, and returned on Monday morning, Bill looking and seeming better than he had in weeks. Later that day I left for Holland with two girl friends to tour houses and gardens; the next evening before dinner I called Paris to be told by Edmond that Bill seemed sleepy, confused, and very unwell. I asked how much oxygen he had been using; when Edmond told me my heart sank as Bill knows the dangers of overoxygenation. I told him to send for Dr. Varay urgently and tore for The Hague in a taxi, caught a plane, and was at the Avenue d'Iéna an hour and a half from the time of my telephone call. In the plane I considered whether Bill would want to be pulled out of this one or not. His suffocating, breathless days and nights seemed to me unbearable, and the intervals of comfort and pleasure are getting rarer. But Bill is a fighter, a lover of life, an adoring father. It would be up to him to decide, I had always thought, and up to me to back him up. In this instance, decision was taken out of his hands. I found him unconscious, with the doctor there and an ambulance outside. Things went very fast. Dr. Varay told me that it was uremic poisoning and that we were on our way to the Hopital Necker, which is an ancient Paris public hospital. He said that he was afraid I wouldn't like it compared to the American Hospital, but as Necker possessed the only artificial kidney equipment in Paris we had no choice.

Necker is a forbidding building; the first thing one notices is a flight of endless stone steps at the entrance, lit by a couple of dim bulbs. At the foot of the steps was a pile of stretchers, covered with dried bloodstains. They don't have enough money to change the canvas of their stretchers, or to have an elevator, or to light the stairs. We went straight up to a ward called the Salle Lefort, which Varay explained to me is for critical cases only, and Bill was put into an immaculately clean bed. Tests were started (the results came back within an hour) and never once was there a formality. The head nurse asked me my name and if I could pay the equivalent of nine dollars a day, which would include everything. I said I could, and she said that she suggested we skip the paperwork and that she was putting two special nurses on Bill's case, giving me their names, that their shifts would be twelve hours, but to continue the artificial respiration which had already started we might need more help, so if I wanted to bring in a friend for the night not to hesitate, as there are no visiting hours in the Salle Lefort. I sent for Elise Bordeaux-Groult for several reasons: she is brave and quick-witted and loves Bill, and her valiant spirit gives her physical strength. Also I wanted an American friend, for already the nurses were talking urgently to Bill, trying to bring him out of his torpor, and I thought an American voice might help. Our doctor and dear friend, André Varay, then told me that after consultation with his colleagues he had decided against the artificial kidney, as Bill could not have survived the shock, also against a tracheotomy, so the treatment was to be artificial respiration, assisted by a breathing machine. He said that the chances were twenty-five per cent, perhaps a little less.

Pierre and Elise arrived and we worked through the night, in teams. Elise was the best, shouting at Bill or alternately coaxing him in her lovely voice that has charmed so many men. The nurses were remarkable, young, gentle, compassionate, highly efficient. As I got to know the Salle Lefort, I discovered that to nurse there is a high distinction, only the elite are chosen. Physically, it must be very hard. The floors are stone, without carpeting. The beds are close together and, during our time there, several of the patients were Algerians, terrorists who had been picked up trying to kill Frenchmen. They got just as good care as everyone else, but they were very noisy and their families crowded the floors beside their beds, moaning day and night. The equipment was either the best and most modern that money can buy or the most shabby and antiquated, there seemed only extremes. Everything that could be was shining and spotless.

During that first night, I became conscious of sound as never before. The sound was the wailing of the Arabs. It sounds to someone like me who has no musical ear like Ai-ai-ai. Monotonous, ageless, echoing and re-echoing from the stone walls and ceiling, it came through to Elise and me, working over Bill not more than two feet away from the nearest Algerian, dying in his bed beside us, with his family there. While it was still dark, the head night nurse came up quietly to tell me that she thought it time for Elise and me to take a walk in the courtyard. The courtyard, she said, was a fine seventeenth-century example of architecture, and the moon was still up, although fading. She thought that we could do with a bit of air. She added, as though it was nothing, that she had put two more special nurses on the case, they were on their way. This meant four special nurses, on the case of one American charity patient. Elise and I went down to the courtyard, which was indeed of arcaded beauty, and in the moonlight we lit cigarettes and sat on a stone bench. We were dripping with sweat, for artificial respiration is tiring, and neither of us weighs much over a hundred pounds. Elise and I talked shorthand, as I do with Marietta. There was no time to waste. I said, "Elise, we've lost the fight. Do you think I could ask these French doctors to give Bill a strong dose of morphine?" She said, "The hell you can. They probably will, if it comes to that, because they are more merciful and less frightened than in an American public hospital. But just you wait—" and we went back to the Salle Lefort. The Algerian keening was worse than ever.

Elise started again on the artificial respiration; at the same time she started talking to Bill in a tone and in a language that I had never heard before. When the next shift took over I took her aside. She was dripping and breathless, and when she could speak I told her that I thought that she had pulled Bill through—for I had seen, just for a moment, a light in his eyes. "Elise, where did you learn how to talk like that?" "Don't you remember, S.M., that I was married to Henry Mortimer and spent the war at Fort Riley? Sorry about the four-letter words, but I thought it was time for sergeant-major stuff, in English."

The next day Bill was put into a little private room giving into the main ward. Here we had a chair, which seemed to Elise and me a great luxury. That night he regained consciousness, and five days later he was taken off the critical list. I went to see the head nurse, who was sitting at her desk wearing her shabby old uniform with the three stripes on her cap denoting her years and years of service. She was working over her charts and her decisions, paying no attention to an enchanting little girl of five who was playing at her feet. This was her niece, she explained, adding sadly, "I know that it's no playground, but what can one do, her mother is ill and there was no one to leave her with." She said that it was wonderful about Bill, that she didn't want to hurry us but it would be a great help to have his bed. We went home the next day, still not having paid one cent; when the bill did come it was for forty-five dollars. The nurses kissed me good-by, and that night, to our amazement, the young doctor in charge of Bill's case at the hospital appeared at the Avenue d'Iéna, to check up on him. This was like having a Bellevue resident drop in on a case on Park Avenue after it had been discharged; he didn't have to, I couldn't pay him as he belongs to the city of Paris, but he said he was worried about the medication and wanted to come. We showed him the Bennett machine,[6] which had just arrived from America.

You will be worrying about the children's reactions to this terrible time. Billy is still in England, thank goodness, and Aline Berlin has seen to it that he knows his father has been ill but is now recovering. Anne has of course been much on my mind, and I managed to come home once a day every day from the hospital to reassure her as best I could. The friends have been wonderfully kind, not only her two godmothers, Louise and Odette, but Dottie and Marina and Diane de Mouchy and others kept her busy and amused.

54 Avenue d'Iéna
Paris, France
September 12, 1958

Words are impossible; one can't find them, and I can only hope that your radar occasionally picks up a fragment of my gratitude and appreciation of all you did for my family in Portugal this summer. If only dear Frankie had been there, too! As it is, Billy talks much of his godmother and do tell Penelope that in the car the other day I turned on the radio to hear a Lucienne Boyer voice singing that romantic song, "La Seine," and Billy said, "That would be one of Penelope's songs." "Oh, does Penelope know that?"

[6] This example of American ingenuity was new in those days. Now every hospital in the United States has a supply of them. By a system of valves the patient inhales the correct amount of oxygen and exhales carbon dioxide, and since its invention, no sufferer from emphysema need ever be so uncomfortable again. Young Dr. Antoine of the Hospital Necker was thrilled by the Bennett, and we ordered one for him, which was a small present from us to the city of Paris.

"Perhaps she doesn't know it," said Billy, sighing, "but it is a Penelope song."

Our news is all good. Bill seems better; I dare not hope too much, but anyway, his morale and his own hope—just these last few days—are a tremendous improvement. He tells me all the time that he hasn't felt so well in years, and says it with such conviction that I think he means it. I feel so much better, too, dearest Marietta; I am not nervous when I don't feel that Bill is unhappy, and he isn't today, September 12, 1958. The prognosis cannot be certain, ever; after all, the great heart specialist gave him two years over two years ago, and the plan for today, for example, is to have Elie de Talleyrand for luncheon, the Johnny Alsops[7] for drinks, Charlie Adams to dine, and possibly a drive to the Bois for an hour this beautiful September afternoon.

The friends continue their loyal support—on paper, if they cannot come themselves. I had a sweet postcard today from Adlai Stevenson, which I plan to answer, saying that he is the visitor who has most impressed and amused Bill this month. People come at great inconvenience to themselves—Fred Warner in a Land Rover on his way to Athens, looking like a young diplomat in a play, japanned tin boxes full of ostrich-feather hats, fishing rods, Thucydides. You never saw such a crowded car. I am very fond of Fred and found it hard to say good-by to him for two years.

But on they come, the loyal friends, and Bill loves it. I enter the house to find Diane de Mouchy delighting him with indiscreet stories; Amory Houghton telling about French politics or Gladwyn Jebb with nothing at all to do but amuse Bill for half an hour with a riotous description of the latest political antics.

Of course, Ronnie helped me more than anyone. He is wonderfully imaginative and practical about thinking of ways to amuse Bill, and the children feel that he is an uncle. And he is so funny. Did he write you about his drive back from Portugal, and lunching with an eccentric Englishman called Peter Pitt-Millward in his gracious finca? The silver on the table had belonged to William

[7] John is the youngest of the three Alsop brothers. Possessed of the family brains and literary talent, he too could have been a famous Washington figure, but he chose to lead his busy and useful life in Avon, Connecticut, from where the Alsops come. His wife, Gussie, is largely responsible for the contentment of his life.

Pitt. The host was a little intoxicated. Ronnie said, "I think you know the Kenneth Clarks?" Host: "Certainly, they're my best friends and thank God I never see them!"

Odette has returned from Venice, traveling back with René Clair and Louise de Vilmorin, who had created a sensation with their new film *The Lovers*. She says that it is considered a triumph of eroticism, but that it won't pass the French censors, adding, "I went with Gaston Palewski and Charlie Bestegui and when I tell you that those two men blushed you will see that it's time to cut a film."

Politically, one is waiting for the vote on the Constitution at the end of the month, which will surely be an overwhelming vote of confidence for de Gaulle. The dramatic events of May have drained the French of political enthusiasm, and they will vote for him because he is the only great figure in France. The immense, surging popularity he aroused after the liberation no longer exists, but to me he has recently become a touching and appealing figure because he is one of the few Gaullistes—perhaps the only one—who really means what he says. The staged demonstrations of enthusiasm grow daily more embarrassing, and Malraux's recent sycophantic speech was more blushmaking than the above-mentioned René Clair film. However, entering the nursery while it was going on on the radio, I found Mademoiselle clapping wildly, with tears in her eyes. Anne Patten lay in her bath, unmoved. I tried to take the children to the birth of the Fifth Republic, a "spontaneous" gathering at the Place de la Bastille, but discovered that tickets were by invitation only to ten thousand carefully chosen republicans. Any alien republican enthusiasts were efficiently taken care of by the C.R.S. (those competent helmeted figures we saw so much of during the troubles in May) so it is as well that I didn't try to crash it with Billy and Anne.

54 Avenue d'Iéna
Paris, France
December 18, 1958

My annual Christmas letter and I feel about as Christmasy as Scrooge. Anne's Labrador puppy is ill, causing dramas, I have a vile cold, Berlin is dangerously alarming again, all the Western allies are meeting here and indulging themselves in a textbook example of an alliance in disarray, General de Gaulle is at his most Olympian and says that he can't be bothered with details—the Common Market, for example, is a detail. Joe Alsop has just come to us from Berlin, and says that the Berliners are staunch as ever but Khrushchev looks like meaning it this time and Joe isn't the only observer who thinks that the Russians are out to take Berlin. If so, it's the Third World War. Merry Christmas.

What do you think? I somehow feel in my tummy that there are ways to get out of this one, unless someone is insane, and I have too little imagination even to be afraid. Also Paris does look beautiful, decorated for Christmas, and at Dior's they are spraying the passers-by with a mist of Diorissima, my favorite perfume, so one has only to walk down the Avenue Montaigne to be showered in glamor. I think of taking the Labrador there to cheer her up. And this dreary conference has brought some of our best friends here; tonight the David Bruces, Freddie Reinhardt, and Tony Rumbold are dining with us. Bill is better than you could believe possible and is looking forward to the party.

Billy returns tomorrow, I saw him last month when we spent a happy weekend together at Oving with Pam and Michael Berry. On the way I had the luck of going to Oxford with Pam to hear Isaiah Berlin deliver his inaugural lecture as he took the chair of political theory and philosophy. You know what star quality he has, there can be no other lecturer in England who could command such attention as he does. If there had been five thousand seats they would have been filled, and no one would have sneezed or rustled a paper. His subject was liberty. Although he never mentioned the name, I felt that the lecture was for his friend Pasternak, fellow Russian, fellow intellectual, who is going through tragedy. He spoke for an hour and ten minutes, slowly for him, and it was a triumph. Aline is going to send me the text, which I shall pass on to you. And I shall read it myself, at least twice, as it was the tightest lecture I ever heard, and it would be hypocritical to pretend that I didn't miss a lot. I am so badly educated and I never heard of Fichte before, let alone understand his relationship to Hegel. Oh, why didn't I go to college like you?

To Marietta from Paris

Christmas will be a quiet one, provided that we aren't blown up, and I feel profoundly grateful that 1958 is nearly over. Without you and Ronnie I could not have got through it.

The children as usual make it fun to prepare for Christmas. Anne is going to adore your present of the diary. She writes amazingly well for a child of eight, and her letters to my mother show real imagination. The Labrador puppy is the center of her life and she describes her to Granny with real flair.

· 1959 ·

Château Mouton Rothschild
Pauillac, Gironde
January 24, 1959

We love our visits to Pauline and Philippe de Rothschild, and I should have described one before. The cast of characters varies: sometimes it is a house party of English critics and writers, sometimes our fellow guests are French, like this weekend; but the scenario is unchanging. Pauline suggests a certain weekend, then the eager acceptance by us is followed by the arrival of tickets for the fast train for Bordeaux, and no amount of arguing with the secretary about repaying him is admitted: one has become a guest of the Baron Philippe and getting out of that one would be about as easy as fishing for a letter one has just mailed in the postbox. Also, one doesn't want to fight—it is delicious to be a couple of mailed letters traveling first class on one of the most comfortable trains in Europe. Nearing Bordeaux, the January sky takes on a southern look, as do the red-tile-roofed houses and farms.[1] Bordeaux we all know well: a sad city with its Anglophile wine merchants prospering secretively behind their high iron-gated courtyards, their great past suggested by the lovely classical theater by the architect Louis; the Flaubert-like ladies who protest too much that they far prefer Bordeaux to the crowded horrors of Paris; the wide silent streets at night; the exodus of eager young people who throng the halls of the visa section at the American Embassy in Paris inquiring about possible scholarships in the United States.

From Bordeaux to the châteaux among the vineyards is a dull flat drive, and nothing could be less dramatic than one's first sight of red-tiled Mouton: a series of plain lowish farmhouses as under-

[1] This picture of Bordeaux is hopelessly out of date. François Mauriac, who wrote brilliant, bitter novels about what he called *le desert français*, by which he meant this region defined in Larousse's dictionary as "gauche, undistinguished" with its lifeblood drained by Paris, lived to see it develop into the powerful and dynamic city that it is now and has been for a generation.

stated as one of Pauline's Balenciaga raincoats. Inside is rather different. Arriving at the end of a January afternoon, one is led upstairs into an immensely long room lighted by rounded windows giving directly onto the vineyards; one is very conscious at Mouton that this is no pleasure dome placed meaninglessly by rich people in a pleasant setting: vineyards are all-important and ever present; this is a working estate. There is too much in the room to take in at once, although sparsely furnished. Pauline has a horror of crowding, but Giacometti is a happy neighbor to a sprawl of books on English gardens, just as in her bedroom the finest of Chinese wallpaper suits an austerity as severe as Carpaccio's rendering of St. Ursula's little room in the series in the Accademia in Venice. Pauline is all contrasts—I think of her as sitting at tea tables, round tea tables covered with muffins and several kinds of honey, probably dressed in corduroy or velvet knickerbockers and a plain white shirt, just as we found her yesterday by the fire at the end of that long, lovely room. I also see her dressed for the evening: a wide satin blue cape, the lady embarking for Cythera, her long fingers and her long elegant figure never fluttering, the composure of her beautiful face as still and serene as Watteau caught them on the banks of his magic lake. The conversation around her is as unserene as possible, and she loves it and makes everyone seem at his best. Yesterday it was uncerebral—we found the party in the middle of the Walther case—this is worth describing briefly if it didn't get into the American press. A very rich woman—her fortune coming from mines in North Africa—called Madame Walther is a well-known figure in Paris (we don't know her but many of our friends do) and delighted everyone there a few months ago when she announced that she was giving her important collection of pictures to the Louvre. The Louvre instantly began doing over the Orangerie, their loveliest small museum building on the Place de la Concorde, in readiness to receive the splendid gift, and the opening was scheduled as a great Paris event. Only the other day, Madame Walther's only son, Guillaume, informed the press that his mother was planning to murder him, in collusion with his uncle; that the pictures in fact belong to him; and that he wishes to keep them. As for the murder plans, his evidence is rather convincing and it is feared that Madame W. is headed for jail, pending trial. One of our fellow guests is a Louvre curator—he is furious and said at tea, "Really, that boy Guillaume, he has no civic sense whatever."

Hours are unusual at Mouton—tea can quite easily go on until eight or nine o'clock and dinner is very late. The luxury and comfort of it all could only be achieved by an American woman married to a Frenchman. It has long been my theory that there is no such combination when it comes to food. Pauline, who comes from Baltimore, mixes the very best American food with the very best French. Philippe's wines are of course unbeatable. One has four or five with every meal, served in plain tall-necked glass carafes tied at the top with a twist of red ribbon so that no drop can escape on the tablecloth while the butler serves the wine. I once asked Philippe if this was an old family tradition; he said that it wasn't but that after the war they had the wine, they had the tablecloths, they had the carafes, but no soap to wash the tablecloths, so they invented the red twist of material and as it seemed pretty they have kept the habit. I wish you could see my bed. The pillowcases have wide blue satin ribbons drawn through them and wide borders of tiny, tiny pleats in sheerest linen. Even Pauline can't get the laundering of these done in Paris, so they are only used down here. Every book I have ever wanted to read is in my room, and in Bill's dressing room is a well-stocked bar complete with delicate watercress sandwiches should we get hungry or thirsty between meals. One drifts off to sleep smelling the softest and most delicious air; the sea is not far away and the wind rustles through the vineyards. One doesn't stay awake long, and sleeps luxuriantly late. Philippe and Pauline are both writing; he is a highly respected translator of Elizabethan verse and she has a magic pen.[2]

Bill and I had many long talks that winter about Anne, without resolving her problems. We had come to dread Friday afternoons, when the school marks were read out in front of the assembled mothers and governesses as well as the class. I did not attend these occasions as Anne preferred me not to go but instead to be waiting at home for the results. Bill used to say that if things had gone badly

[2] Pauline's book on a trip they made to Russia in the sixties was a great success in France, England and America.

one could hear the howls from the school all the way to the Avenue d'Iéna, about ten blocks. I now feel that we should never have subjected a sensitive child to such a system, but it was worse at other schools. Anne's was considered the gentlest and most humane French school in Paris, with small classes and dedicated teachers. She has made notes for me, in 1974, about her memories.

"In first and second grade I was always first or second in my class. Then I slipped, I don't know why, and in third to fifth grade I would be fifteenth or sometimes twentieth, and there were only twenty children in the class. On Fridays there was an examination, from 1 P.M. to 4 P.M., on all my subjects, which were math, French, Latin, history, and geography. Every other day Mademoiselle and I would have lunch with Daddy and Mummy, when I came home from school at one o'clock for an hour, but on Fridays Mademoiselle and I ate at noon and we always had fish because Mademoiselle said that fish would help my brain. I was scared of the fish coming alive in my tummy, so I would not eat, but I never told Mummy or Daddy about this. I still don't like fish. After the exam the grades were read—'Florence Richard number one, down to Anne Patten number sixteen, or whatever.' Sometimes the teacher would say in an aside, 'Mademoiselle Patten, we are disappointed.' If they were mad with you they called you Mademoiselle, instead of Anne, as usual. The mummies and the governesses were in the back, but one saw them straining forwards competitively as the grades were read; later they would come up to Mademoiselle right in front of me to offer condolences, assuring her that I would do better next week. No one ever condoled with me, until I got home."

54 Avenue d'Iéna
Paris, February 18, 1959

Oh, such a lovely letter. I loved the tempo of it, and it was very good of you to sit down at your blue and white desk and describe everything from the character of Hubert Humphrey (I wish I knew him, he sounds outstanding) to what you were having to eat that day in Barbados. The lime ice and the rum punch make me drool with envy on this foggy winter day. You are much too modest about your new job which is a great tribute to your years of hard work for New York City and could not sound more interesting or important. Arthur Schlesinger has been here and told me about it. I liked the Schlesingers more than ever and was amused when I asked him for his chief impression of England, where he is much admired as a historian and appreciated for his wit. He said that what had struck him most was that everyone talked of nothing but sex. Sex in the parks, what to do about loiterers, what to do about the Wolfenden report (a study of homosexuality), what about female prostitutes, etc., as well as a cheery amount of gossip about who is sleeping with whom. I wish we had had time to pursue the subject, as I would like to know what he makes of it as a historian—is it a good or a bad sign? Under the puritanical rule of General de Gaulle, sex is at a low ebb in France and even the *chansonniers*[3] are said to be muted. Instead, as I was telling Arthur, the chief subject of conversation here is the school of new novelists, Butor, Sarraute, etc., who write what they call anti-novels. Their aim is to break the mold of classic fiction that has gripped French writers for three hundred years—they sell well but I strongly suspect that not everyone reads through their dreary length. I can't, for one, especially the works of the leader of the school, Alain Robbe-Grillet. One of his recent books contains pages in which things and objects are just listed. This seemed to me far less thrilling than the Sears Roebuck catalogue, but even the English critics have written of the technique admiringly and have invented a name for it—"thingishness."

In reaction, Bill and I have returned to Balzac with never ending pleasure. We also have become maniacs about the game of Scrabble. Yesterday we played for nine hours without stopping!

Bill no longer goes out in the evening, but we entertain cheerfully here and I occasionally go out to fill in as an extra woman, for he likes me to bring him home such gossip as I can collect. The other night I dined at our Embassy, and marveled once more at what a superb diplomat's wife our old friend Dottie Kidder is. On this occasion Dottie and I had between us a terrible old congressman from Iowa who had partaken well of the Ambassador's predin-

[3] *Chansonnier* is an untranslatable word. The nearest I can come is a night club singer who holds his audience by an improvised running commentary on the events of the day.

ner hospitality. I had no message for him, but he was fascinated by Dottie and was determined to unzip her dress and do appalling things with his hands under the tablecloth during the dinner. I admired Dottie no end for saying sternly, "No, Congressman, not before dessert!" with the soup course, and repeating this at intervals. I suppose that at dessert she said, "Not before coffee," and so on. In any case, she handled him ideally and as you know one has to watch it with congressmen if you are the wife of a career diplomat as Dottie is. For all we knew, this old buzzard might have been on the Foreign Affairs Committee and would have remembered Randy Kidder, presently political counselor in Paris but certainly destined to go on to ambassadorial level. Dottie gets up and out and into the Bois de Boulogne every morning by eight forty-five with her dogs, no matter how late she has been up. While walking, she reads the leading French newspapers and retains everything that is important. Her French is bilingual, and her knowledge of every facet of French life, history, art, politics phenomenal. She is surely the most admired and successful American in Paris today and one of the most modest. Bill loves her visits, which are frequent. She is determined to take me on a holiday to Spain, where we are to visit Seville during Holy Week. I hope I won't let her down—hearing that in Seville even in Holy Week one never goes to bed before 5 A.M., I said that I didn't imagine this sort of life for us, two women without one friend in Seville. Who would take us to flamenco caves? "Wait and see!" answered Dottie, with a gleam in her eye. "I don't feel middle-aged, hot diggety dog!"

American Embassy
Bad Godesberg, Germany
June 10, 1959

We have had a lovely month of perfect weather; Bill much better and his morale excellent. Nearly every day we have taken a picnic lunch out, discovering new surprises like the little shell house at Rambouillet where we drank white wine on Marie Antoinette's terrace and set up our Scrabble board under the lindens that she had planted. I went to England once to take out Billy, who is beaming and well. This time I stayed overnight in London with the van Kleffenses, Dutch diplomatic friends who inhabit one of those immense Edwardian houses in Kensington Palace Gardens; the Russian and French Ambassadors their neighbors. Eelco van Kleffens has an ageless van Eyck face off the walls of the National Gallery—the fifteenth-century merchant Arnolfini and he could be brothers. He has held every important post that his country could give him, and he and his wife, Margaret, are a serene, wise pair. When the Germans invaded Holland with their lightning blitzkrieg in 1940, van Kleffens was Foreign Minister. One day he went to his office as usual, to be informed that the Queen and the government wished him to fly at once to London to see Churchill and Eden, informing them of the situation, then to remain in England helping to set up a Dutch government in exile. He asked if he could go home to say good-by to his wife and was told that there was no time, as the Germans were on the outskirts of The Hague. So he set off for the military airport and while driving through the city had the extraordinary luck of sighting Margaret, who was out shopping, carrying her market basket. He scooped her up and they proceeded to the airport where a little army fighter plane was awaiting them. The pilot was very young and inexperienced, without maps or knowledge of the English coast. The van Kleffenses recognized Brighton as they flew over it and decided to tell the pilot to land there. Being a beautiful early summer day and a bank holiday, the beach was jammed with merry holiday makers, quite unaware of what was happening just the other side of the English Channel. The Dutch were taken in charge by a suspicious policeman who didn't believe a word of their story, and they were led off to the local police station where they were permitted to make a call to London—and reached Anthony Eden, who did believe that it was quite possible that the Foreign Minister of the Netherlands could be wandering around Brighton without a passport, a suitcase, or indeed any personal possessions at all.

As you can see from this writing paper, we are now staying with the Bruces in Germany. The residence is an undistinguished but comfortable house on the banks of the Rhine; watching the barges go by at the end of the lawn is mesmerizing. The tempo of the visit is ideally arranged for Bill's health and pleasure: our kind hosts make everything easy for him in what appears to be an effortless way. David has a small private train, as do the other representatives of the occupying powers. This luxury will soon disappear so we were delighted to be included yesterday when he took the train for the day in order to attend an official occasion that brought us to Aachen, or Aix-la-Chapelle as the French call it. It was the greatest fun to tootle through the sunny Rhineland arriving, after a delicious picnic lunch, at Aachen where we visited Charlemagne's dark and holy church—a most haunting and evocative place. The Bruces completed their job and we started for home; Bill resting and looking happily out of the window, David working on some papers, me asking Evangeline all sorts of ignorant but eager questions about what the Germans are like today. Did you realize, for instance, that the school children learn history from textbooks that stop with the rise of Hitler and begin again only at the end of the war?[4] She told me much that was curious but much that was hopeful. When we got back to the Embassy in time to get dressed for a dinner party, we were met by one of the staff who told the Bruces that several of the German guests, all politicians, had telephoned that they couldn't come after all. Evangeline seemed quite undisturbed by this, it appears that it isn't rude in Germany to give out on an Embassy dinner at the last moment. But it makes it hard on the hosts: members of David's staff had to be hurriedly summoned from their homes to fill in and Evangeline had to do the seating all over again in about ten minutes, but promptly at eight she and David came down the stairs laughing to each other and looking as distinguished and beautiful as they always do. There were plenty of politicians who did come to make it an interesting dinner, and I sat by a probable future Chancellor, Erhard.

Today we visited the baroque castle of Bruhl, near Cologne, full

[4] The history books were later revised and the Nazi story told, but there remain the Germans in their thirties who are yet uninformed. In the summer of 1972 Ronnie Tree and I did a trip together in northern Italy; our chauffeur was a delightful young man whose father had been a general in charge of the Berlin air defenses during World War II. He knew nothing about the German campaign in the country through which we were driving and was surprised by the many war cemeteries. He told me that his family never discussed the war, and only as a postgraduate university student had he begun to learn about the most unhappy chapter in his country's history.

of cherubs and sky-blue ceilings and twisted marble columns; lunched at the French Embassy, which as usual is the best house in town; and tonight we return to Paris.

That summer, for the last time, our little family joined my mother at her cottage in Northeast Harbor, Maine. Bill loved Maine and always looked forward to breathing better in the diamond-clear air, but I had been told by Dr. Varay before leaving Paris that the most recent tests showed that he was now breathing with one-third capacity of one lung, the other was useless. His courage never failed him but he grew discouraged and decided to return to Paris earlier than we had planned. His great desire was to stop at Groton School near Boston in order to apply for Billy's admission the following year. Knowing that this effort would exhaust him, I telephoned Marietta on Long Island to ask if she and Ronnie could possibly take us in for a few days in order to break the trip before embarking on the *Queen Mary* for France. Typically, she said that nothing could be easier than to have all five of us, for as long as we cared to stay. (The fifth was a young French maid, Jeanine Saunier, who had accompanied us instead of the governess. I was so lucky in my servants all those years—Jeanine was highly intelligent and nursed Bill as well or better than I.) A letter to my mother from the Trees' describes this sad little trip.

Summer Cottage
Caumsett
Huntington, N.Y.

I do hope that you are having some well-earned rest; for I fear that the last month has been a strain for you, worrying about Bill and having to put up with all the daily difficulties involved in keeping house for an invalid. You did it so beautifully, and the fun the children had would alone have been worth crossing the ocean. You made so many kind and generous arrangements, and as I tried to write to you from Boston I don't know how to begin thanking you.

Groton was successful but painful, requiring a great effort of will power on Bill's part. I think that they will probably admit him. The headmaster, Mr. Crocker, said to Bill, "You have a real star, a most exceptional boy." It was fun for Billy to be greeted as a son of a member of "the legendary class of 1928" and the grandson of William S. Patten of the class of 188? (I have forgotten) and the walls are hung with pictures of his godfather, Charlie Devens, one of Groton's most illustrious athletes.[5] Billy asked if they had a picture of his other godfather, Joseph Alsop, and was told that, while they had no picture, the records of the Alsop brothers at Groton would never be forgotten, and that when Joe's college entrance marks came in the then headmaster, Endicott Peabody, had given the whole school a day's holiday to celebrate the occasion.

Bill was very tired that night and the next day, but he was up to seeing all his best Boston friends, who came to pay visits at the hotel. He didn't feel up to having meals with them, but they were most understanding. Dear P. L. Harrison sent up her own car and driver from Long Island to bring us here, and we are ideally settled in a quiet little cottage with Jeanine, oxygen of course, and just the right number of visitors. The weather is divine and the children are adoring it. Ronnie is very interested in Billy's tennis and has engaged Mrs. Marshall Field's professional to give both of the children lessons every day. Anne and Penelope get on beautifully,[6] and the swimming is great fun too. We shall stay here until Wednesday and then Marietta is going to drive us directly to the boat. To show you how peppy Bill is, he said today how annoying it was to leave America the very day Khrushchev arrives on his state visit and de Gaulle makes his important declaration on Algeria.

[5] Charles Devens, a most loving and devoted godfather and our intimate friend, was the best all-round athlete of his time and the best-looking among Bill's many handsome classmates. Unlike many golden youths, he went on to a highly successful business career in Boston.

[6] Anne showed courage on this visit. While swinging on a four-poster bed, pretending that they were monkeys, she and Penelope crashed to the ground. They reported that they were a bit bruised, and that Anne's arm hurt, but not enough to bother about. Marietta and I were so concerned with Bill that we didn't bother, and we were at sea on the *Queen Mary* before I put my mind on Anne's arm. It turned out to be broken; the ship's doctor put it in a plaster cast and congratulated her on her fortitude.

• 1959 •

54 Avenue d'Iéna, Paris
November 2, 1959

Ronnie's visit was wonderful fun for all of us, his understanding of the children and their affection for him grows yearly; as for Bill, everything has been easier since we got back, for Dr. Varay has new and hopeful ideas for his treatments, some from Sweden and some here. Believe it or not, I am writing letters in Swedish, using a dictionary. The answers come back in perfect English, making me feel like a fool, but at least I have the fun of trying to learn a new language. Billy is on the football team, which means that my last visit to his school was sheer torture: first he was ashamed of me because I don't understand English football, then more ashamed because of my cowardly shivering cold standing watching the match while the icy winds of Oxfordshire made mock of my heaviest clothes. The English parents didn't even wear overcoats and I hated them all for their heartiness until I found a pair of sympathetic companions who made the day possible. They were a Foreign Office couple, recently transferred from Bahrein in the Persian Gulf, so their blood was as thin as mine, their ten-year-old son just as ashamed of them. We all went to tea in Buckingham, poached eggs, potatoes and bacon, quantities of toast and jam, then back to school. I always feel sick for a day or two after leaving Billy in England but he did seem well and happy. Thanks to Pam and Michael, I had a lovely comfortable Saturday night at Oving and the next day they let him bring two friends for lunch and we visited Waddesdon, which is the Rothschild palace nearby. It's Chenonceaux and Upper Fifth Avenue and the Breakers at Newport, hideous beyond description, but filled with wonderful things. Billy was bored but his friend David Sulzberger has an extraordinary eye and was thrilled. Faithful, kind Pam provided the kind of tea the boys love and they all went off cheerfully.

Just before I went to England we had our twentieth anniversary party on October 28. Diana Cooper spent the night, and all our best French and American friends in Paris came. We were twenty-four for dinner, and the ladies wore their very best: Dottie was superbly elegant in a Lanvin brocade dress and Elise looked a seductive twenty years old, dressed by Balenciaga. Bill made a toast to me which was too moving for me to dare to write about for fear of tears; and nobody went home until very late so we hope it was a great success.

54 Avenue d'Iéna, Paris
December 22, 1959

This has been a very happy ten days: Paris full of old friends who come to see Bill no matter how busy they are, Billy's return for the Christmas vacation in long trousers, which deeply impresses Anne; they have rather formal conversations as if they were two strangers getting to know each other, talking politely of the comparative climates of Paris and Northamptonshire. This won't last; I predict the usual sibling row by Christmas Eve. The night Billy got home Joe got passes to take him to the station for President Eisenhower's arrival, which wasn't at all an easy thing to do but wonderfully exciting for Billy to see de Gaulle and Eisenhower so close at hand. Apparently it was a very cold public occasion. Curious de Gaulle—I discovered a side of him the other day from Gladwyn Jebb which astonished me. The Douglas Dillons were dining with us and the Jebbs joined us after the wedding reception of their daughter. Gladwyn said that he had been most surprised to receive a lovely four-page letter written by the General in longhand about Stella Jebb's marriage and the sadness a father feels on such an occasion, etc. This, at the end of a year of highly strained Anglo-French relations, from the most icy, remote statesman in Europe. Gladwyn said that he thought it was because it had occurred to him the other day at the presidential shoot to ask de Gaulle if by any chance as a young man he had been fond of writing sentimental poetry, possibly sonnets? This random shot provoked an outburst of pleasure: indeed he had, said the General, he had even had a few published in the local paper, but everyone had thought them so poor that he had never liked to talk about it since; however, since the Ambassador had guessed it, there it was, he is a poet manqué, a romantic at heart, an artist. I don't know if this has ever been put in any of the many books about de Gaulle; certainly I had never heard of this side of him before, although of course we all know and admire his prose style.

Mac Herter, wife of our Secretary of State, came to say good-by to Bill on her way to the airport. She has made a great impression on the French, who say that she looks like a Gainsborough portrait, and I agree completely. She is very sweet and elegant. Charlie Adams has been with us too, as well as Joe, and on Sunday I sent them out to Diana's as Bill was in bed and a bit blue. Their report on domestic life at the Château de St. Firmin at Chantilly is more Diana-like than ever. The last cook, an Algerian, was shot to death on the streets of Paris a couple of days ago, poor fellow,[7] but she has a new cook, and luncheon was absolutely delicious.

Think of us on Christmas Eve dining quietly at the Bordeaux-Groults' as we usually do—Elise is a great girl for making Christmas sparkle. I shall be thinking of you and blessing you for all you have done for us this year.

[7] It was impossible to determine what happened to the cook. The Algerian war raged in the back streets of Paris, and the man could have been a member of the F.L.N. (Algerian nationalist movement) brought down by the police for an attempted act of sabotage or murder, or he could have been a Harki. These unfortunate men were Algerians who remained loyal to France and fought with the French army; many of them lost their lives at the hands of their own people.

• 1960 •

I don't seem to have written any letters in the early part of 1960, or if I did they are lost. But I can remember that as the end approached I was particularly touched by several kind, very French, things that happened. The servants came to me together and said that they no longer wanted days out. The great dressmaker Pierre Balmain sent me word that he was hurt because I hadn't been near his collection that winter, and when I told Ginette Spanier, my friend who is the director of the house of Balmain, that there wasn't any point as I never went anywhere, the word came back that Monsieur Balmain and she both thought it was just the moment to have some new dresses as Bill would be tired of seeing me in my old ones. So I had a whole wardrobe of beautiful Balmain clothes, and there was no bill. I remember the man who ran the oxygen company ringing up and asking me if I realized how much oxygen we were using. It was his business to sell oxygen, which is not a cheap commodity, but he was an old friend and he was worried. I told him that I had noticed, of course, but we were now running the Bennett machine eighteen hours out of twenty-four and I wanted to always have four reserve tanks at hand. He sounded so sad and nice. Bill died of cardiac failure in the early morning of March 26. The day before had been a lovely early spring day and he had seemed particularly comfortable. I took a walk in the afternoon and had the luck to see Khrushchev driving through the streets; Bill was most amused to hear my description, and we had a nice evening first of all with Anne, hearing her news of school which had been particularly successful that day, and all of us looking at our brand-new toy, television. His pulse failed later that night and he became mercifully unconscious. I was not alone as my own obstetrician, Professor Maurice Mayer, lived in our building and was with me three minutes after I called him, equipped to do everything that anyone could do.

My first duty was to tell brave little Anne, who was just ten, and then to fly to England to break the news to Billy, for I thought better that it should be I who gave the shock rather than the headmaster. Marina Sulzberger came with me and we brought him back to Paris the same day. Thanks to my kind, competent friends, the service in the American Pro-Cathedral was beautiful, and my mother flew over to be with us. Later, Marina and Cy carried the children and me off to a lovely hill town in Provence for the spring vacation with the Sulzberger children and Jane and Bob Joyce, two old and dear friends who came up from Italy to be with us.

My letters of condolence were many and I don't know who writes the best letters of this kind: the French, the English, or the Americans. The English have the graceful habit of writing open letters to *The Times* as well as personal ones. Bill would have been very pleased by two letters to the editor of *The Times*, one from Lord Salisbury, one from Frank Giles.[1]

Our own children were shattered. I think they were most helped by something that my little godson Sebastian Giles said. "He's all right now—he's with Jesus—no more coughing there."

But Anne herself wrote to me. It was the first time she had attempted a letter in English[2]:

Dear Mummy
Try to bee raisonnable. It
happen before then wee thort it
would.
Be courageous, I'm here, Billy,
Granny, Mazelle. I shell not
Sleep before all is quiet.
Sleep welle dear
little mumy. Everyone
Love's vous, and me the
most of all.
I'adore you
Little Anne

That summer we took a cottage in the Pays Basque country in order to be near Elise and Pierre Bordeaux-Groult and their family.

[1] See Appendix A.

[2] Anne wrote to me recently to say that she wanted the letter included because "in the book you are too hard and brave. I heard you crying all night." I should also explain that *raisonnable* means in English sensible, intelligent, facing facts as they are.

The cottage was above a wide, long empty beach on which I walked endlessly, breathing in the sharp Atlantic air. By about August my mind was beginning to work again and I was reading the newspapers and receiving interesting letters from Marietta about the American political scene. It was the summer of the Democratic convention at Los Angeles at which Adlai Stevenson lost the nomination to John Kennedy. I grieved for Stevenson, whom I much admired, but the more I read the more I became impressed by this new young man Kennedy. When we returned to Paris in the fall I joined a little organization called "Americans in France for Kennedy" and helped raise money. My friends were by now tactfully giving me their advice about what to do with the rest of my life; it didn't seem to me very important then, but the children were important. Billy would be going to Groton in 1961, and although he unselfishly assured me that he would quite understand if I remained in our beloved Paris, I thought that we should all stay together and that America was the place for us. So they went back to school for their last year abroad, and I too went to school, with Dottie Kidder. We enrolled at the Ecole des Sciences Politiques as auditors, for, alas, we lacked the degrees necessary to become full students at this great postgraduate school from which the elite of young French minds has emerged for generations to govern the country. Our subjects were history and government, and it was a fascinating experience to sit cramped in the overcrowded lecture rooms listening to our teachers—all towering names in Paris intellectual life—thundering away from the rostrum. The students were tense, harassed, the physical conditions unbelievable by American standards. Except for one inadequate library, there was no place for them to work, so they would struggle home, often hours by subway, having grabbed an inadequate meal in the canteen. French students have told me how lonely life is: no time to make friends; although I would hang about after a lecture longing to compare notes over a cup of coffee. The only social success I had was to be asked to join a Communist students' union, and also a non-Communist one: I reluctantly declined, thinking that I was a bit old for this sort of thing. It was no surprise to me when the great students' rebellion broke out in May 1968; I was only surprised that it hadn't come sooner, but I wouldn't have missed those courses. Some were brilliant, some seemed to me negative and sterile. I remember a professor of government drawing a series of sharp zigzags, like lightning strokes, up and down a blackboard. His point was that France was ungovernable and unsuited to democracy: its history showed that it swung from anarchy to dictatorship; that we were presently living under a dictatorship (de Gaulle). I looked around at the clever, tired young faces around me scribbling notes, and wondered if one of them would jump up to scream at our arrogant teacher that this was not a dictatorship. I was no Gaulliste, but could one imagine a professor in a government university in Russia getting away with this kind of hypothesis? But, of course, no one jumped up: it would have been unthinkable.

While I was regaining strength and courage in Paris, Marietta, with whom my life had been closely interwovern since those early days in Bar Harbor, was becoming one of the best-known and most admired women in public life in the United States.[3] For many years her career had been fully appreciated by those who followed New York's politics and civic causes. She had fought heroically during the presidential campaigns of 1952 and 1956. But her career was a private one, interrupted by her correct judgment of her priorities. Ronnie and the children came first. They still did, but they applauded and were proud when in 1961 she became a member of the United States delegation to the United Nations serving as U.S. representative on the Human Rights Commission of the U.N., until 1964, when she was elevated to the Trusteeship Council with the rank of Ambassador. She still managed to find time for all of us who needed her, and always will.

In this same year of 1961 I married Joseph Alsop, and the children and I moved to Washington. In him, they found the wisest and most generous of stepfathers. Anne will never forget tenth grade, when she was failing in Latin and Joe gave up all appointments between 5 and 7 P.M. for a whole winter in order to tutor her. Anyone who has lived with a busy reporter will appreciate what this, which sounds like a small sacrifice, really means. Billy would certainly agree that he owes as much to Joe as Anne does for helping him through

[3] Positions held by Marietta Tree during the years referred to: Member of Board of Commissioners of New York City Commission on Human Rights, 1959–61; United States Representative to Human Rights Commission of United Nations, United States Delegation to United Nations, 1961–64; United States Representative to Trusteeship Council of United Nations with rank of Ambassador, 1964–65.

the hard, transitional years of adolescence. A wing was added to that beautiful Georgetown house for us, a swimming pool built, and Joe encouraged the teenagers who began to surround my lovely Anne as the years went by, never wincing at the Coca-Cola bottles forming dank, ring-making battalions on the surfaces of his glorious eighteenth-century French tables, or when the house shook to the sound of the Beatles as he was trying to write an important article on deadline.

Another joy about coming back to America was to have a family. My mother lives in Washington, and in New York there were all my dear cousins and there was Bill's first cousin Nat Winthrop and his wife Eleanor, who were like an uncle and aunt to the children.[4] The Alsops, a close-knit tribe, consisted of Grandmother, living in Avon, Connecticut; Uncle John and Aunt Gussie, who also lived in Avon; and in Washington there were Uncle Stewart and Aunt Tish. Avon provided marvelous vacations and during Billy's school and college years in New England he took his friends there as if it had been his own home. In Washington Uncle Stew taught Billy to shoot and later allowed him to join the men's tennis games at Springland Lane. Aunt Tish kept open house in town and in the country, and we all agreed that she had the best food in the family and it was more fun to go to the Stewarts' than to any house in Washington. Elizabeth Alsop[5] became Anne's best friend at once, and through the years when the little girls were late for supper Tish and I had only to call each other up; they were sure to be in one house or the other. I was equally congenial with my beautiful sisters-in-law and very grateful for their generous adoption of us.

Apart from our personal contentment, it was exhilarating for me to be in Washington in 1961, smelling the air of Kennedy's Administration. Our American record in the post-World War II years had been one of which I was immensely proud. I have written earlier of the Marshall planners sweating away under the glass roof of the Grand Palais in Paris during the summer of 1947, driving through eighteen-hour days on adrenalin. There was adrenalin everywhere in

[4] Mr. and Mrs. Nathaniel T. Winthrop.

[5] Elizabeth is now Mrs. Peter Mahony. She has inherited the family talent and has already published two books. Her husband Peter, an able young architect, is also an able suitor. While already in college he met Elizabeth in Northeast Harbor, Maine, where we were staying with my mother and instantly fell in love with her. She was only fourteen at the time, but he pursued her despite many later rivals. Tenacity paid off: it is a very happy marriage.

Washington in 1961, and the sparkle in the eyes of the men of our generation—those great public servants Bohlen, Bruce, Nitze, Thompson, and others like them—impressed me even more than did the enthusiasm of the young men new to office, brilliant as these latter were. It was the combination that was so heartening—surely with McGeorge Bundy at the White House and Chip Bohlen in the State Department one couldn't go wrong. But that other great public servant, Averell Harriman, summed it up for many of us when he said to me in 1963, "When Kennedy was alive was the last time I felt young."

As for France, although the National Gallery is one of my favorite museums, it was many years before I could force myself to visit their splendid collection of French Impressionists. Those diabolical geniuses carry the high skies of the Ile de France onto their canvases and make one smell the air again, just as one's heart turns somersaults when some silly orchestra plays a tune of which one was fond when one was in love.

France has changed. For the better, in many ways. The young are international and travel widely, as they never could in my day. They are believers in Europe: it is impossible to imagine this generation accepting a narrow, chauvinistic France again. People, including myself, find inconveniences. Bill and I used to love to go to Beaulieu, then a little harbor on the Mediterranean. I read the other day that now they have parking meters for boats, and are so crowded that one is grateful to have a parking disc which lasts ninety minutes, so crowded is the harbor with yachts. But when Marietta and I were girls we used to drive all over New York and park wherever we wanted to. I refuse to moan about the things that have disappeared, and have already offered my children fifty cents each for every time they catch me telling stories about the good old days, or indeed for each time I repeat any story. The fact that this offer has been so eagerly accepted confirms my suspicion that it is time to close this series of impressions of a very lucky life in Paris and Washington, 1945–61.

Susan Mary Alsop
Washington, D.C.
November 1974

APPENDIX A

Mr. W. S. Patten
F.T.R.G. writes—

Bill Patten whose death in Paris last week put an end to years of suffering most courageously borne, was a man in the great tradition of those New Englanders who, while remaining sturdily American, have been able to appreciate and derive the best from their adopted homes in Europe. For the last 15 years his home in Paris has been a common meeting ground for French, American, British and many other friends, who found in Bill's generosity (both material and of the spirit), his regard for friendship and good talk and his tolerance and understanding a constant source of enjoyment as well as a heartening experience in human relationships.

The burden that he had to bear, in the form of his illness, might well have reduced another man to a state of invalid querulousness. For Bill, however, the increasingly difficult business of remaining alive was subordinated, with extraordinary courage and resolution, to the more important one of getting the best from the strength left to him. And he got it, many times over, in the shape of the admiration, respect and affection of his friends. It is to be hoped that in the dark days of his loss his devoted wife, Susan Mary, may find consolation in the knowledge that Bill's memory will live on in the minds of the large and varied company of those who had the privilege of knowing him as a shining example of courage, steadfastness, and unaffected dignity.

The Times, April 4
From Frank Giles

Mr. W. S. Patten
S. writes—

The short account of Bill Patten's life which appeared in *The Times* of March 29, will have been warmly welcomed by his many friends in England. But such a record, in the nature of things, could only give the bare facts of his career, and I feel that some reference should be made to what, to those who knew him, must assuredly be the main quality by which they will always remember him, his unquenchable courage in the face of a physical disability which would have utterly crushed most of us. He suffered from a form of asthma so severe that it amounted almost to torture. He was nearly always miserably uncomfortable, and often could hardly breathe. Yet in spite of all, he managed to carry on with his work and the other activities of a normal life. Only by an occasional twisted smile could one know how much he must be suffering. With his beautiful and talented wife, he gave much happiness to those who, either in London or Paris, were privileged to come to their house. All our sympathy goes out to her and his son and daughter in their cruel loss.

The Times, April 6
From Lord Salisbury

APPENDIX B

William Samuel Patten, Jr., was born on November 29, 1909, at South Natick, Massachusetts. He was the oldest son of William Samuel and Anne Thayer Patten. He was educated at Groton School, 1924–28, but was unable to graduate with his class due to prolonged attacks of asthma which necessitated leaving school in his last year to winter in Arizona. However, he attained the necessary credits to enter Harvard in the fall of 1928, and graduated with his class in 1932. His desire had been to enter law school, but with the depression at its height he felt that he could not ask his family for the money to pay his fees, so instead he moved to New York and obtained a small job in a brokerage firm. He remained there for three years, sharing an apartment with a college friend, Joseph Alsop. In 1936 he moved to an insurance company with offices in New York and Boston, Marsh and McLennan. He left the company due to ill-health in the spring of 1939, and on October 28, 1939, married Susan Mary Jay in Westbury, New York. From 1940 to 1942 he worked for civil defense in Boston, Massachusetts, joining the State Department in November 1942 as Foreign Service Reserve officer, attached to the office of the Under-Secretary, Sumner Welles, and subsequently the office of Economic Affairs. In August 1944 he was named to join the American Embassy in Paris, where he remained until 1955, first as an economic and financial analyst, then in 1948 he joined the Military Assistance Program and in 1949 became an assistant to the Minister of the Embassy, Charles E. Bohlen, who was in charge of the Military Assistance Program for France. In 1952 he was made assistant to the then Minister, Theodore C. Achilles, covering French political affairs, and in 1953 was sent to Strasbourg to cover the new European Constitutional Assembly. He left the Embassy in

1955 and in the same year joined the Paris branch of the World Bank, where he remained until 1958.

He died on March 26, 1960, in Paris, leaving a widow, Susan Mary Patten, and two children, William Samuel and Anne Patten, born respectively July 4, 1948, and January 20, 1950.

I hope so much that anyone who reads this book will realize that Bill Patten taught all of us who knew him the essential lesson: life is a great gift and anyone who doesn't make the most of every moment is a tragic figure. There was nothing tragic about Bill, and when his friends formed the William S. Patten scholarship at Harvard which to this day, and in perpetuity, puts a boy through the university I was much moved by the terms, written by Joe Alsop, or Cyrus Sulzberger, or Charlie Adams, I don't know which. It begins, and I am paraphrasing, for the text is at Harvard; "The Patten scholarship will be given yearly to a boy, handicapped in some way physically, who deserves and intends to make the most of his life." The results have been marvelous. Black and white men, the Dean of Harvard informs me, have been helped on their way through the years since Bill's friends gathered together from France, England, and America to make this generous gift in his name.

Index

Index

Index

Index

Index

Index

Index

Index

Index

Index

Index

Index

Index